Underground : USA
The lower 48 states of America

First published in 2014 via Lulu.com
(First edition, revision ten)

Copyright © Geoffrey Marshall 2009-2015

ISBN 978-1-304-63392-7

Geoff Marshall has asserted his right to be identified as the author of this Work in accordance with the Copyright, Designs and Patents Act of 1988

All rights reserved. No part of this publication may be reproduced, stored in a retrieval system, or transmitted in any form or by any means, electronic, mechanical, photocopying, recording or otherwise without the prior permission of the copyright owner.

Cover Photo : Highway US-26, Washington. 7th August 2009

'Never go on trips with anyone you do not love.'
Ernest Hemingway

End of the Road

*'Here we are now lay the burden down,
we're coming to the end of the road
Sorrowful yet glorious somehow,
to be humming this one last ode'*

It is weird how life really does go into slow motion during a particularly intense moment of your life. People say that your 'life flashes before your eyes' when you die, and I guess it's akin to that – when something is happening that you know is going to affect you in an extreme way is happening and there's a lot to take in all at once, the world actually seems to slow down around you.

I had a physical slow down as well as a mental one as I walked barefoot towards the car. *(I don't have any shoes on because I've got out of bed about five minutes beforehand and have only just about managed to drag on a t-shirt and some trousers)* and at about 100 yards from the car, for some reason the thought that first goes through my head is 'That's odd ... the sun isn't reflecting off of the driver's side window like it is on the rest of the windows of the car', and as I take a step forward on the still somewhat dew-infested squishy grass my pace slows.

The next step brings a new thought – 'Duh ... I've been a silly fucker and left the window wound down all night ... Shit! I hope that ...' and as my other foot gets slightly wet on the grassy mush, my pace slows again.

It wasn't until I took the *next* step that I realise that my legs had started to slow down – soon to be locked frozen still – as I found myself facing the sight that I knew I didn't want to see.

The sun wasn't reflecting off of the glass of the drivers windows because there is no longer a driver's window. I haven't left the window wound down. The evidence of what has happened lays in shards of glass on the ground of the concrete parking lot, glistening in the sun, shiny blue fragments of compressed sand that all huddled together and shouted to me *en masse* the line that had made me stand still ... 'Yes', they all echo together 'Your car has been broken into'.

The next minute is when the weird slow motion stuff happens. A lot of extreme emotions, but with time slowing as it occurs. I remember I start to shake. I also didn't want to go near the car. I remember that I found myself back inside the house as I ran there screaming ... *something* ... out loud alerting Katie and her sister Courtney about my discovery outside.

And as the world span and people and noise happened around me, I stand and just look – look on from a distance trying to deny what has happened as if by not acknowledging what had been stolen, then maybe it wouldn't be real.

Truth be told – I'd been a bit of an idiot, and a bit lazy too. And tired. The previous day I had driven all day, and ended up in Greensboro, North Carolina for the night where I planned to spend the whole of the next day editing the latest batch video shot using all the nice expensive equipment I've brought with me, and having a day off from the road.

When we'd pulled up and parked Katie had even said to me 'Shall we bring the stuff in now?', and I'd lazily replied 'Nah, it's ok, we'll grab it later', and we go inside and eat, drink and relax. But we relax too hard, and by the time our stomachs are full, and I'd had a couple of beers and played cards, the thought that maybe I was leaving several thousands of dollars of equipment practically begging to be stolen of equipment in my car had slipped my mind, and I'd gone off to sleep leaving it all in the car.

And now it was all gone.

The next couple of minutes go from slow motion to fast-blur. So fast that I don't really remember much about it. But Katie tells me that I'd ran back into the house with a scared look on my face and blubbed the words 'They took it, it's all gone! They took it all!' I didn't need to explain who *they* were or *what* was all gone – the painful expression on my face made it all too terribly clear.

Katie's sister on hearing the commotion appears from her bedroom door – her mobile phone already in her hand dialling 911, and they both go outside to look, as I start to shake and remain rooted inside, not wanting to go back out and survey the damage.

It doesn't take them long to figure out the obvious. They poke their heads into where the driver's side window used to be. The SatNav, iPods and point-and-shoot camera that had been out on the dashboard were all gone. But what about the back of the car?

Katie had to come back and get me – I wouldn't go near the car. Courtney was being asked on the phone by the police to state exactly what had been stolen, and I only I can comprehensively tell them – once I've looked. She takes my hand and leads me over to the car, I'm still tentatively walking in my bare feet.

'I wonder if … 'I say, and open up the back door and let out a noise which Katie later can only describe as a 'defeated moan'.

'It's gone. It's all gone. It's over', I say – part sobbing and part screaming as I say it. Katie looks at me desperately. There was *nothing* that she or anybody can say to me right now that would make any sense at all. What is the point? I just want to go home!' Katie looks scared ... I am angry, but not with her. And there was nothing anyone can do.

No one says anything for a few seconds which feels like a long longer. I try to make sense of the thoughts in my head right now.

The *whole point* of my trip was to give me time out – an extended holiday – to see the country I've lived in for three years, and decide whether it was the country I wanted to stay living in for a lot longer, or if I should go home. Same named-stops and attraction visiting aside, this was the *true* raison d'etre of the trip, a bit of soul searching, and with everything now collapsing around me I could see I was going to have to end the trip early.

'This is going to fuck with everything, it's all fucked up. They've ruined it, they've ruined me figuring out what the hell I'm supposed to be doing and ... and ...' And I didn't know what and. But after a moment Katie convinces me to stop walking all over the glass, get away from the car and go and sit on the grass verge instead.

Sitting down with a deep breath I take stock of the situation. What they'd done was to smash the driver's side window *(why hadn't the alarm gone off? Did I not set it?)*, and just unlock the rest of the doors from there. From it, they'd taken my digital stills camera and lenses, my video camera and accessories and all the footage shot so far, my kick-ass desktop video editing PC and widescreen monitor, my SatNav system, my little point-and-shoot digital camera, my beloved iPod, and Katie's iPod. I estimated about $8,000 worth of stuff – all gone.

Everything *was* messed up, everything *was* ruined, and I'd meant what I said minutes before – I wanted to give up and go home right then and right now. The whole *point* of the trip – that I've been so candid in telling everyone in the build-up, is that it would it be the answer to all my questions. The perfect time out from my regular daily life and the space that I needed to work out what the hell I wanted to do next, shattered – literally shattered – and broken and destroyed and crumbled, and I felt like shit.

Weirdly, I put my hands to my pockets. In an instinctive move of wondering what had been stolen and what had been left behind, I can feel that I have my wallet in one pocket and my mobile phone in the other ... thankfully I hadn't been a complete idiot.

I realise that as I'd got out of the car last night last night I've also grabbed my laptop bag and taken that in with me, so I still had a couple of things – most importantly, my phone – my communication device to the world that I'd been using near-religiously to send tweets out for the past three weeks.

I turned around and look at Katie sitting on the grass. And I started to move – with pace, and vigour, not at all in slow motion, and determination, and this time I go faster as I walk towards her, because I know what I have to do.

'You don't want me to quit?' I say to her, perhaps a little tersely. 'Well then I'm not gonna quit. I know what I'm gonna do instead!', and leave her with a puzzled expression. I walk quickly, then pick up pace as I can feel the adrenalin now pouring through my veins and eventually speed up to a full on running pace to go back inside the house.

My laptop is sitting on the kitchen workbench, I flip it open, frustratingly wait for it a few seconds to connect to the Internet and go to the Twitter webpage. And then I type in an update. One which I know will get people's attention.

> **10.59 AM Jun 29th**
> well. i got my drama. and the journey may be over. i am somehow producing one very rough video cut. standby.

I then dive into my laptop-bag sitting on the chair. In the side pocket where it has been kept unused on the three weeks of the journey so far was my 'backup' video camcorder … a crappy quality hand-held shaky-cam, but adequate enough for what I wanted to do right now. I open up the side monitor panel, and flick the 'on' switch open and as I run back outside as it whirrs through the motions of powering up. I get to Katie, and thrust it into her hand.

'What …. What's this for?' she says looking quizzically at me. 'We're going to make a video' I say, the terse tone actually helping *me* through what I was about to do next.

I stand by the car, make a bad attempt not to stand in some of the broken glass and prompt Katie.

'Geoff, do you really want to …' she starts to say – but before she can finish her sentence I cut in. 'I've got to. Just … record everything okay? Press the red button. Press it. Now. Ready? Is it on?' Katie nods.

And I stand by the car, with its missing windows. With its empty back seats where my equipment had been, I look directly into the video camera that Katie now holds in her hand pointed at me with the red light glowing.

And I started to talk.

Six months earlier …

Londinium

'London never sleeps, it just sucks ...
... the life out of me, and the money from my pockets'

I'd been living in America for exactly two years now, during which time I have been married, divorced, eaten a lot of strawberry Twizzlers and acquired a taste for root beer which you can't really buy back in England, but in America it's everywhere.

And I'd been thinking about going home. Ever since the marriage in fact had gone horribly wrong, the thought of packing up and going home was always present in my mind, except now I had a job and friends and people and things that I'm involved with here, so some days I 'd think 'Well why don't I just stay here and live out the rest of my life!', only for the next day to wake up and think 'No, I miss London too much I think I should go home'.

What I *did* know though, is that when the time came to go, I'd already decided that I would not go home in a straightforward way. Just flying eight hours east back over the Atlantic seemed a bit ... well, dull. And I knew that I want to do something more ... interesting, because I could, because I will probably never live in America again, and so this is literally a once-in-a-lifetime opportunity to do something that I will never get the chance to do again. To coin a phrase that's been overused in the past – I would want to go home *the long way round*.

Various ideas had come to mind. First I planned to drive from east coast to west coast and then fly back to England via Hawaii and Japan. I thought about flying out to the west coast and then just driving back to the east and going back from there. And after chatting about all these ideas to friends and family, someone came up with the idea of linking it up with something, which in some way, I was already niche-famous for.

Between 2004 and 2006 I'd held a World Record. No, really. A proper 'Get your name in the Guinness Book of Records', World Record that had involved much of my time, money and considerable effort to undertake and achieve. Back in May of 2004 – and at my seventh attempt of asking – myself and a friend had managed to travel around the whole of the London Underground – The Tube – in the fastest time possible. Eighteen and a half hours to be precise. Or – in fact – Eighteen hours, 35 minutes and 43 seconds to be *very* precise.

Now I know that you're thinking 'What the hell!' at me on this one, but you need to understand that I am not the first person to do this – and certainly not the last. In fact, people have been trying to attempt this ever since the 1950's ... travel to every Tube station on the map in one day, in the shortest time possible.

I had also been fortunate enough to do it at a time when the TV companies were interested in it, and managed to get myself onto the telly doing it. I wrote about it a lot on my website which pushed it into the 'mainstream' a little more. I helped start up a website forum about it where other people wanting to attempt it could discuss routes and tips. People at work coined me the nickname of 'Tubegeek' and I would regularly get asked for travel tips and advice as I would indeed know the fastest way between two points in London. I know my Tube system, I got a kick out of it, and knew that people had me down for that.

So one random Tuesday in the summer (because I like to think that all the best ideas happen on random Tuesdays) I am chatting to a friend of mine – Simon – over email who asks if I am coming back to London, and I tell him that I aren't sure when, but when I do, I would have an interesting 'angle' to it, not that dull flight.

Simon – my friend because just like me, he *loves* doing random quests and things which aren't dull – gets on board straight away, and we immediately joke about over the course of an email thread various things that I can do, rather than just drive from one coast to another.

'How about Super-State-Me? You eat a Big Mac in every state of America!' he writes in a one-liner.

'Or a music themed road trip? One Classic song per state. Dakota by the Stereophonics ... that sort of thing', says his next email.

'I did think of going to every capital of every state' I reply. 'Capital cities are usual boring though, small town America is much more interesting' he fires back.

'Although you could go to a Starbucks in every Capital City!' he writes back, cleverly picking up on my known lust for the popular coffee giant.

But then Simon goes quiet ... We've been bouncing emails to each other every two minutes across the Atlantic, like a staggered phone conversation with massive delay, except now two minutes has passed and he hasn't replied. Shit, where's he gone?

It turns out he's come up with an idea which is to shape the whole of my next summer. And he's spent time typing it out carefully and doing some initial research for me. And so ten minutes, and one cup of tea later *(on both sides of the pond as it later transpired)* my laptop gives its new eMail 'Bing' sound, and a line of bold text presents itself to me at the top of my screen, and I can see a fresh missive from him with the words in the subject line that reads:

> **From:** Simon
> **Subject:** Or you could do this ...

I may have paused for a split second before double clicking on it. Because I know from the fact that it has been ten minutes that he must have been thinking, and typing out an idea that he really likes.

And he has.

> You, Geoff, once held the Guinness Record for visiting all 275 Underground stations in the fastest time. Doing all 48 states in the shortest time just isn't feasible.
>
> So, underground stations it is. Why don't you find 48 American locations with the same name as underground stations, and visit them.
>
> Could take a lot of research, but there must be some 'Temples' and 'Banks' out there for when things get desperate.

Tube Stations that shared the name of American towns? Now *that* is brilliant. I remember actually chuckling out loud to myself and looking round my empty bedroom to see if there is anyone that I can share this crazy idea with. There isn't. So I hit 'reply' instead.

> **From:** Geoff
> Tube Stations as American towns!! ha ha, ok.... now THAT is quite funny. Don't make me research it though, or I'll probably want to do it....
>
> **From:** Simon
> I'm not going to research it either, but I bet it would be easy in New England, and rather harder in the Mid-West.
>
> **From:** Geoff
> I've found a 'Temple' already.... God help me. No sign of a Theydon Bois so far though. Bah.
>
> **From:** Simon
> This ought to sort it.... **www.placenames.com**
>
> And I've done you two already – no more! So that's:
>
> > Vauxhall: http://www.placenames.com/us/p1931663/
> > Brixton: http://www.placenames.com/us/p1778077/

From: Geoff
No no no no no! Stoppit! Otherwise you'll get me started!

From: Simon
OK then, pretend I never mentioned it

Too late.

He's mentioned it.

And he's got me thinking.

He even gives me a website – **placenames.com** where I can look up matching names. I try it out a few times and discover that yes – if you type a word – any word – into it, it searches a database that covers the whole of America that knows of every place name in the country.

e.g. type in the word 'Banana' and it tells you that there is a Banana Spring in Arizona, and a Banana Mountain in Colorado and even a Banana Gulch in Idaho – you get the idea.

And he gives me 'Victoria'. – A station *and* a line on the London Underground, but also shares its name with 235 places in America.

I stare at the screen for a few seconds, and then click on the link and try a few more Tube station names at random... 'Barking', 'Hampstead', 'Golders Green' don't find places in America that have shared names, but 'Epping', 'White City' and 'Holborn' do. Love it!

And then the phone rings, or I get another new email asking me to do some work, or – I can't remember – but something happens at that point which distracts me away from researching it anymore, but enough for it to lodge in my head as a kind of 'Yeah, that's funny ... Maybe I'll do that at some point .... We'll see'. And I think no more about it.

~ ~ ~

The summer of that year comes and goes, and winter and Christmas rolls around, and I pop back home for a week to visit family and friends as you do. London it seems has carried on just fine without me, huh – does it not miss me at all? In fact, annoyingly - in my time away living in America someone had *beaten* my world record time, and I can no longer say that I am the current world record holder of the tube – merely, the *former* world record holder. Damn it. People continually ask me if I am going to go back to London to have another attempt – but I know that it won't be possible to have a proper crack at the record time until I move back to England permanently, and am able to make plans properly.

'Are you making plans to come back permanently?' a voice says to me across the room. I look up from my laptop, and find that it is being asked by my old friend Jono – no real surprise really as I've gone round to visit him and his wife on those tricky days between Christmas and New Year.

We have dinner, catch up on the gossip, send their two children to bed[1], and now I am sitting in their lounge, with a tea on the go, my laptop out connected to their Wi-Fi and generally relaxing in their house.

This is the best thing about them – they always make me feel at ease whenever I pop round to see them, as they are the sort of people that will say 'Make yourself at home', and *they really mean it*. There is no agenda, there is no 'You just get on with your own thing', but then they just spend their time trying to get you to do what they want to do ... *they* really do let you get on with your own thing, which is brilliant.

And it's that brilliance that I am convinced to this day is the whole key to what turns into a very productive few hours after Jono asks a seemingly innocuous question.

We have our respective laptops out, we are onto our third tea of the night, ignoring a repeat of something-or-other on the BBC and fucking about on Facebook (because let's face it, no *work* is done on Facebook – you just fuck about) when Jono pipes up with a question – which unbeknown to me then is about to make it all happen. Simon may have put the explosive in place, but it's Jono that in effect lights the fuse for me.

'Well I do keep thinking about coming back' I reply, 'But you know I'm trying to think of an interesting way of doing it'. 'Like what?' asks Jono.

'Well there is one this *one* sort of idea that someone suggested to me' I say. 'But it seems like a lot of work and I just haven't got around to researching it yet'.

'Oh? Which is?'

I shuffle over on the sofa to Jono. Two geeks – side by side with their laptops, and I quit Facebook and fire up **placenames.com** instead.

I explain to Jono about the site, show him how it works by typing in any word that you can search on, and before I know it ... I find that out of nowhere I am getting excited about the idea for the first time in months, and perhaps if Jono hadn't of mentioned it then nothing would have ever happened.

'So I type in Am-er-sham' says Jono slowly speaking the word as he physically types it on his keyboard, then it should ... *Click!*

---

[1] When I first started to write this book, they had two children. By the time I'd finished it they had three. So if you're ever wondering how long it takes to write a book, 'At least nine months' would be one possible answer.

He hits the 'search' box, and it pops up with one instantly – the only one place in the USA that shares the name as the last stop on the Metropolitan line – Amersham, Tennessee.

Well that was it, isn't it? If anyone is going to work these out, surely it should be me! Not Jono! Does he have a certificate from Guinness World Records hanging above his toilet in his bathroom? No![2]

But he acts as an inspiration (Well that and a supply of constant tea) and immediately and with a certain level of fervour over the next twenty minutes we both tap away at our respective laptops going through the names of places on the Tube map to see if we can find places in America with a matching name.

By the time I leave that evening I think we have just over twenty in the bag – about half of the forty eight. Yes – 48. I know there are fifty states in America, but considering that you can't drive to Hawaii from the mainland, and that you *can* get to Alaska via road but it takes three days to get there and back as you cross half of Canada, I've decided to 'just' do the lower 48 states, the contiguous 48, the mainland 48 states – which I've typed out into a neat list, and am now staring at now on my laptop screen.

On the train back from Guildford where Jono lives to my mum's in Redhill that night where I am staying I stare out of the window into the mostly dark – yet just about visible in the moonlight – Surrey countryside.

Trees and hedges and hills and little communities lit up by a post office and a pub and a telephone box. I let my mind wander and I close my eyes and I try to imagine what it would be like to travel though the plains of Idaho or the countryside of Kansas and what *their* trees and hills and rolling landscapes might look like. I blink my eyes open, the glare of the laptop screen shining into my face, and an old man sitting across the aisle from me looks at me oddly as if he's been wondering what I've been daydreaming about, and I look at the list of names and think 'Well that was fun, but ... Really? *Really*, can I do this?' and at that moment decide that – yes. I think I probably can.

I get back to my mum's that night on the last train, and stay up another hour trying to find a few more, before tiredness eventually gets to me.

The next day – I pretty much ignore my poor old mum as I tap, tap, tap away on the laptop to find some more. At one point she even goes out

---

[2] Although Jono did once come with me on a failed attempt to get round the whole system, and acted as a supply man on a subsequent attempt. That's another reason *(apart from our bad haircuts)* why we get on – he's a secret Tube geek too.

for a few hours, and returns to find that I haven't moved from my screen and her internet connection as I research it all the way through.

By the end of the day after though, I have it complete. I've been through several revisions, changed a few towns along the way for a shorter route – or a place that just looks more interesting, and draw up a rough route in Google Maps. I've worked out how long it is going to take, and I start to wonder about what dates I may like to do it.

By the end of the third day, I have a complete schedule, – eight pages long – I sit back, draw and exhale a deep breath and look at it on screen. I have a plan. One that will last eight weeks, spanning the summer of months of June, July and August when it will be warm across the whole country – even up in the far northern states. I have 48 place names listed out, and rough dates that I am going to do them.

Shit – I am actually going to do this. It is the end of December now, and I will leave in the middle of June.

I have five and a half months to prepare.

Day 1 – Tuesday 16th June

Take the long way home

*'So you think you're a Romeo,
playing a part in a picture show, take the long way home.
Then your wife seems to think you're part of the furniture,
oh it's peculiar, she used to be so nice'.*

I've been quite busy in those five and a half months, getting everything ready.

For a start, I've refined my route a few times. Out of the three of the 'same names' places that I had found I've changed (one – the place in in Massachusetts just a week before I set off!) because it makes it less travelling for me. For example, I had first found a place in Florida which shares a name on the place of the Tube map, but it is half way down in the middle of the state. I don't really want to drive several hours into Florida, only to turn around and go back again, so I am happy when after some more extensive research I find Lancaster (Lancaster Gate on the Tube) which is just in the panhandle (at the top) of Florida – much better.

That same extensive research also turns up a whole bunch of places that I want to go and do along the way. The world's largest ball of twine, towns with populations of just one person, and the 'classic' sights of Graceland, Yellowstone and Grand Canyon are all on a much-refined route. You know – you can't do a road trip of America without going to some of the classic spots as well. Right?

And the car I am driving isn't even mine – it is borrowed. My original plan had been to sell my own car (a Ford Focus), and spend half the money on a car/van big enough for me to sleep in so that I wouldn't always have to camp each night or spend money on accommodation. In the end, Beverly – my landlady (who I also live with) comes up with the idea that we just *swap* cars for the summer. She has a 4x4 Jeep Cherokee which is certainly big enough for me to put all my stuff in, and just about big enough for me to sleep in (if I lay in it diagonally!), and so rather than question why she thinks that saving a few dollars on gas (her car gets about 18 miles to the gallon – mine a much better 32) is better than the 20,000 miles that I am about to add to her engine clock is better – I accept her offer, and a few days before I set off, we swap cars for the summer, and I find myself driving a much-less-economical Jeep.

So my plan is for Day 1 of my journey – starting in Maine – would be on an odd day of the week, a Tuesday. Tuesday June 16th to be precise, because I back-calculated that this would mean that I would pass back through South Carolina and Charleston (where I live) on the July 4th weekend – and because it's a random Tuesday that Simon had come up with the idea – and I like matching things up like that. Oh, and it means that the back-timing into Charleston, will give me a nice weekend to chill out, and have a few days respite before cracking on with the rest of the journey.

I've also sorted out my companions to come with me along the way. Since I've got back to Charleston at the beginning of January after my trip home was over, my planning had started in earnest. I'd told a few select friends about it and ask those who I want to come with me, some had agreed then dropped out, one had said no and then said yes, and one said 'yes' continually only to say 'no' very late on.

Some parts of the trip I will be alone on though – and that was fine with me. I reckon that I would go crazy after a while with certain people all the time in the car –whether they are my friends or not, so I was OK with having a week at the beginning where I would be with myself, and a week in the middle where I would also have time to breath and have some sanity.

Driving up to Maine to the start takes four days, as the pace I've set myself is around four hours of driving per day. The rough plan is to be on the road by ten o'clock each morning, and get to where I want to be by two or three o'clock (break included) in the afternoon. That then gives me time to find somewhere to stay, and have a look around the area that I am in. I'm also scheduling in 'rest days' – every week or so, where I plan to do no driving at all, which will allow me to sleep or catch up with video editing that I want to do along the way.

So in the end I leave Charleston on a Thursday evening about 10pm, when it is dark. About twenty minutes into the epic journey and it starts raining, I call Beverly in panic because I can't find the control knob for the windscreen wipers – not a good start!

On the way up to Maine I visit my friend Rudi in Washington D.C. and stay with more friends – Mike & Melissa in Boston – where I manage to get the car *towed* for parking in an illegal spot. Yeah – even before the trip has properly started I am $150 down on a towing tax. 'They don't call it taxachussetts for nuthin!' observes Mike, grimly.

I also drop in on one more rather wonderful person ... in New York, I meet up with *Chris Searle*, a man who had out of the blue emailed me about a month before I am due to leave. It transpires that he's the man who currently holds the World Record for going round the *New York* subway system in the fastest time possible. More serendipity at play? I like to think so! So I spend a pleasant Sunday afternoon in a beer Garden in Queens having a cool drink with him being slightly geeky comparing the USA to the UK subway system.

And finally to Maine, to Bar Harbour, and to a KOA (Kampgrounds Of America) campground for the night where I arrive at on a Monday evening. I treat myself to lavish meal in a dead posh restaurant (even though it looks a bit strange that I am sat there eating by myself with no company) as I figure I am about to have many weeks of bad roadside Diner food and sugary snacks. So I eat like a king, and feeling fat head back to my tent and get some sleep ready to up & at 'em in the morning.

~ ~ ~

I wake up at exactly six o'clock according to my watch. Technically speaking thought it's the third time I've woken up at that morning, because it has got light at 04.30 when I'd first woken and then rolled over under the hood of my sleeping bag, and then the second time at 05.15 when the same thing has happened ... but a few minutes after 6am on a dry fine morning in Maine, I concede that sleeping in a tent and sleeping bag is going to take some adjusting to and that as it will surely be better on later days, I might as well start my day. And so I get up.

Actually, what I *really* do is get up, open the car, get the video camera and tripod out and set it up pointing at my tent, hit RECORD, go back inside the tent, and then 'get up' for the day, announcing my arrival on tape for me to edit later for the rest of the world to see. And then I decide that I don't like what I've said, so duck back inside, zip up the tent and do it all over again – Take 2, much better.

There is still no one else about. In the fading light of the evening before I know there's been no one else about, but the bright daylight somehow re-enforces this fact. I like it, and wonder if all the campgrounds I will stay at over the summer will be like this ... I suspect not, but I am thankful because it means that when I find four bits of string and plastic doohickeys left over ('doohickeys' by the way, is a perfectly real word no matter that my word-processor is right now putting a red squiggly line beneath it, OK?) from my tent kit and I don't know where I am supposed to have used them, it means that there isn't some outdoor expert in the next tent spot one down from me to snigger at my novice level.

Somewhere though, I remember that there is an instruction manual for the tent, I must dig that out and read it at some point.

> **7:03 AM Jun 16th**
> it got light at 4am. then the birds at 5am, so i conceded at got up at 6am, welcome to camp life. oh, and then the car wouldn't start

I walk to shower block and get clean, shave, brush my teeth and wonder about what the hell I am going to eat. I have no food. I have tea to make a drink with, but last night on the way back from the restaurant downtown I figure that the Exxon[3] gas station opposite the camp ground would be 24 hours and sell milk all night – it doesn't. It closes at 10pm, and I get there about five minutes after – annoyingly close enough for me to watch the girl inside go through the motions of packing up and closing down for the night, and no amount of gesticulating or motioning 'I'd like to buy some milk please' will make her open back up just to serve me. Black tea it is then.

I pack up the tent and all my stuff and decided to splash out again and go and drive somewhere for breakfast. Except for one major hitch: The car won't start.

Every time I turn the key it makes the regular sound of an engine turning over and then a whirring sound as if something electrical is failing, definitely not mechanical. And then the ignition dies and it fails to start. The needle on the rev counter goes crazy, and spins all the way round hitting the red-stop marker before gently coming back. This is not good. I am not going to drive somewhere and get breakfast it seems.

Instead I walk on foot up to the KOA store only to find that at 07.30 in the morning I am half an hour too early for it to be open at 8am. So I return back down to the car and pack up my tent instead. The car has to start at some point one way or the other and so I figure that leaving it for a few minutes might make a difference.

With everything packed up, I pause for a moment and just look around me. It is *completely* quiet. There is no one else about, no cars not even in the distance to be heard, just the slight ruffling of the leaves in the branches as a gentle morning breeze works its way amongst them. The air is clear, and I breath … deep … suddenly from somewhere remembering that old yoga exercise where you count up to seven for the inhale, but count out to twelve for exhale. I shut my eyes, breathe some more, and I feel refreshed.

The karmic effect obviously works on the car to some extent as when I try to start it again, the engine turn over and starts although I find that I have to keep my foot on the gas to keep idling over (or I fear) that it will stall and die on me if I don't. And so after a minute of gently revving, I creep up the mud track, away and out of the campsite.

> **7:49 AM Jun 16th**
> on the road before 8am! Epping is an hour away …

---

[3] Esso

And I head for my first stop – my first *same named* stop of the trip – a tiny little town called Epping, which is an hour away from Bar Harbour where I stayed the night, but it takes me a little while to find it when I get there, I know this sounds strange – but less so when you realise what sort of 'town' Epping actually turns out to be.

When I'd planned this six months ago, I'd done my research on all the places I was going to go to and zoomed in on Google Maps to see what it was like. There are a few Epping's in America – but when I saw that there was one in Maine, I knew *immediately* that it was going to be my starting point.

Epping – at the far east of the Central Line on the Tube in London – is this relatively remote place on the top right hand corner of the Tube map.

Epping, Maine is this remote place in the top right hand corner of the USA.

Two places called Epping both in the top right hand corner? It has to be done. At some point a vision of drawing a custom Tube map within an outline of the USA, and plotting onto the map just the forty-eight places that I will visit comes to mind, but then I realise that this might get me in trouble with TfL's lawyers again[4] and dismiss it.

But until you actually *go* somewhere, you can never really have an appreciation of how quiet and remote somewhere can be, and although I have an idea that Epping might be a bit of nothing town, I don't really realise how nothing it is until I arrive.

---

[4] They tried to sue me in 2005 for some alternative Tube maps that I had on my website

In the USA
Epping, Maine

On the Tube map
Epping (Central Line)

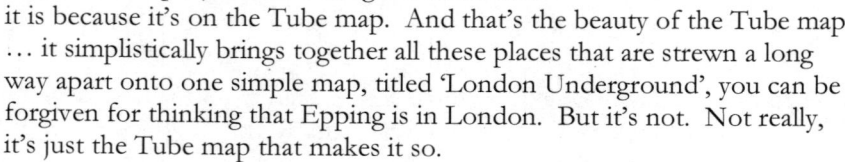

Epping in London, England isn't really in London. People just sort of might assume that it is because it's on the Tube map. And that's the beauty of the Tube map ... it simplistically brings together all these places that are strewn a long way apart onto one simple map, titled 'London Underground', you can be forgiven for thinking that Epping is in London. But it's not. Not really, it's just the Tube map that makes it so.

Epping on the Underground is also one my earliest memories of travelling on the Tube. There used to be a single-track extension on the Central Line from there to a place called Ongar, which eventually closed in 1994 due to low passenger numbers. In fact, steam trains were running on this shuttle as recently as 1957 – one of the last sections of the underground to be using steam powered trains.

And Epping to Ongar is actually the whole reason (I think) of my little love affair with the Underground as I came here as a child – when my cousins had taken me on a day out.

I must have been ten or eleven, and with my mum glad to get me out from under her feet for a whole day on a Saturday, she would set me off packing at 8am with my two older cousins – who were 14 and 16. I was given 50p to buy a 'Red Bus Rover' ticket – which let you travel on any red bus in London, and a packed lunch, and she sent me out for the day with them. It would never happen now but I do remember that I had to be back by 5pm which now seems ridiculously early.

One Saturday, they decide that they wanted to make the most of their Red Bus Rover tickets and ride the most *extreme* bus route that the ticket covers. The bus in question was the 247B which goes from Ongar station at the very end of the Central Line. So to get there, we took the Tube all the way out (one of my cousins bought me a single ticket), and we travelled out ... and we miss the bus.

And that's what I remember the most – the friendly ticket inspector at Ongar station letting us back in onto the train when he finds out that we've missed the bus. So I never got to ride the 247B, but I did get to go to Ongar station – I just wish I can remember more of what it was like.

But it *was* a terribly exciting journey to make as at that time I'd not really been on the underground much. I'd been on plenty of British Rail trains with my parents, but not really the Tube.

As we made the long trip back down the Central line, towards Epping and into London, with me complaining along the way that I really want to use the toilet, something obviously instilled itself within me then that the Tube was a cool thing. The word 'Geek' (or for that even to be a good thing) was years off yet, but that's what had happened that day.

Years later when I get my first job in London, I start to discover things about the Tube that I'd never realised – How ridiculously close Embankment and Charing Cross stations are together. That the topological map bears no relation to the real geography that the lines take. I remember spending one bored Christmas at a girlfriend's family with an A-Z of London and a pack of tracing paper which I'd specifically bought, drawing the real layout of the Tube lines in London. Back at work, I taught myself how to use a vector-based drawing package, and start to design the Tube map on screen, and make variations of it.

So all of these memories go through my head in perfect clarity – me as that ten year old child with a weak bladder and a bag containing a soggy cheese packed-lunched sandwich that his mum has lovingly made for him that morning, the geek-in-the-making with his Tube map designs and tracing paper – how surreal it would have been to have told him then that in the future in the year 2009, he would be at another town called Epping – but the one in America instead.

To be honest, it isn't even really a town. It is just a road. A road that intersects with another road with farmland all around and a few houses dotted within a few minutes' walk in all directions. I'm not really sure where 'Epping' starts or finishes, but after a few minutes of driving up and down I stop to take photos and shoot video at the junction which to me seems to be the centre.

And I stand. Quiet. Motionless.

And there is nothing to be heard.

Nothing.

And I have a moment to myself where I realise that almost six months' worth of planning has come to this, this point. And so it is time to tweet.

10:16 AM June 16th
i'm in Epping, Maine. And there is nothing … literally NOTHING here!

And then I wonder if everywhere in Maine is like this … and that thought takes me to another worrying thought that a lot of the 'small town' places that I have planned to visit might just be junctions and dusty roads in the middle of nowhere too, and there might be zilch to see and no one to talk to. And just as I can feel my calmness receding and an anxiety taking over about what I have set myself up to do, I see something that makes me smile – a lot.

Is that a *railway sleeper* over there? And … another one? And – hang on, a whole pile of them! I walk briskly over to where they are about 50 yards away, up a road that I have not driven up, and take a closer look.

Yup … sleepers. Lots of them! Big hulks of heavy wood as tall as me but certainly a lot heavier. And beyond them? A faint trail … a track …. *where a railway line has once run.*

Now this is funny, because when I'd picked Epping to be my start place – in fact when I had picked any of the places to visit, it had been purely on the name only. I'm no uber-geek (really), and at no point did I think that there might have to be a train line there (or evidence of one) as well. But here it is … an old abandoned train line that used to run through the nothing village of Epping.

And those familiar with the state of London's Underground will sense what I'm getting at, for as if to further match up to the Tube line where Epping is, it's worth knowing that there is too an abandoned line at the Epping in London - the line which in 1994 was closed up to Ongar, and here I am in Epping, USA … looking at the path of an old line that used to run … where? Who knows?

The lady in the gas station a mile down the road doesn't know either. I realise that I need to talk to *someone*, I want to say that I am from London where there is an Epping, and this is what has brought me here to Maine to their Epping. Trouble is, the gas station server is insistent that the 'Folks round here call this place Colombia Falls', and it is then that I notice that the gas station is indeed 'Colombia Falls Super Gas!' and not 'Epping Super Gas!' as I might have expected it to be called. The conversation doesn't go much further, it seems that not everyone in America is super friendly and chatty, or maybe she just wants to serve the big burly bloke standing in line behind me, who really is wearing a classic lumberjack style shirt.

I suddenly feel a bit lonely. And almost a bit stupid? What *am* I doing here … am I really going to see this all the way through to the end. And there would be far better people to talk to and interesting places to see on my way round, right?

I look at my watch. Time is getting on, and I know that I have a long drive ahead of me for the rest of the day. I turn the key in the ignition and the car fails to start ... ah, shit. Not *again*. I wait a moment and try again – still nothing. So I go back inside the gas station to use their toilets, buy another drink for later and try for a third time – and it starts, just.

Mind the Gap please, you are now departing Epping.

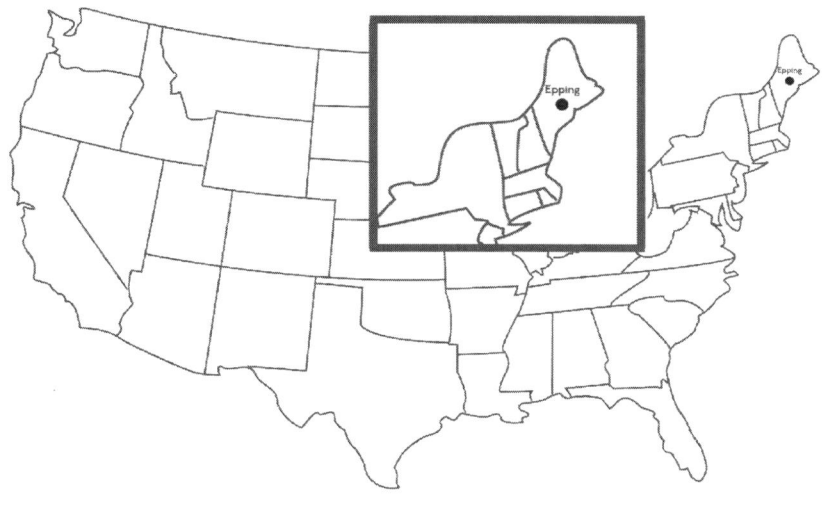

Day one and one 'stop' down, and I head for the second by the end of the day – trouble is it's several hours drive away - and I will learn the hard way over the next three months that America is just so hugely big that it's hard to get your head around *how* big until you've travelled all the way through it, from one side to the other.

I still recall how in England, a drive of four hours will get you via a congested M1 nightmare experience from Manchester to London. Four hours in America is considered a short-trip taken to visit some family or friends, along a relatively congestion-free two lane highway.

And so whilst I have six hours of driving to do today that to me is a chore, I've since met many Americans who wouldn't bat an eye at that, as they consider it as just something that you have to do if you live here, and definitely something that you have to do if you want to explore.

I think of this all during my long drive - six hours in total - except that five hours into it I find myself cursing – out loud, all down to my stupidity.

> **6:51 PM Jun 16th**
> stopped on Hwy 4, New Hampshire (Concord), trying to make my campsite in Vermont before dark, eating from a terrible and terribly well-known fast food 'restaurant'

I'm going to say something here which you're going to laugh at, and in retrospect I'm able to laugh at it myself, but when I give you my reasoning I hope you'll see why it's the way it is.

I've just embarked on Day One of an eight week road trip across the third largest country in the world, where I would drive thousands of miles across roads, to many new places that I have never been to before, where I would literally not know where I am going until I get there, and ... I don't have a map with me.

Well not a *paper* map at the very least ... oh no, because I have my laptop which connects to the Internet and thus Google maps, and I have my SatNav system with me which is capable of looking up any place and any address at any time ... and it takes you there, right? So I feel like I am covered. Except that's where I get a bit unstuck, because I realise as I enter the town of Brattleboro, Vermont - that I don't where the KOA campground is that I want to stay in that night.

I've booked it online that morning using their website, noting that Brattleboro is just a short drive up the road to Putney – the same named town of Vermont that I want to be in the next morning – but I have no record of their address, or a paper map onto which I can point my finger and say, 'It's there'. When I'd rolled into Bar Harbour the night before, the nice big shiny yellow 'KOA' sign has been at the side of the road and I just found it that way ... and I've foolishly assumed that Brattleboro would be the same. But it isn't the same ... Brattleboro is a much larger town than Bar Harbour and also seems to be integrally entwined with Interstate 91. I make a wrong turn at a badly lit intersection[5], and find myself on the slip road leading down to the Interstate where I have to drive along to the wrong junction, come off, turn around and then drive back again.

---

[5] I almost don't have to qualify that. I'd like to make a sweeping statement early on in the book and say that all intersections in America are badly lit.

8:43 PM Jun 16th
filling up with gas for second time in a day! Another $50 spent

Eventually I let my macho pride swell down, I ask for directions at a gas station, after which I am there in less than five minutes, down a road I haven't looked – and I've wasted about 45 minutes driving round. And so at ten o'clock at night with all light gone, and a slight drizzle falling from the sky, I miserably pitch my tent under the headlights of the car.

10:15 PM Jun 16th
made it to KOA battleboro Vermont. 3 hrs later than planned. No video editing tonight....

The moment I get my tent up, the rain obviously stops and I am able to get my camp stove out and make some tea. I take a sip recount my long first day to myself. It isn't so bad after all – I can still get a decent night of sleep right now and I will make my same-name destination in the morning and still be away on time. It just feels like that the main thing that I have done today is drive, and not a lot else.

Day 2 – Wednesday 17th June

The Second Day

*I woke up in the night, wishing it would rain
The morning light had shown, that I was not alone
You don't even know, that my love for you is real, the second day'*

I am going to have to get a pillow if this is going to work, as somewhere at around 6am – when I can smell the wetness on the grass outside – I wake up with a pain in my neck. I pull a jumper from a nearby bag and stuff it under my head for support, but it's too late – I'm already awake, and half an hour later I get up properly, and survey the morning.

> **6:38 AM Jun 17th**
> a little too cold for my liking this morning Vermont. you'd better warm up some
>
> **7:29 AM Jun 17th**
> hot shower, shave, clean teeth. ohmiGodthatfeelsgood. #camping

I am now quite adept at screwing together my camp stove, and within moments I have boiling water bubbling away to make some tea, nectar to my throat, and as I drink I realise that I need to do something that I should have done before I'd left, namely – get a map. And as it turns out, the lovely *Betty* in the reception/shop of the KOA campground is more than helpful with this matter.

'The one in Spearfish is just lovely', she says as her finger – perfectly manicured with a deep purple coloured varnish – points at locations all over America. I realise that if KOA is going to be the way to go for me, then a guide to all their locations and a map showing where they all are is going to be very helpful indeed – I can just type the ZIP code into my SatNav and it will guide me in without all the hassle that I've had the night before.

She also gives me a whole bundle of other literature, and to top it all signs my T-shirt. Oh did I not mention that? Sorry. OK – alongside everything else I am doing, I have had a T-Shirt printed out with an outline map (including the states) of the USA on it, and I am getting one person per state to sign and date it as I travel round.

I really want to stay and chat for longer but I know that I have to crack on early with my day as I have a few locations to go in a short space of time, and I want to get an early start. I say my 'Goodbyes' pack up my tent, and head off. Well, not until I can get the car to start again that is. Again, as per yesterday it shows the same weird signs of the rev counter spinning around like crazy, and it takes a few attempts of me pumping the gas pedal and turning the engine over until it starts properly.

I should probably get that fixed.

In the USA
Putney, Vermont
On the Tube map
Putney Bridge / East Putney (District Line)

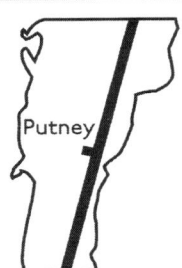

Now in London of course there's Putney Bridge Tube station, and East Putney stations (as well as just 'Putney' – a National Rail station), but as I find myself standing on a bridge in the Main Street overlooking a small waterfall and waterwheel that appears to be powering a nearby lumber mill I decided that I like *this* Putney, and this would be the one for me. (Later that night on Google maps, I discovered that there is an East Putney but it is a little way of where I currently am, and looks like another crossroads in the middle of nowhere, and coming off the back of Epping, I really don't want that).

I wander up and down the main drag of the town ... and when I say 'town' I really mean about three business locations on one road, consisting of a laundry store, a Pizza Shop, the 'Putney Diner' and Mountain Paul's General Store, where a large figurine of a hefty man with a lumberjack shirt and an axe over his shoulder towers above the entrance door.

I enter inside. And soon discover that it is one of those shops that I would soon be accustomed with in America, as it seems to sell everything. Really, *everything*. I'm beginning to wonder why they even bother to have a sign up that promotes anything in the windows, as to anyone in this town it would soon be obvious that this is the shop for everything – If you want it, they've probably got it.

Behind the counter, an elderly man – without a red checked shirt or axe over his shoulder unlike the figurine by the entrance – serves who is obviously a local, and they both smile at me as I approach.

'Can I help you sir?' he asks with a smile. 'No, no, just ...' and I really want to say something other than 'looking' but what else do you say In that situation? Until that is I remember what I really want to say. 'No, no, just … passing through your town because it's got the same name as one on the Tube Map back in my home town in London.'

Except that I don't say that – because I chicken out. Honestly Geoff, you're *rubbish* sometimes, but my sixth sense also tells me that if I'd tried to have this conversation with the sweet old man in his shop, I think it would have confused him very quickly. Instead, some regular small talk ensues and a few minutes later without me purchasing anything I skulk out of the shop wondering why I'm not having the conversation I know I should be having – with a local in Putney.

Back outside in the mountain air that I realise I have climbed up into, it fills and refreshes my lungs, and armed with a coffee that I don't really need, I go for a walk to see what else I can discover. Leaning over a brick wall I find a gushing torrent of water from a river turning a huge wooden water-mill wheel, but it appears to be attached to the side of a normal house and not a business such as a bakery like I'd hoped.

There's an old man wearing a cap out walking his dog. Two men in a pickup truck – both wearing caps – pull up, and head towards the Putney store. And then a young woman, puffing so hard, red in face and clutching an iPod because of the tell-tale white earbuds comes jogging past. Oh and she's wear a cap.

Maybe I should get myself a cap to wear?

Back in the car, I punch my next destination into the SatNav, and then remember to fire out an update unto the world of twitter.

> **8:59 AM Jun 17th**
> no.2 Putney, Vermont complete! I'm happy to report this is an actual town, unlike Epping, ME.

And turn the key to start the engine – first time.

Putney to Plaistow on the Tube – on a direct train on the District Line would take about 45 minutes I work out in my head, visualising the Tube map as I make the same journey in real life – but in the USA from Vermont to New Hampshire, along US Highway 2, is just over 2 hours, which is about as long as a journey can feel like on the London Underground sometimes. There have been six hours between stops yesterday – so it feels much nicer to be at this one in just a third of the time. As I drive past the 'Welcome to…' sign, and turn a bend in the road I can already see that I am going to like it – it looks pretty.

> **1:19 PM Jun 17th**
> i'm in Plaistow. that's Plaistow, New Hampshire & not district line stop. It's pretty. Church, bandstand, clock tower etc.

In the USA
Plaistow, New Hampshire
On the Tube map
Plaistow
(District and Hammersmith & City Lines)

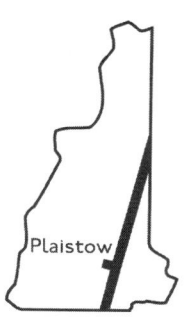

I park in what seems to be the town square, grab my camera and go for a wander around. My first impression is that there are a lot of flags up – but that doesn't really surprise me because America is a country that likes its flags, likes having lots of variations of them, likes hanging them up, and then organises tours of places where a friendly guide points out all the flags to you.

What I think is the state flag for New Hampshire (A boat surrounded by a golden circle and then golden laurel leaves) hangs outside a very brick and wooden building which very much looks like it might be some sort of visitor's centre. Hey, I'm a visitor! Perfect for me to pop into.

Oh. No. I am wrong ... although there *is* an information board with some local events, there are far more signs saying 'chamber rooms this way', and notices about new developments up, than there are about local miniature railways instead. I appear to have walked into the town hall – doesn't stop me walking around and having a nose though.

'Can I help you?' says a friendly voice. As I walk down a corridor and poke my head into an empty meeting room. Turning around, I see another room – an office – off of the corridor where the gentleman inside is also getting up and walking over to me.

This it turns out is *Malcolm* and he is the extremely pleasant Town Hall manager of Plaistow! 'Can I help you?', he asks again – and I know in a moment that I either have two ways of going about this, mumble an apology about being in the wrong place and scuttle off, or actually going for it this time and explain what I am doing there. I suddenly remember the nice old man in the shop in Putney this morning and how I'd bailed ... and I know I must not bail again.

Do it Geoff, do it. Explain why you're here – tube trains 'n' all. So I take a deep breath, and go for it.

'Hello!' I say with a cheery smile on my face, 'I'm from London, England where there's also a place called Plaistow…' and before I know it, I launch into it all.

Half an hour later, I am climbing back into the car, and I am *delighted*.

> **2:58 PM Jun 17th**
> the town hall manager of Plaistow just signed my t-shirt and gave me a free 'Plaistow' cap! I'm wearing it now.

I explain to Malcolm why I am here, what I am doing, and he has lapped it up. 'There's no railroad station here though!' he jokes at some point, but we talk, he tells me about the town's history, how it is thriving, and best of all – he gives me a 'Plaistow' cap. Yes – a cap. Like some Putney-cap-wearing haven had worked it's voodoo over here to Plaistow, but also reader take careful attention now of just how easily won over I am sometimes, and that if you know me in real life and want me to do something, all I'm saying is that you can do a lot worse than give me a free cap with the name of your home town on it. I put it on as I leave the town hall, and wear it for the rest of the day (and several days after, in fact).

But basically, I am charmed. I suspect that coming up later on the trip there will be more desolate crossroads (like Epping), or more Putney moments (where I wouldn't engage with any people), but here on my second day and third same-named place, I feel like I've done a little of what I'd set out to achieve and that makes me feel really happy.

It's also worth pointing out that in the rest of the several thousand words that lay ahead of me that I am going to write about America, I am going to say some negative and cynical things – things which people usually remember and overlook the nice stuff.

You might know me and after having read this book you'll say to me 'But all you did was whine and complain about things Geoff!', but that's just because I'm British and if there's one thing that we *excel* at, it's being cynical and complaining about things, OK?

So let me take this opportunity to stress and point out that this is a moment that is pleasant and delightful. There is a veteran's memorial garden, nice flowerbeds that obviously are kept well, a children's swing and play area in the park – it's a cute town. But best of is that Malcolm takes time out of his day to chat to me and be nice for no other reason that he can, and I walk away and leave Plaistow thinking what a lovely town it is and what a lovely man he has been. I really like Plaistow, and best of all – that's two 'stops' done today, and to cap it all off (a 'Plaistow' emblazoned cap too) I know I can knock out another one quite quickly too as it's only a short drive away.

A short few miles down the road and I cross the state line from New Hampshire into Gloucester, and I am reminded of something else that Malcolm has told me – that New Hampshire has no sales tax on goods compared to Massachusetts, so basically a LOT of people from MA, make the drive up to New Hampshire (and often to Plaistow!) to come to shop for things and get them a little cheaper. A crazy thing about the USA is the different laws all over the country between states mean a lot of 'border hopping' between states for things like this – as I would discover more later.

4:10 PM Jun 17th
i'm in Gloucester, MA. It's a cute little fishing/seaside town. Very British-esque

4:18 PM Jun 17th
this is three places in one day. If all days were like this, I'd be done in just over two weeks

---

In the USA
Gloucester, Massachusetts
On the Tube map
Gloucester Road
(District, Circle and Piccadilly Lines)

Driving down the main drag I instantly decide that I am also going to like Gloucester.

Hang on – that's two in a row isn't it? That's good. I've been in Gloucester for just five minutes and decide that I like it because – as with Plaistow – there are flags hanging from the street lamps, the sun is shining, and I see a kid being pushed along in a stroller eating an ice-cream, with the typical situation of more ice cream going onto the outside of his mouth that in it.

All of that, and probably because a car exits out of a space right outside the coffee shop that I've decided looks more than likely to give me free Internet, and as I pull up outside the Lone Gull coffee shop, there is indeed a sign in the window saying 'Free Wi-Fi' here, perfect.

Erin & *Castille* that are working here behind the counter are busy, but they talk to me more when I ask if they have a Massachusetts quarter in their cash register which they can give me as part of the change. 'You want what kind of quarter?' asks Castille – the American verbal disease of making T's sounds like D's means that it comes out as 'Quarder', but I forgive her. And explain why I am collecting quarders. I mean – quarters. Oops.

The US Royal Mint has a 'State quarter program' running, where four times a year they release a 25 Cent coin with a picture of a different State on the back of it. You have to remember that I am the person who's been to all the Tube stations, is now driving to all the states, is getting a T-Shirt signed, is spotting license plates and also trying to get a Geocache per state as well - so yes, I have an OCD tendencies to collect things, and there is no way that I am not going to get one of every state quarter as I drive around the country.

And I remember that I don't have a Massachusetts one yet, and seeing as I am *in* that state, it seems a good time to try and get one.

I chat to the barista some more when she comes to bring out my drink at the table where I am sat at a few minutes later and discover that Gloucester – predominantly a fishing town – is famous for being the location where 'The Perfect Storm' film has been based and shot. 'My mom saw George Clooney one morning!' she tells me excitedly, 'But I was only little at the time, so I don't really remember it' she notes, a little sadly afterwards.

She also tells me the story which every American seems to relate when talking about the movie – that somehow, one of the relatives of someone who has died in the real storm (which the movie is based upon) had been to see the film *without realising what the film is about*. And halfway through when they realise –get upset, walk out, and then later try to sue the Hollywood company that had produced it. Is that last part true or just an Internet rumour? I'd love to know.

Post coffee, I take a walk down the sea front and find a small harbour part where there is a whole line of fixed 'look out binoculars'. I am reminded of the cover of the Bill Bryson book 'Neither here nor there' and consider for a moment that this may be the point where the photo is taken for the cover of his book.

A huge line of Star & Stripes flags flutter in the breeze … and I look out to see but can't quite make out the horizon. So I deposit a quarter into one of the look-out machines, and with a now magnified view realise the reason I can't see the horizon clearly is because there is a fog/mist out to sea, and all I can

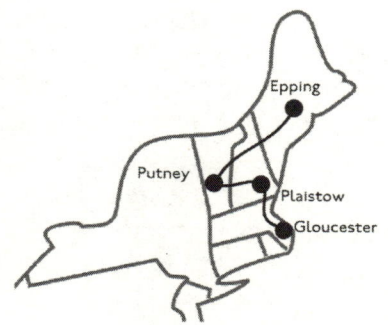

34

see now is a magnified view of some fog and mist obscuring the horizon. I tut, lean back up straight, and then have a moment of realisation where I grab at the change in my pocket ... and yup, sods law has it that out of all the quarters in my pocket, the one I have just used is the Massachusetts one that I have just collected and wanted to keep ... damn it!

Moving along the seafront, I find the Gloucester Fishermen Memorial nearby detailing the deaths of over 5000 fisherman and home history about the town. English settlers (presumably, from Gloucester?) have first come here in 1623. 'They that go down to the sea in Ships, 1623 – 1923' is engraved on a huge monument of a sailor at the 'Steering Wheel' at the ship, and I am lost in awe for a moment imaging being a fisherman clinging onto his life out at sea in a massive storm, and how easy I have it now in comparison.

The seagulls chirp in the air, the water crashes against the concrete harbour wall behind me, and in cliché to end all clichés I genuinely breathe in the salt-sea-air, before the female shrill of a mother shouting 'Daniel, STOPPIT!', as the sea-silence is broken by two children playing, a younger brother chasing after his older squealing sister, water-pistol in hand as he pumps jets of water in her direction. It is my cue.

Back in the car, I get out my notebook and for the first time, start to write a list of the places that I have been to so far, and start to categorise them too.

SAME NAME TOWNS TALLY

Something there and enjoyable
Plaistow, Gloucester

Something there but not that exciting to be honest
Putney

Nothing there but somehow being in the middle of nowhere made it OK
Epping

Yes - I decide that I am going to make a list of the places that I go and categorise them accordingly – so at the end of the trip, I can see just how many places were great – and how many were just big nothing's. Gloucester? Gets a tick.

Bring on the next same named place!

Get. Me. Out. Of. The. Car.

Now.

Please.

Oh my God, oh my God, oh my God.

I can feel the anxiety bubbling up inside of me that starts with my legs shaking slightly, followed by a slight prickly feeling of a possible panic attack rising up in heat around my collar towards the back of my head.

I've entered the highway into the centre of Boston about half an hour ago, fifteen minutes of which is slow driving, and then the last fifteen has been just constant stop-go crawling along, and weirdly I find this worse than being stopped altogether as it is agitating me not be able to relax but have my foot constantly hovering over the gas and brake peddle, stopping and starting and inching towards what looks like to be a very fancy bridge, that is already crammed with traffic.

Now I know it's a cliché to moan on like this, and it's an easy conversational starter to say 'Oh, the traffic is bad', and 'I got caught in a jam', but please – *seriously* – please don't ever make me drive in Boston again. Bridges and tunnels and ramps that twist and turn, chock-a-block with cars, and intersections and junctions and slip roads that suddenly appear out of nowhere all so close together that the SatNav hasn't got time to catch up and be able to differentiate between them all and so you miss your turn or take the wrong turn – at one point, I miss the turning I am supposed to take *three time*s in a row, and loop back round on myself, only spotting the small slip road leading to the highway that I want to take on the fourth time of trying. In case you haven't got the point yet – I am not enjoying driving in Boston.

Suddenly, another slip road appears! What!? That's not on my SatNav, and I then I realise that I'm on a road above another road and the SatNav thinks I'm on the one below and I haven't seen it coming. The bridge seems to be on multiple levels, confusing my already addled brain, and I'm not thinking straight and feel not right to drive, so I shoot down the slip road and turn into a sketchy looking back street, and park up in a place where I probably shouldn't, and get out of the car so that I can stretch my legs and breath calmly again.

> **6:31 PM Jun 17th**
> Boston in 5 : not a traffic friendly city.

> **6:33 PM Jun 17th**
> oh hang on, i can do it in 2 : shitty traffic.

I make a few phone calls and fire off some text messages, and leave it a good hour during which time the only thing to come down this back road with trash cans that need emptying is a stray dog, that comes up, sniffs around the tyres of the car, licks at an oil patch in the road, and then runs off again.

I get back in, and turn the key. I turn the key again and again and it takes several attempts for the engine to cough into life ... it is still playing up, and once started, I plot a course on the SatNav that avoids going on the Interstate, and slowly – through backstreets interspersed with many intersections I drive towards my friends Mike & Melissa with whom I am staying the night with again.

They live near Fenway Park – the massive baseball ground, and as I get close I literally start to see signs that there's a game on tonight – billboards, posters and most of all lots of men out on the street saying 'Parking this way for the game!', making it obvious.

> **6:50 PM Jun 17th**
> sign on '99' diner. 'kids eat free if red sox win', cute.

I have to park the car (Hang on, would you like that in a Boston accent? Sure ... here goes), I have to paaaark the caaaaah several blocks away from Mike's house, but of course don't want to have to lug all the equipment with me. So this means stopping outside of his house, taking in all the equipment quickly, and then driving several blocks way to pay lots of dollars – better than being towed again and paying a fine to park overnight. Once inside Mike gives me a cold beer from the fridge, and announces to take my woes away that we are all going to the game.

'So, you've got tickets then?' I ask. 'No', he replies 'But I figure we can get some from a scalper pretty easily'

'Oh ok' I say, and we all walk along for a few seconds, before it occurs to me that I should probably ask.

'What's a scalper?'

This time Mike's wife Melissa looks at me like I am a little odd for asking such a question and speaks up. 'A scalper? You know ... a guy that stands outside the ground selling tickets!' 'Oh you mean a ticket tout!' I reply eagerly finally getting on board with what they really mean. 'A what?' 'A tout'. 'A Toooowwt?' she tries, her Bostonian really coming through strongly. 'Almost... try... towt!'. 'Towt?' 'That's it! Only spell is with a U though if you ever write it down'.

> **7:26 PM Jun 17th**
> new US/UK word comparison! A 'scalper' is a 'tout', as in ... ticket tout. Brilliant! #redsoxrules

And thus starts the conversation that sooner or later always starts after a period of time when an Englishman and Americans get together – the difference between the words and the language. Because whilst everyone knows that trousers are pants, and a lift is an elevator, and the pavement becomes a sidewalk on the west side of the pond, it's only when you've lived here for a bit and immersed yourself completely in the culture that you discover that a tout is a scalper, Perspex is called Plexiglas, a cagoule is a poncho, a balaclava is a ski-mask, tippex is call white-out, and cotton buds are better known as Q-tips.

Oh, and if you want to completely freak an American out, try using the word 'forecourt' when referring to the area of a petrol station that you pull up and come to a rest before you fill up – they have no idea what this means. They don't use it. There is no equivalent. To them, the whole thing is just 'A gas station' – nothing more, nothing less. It's freaky.

> **7:52M Jun 17th**
> there are TV's in the urinals at the pub/ bar across the road from the Red Sox stadium, so you can watch the action whilst you pee.

When I get back from relieving myself, Melissa's sister and girlfriend have joined us and more drinks and beers are ordered, amongst a general discussion of when would be the best time to try and 'scalp' some tickets. Five minutes before the game is about to start, or five minutes after the game has started? The chat carries on, and before we know, it's twenty minutes into the game, and no one has really made a move to get up and try and find a scalper to get some tickets, which is fine because it is nice ... pleasant ... and suddenly it becomes not about going to the game, but about hanging out with people in a bar in Boston, just chatting about stuff and having a nice time.

I ask them questions about living in American's supposedly most Anglicised city (though I fail to see any red phone boxes, or cars driving on the left), and they in turn all ask me about that places I have been to so far, and how Epping has been nice but Plaistow is currently 'winning'. I suppose? There shouldn't be a winner, should there? Maybe just a favourite.

As we leave the bar though, I feel as if I should record some of this though and remember that all this time I've had my video camera slung over my shoulder. I give the camera to Mike and get him to shoot some video of me.

---

[6] There's a Nickleback song that refers to 'Bottom of the Ninth' and for years I had no idea what it meant, or in fact it was a baseball reference, even though I used to sing along with it whenever it came on the radio. It was when I came to the USA that I learned it's the English Football equivalent of 90 minutes being on the clock, or perhaps in injury time – there's not a lot of time left in the game to salvage something if your team is losing – PS. I am not condoning the purchasing of any published music by Nickleback by the way, I just unavoidably hear it on the radio sometimes.

I take some photos too, and we walk around the outside of Fenway, soak up the atmosphere of the people that are still around outside and the roar of the noise from the people that are inside, I wonder if they are at the bottom of the ninth yet[6], we head back, grab one of the many pedicabs that are waiting outside, and again I grab some video interviewing the guy as he rides us home. Still in a super video mode, I get Melissa to shoot me whilst talking to Mike back in the kitchen of their place, as Mike is a road trip veteran himself, having driven around a lot of the country a few years ago and he gives me a few tips of things to do and not to do. And finally, after another drink, sometime quite late, we decide to call it a night and I crash out on the air mattress in their lounge.

Day 3 – Thursday 18t June

The Lonely Rhode

*'I'm going down that lonely road , I wish I was going home
I would do it all again, if i just could be someone.
It's been like this for ages, I can't hear a word they say
I'm crying on a sunny day'*

In the morning, over a very strong coffee that Mike makes me, I plug up my PC and awkwardly sit on the mainly deflated air mattress, and with a grim determination, start to edit up my first ever official 'on the road' video.

> **7:28 AM Jun 18th**
> finally cutting together my first road trip video! you think it's EASY doin' this shit on the road people? ha. expect it in 2+ hours

Back in the luxury of Charleston, I thought back to my old job – a nice little snug studio room with some sound proofing. A comfy chair. Video editing keyboard with jog-wheel that I'd bought. I even think back to my home setup with all the cables nicely organised, soundboard mixer at my side and amplified speakers making it easy to hear what is going on.

Here, on the floor of Mike's lounge I look at the mess of tangled cables that are everywhere. I end up awkwardly changing from a kneeling position to a cross-legged position every few minutes, and the mouse is on an uneven surface making it difficult to precisely edit the video where I want it. Editing video on the road in a temporary setup? Yes, I'm whining, but that's because it is around that moment that I think I start to realise the challenge of what I've set myself up to do. It is not going to be as easy, or as comfortable as I am used to, or how I thought it might be. I feel a little grumpy.

Just less than two and a half hours later though, and I finish cobbling something together – three minutes worth – and upload and publish it to the world.

> **9:54 AM Jun 18th**
> FIRST VIDEO IS UP! Go play people: 'The Maine Reason for Being Here'
> http://bit.ly/mSm7B

I get a few tweet replies almost immediately back from some people, a couple from some nice folk who appreciate the technical difficulties of cutting stuff together on the move and what equipment am I using to do it? And that makes me feel a little better. I feel like I've been spending all my time this morning doing this, and that time is against me and that I need to push on, so I say my polite goodbyes to Mike ... knowing that I might not see him again for ... well I don't know when. It might be years, and I hit the road.

> **11:36 AM Jun 18th**
> mmmmm.... dunkin' donuts breakfast, coffee, donut. delicious. Rhode Island next.

I swing by the nearest Dunkin' Donuts and I swear I can feel the vanilla-infused caffeine mix swirling round my body, attempting to lift my spirits. I negotiate the Boston traffic as best I can, loyally following the Satnav's instructions to head south, west and south a lot more as I head towards Rhode Island, and my next 'Tube' stop.

Two hours later, I cross into Rhode Island somewhere on the I95, noting that I haven't crossed an expanse of water or even a river to get here ... so is it really an island, I wonder? And into the brilliantly named town of Pawtucket, feeling like the only thing that can keep me going at this point is another coffee.

> **2:00 PM Jun 18th**
> hello Rhode Island, you are tiny. I feel a Starbucks coming on ....

Except I can't find a Starbucks, and it starts to rain, and I realise that I feel a bit ... depressed now? Why? I pull in at a gas station to use the loo and have some of *their* coffee, but it doesn't really taste the same as what I crave, and I drink only a few sips, before sitting back in the seat of the car feeling fed-up, alone, and even more grumpy. What *is* wrong with me?

And then I nod off.

Twenty minutes later after my unscheduled power nap, I awake with a start, because the *slam!* of a car bonnet being closed from the car next to me where the driver has a big wiry wispy beard that looks like you can keep small creatures inside of it. He gives me a funny look back as I guess I am inadvertently giving him a 'Hey you just woke me up!' kind of look at him. I'm not to know it then, but pulling onto the forecourt of a petrol station into a parking space and having a short nap is going to become quite a common thing for me to do on this trip.

It has also started to rain whilst I've been asleep and the sky is very grey. My grumpy mood has not been lifted by the nap, but I know I should push on. I turn the key and the engine starts (successful on the third attempt), and head for Warwick, my next stop.

> **1:12 PM Jun 18th**
> Warwick bound. I bet you 50 cents there's a railroad there.

I hope as I drive that the weather might improve, but the rain is not letting up, and nor is my mood. As the SatNav counts down and we get closer to Warwick, my spirits raise a little only for them to be massively damped again the moment I get there. For Warwick is ... well ... it is ... well, just sort of a non-descript nothing. In the rain.

In the USA
Warwick, Rhode Island
On the Tube map
Warwick Road (Bakerloo Line)

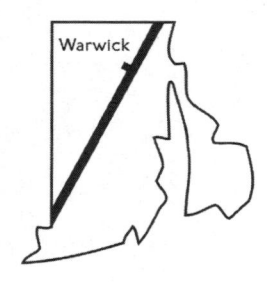

2:57 PM Jun 18th
i'm at Warwick, Rhode island. it's ... umm, sparse.

This is weird. When I've been at Epping in Maine, there really has been nothing. Here in Warwick there is more 'stuff' about than there has been in Maine, and yet somehow it feels emptier.

To summarise – Warwick appears to be a crossroads. In a built up residential area, and there are traffic lights. What is odd, is that there is a constant stream of traffic in all directions on the cross roads, and there are houses – residential houses – on all corners, but ... that's it. There is no life in that there are no people. No shops. No cute coffee houses. No one walking their dog. Just lots of people-carrying cars – Soccer Moms taking their kids home from school – splashing through the puddles by the kerbside as they turn to take them home in time for their dinner.

I get out – but not for long because that involves getting wet – and look in all directions and can see nothing but traffic. I snap a hurried photo, shielding my camera as I go, and climb back into the car and used the cuff of my sleeve to wipe the windscreen where the condensation is forming on the inside of the glass.

I think about my stops so far – I've enjoyed Epping as it had been the first and even though it was lonely and nothing there. Putney has been pleasant and I am amused by my cowardice at talking to a local. Plaistow has also been brilliant and Malcolm friendly, and by Gloucester I'm feeling like I am really motoring along – exploring the town, talking to people and really getting into it. But now with Warwick, it has all come to a halt. May I say I have hit the buffers to use a train metaphor? Perhaps not. So I won't. And so I just stay put in the car, sitting.

I sit with the engine and radio off. I sit there with the patter of rain on the roof of the car. I sit with the inside of the windscreen starting to fog up again as my breath starts to form and condensation hits it. I wipe it with a classic swipe of the end of my sleeve again bunched up in my hand, and stare out as a rainy crossroads with boring traffic going over that is Warwick. And continued to just sit.

This isn't meant to be happening. This isn't how I've imagined it. I'm not supposed to be sat, by myself, in a car which doesn't start every time in the rain looking at a crossroads of nothing. This is not the road trip that I have imagined. There is meant to be something going on here that I can indulge myself in – a local museum or friendly people I can talk to – not a dull, dreary rainy crossroads with nothing going on. I really thought there would be more to Warwick.

Shit.

> **3:06 PM Jun 18th**
> Rhode Island, officially 'Ocean State' according to the license plates, whereas 'Pissing down with rain State' would be more appropriate.

For a moment, I became ensconced into a drizzly trance with the raindrops hitting the windscreen in a random and yet somehow organised pattern. It reminds me of the floor of Tube trains back in London, where a random fleck pattern of colours is used on the floors. They look seemingly random, but I bet there must be some order in there to them somehow. I realise I have my eyes closed, and I am picturing Tube carriage floor patterns in my mind. So I open my eyes.

I stare out in the gloom of traffic passing by, wondering if there is something more to this place, and can come up with only one thing – It seems like the majority of cars have customised license plates.[7]

> **3:12 PM Jun 18th**
> RI: almost every other car has got a personalised license plate. weird.

This reminds me of another thing that I want to do – take a photo of one of these license plates. As well as visiting the 'Same Name' town in every state, I also have a few other minor objectives on the side that I've decided that I want to try and do, those being to find a Geocache[8] in every state, get a picture of every 'Welcome To…' state sign, as I cross the

---

[7] Weeks later, back in Charleston I bumped into someone from Rhode Island who confirmed that this was the case – apparently more people in Rhode Island have customised car license plates than any other state.

[8] A Geocache is a GPS based treasure hunt game. People hide 'caches' in secret locations all over the world, publish the GPS coordinates online on a website, which you sign up/into get the coordinates and then try and locate the cache.

State line, and also to get a picture of a license plate of at least one car in every State —as they are all different, with their own designs and slogans[9].

Taking a picture of a parked car with its Rhode Island plate though, makes me suddenly recall if I've got one in every state so far or not, so I go back through on my camera and check ... I have them all – *except* for one in New Hampshire, which I've forgotten to snap , dammit. Ok then I tell myself – I must look out for a car which has a New Hampshire plate and take its photo.

But back to Warwick. Ok. To be honest – it's a bit miserable. This isn't the all-singing and dancing fun road trip that I have imagined. When I'd been on the train back to my mum's from Jono's house that night at no point had I envisaged sitting at rainy crossroads with my hands on the steering wheel watching my breath cloud up the windscreen. Not one bit.

I need to move on even though it feels like Warwick has been a failure. It's time to go to Wapping instead. The engine makes a weird whining noise as I start it – just about on the first time – I indicate and pull out onto the road flicking the wipers on as I go, and head west.

A change of State did not bring about a change in the weather. Two solid hours of driving alone in the rain, plus a 15 minute power-nap at a gas station where I also fill up, and the Connecticut 'Welcome To!' State sign whizzes past my right hand window, in the inclement gloom.

> **5:26 PM Jun 18th**
> Connecticut : Raining, *sigh*

I dutifully follow the direction of my SatNav, but with 10 minutes to go I start to fear that it's going to be another Warwick ... I doesn't appear to be in much of a built up or interesting area, and the gloomy rain really is getting my mood down now. It gets darker – and as it does my SatNav glows brighter, five minutes to go, and I may have silently prayed for a sudden change in the roadside landscape and for a cute town to suddenly appear.

One minute away, and I know it's not going to happen as I am driving down a non-descript road with trees towering overhead blocking out most of what is left of the daylight 'Wapping' appears as a blob ahead on the SatNav, and I prepare myself for a massive let down.

---

[9] I once discovered through most Americans that I talked to, that more people could remember the slogan on a States' license plate than they could tell me what the Capital city for that State was.

In the USA
Wapping, Connecticut
On the Tube map
Wapping (Overground)

It is a massive let down. As I find myself staring at a barn.

> **7:36 PM Jun 18th**
> stop number six – welcome to Wapping, Connecticut. it is raining, and Wapping appears to be a barn.
>
> **7:37 PM Jun 18th**
> Wapping, Connecticut is soul-less, a little depressing and I think I need a coffee and some Wi-Fi badly.

Except … is it really a barn? From a distance, it looks like a barn … but then I realise that it is too new and shiny of a building to be an old barn. It is wooden, slatted, and painted brown, and it has a sign up the top saying 'Post Road Stages' and a wooden wheel out front, given every indication now that I thought about it that this is a re-constructed building of some old horse-drawn staging post, and yes … this … *this* is all that there is to Wapping. Really? Surely not.

But the longer I sit there – the longer it dawns on me. Yes, this is all there is. And there is nothing else to see. I check by not getting out of the car (as it is still hurling it down), but driving around for a few minutes – up the road and back again, to the 'barn' where are a few other non-descript outbuildings, but it isn't clear what they are. Is this some kind of tourist attraction some reason closed, or am I just out of hours?

I drive around an empty car park trying to work out more to it – there is a rusty old white truck parked here, but no-one about. I drive a little up the road one way further in case there is anything else … but there isn't. I drive a little back the other way – the way I have come and there are just a couple of houses set back from the road, but that is all – nothing else, just this modern re-done staging post.

I start to wonder why when I'd picked my 'same name' places from the website, that I haven't done more research to make sure that these named places are actually *something* and not just a crossroads in the middle of nowhere. But hang on – a crossroads in the middle of nowhere is kind of exciting, but this … is a sort of nothing in the middle of nothing, and I'm really sure *what* it is.

45

And here's the shocking part to which I must admit ... I don't even get out of the car. It is raining so hard now – the sort of hard where you'd be soaked to the bone after 30 seconds, so I don't want to. And nothing that I can see in the gloom of whatever the hell Wapping is tempts me to get out and get that wet, and so I don't. And after a few more moments of wandering what Wapping may have been or is now, I start the engine and move on again.

SAME NAME TOWNS TALLY

Something there and enjoyable
Plaistow, Gloucester

Something there but not that exciting to be honest
Putney

Nothing there but somehow being in the middle of nowhere made it OK
Epping

Nothing there, and not that exciting either. Oops.
Warwick, Wapping

Back onto the highway and a few miles down the road in search of hot sustenance in solid or beverage form, I find the world's most deserted shopping centre. Well I say shopping 'centre', but it isn't a 'Mall' style of centre – rather instead lots of individual shops all built close together and linked together by a series of small roads with a plethora of parking spaces dotted everywhere. There is a sign on the highway indicating that it is open until 9pm, but in the fading evening light there seems to be very little patronage.

On the plus side, the rain reduces down to a slight drizzle which encourages me to get out of the car and go for a wander. It is only when I do this I realise that there is music playing – all around. A cheesy instrumental version of some 80's ballad or similar, but the music is being played *outside*. I look and see that there are speakers buried in the ground – amongst the small trees plants and shrubbery that makes up the dividing verges keeping pedestrians and cars apart. That's if there are any cars or pedestrians about that is, as there are hardly any. It is surreal – it isn't as if this place is old or run down or abandoned, it is modern, with modern shops but it is just empty. And drizzly. And a little cold too.

Not all the businesses are booming though. I stand staring at the empty shell of a building that has so once clearly been a Starbucks – you can tell by the colouring and remnants of the façade left behind that that's what it has once been, but no more. Hard times are hitting the coffee giant too, it would seem.

> **7:45 PM Jun 18th**
> For the 3rd time today, my TomTom has taken me to a Starbucks that is shut down. Are the coffee Gods against me?

I press on and twenty minutes down the road, see another Mall – this time more traditional and set back from the one with one giant parking lot in front of me, and in the middle of that parking lot? A Starbucks! The glow of green draws me in with its hot liquiddy goodness and the promise of some free 1's and 0's in their thousands bring me deliverance of information and connectivity with the rest of the world that I so badly crave.

> **8:12 PM Jun 18th**
> Six states/same name places complete. Progress map: http://is.gd/15JtB

Over a steamy cup of coffee which literally turns my damp and cold lips and cheeks warm with prickles of heat hitting it, I open up my laptop and get online. I catch up with my email. I check the Underground : USA Facebook group that I have setup, I blog a little. I update my map. I upload some photos, and I feel a little connected with the virtual world – which is what it takes to make me suddenly realise why I am very gloomy, it isn't just the weather.

I am very alone. By myself. With no one to talk to, bounce things off or even be able to say 'Is it just me, or is Wapping a bit of a let-down?'. I have no real human contact or companionship and I am starting to feel lonely. I need to have someone with me.

> **8:34 PM Jun 18th**
> Small salvation found at http://is.gd/15ljT (SBX). But I *need* people, people. It is still raining. Mood=gloomy.

I need people. I need to talk to someone. And not just on the phone, but just to have someone to fire silly comments to, or have someone point things out to me. It is time to go get that – maybe New York will have it.

Day 4 – Friday 19th June

So good, I made a New York specific playlist

*'New York you're safer and you're wasting my time,
our records all show you are filthy but fine.*

*But they shuttered your stores, when you opened the doors,
to the cops who were bored, once they'd run out of crime'*

> **8:14 AM Jun 19th**
> I just spent the night in room of a guy who'd i met just 2 hours before. expand on that? sorry can't, got to go to Kew Gardens stop!

I wake up about eight o'clock. I check for a wireless signal, but there is none. And suddenly I realise I am staying in a complete stranger's bed and immediately feel very awkward about the prospect of meeting him again, so I make the bed as best as I can, and get the hell out of their place.

Obviously I go and find myself a Dunkin Donuts to go and get breakfast at. On the way out, I put the coffee cup on the roof of the car, and as I fumble for the keys in my pocket I realise it will make a really good picture with the Dunkin' Donuts sign in the background. I snap a shot of it, and it turns out to be one of the most random, but one of my most favourite photos of the whole trip. I sip coffee. I start to warm up and wake up. I feel good. I go to the car and put my 'New York' playlist on my iPod, and start to sing along to Simon & Garfunkel at a not-entirely quiet volume.

> **8:07 AM Jun 19th**
> Geofftech – is the only livin' boy in New York.

> **9:08 AM Jun 19th**
> Just passed a 'Warren Street' in Brooklyn, but that's not the Tube station we're looking for !

The station I am looking for really is an actual station! As in ... there is a railway station in New York that shares the name of a station on the Tube map, and I am going to take a train there to get to it! Except there is a twist that I fancy trying out.

Kew Gardens – in the New York borough of Queens - has *two* stations, a Subway one and 'mainline' train one too – as part of the Long Island Rail

Road. The LIRR is the train system that is featured in one of my favourite films – Eternal Sunshine of the Spotless mind. Right at the beginning, there is a scene where Jim Carey should be getting the train into work to go to downtown Manhattan, but instead goes the other way and takes the train out to the beach … in the middle of winter … to the end of the line at Montauk. Part of me wants to go all the way to Montauk, but I know I don't have time for that, so getting a train to or from Kew Gardens will have to do.

I decide though that as it's a train station, I need to arrive there *by* train – so I drive to the station one stop back up the line – Forest Hills, put the car on a parking meter for couple of hours – worry about leaving all the equipment in it in a New York side street for everyone to see – then run to the station … where I can hear the rumble of train leaving, but by the time I purchase a return ticket and get to the platform level I can't tell if I've just missed one going the way I want to go, or whether it has been in the opposite direction.

> **9:55 AM Jun 19th**
> Am at Forest Hills station, Queens on the Long Island MTA Railroad. Next stop: Kew Gardens.

I look up and down the platform for a 'Next train' indicator but there isn't one. After much searching I eventually find a faded and torn poster back down by the machine where I've bought my ticket, and deduce from the tatty timetable that trains are every half an hour.

Whilst I wait, I setup my video camera on a nearby ledge that acts as a tripod and record myself on video reflecting upon the past few days. It passes the time.

> **10:37 AM Jun 19th**
> i've been waiting 45 minutes for a train that is meant to be every half hour. And people complain about the Tube! Ha.

In the USA
Kew Gardens, New York
On the Tube map
Kew Gardens
(District Line / Overground)

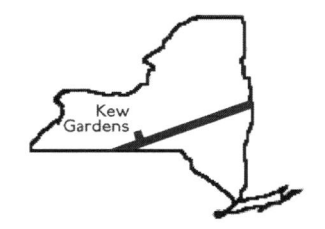

After a few fast trains have annoyingly whizzed through the middle without stopping, eventually a gleaming silver train slows to a halt in the platform, and I climb on board for my six minute journey. I have my video camera still as I definitely want to capture some of Kew Gardens – the only same name spot that is also train station – on video to edit, but realise I am suddenly presented with a problem, how am I going to video myself now?

By asking a complete stranger, that's how! And so I scan the carriage that I'm sitting in and come to the conclusion that the most likely candidate is actually a chap that has been standing by the doors when I'd got on, and is still standing there now.

I introduce myself to him and find that I am talking to *Charles*, or Charlie, or 'Chaz really, as everyone calls me!' he says in a very friendly way, and discover that he is more than happy to shoot some video of me looking poignantly leaning against the door looking out of the window of the scenery outside.

Charlie tells me he's going to Jamaica, he's stayed the night as his girlfriends and is now going home for the day to study – he says with a laugh that makes me think that as it's Friday he's looking forward to the weekend and probably isn't going to be doing much studying. 'Especially as she's coming over too, to mine later for the weekend', he adds with a cheeky smile.

'So what's the video for?' he asks, and without getting into the whole story as I want him to film me rather than chat to me, I simply tell him that there is a Kew Gardens station in London where I am from, and I just want to come here to see what it is like, which he smiles at.

'So what is it like?' I ask him. 'No idea!' he laughs again 'Never got out here!' which again makes *me* smile because it makes me realise that this is exactly the same that happens in London. Every year millions of people commute to London on their season ticket passing through stations that they never ever get out of the whole of their commuting life – they only ever see it from the train window.

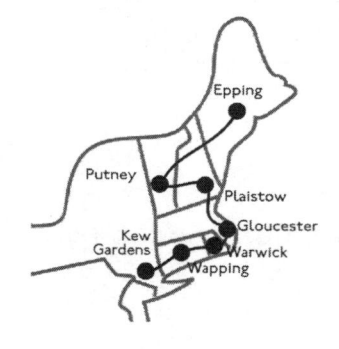

I think about this some more as I get out at Kew Gardens and explore the local area – an area dominated by houses and apartment blocks, and it looks like a typical Zone 3 or Zone 4 area back home in London – you would live here in Queens and commute down into Manhattan.

50

But something that always got me back in London is that people would often buy season tickets – annual passes – an entire years' worth of travel, and yet only ever in the *whole year* make the same journey Monday to Friday, to work and back again, never getting out at the intermediate stations, and never going anywhere else at the weekends either.

If you've already got *and paid for* a ticket that lets you travel at weekends, why not use it on your non-work days to get out in the town where you live (whether it be London or New York) and explore a little?

Why travel through Kew Gardens everyday but not get out there just once to have a look around?

After 20 minutes of walking around though – including finding the 'Kew Gardens' on the MTA/Subway stop too, I walk back again and I come to the conclusion that there really is nothing special about the Kew Gardens here - it's an urban populated area with nice houses which have nice lawns, and kerbsides with fire hydrants that you're not allowed to park by, but that's about it - but am still pleased that I've got out and had a look around, and have also talked to Charles on the train.

> **11:22 AM Jun 19th**
> Kew Gardens, NY complete! That's 7 out of 48.

I have to wait less than a minute to get a train back which feels lucky, and back at Forest Hills station, I check my watch, I still have twenty minutes to spare on the ticket where I've parked my car. I am slightly worried about its safety too, but figure that on a busy shopping street in broad daylight, no one is going to break into it. I get back to it and its fine, well except for the fact that it won't start properly again.

It takes two or three goes to get the engine to start and tick over, and I resolve to myself that I really must get that looked at the next time I see a garage that would do just a thing. I really will, definitely, yes. No I mean it this time. Must look for a garage.

> **11:22 AM Jun 19th**
> I haven't showered or cleaned my teeth in over 24hrs. It's time to check into a motel. And maybe get the car fixed, it's playing up

I drive to New Jersey that afternoon and treat myself to quite an expensive luxury hotel for the night. You know you're in an expensive hotel when you have wired Internet access (complete with Ethernet cable), and you don't have to rely on a dodgy Wi-Fi signal. I put some washing on in the laundry, and watch it in a circular motion as it spins round.

> **4:39 PM Jun 19th**
> Clothes cleaned in Days Inn laundry, Total cost = $4.25 for detergent, wash and dry. High living, eh?

That evening, I finally make some proper human contact that I've been craving, as I catch up with a friend of mine – *Tatiana* – at a movie theatre in New York. In a few weeks' time when I get to California on the West Coast, she's offered me her place to stay to crash for a couple of days to recover. In the meantime, she's recently been the screenwriter on a film that's just come out and there is a launch party at a hotel in New York. So I meet her, I meet other random people, drink, eat nibbles, and watch her movie, and generally had a lovely, social evening, and I feel a *lot* better. I play the songs from the soundtrack to the movie I have just seen as I drive back to my hotel through the crazy streets of NYC.

> **12:32 AM Jun 20th**
> NYC traffic may be bad, but not as bad as Boston. I'm not letting the Boston thing go, am I?

I have to fill up with gas on the way back, only to find that I am now in New Jersey and I'm not allowed to do that – the attendant must do it for me. I talk to him a little, and in the end he relents – a man with a British accent but with South Carolina plates probably does it, and confuses the hell out of him enough to let me fill up myself.

> **1:13 AM Jun 20th**
> Filling up with gas in New Jersey. The attendant thing caught me out AGAIN, gah!

It costs me to drive onto Staten Island, drive along the expressway and then pay again to get off it and officially enter New Jersey. I remember when I'd first come to New York a few years ago, I'd deliberately got a ferry across from Manhattan – and straight back – just so that I could say that I'd been to New Jersey. This time though, I am doing it properly.

Back in my posh hotel room, I literally kick off my shoes so that they fly through the air and 'thump!' as they the hit the wall, and lay back on my bed and investigate my own thoughts. I start to do some sums in my head ... how often can I and how much is it going to cost me to have a nice hotel room like this instead of camping out like this? I fire up the calculator application on my laptop and do some rough sums. I can afford it once a week. Probably.

I fire up my computer, and set about editing the video that I've recorded that day – it shouldn't take too long.

Day 5 – Saturday 20th June

Harrow, I must be going

'Hello, I must be going. I cannot stay, I came to say, I must be going. I'm glad I came, but just the same, I must be going.

I'll stay a week or two, I'll stay the summer through, but I am telling you, I must be going.'

The day is not starting well. I am not able to upload my video.

> **8:44 AM Jun 20th**
> my motel internet connection isn't working. Not impressed. Having to use AT&T usb stick instead. hmm.

I've finished editing it by staying up late last night – later than I intended – but come the morning, I want to tweak a couple of things before I upload it, except that when it comes to the all-important 'connect to the Internet' part, I find that the whole of the hotel internet connection is down. I've been quite thrilled at the prospect of having a wired connection yesterday, and now it is dead. I quickly pop down to reception to find a very friendly person to tell me that that Yes! It is dead. But No! It is unlikely to be fixed anytime soon.

So instead I drive across to the Starbucks across the road, which I can see directly opposite me and yet if I want to walk it there, it would have taken as most ... ooh, 30 seconds. Except I can't walk there because the road is in the way, but that road doesn't allow me to cross in my car either because this is America. Instead I have to drive down the four lane highway for a bit in one direction, come off at the first turning, turn around, go over the junction (because no turning is allowed from that direction), turn around again, *then* turn onto the highway and drive back towards the hotel only on the other side of the road this time where the Starbucks is – to use their Internet connectivity to upload the video. Only thing is ... I don't really fancy a Starbucks coffee. WTF?

> **9:59 AM Jun 20th**
> Dunkin Donuts brekky third day running. How have i survived without DD before???

Yup, because twenty minutes later with my second video now online and I am back on the road this time having gone via a Dunkin' Donuts to get my morning sustenance.

I leave New Jersey and as I do it's nice to feel like I am leaving urbansville and industry and towns and people and places. I know that the East

Coast of America is generally more built up than the west, but I am starting to tire of it a little. I think ahead to next couple of months and look forward to driving in the desert in the middle of nowhere of Arizona. I press down a little harder on the gas, feeling as if that will somehow help me get there a micro-percentage quicker.

Pennsylvania cheers me as it does provide winding country roads, albeit giving me some bad weather along with it – and a lot of greenery too. Although as I drive past the 'Welcome to Pennsylvania!' sign, I realise that there isn't a convenient place to stop and take a photo of it.

Before I'd set off on the trip, I'd made myself a list of 'things to do', per state and one of them is to take a picture of the state sign as I drive into it ... but that just isn't always possible, as if there is a car behind me or no place to stop then it just isn't always possible ... and some of the major Interstates don't even have them.

So as I miss out on taking a photo of the state sign on the state line, it also occurs to me that I haven't been using my fridge magnets – At a service station on the way up through New York I'd bought a map of the USA which is comprised of stick-on fridge magnets... and every time I 'did' a state I'd told myself I am going to stick it onto the side of the car and take a picture/video of it ... and yet, I haven't. And it is bugging me. It's bugging me that I'd planned to do a whole load of 'fun' things on the side, but the reality of what I am doing is of course far from what I'd hoped to happen. As it turns out – the days are long, the driving is tiring and doing everything by myself all the time means that I've just sometimes lacked the motivation and energy to do anything. It isn't as straightforward as I'd envisaged.

And to top it all off, it starts to rain *again*, and I am very bored of driving in the rain now, who can I rant to? Oh that's right ... Twitter.

> **1:34 PM Jun 20th**
> i have had ENOUGH of driving in the bloody rain. On I287, north.
>
> **2:49 PM Jun 20th**
> heading for Harrow, PA. population: as yet unknown.
>
> **2:52 PM Jun 20th**
> PA in 5 : It smells of damp countryside.

Now my route today is an interesting one ... I have a 'Tube' stop to visit, but ultimately I also want to drop in on a town called Centralia that is in Pennsylvania too ... I'll get to that later, but first I have my obligation of a same-named-place to visit.

As I approach Harrow, my phone rings. I like how it actually 'ring ... rings!' in time to the wipers going left to right, and I glance at the screen and see that it is my old friend and colleague Melissa – I'd worked with her in Charleston but she has now moved to North Carolina and I've told her that I would give her a call to let her know when I am passing through her neighbourhood. I haven't called her yet ... but don't have to now as she is calling me!

'Hello!' I say, happy to have a friendly voice to talk to. 'Heeeeey!' she says back in her soft southern drawl, and we proceed to have a pleasant conversation for the next ten minutes, the rain eases up to a drizzle, and with my SatNav saying '1 minute' until I get to Harrow, I sit and park up on the side of the road – it appears that I've pulled into an open drive of what looks like used to be a convenience store that is no longer open.

We chat for a while, and I arrange to meet up with Melissa when I am down her way next week – and it spurs me on, I turn the key in the engine – happy to get to Harrow which is just seconds away down the road, except ... the engine does not turn over at all.

There is nadda ... nothing ... *completely* nothing, and none of the tricks that I have used previously to get the engine to turnover help, and I am sat there with a car that won't start.

And I realise that I have been very stupid, and that instead of thinking 'I'll get that checked out at some point', I should have got it looked at *immediately*. I have been riding my luck. And it has just run out. Shit.

> **3:02 PM Jun 20th**
> oops. I stopped to take a call, and now the car won't start, seriously. battery may be flat! #drama

I get out the car and look around. I am at a junction with an unnamed building. A small yellow school bus (short bus) is parked nearby. My SatNav says that the centre of Harrow is half a mile further down the road ... and it is still drizzling slightly. I have no option other than to go on foot and see what I can find.

As I walk down a road with no pavement I curse that that there is no one with me to capture this on video. If this is to be my mini-drama with the car breaking down, isn't this the sort of thing that I should be capturing? And that makes me even more annoyed that here is something else which I can't do alone, but I do take my stills-camera for any photo opportunities.

What I do find is The Turkey Hill Mini-Mart, which also has 'Harrow' written into the address of its sign – so at least I know I'm in the right area, although it worries me that when I get here there isn't a sign saying 'Welcome to Harrow', but one saying 'Welcome to Ottersville' instead.

The mini-mart gas station is super-modern and gleaming and is more like a grocery store inside. What I really want is a rustic-old garage with some old timer leaning behind a counter who can dish out some local advice and help. The super slick efficient counter staff in the shop don't really fit my idea of help. So I go back outside and have a further walk around to see if there are any other places that can help.

I get my hopes up when I see across the road what looks like a garage, and a battered 'Auto' sign, but it turns out just to be a sales place ... that doesn't appear to be open anyway even though it is a Saturday afternoon. I sigh, dodge a big muddy puddle as I cross back over the road, and turn towards instead back to the mart.

I queue up with everyone else with nothing to buy and nothing to pay for and when I get to the front of the line explain that I've broken down and is there a garage nearby? This seems to confuse the guy working behind the counter, but his more helpful colleague overhears and offers me up their phonebook so I can look some places up. 'Thanks' I say, and shuffle outside to make some calls.

As I call around the places in order listed under 'Autos' I do start to think then that I don't really know what I would do if I am completely broken down and stuck here. Supposing there is no one here to help me? Supposing everything is closed until Monday? What if it has been a Sunday today and everything had been closed? Would I have slept in the car overnight broken down where it is until things open again on Monday? I suddenly feel very under-prepared.

Three failed phone calls later and I am starting to actually worry that I may be stuck here for a while, but on the fourth phone call though ... something a little magical happens. Someone answers! From a garage that is listed locally, and I rather rapidly explain my predicament. A little too rapidly apparently, or maybe it's just my accent that confuses him because I have to explain it all over again for a second time, only more slowly.

'Where are you again?' he asks, and I explain I am at the Turkey Hill mart shop. 'Ok, he says, that's just around the corner'. 'But you know ... you're lucky because I don't normally come in on Saturday, I'm normally out riding motocross on my bike, but it's been cancelled today so I thought I'd come into the shop to work on my car'. None of this really makes any sense to me – but it is about to in about half an hours' time.

All I know is that I've made contact with someone that says they are coming to help, and I feel like I might not be stuck here after all.

> **3:21 PM Jun 20th**
> I've called a local garage, had to coerce the dude into coming out to rescue me! I'm waiting at a gas station for him.

3:25 PM Jun 20th
s'funny, coz i said 'i need a baTTery', and didn't understand me. So i said 'i need a baDDery', and he did.

Ten minutes later, and the largest white truck I have ever seen in my life pulls up into the forecourt of the gas station. Out pops a man who I only then learned name is *Mike*, who runs a local garage nearby and seems more than willing to help me.

I take him up the road to where the car is – explaining on the way that I am on a cross country American road trip, and this is only at the beginning! The ice broken, I relax, he relaxes, and before I know it we are chatting away whilst he tries to get my car started. After a few attempts with his jump leads he manages it, slams the bonnet of the car down and says 'And now you're going to follow me'.

3:39 PM Jun 20th
i have been rescued! Jump started....

I'm going to *what?* Follow him! Where to?

To his garage, it turns out ... which is a mile down the road and I follow him tentatively down an unmarked side road, and the right into a muddy road where eventually there is a battered sign and an area that leads into a place with a big workshop. *This* is more like it – more like the local garage place I'd had in mind.

For the next twenty minutes Mike works his wonders on the car which basically involves changing the battery out – but I feel suddenly underprepared for something that sounds so simple, and I am resolutely glad that he is there to do it. Turns out that the battery that is in there is the wrong one anyway.

'The one that's in here now is the wrong type, someone's put a cheap one in – you need a heavy duty one, and I've got one you can have!' he explains.

As he changes the battery out it occurs to me that I really have been lucky with the whole incident, and how stupid I've been for not getting it inspected earlier. What if this had happened at 11pm on a country road in the dark, or at a same-named place in the middle of nowhere with no one around?

As he finishes up, I open up a side-door to his workshop, wondering what is on the other side. 'Oh' says Mike 'You'll probably want to have a look around in there'

I pop my head in and am not prepared for what I see – a private collection of old vintage cars in pristine condition. This isn't a garage it is more like a museum! There are at least 8 vintage vehicles – including a fire truck (Which worryingly has 'Ottsville Fire Department', not 'Harrow Fire Department' written on the side) all that have obviously been salvaged and lovingly restored. They are lovely. I run round, snapping photos.

'So these cars ... all yours then?' I ask as I can see Mike is finishing up. 'Sure are' he says, 'Well me and the boys, it's a little hobby on the side that we have to look after them', and goes on to explain how he's salvaged them from auction and does them up in his spare time. I am beginning to suspect that Mike may not be a married man.

> **4:22 PM Jun 20th**
> i have a new battery! Am back on the road! All hail www.vandergear.com for saving the day! Ottsville, PA.

Mike is happy to chat for a little longer, but I also sense that he has things to do and he wants to get on with his day, so I settle up and pay in cash – plus a sizeable tip for the battery, and I ask my last question of him of the day.

'So where's Harrow then?' I say nicely 'All the signs round here seem to call it Ottsville, including that old fire truck'

In the USA
Harrow, Pennsylvania
On the Tube map
Harrow-on-the-Hill (Metropolitan)

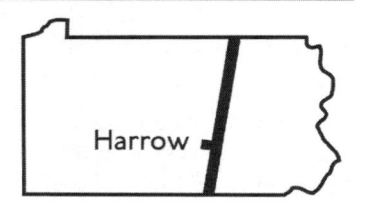

'Harrow?!' says Mike. 'Well no one's called it that for years' he says 'Although Harrow Hall is still there I think'. And it transpires that the tiny town of Harrow has been swallowed up by the larger populous of 'Ottersville' and that the name doesn't appear on maps anymore, but is known to just some of the locals that still live here. The big plastic sign outside of the gas station though *does* say 'Harrow Station' on it (I have taken a photo), and it turns out that the community hall across from the street of exactly where I have broken down is what all the locals called 'Harrow Hall'. It works for me; it just wouldn't have been obvious to anyone casually driving through that this is a place known as Harrow.

I shake Mike's hand – firmly, with vigour, and a look from my eyes to his that really says 'Thank you', and as a final tip, he recommends I take a picture of a secret waterfall just down the lane from where he is which I do, but in the drizzly rain doesn't want to make me explore it any more up close.

I plot my route to the campground that night on the SatNav, and once again realise how essentially I've totally lucked out that I broke down in a random place where luckily – very luckily – there'd been a friendly mechanic just around the corner who shouldn't have normally be there able to pop round and have just the right battery to set me up and get me going on the road again.

Something comes out of it though – that Harrow, PA gets a huge 'tick' on my list of same named places. A friendly guy has given up his time to come out and help me, and I've seen a small corner of America that I wouldn't have otherwise – and for that, I really *really* like Ottersville. Err, I mean – Harrow. I add it to my list, along with Kew Gardens from the previous day.

SAME NAME TOWNS TALLY

Something there and enjoyable
Plaistow, Gloucester, Kew Gardens, Harrow

Something there but not that exciting to be honest
Putney

Nothing there but somehow being in the middle of nowhere made it OK
Epping

Nothing there, and not that exciting either. Oops.
Warwick, Wapping

I think about it some more as I make my non-Tube-station stop for the day - as I take a two-hour detour via the town of Centralia.

Centralia is a near ghost town as its population has dwindled from over 1,000 residents in the 1980's down to officially just 10 people at the time of the last census. The reason? Is due to a mine fire burning beneath the town since the 1960's. Cracks and holes started to appear in the town since 1979, and in one famous case a 12-year-old boy fell into a hole that was measured at 150 deep that suddenly opened beneath his feet in the back garden. He was pulled out by his cousin that was playing with him at the time and saved his life. From the hole, a plume of hot steam was measured and was found to contain lethal levels of carbon monoxide.

I actually expected it to be *more* ghost-towny – buildings falling down, etc... But a lot of the buildings are still standing, and to be honest it's just a mainly deserted town. I park the car up... and sure enough there is steam rising through cracks in the ground.

> **7:15 PM Jun 20th**
> i'm in Centralia, PA. Weird ghost town due to 45 yr. old mining fire deep underground.

With light fading, I head for Allentown where there is a KOA on my map that I know I can get to before the end of the day. I think I've passed by the outskirts of Allentown on the way up. I stop at a Gas Station about twenty minutes out and have a pleasant conversation with the guy behind the counter ... tell him what I am doing and give him one of my cards – he promises to check out the blog. I also buy a fire log – one of those self-lighting, hard fuel burning thing which starts you a fire with just the touch of a match – I don't really *need* to light a fire that night, I just feel that I want to. Oh, and they have a mini Dunkin' Donuts coffee bar too, so I help myself to some of that as well.

> **8:42 PM Jun 20th**
> considering that all that might actually come of this road trip is that I'll end up with a Dunkin Donuts addiction

I make the KOA campground just ten minutes before it shuts, and it has a very 1980's retro feel about in terms of décor. A video game room too, with what may have been an original Pac Man game in it ... that takes quarters of which I have plenty, so there is just time for a quick game (or five) before I settle in for the night.

I set up the tent under the light of the car headlamps again (and take a moment to be proud about the battery now under the bonnet knowing I would have no problem starting it up tomorrow), and wanting to feel manly, I start my fire log. I have nothing to cook and I'm not really that cold ... in fact, there is a vague warm drizzle in the atmosphere to be honest, but I think I want to make a tea whilst I sit and look at some crackling flames, and so I light a fire.

> **9:48 PM Jun 20th**
> i'm here for the night: N40 39.561 W75 41.664 koa campground. I've lit a campfire & am next to a stream, nice.

I don't mention the fire log in my tweet. It would make it sound as if I've gathered for wood myself and lit it without cheating at all, wouldn't? Still, the tea is good though as I cook some up on my gas stove, and sit there - just sit ... in the slight drizzle surveying the rest of the campground in the darkness, wondering what it will look like in the morning.

I think back on the day- from industrial New Jersey leading to rainy Pennsylvania. To breaking down and being rescued in Harrow. And the strangely deserted town of Centralia. Alone, but OK.

I think I am starting to appreciate what I have undertaken, and how much further there is ahead of me.

I finish my tea. I sit quietly by the fire almost half an hour with it keeping me warm in the drizzle, and when it gets down to a safe level where I know I can leave it unattended, I climb into the tent, zip myself up, and get cosy for the night.

Day 6 – Sunday 21st June

Acton Stations

*'We never went to church,
Just get on with work and sometimes things will hurt,
But it's hit me since you left us,
And it's so hard not to search. We never went to Church'*

The fire log is still smouldering from the night before when I arise just after eight o'clock. I scratch my ruffled hair and survey the scene. Yup – just as I thought, it's a camp site.

I get all my stuff together, wishing that there is someone else here just to help me as it seems like I spend half my time loading gear in and out of the car all day. Grumpy me, I need tea - I fire up my stove.

The gas burns away nicely for a few seconds with the water starting to warm when – whhhuump! It dies on me. What? Has the gas run out *already*? I've only used it about four times, I can't believe that the gas container doesn't last that long. How annoying! Ok, I'm going to have to get a new gas canister then at the next camping place I find.

Trying to find something to be non-grumpy about I concentrate on today's destinations. Today is a day of two same-name places! Yet again, the benefit of the States being so close together in the north east means that I figure that I can make my first stop – Acton – this morning, and my second one – Camden – down in Delaware later this afternoon. Sorted.

> **9:44 AM Jun 21st**
> Pennsylvania in 3 : Hilly, Green, Pretty.

There is nothing much to do today except drive, drive … drive some more and get to my next destination as quickly as possible. I am aware that I've wasted time by visiting Centralia, but I also figure that I would have ended up at the same campground, so surely I am still on target? During a gas station fill up I check against my pre-trip schedule that I've drawn up to make sure that I am making progress as much I should have been – I am. I drive on down the Interstate.

> **11:33 AM Jun 21st**
> there are huge billboards everywhere in PA along the Interstate asking 'What have you done for your marriage today?'

I find myself searching on my iPod for the Janet Jackson song 'What have you done for me lately?' so I can sing along to that, but with alternative nuptial lyrics.

12:17 PM Jun 21st
road trip fast food option: Wendy's is acceptable. BK/McD's/Arby's is not, right?

1:02 PM Jun 21st
just saw my first Delaware license plate. This excites me for some reason.

The rain finally stops and the sun comes out as I traverse south, and I notice that I 'bum-bumped' over some train tracks of a rusty old level crossing as my SatNav informs me that I am getting close to Tube stop No.9 – Hello, Acton.

In the USA
Acton, New Jersey
On the Tube map
Acton Town
(Piccadilly and District Lines)

Well. At least it isn't raining. But I can see it is going to be a mild let-down again. From the friendly mechanic in Harrow I'd hoped to be back on a roll with some small-town community, but it appears otherwise. Acton, NJ is just a crossroads of two country roads.

3:31 PM Jun 21st
there's a train line here, the road is even called 'Acton Station Rd'. but just one house here & that's i.

There is a house though – a large expensive house – with wooden slats across all the windows that for some reason looks as if they've been added as an afterthought to the design of the house and not originally there.

A bee passes me in the breeze as I open the car door, scrunch my foot onto the gravel of the side of the road, and I go and take some pictures with my camera.

Click!

A picture of a crossroads. Thank heavens for my wide angled lens.

Click!

A picture of a road-sign in the distance. Thank heavens for my zoom lens.

Click, click, click!

I see a sign in the distance which I wander down to see what it says and to take a photo of it too.

Click!

> **'EMERGENCY SIREN'**, it says.
>
> **'IF SIREN SOUNDS FOR 3 TO 5 MINUTES, TUNE TO RADIO STATION 101.7 FM FOR EMERGENCY INFO'.**

For ... *what* emergency, I wonder. Flooding? Is there a river near here? Or a tornado, or hurricane? Must be for some sort of extreme weather condition but it isn't obvious which one, and to this day I still don't know which.

Three more photos later and I've run out of things to take picture of in Acton. So I go for a walk a little way back to where the rusty railroads have been and try to take some arty looking shots, or as arty as one can be on a deserted gravelly road. *Click!* And walk back to the crossroads.

Standing in the middle of where the four roads meet, I do a slow 360, expecting ... hoping ... for another car or someone or something to come along, but nothing does. There are birds in the trees, wind in the air, and maybe now someone peeping out from behind one of those wooden slats with them thinking 'Why is there a guy standing in the middle of the crossroads with a camera taking photos', but really that is it. Really.

Back in the car, I tune into 101.7 FM but there is nothing but static – no emergency would be coming today then, thankfully. I fire up my 3G dongle on my laptop and get online, I'm not sure how or why I am expecting the Internet to save me, but there is a distinct lack of emails or tweets to reply to, so after five minutes I give up on that avenue and conceded that Acton is going to be like an Epping – nothing going on. It's time I think for the next stop.

> **3:51 PM Jun 21st**
> on my way to Delaware Road kill count : 8.

I recall the Smith & Jones sketch where they put stickers on the side of their truck every time they ran over another hedgehog, or other wildlife.

> **3:59 PM Jun 21st**
> welcome to Delaware. Memorial bridge toll – $3.

It's going to be ok. I *know* it's going to be OK – I wouldn't have two quiet and dead crossroad places in one day, will I? Camden is going to be lovely busting little town or village full of life. A conjuring up of small town in America that will fill me with joy.

Oh, shit.

5:09 PM Jun 21st
i'm at Camden, Delaware. It appears to be a bit of another nothing.

In the USA
Camden, Delaware
On the Tube map
Camden Town (Northern Line)

I pull into the gas station. The 'Valero' gas station which for some reason to me sounds Spanish, and I let out a Spanish expletive.

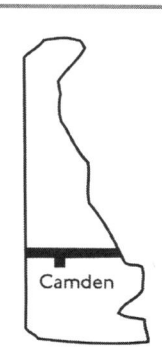

A couple of hours to drive here, and I can see without getting out of the car that it's going to be a let-down. To be honest, I don't even get out of the car, instead I fire up my laptop again and edit my list by adding Acton from earlier, and Camden from now, and then – for the first time – I start to analyse it.

SAME NAME TOWNS TALLY

Something there and enjoyable
Plaistow, Gloucester, Kew Gardens, Harrow

Something there but not that exciting to be honest
Putney

Nothing there but somehow being in the middle of nowhere made it OK
Epping, Acton

Nothing there, and not that exciting either. Oops.
Warwick, Wapping, Camden

Ok. So only three bad ones so far, but it is Warwick and Wapping all over again where a brief drive up and down the road and back to the intersection reveals that Camden appears to be just a T-junction with a gas station on one of corners. I get out the car. I buy a drink and use the facilities, and come back to the car and look at Google Maps a bit harder, and work out whether South Kensington is going to be a blow out or not – I'm not sure I can take another day where I get let down twice.

It is then that I notice that a little further away, a 'Camden Wyoming' nearby on the map. That's strange – Wyoming I only know as a state, here it is liberally being tagged onto the end of Camden as a subsidiary place name. Maybe there is more to this place?

I check it out – it's another ten minutes up the road and does indeed appear to be a spin-off suburb. Although, is Camden a spin-off of Camden Wyoming, or the other way round?

> **5:10 PM Jun 21st**
> so there's houses, gas station, church. But not a lot else. And I now I feel like I need a nap.

I sit back, and with the sun beating down and warming up the inside of the car, I relax and within moments feel my eyelids go heavy and know that I am about to sleep.

In the USA
South Kensington, Maryland
On the Tube map
South Kensington (District / Circle and Piccadilly Lines)

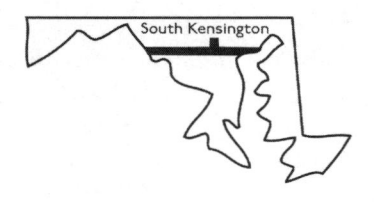

> **7:10 PM Jun 21st**
> no I am not trying to break into a LDS church, Mr nosey parker

South Kensington, I have decided I am going to do a bit more research on. So when I wake from my fifteen-minute cat nap (or is that a power nap?), I check in advance on Google Maps that South Kensington where I am headed next has something there that I can look at. It does! The first thing that catches my attention on the map is a *huuuge* building which upon closer inspection turns out to be a church – a church that is of the Latter Day Saints.

Now I'm not going to get into the weirdness of their beliefs. No – mainly because when I get to Salt Lake City later in the book, I'm going to go into it all then, but unfortunately for me, what I really want to do is go and have a look at their church – something I can't do because the gates are shut.

Whilst being completely non-religious or believing in a God of any sort, I can't help but fail to be impressed by an old church or any building that is a place of worship. They've so often been crafted in magnificent style, by hundreds of pairs of hands into a fabulous building that even – like I say,

I don't – believe, always bring with them a feeling of peace and serenity that is unmatched. It's not been unusual for me to go and sit inside a church – again I stress not to *pray* – but just to take a moment out of the hectic madness that is the everyday world, and enjoy being able to contemplate my thoughts. Some might argue that that's what praying is all about, but I would argue that when you pray you're obviously directing your words towards a deity that you believe in, whereas I can quite happily spend a few minutes in a church, talking to myself, with my own thoughts swirling around my head.

So I really want to go inside, and see what a modern-American-built LDS church is like, and have that moment where I can collect my thoughts, but the gates really are locked and shut.

It's whilst I'm standing on tip toes craning my neck over the top of the gates, that I catch the attention of someone who is obviously a local who (granted, I supposed) wonders what I am doing – perhaps rather suspiciously as if I am trying to break in.

'You can't get in, the gates are closed' the voice comes from behind me – polite, but also pointing out the bloody obvious – the gates are shut and thus obviously I can't get up the driveway to have a proper look.

'Yes, I can see that. I just wondered…'

I don't know. What am I wondering? What am I hoping to achieve by peering down the driveway? As if someone at that moment is coming to unlock the gates and let me in? '… If they might be opening soon', I finish my sentence – suddenly aware that this might sound a bit stupid.

'No I think they close them once the service has started' says the man to me, whom I am now starting to study more closely, and only now do I spot that the coat he is wearing is slightly grubby, and oh – he has no shoes on.

Hang on. What time is it? I check the clock on my phone – just after seven o'clock. And it *is* a Sunday right. Right? Being on the road kind of makes you lose track of what day it is. Is the LDS Church one of those that celebrates on a Saturday and not a Sunday? I know that there is one brand of religion that does that, but I am not sure if it's this one. Wow, my religious knowledge really is appalling. I probably shouldn't write about it.

I chat to the man some more – who it is rapidly became apparent is homeless and sleeping rough on the streets, although quite knows what he's doing wandering through this seemingly nice suburban neighbourhood isn't apparent. He doesn't have any bags or anything with him, in fact his face looks quite clean for someone who is homeless. He *is* homeless, isn't he? Why else would you have grubby bare feet and a tatty old coat? I want to ask, obviously I can't.

Instead the man – I never get his name – decides that this is his cue to launch into his own beliefs which is rambling story of how he has been brought up a strict Christian, but after several things have gone wrong in his life, he loses his faith and decides that his God should not have allowed anything bad to happen to him. He starts to mumble, and I lose parts of it in his incoherent mumbling, but I 'Ummmed' and 'Uhhuuh' I think in all the right places, and after a few moments he just shrugs his shoulders, happy that he has told me his story, and with a deft wave of his arm in the air, shuffles off down the pavement.

I watch him walk, still devouring his story and trying to figure out what he is doing here. I walk for a few minutes, up and down the suburban back streets of South Kensington – but really all I can find are houses, set back on driveways with impossibly high street numbers (4532, followed by 4541, followed by 4560 which I can't fathom out the logic behind), before looping back to the car, content that I have at least seen and done something in South Kensington. But strangely disappointed that I haven't been able to go to church.

> **7:32 PM Jun 21st**
> South Kensington : tick. Have sudden urge to play the Streets on my iPod, I never went to church.

> **9:16 PM Jun 21st**
> in the hilly green rolling countryside of North Virginia. It. Is. Lovely.

That night, I stay in the home – a farmhouse – of an old colleague that I know from the BBC. She'd moved to America, married a local and come to live on his farm – a beautiful old wooden farm building tucked deep into the Virginian countryside, with creaking timber all over the house as you walk around, and the proper smell of a coal fire and stove trickling heat through the joists up to my very comfortable bed in the guest room.

I've liked today over all, three towns ticked off, a nothing-there-but-good one, a proper disappointing boring one, and a random-encounter with a homeless guy one. That's a good day's road-tripping as far as I am concerned. Plus – tomorrow, my first official companion is joining me, so things are definitely looking up. My eyes feel heavy again, the onset of rapid eye movement approaching, and as I vaguely hear the animals making their noises on the farm outside, I start counting sheep of my own.

Day 7 – Monday 22nd June

Along for the Ride

'Go and taste them one by one, until that time, you can't be done
Know your station you just can't direct
Tune in me tonight, Turn down all the lights, I'm just along for the ride'

Today is the day that I would finally stop being grumpy. Today is the day that I finally get my first proper companion, someone to help me move all the stuff, share the driving, keep me awake and entertained, and generally share the road trip experience with! At last. Today – the first of my companions is coming to join me – yup, Katie is coming along for the ride.

> **7:29 AM Jun 22nd**
> this morning: leaving Virginia. got a 4-hour drive NW to Pittsburgh though to pick up my first companion! No idea where I'm spending the night tonight though

So here's the deal on Katie. She's my girlfriend … not. That's not to say that we haven't been hanging out and doing the boyfriend/girlfriend sort of thing, but at the time of Katie joining me on board my road trip, I'd only known her six weeks – during which time we'd not referred to each other as 'boyfriend' or 'girlfriend'. So she's my girlfriend … not. No one's said it yet!

Getting to Pittsburgh is going to be easy … 'just' a four-hour drive, except that instantly after hitting the first highway to take me to an Interstate, I am presented with a work truck, a line of cones, the smell of asphalt in the air, and guy in a high visibility jacket with a simple 'Stop/Go' sign in his hand.

> **10:50 AM Jun 22nd**
> stuck in traffic works, but i just interviewed the guy holding the 'stop/go' sign on video. Classic!

After a few minutes of just sitting there not moving against a 'stop' sign, I roll my window down and smile at the guy holding it. He instantly says 'Good morning!' back, I think pleased that I am smiling at him and not moaning like maybe others have about the delay. He explains that there is a long stretch of road being worked upon and I would be held for a few minutes.

Those few minutes gives me enough time to chat with *Brad* (after he asks where in England I am from) and from me to explain my road trip, give him one of my cards with the website and twitter address on, and I'm just getting to the point where I am thinking of getting him to sign my t-shirt when his walkie-talkie crackles into life, and his 'Go' counterpart at the other end of the works crackles into life too, telling him the last car has gone through at his end. A few moments later when we see it come though, I hit the cars gear back into drive, wave goodbye to Brad, and get on my way with several hours of driving.

Two hours or so later, my phone to the side of me on the passenger seat beeps, and I know without looking it's most likely going to be Katie. I check my watch - 3.22pm. Shit, her plane landed at 2.30 and so I am late.

I read the message. 'I'm outside' it says. 'Ten minute away!' I fumble back with one finger trying not to swerve into the lane on the other side of me and cause a massive pile-up as I faithfully follow the instructions on the SatNav guiding me into the airport.

About eight a half minutes later, I'm pulling up into the pick-up-air of the airport, where Katie sees the car approaching and smiles,

'Hello' I say with a smile back, 'Hello again!' says a smiling Katie back to me. 'Welcome to Underground USA' I say as I help her up with her bag, load it into the back of the car, slam it close with a re-assuring THUD. Hop back in, and – all of a sudden, I officially have a companion with me. And – all of a sudden – my mood gets a whole lot better.

> **3:48 PM Jun 22nd**
> we have a companion arrival! Just left Pittsburgh airport, and for the first time in eleven days someone else can drive!

In the USA
Greenford, Ohio
On the Tube map
Greenford (Central Line)

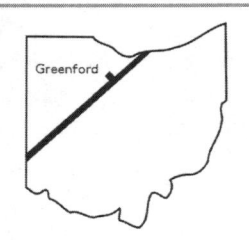

We get to Greenford just after five o'clock which is a little annoying because it seems to be one of those towns where everything shuts right on 5pm. The local store and café, 'The Greenford Cupboard' is closed but has *only just* closed and we can still see the staff milling around inside cleaning up, dammit.

> **5:04 PM Jun 22nd**
> hello Greenford, Ohio. I'm betting there's no sole remaining wooden escalator here

Greenford is cute though, even the sign advertising nearby religious services. 'YOU MATTER TO GOD' says a friendly sign with an arrow directing me towards Greenford Christian Church. A Star & Stripes flutters at the top of a flagpole with commemorative stones at the bottom for those who have died in numerous battles, 'IN HONOR OF ALL VETERANS' it proudly proclaims.

Back at the café, the sign outside advertises 'Grilled Cheese and Bacon Milkshakes', and there's part of me that honestly believes that they just might still be serving bacon flavoured milkshakes, and not grilled cheese sandwiches topped with bacon. One can hope.

But it is just essentially a crossroads with a few shops and buildings on all corners – a bright and breezy and happy place, and with sun out we stroll round, snap photos, and sit in a construction which appears to be a cross between a bandstand and a gazebo and chill out for a few moments.

'So is this the perfect small town America that you're looking for then?' asks Katie. I consider for a moment. 'It's cute', I say, 'I'll give it that… but… it's not really got that small town vibe feel, it still feels like we're in just a nice pleasant well-kept suburb of somewhere bigger, and that a *proper* small town, is yet to be discovered'.

Katie nods her approval, and we discuss the virtues of living in a small town against that of a big city as the sun warms us under the bandstand and casts shadows onto the concrete plinth below.

SAME NAME TOWNS TALLY

Something there and enjoyable
Plaistow, Gloucester, Kew Gardens, Harrow, South Kensington, Greenford

Something there but not that exciting to be honest
Putney

Nothing there but somehow being in the middle of nowhere made it OK
Epping, Acton

Nothing there, and not that exciting either. Oops.
Warwick, Wapping, Camden

After a while, it is time to go – there is nothing else to see here, and no one around to talk to, so we hit the road north and west – a little north but mainly west and discover that the turnpikes are not just restricted to New England and the I-90 which also seems to be confusing joint-named the I-80, and is even more confusingly called the Ohio Turnpike and they charge you a few dollars for the pleasure of driving down it – probably to pay for all the signs that label the same road twice.

I am still driving and enquire if Katie would be up for taking over. She is.

> **6:08 PM Jun 22nd**
> Ohio Turnpike (I-80, westbound). 'nine you're fine, ten you're mine' the mantra of the cops getting you for speeding.

I grapple with the map, and look at the SatNav and flick through the KOA guide to see if there is anywhere local that we can stay for the night. A place called Sandusky along the northern edge of Ohio and right on Lake Erie looks good enough and I call ahead to book us a camping spot for the night.

'Ooh! A Giant Eagle!' says Katie excitedly, just as I put the phone down, and I see that we are pulling off, into a mall and towards a large store called, err ... 'Giant Eagle'

'What's a Giant Eagle?' I ask, 'A kick-ass grocery store!' she replies.

It's at moments like this that Katie (and other native companions in the weeks ahead) would prove their true worth with local knowledge. And by 'local' what I really mean is 'national', except what I *really* mean is just four states – Pennsylvania, Ohio, West Virginia and Maryland which are the four states in which you'll find a Giant Eagle, but with each state being as large as it is, it feels national. I'd would have never of known that something called a 'Giant Eagle' is the equivalent to a Sainsbury's.

> **7:28 PM Jun 22nd**
> shopping for groceries in a 'Giant Eagle, Cleveland OH. No piggly wiggly in the north ....

It's dark by the time we get to the campground, and as I am determined to attempt to use my camp stove again, I buy some gas in the shop which the assistance assures me 'Will fit my stove', but turns out that it doesn't, bah. I will have to go to a proper camping shop to get some gas for it, it would seem. Note to self : take camp stove in with you next time to the shop, to ensure connector fits.

So then with some damp wood, we have a failed attempt to light a proper fire – not a cheating one from a fire log – not that we have any food to cook anyway, but just because it's always quite cool to light a fire, right?

But then it starts to drizzle a little anyway, and the wood isn't lighting so we concede that it might just be time to turn in for the night.

> **10:47 PM Jun 22nd**
> at Sandusky, OH for the night. Camping again. In sleeping bag. It's just occurred to me I haven't showered in over 24hrs. Oops.

Day 8 – Tuesday 23rd June

Shutting Down

*'My daddy taught me that in this country everyone's the same,
you work hard for your dollar and you never pass the blame.*

*Now I see all these big shots whining on my evening news,
About how they're losing billions and it's up me and you.*

*While the boss man takes his bonus pay and jets out of town
In the real world, they're shutting Detroit down'*

I think it's a train that wakes me up.

> **6:36 AM Jun 23rd**
> camping = 6am waking up all the time. Grrr. Still in Sandusky, Ohio. Heading for Detroit, MI today

The trains have been running all through the night – about one an hour I would say from the rumblings of heavy freight that attempt to disturb my heavy slumber, but it isn't until gone six o'clock in the morning that they start to sound their horns, and so better than any avian wake up call, the morning procession and clatter of half a mile of metal with coal inside does the trick.

Leaving Katie asleep, I get up and use the alone time to get online to the campground wireless, and update my progress map and stats. The geek inside me is secretly thrilled to now be building up a good enough pattern of averages on gas consumption.

> **8:27 AM Jun 23rd**
> new progress map online: http://is.gd/1aamb I'm also VERY excited to have got over 21mpg on the car yesterday. i'm so geeky!

With the map done, Katie is awake and we hit the road. We check out the local theme park, and have breakfast in the 'Better Half Diner' where signs hanging up inside cheekily suggest that perhaps men should sit on one side of the restaurant, and females on the other. We chat to our server, and then the owner, get them to sign my t-shirt and generally have a very social time for an hour as we eat delicious food.

Feeling very full and very happy to have met such lovely people, we leave Ohio in good spirits. I don't want to go on the Interstate if I can help it, so we pick up Highway 2 instead, and head out over a bridge that takes us over Sandusky Bay and down towards Toledo and towards Detroit.

I'm also very happy again to let Katie drive this part. I'm still getting used to the fact that I am now not by myself, and I can take the chance to put my feet up and let someone else have the stress of driving. I drift off into a small dream on the passenger side of the car.

'Wake up, we're approaching Michigan' says Katie as she nudges me in the side. I awaken quite quickly, having not really been in proper deep sleep – more like a lazy companion slumber, and I easily have time to reach for my camera on the floor, and snap the 'Welcome To Michigan' sign as we cross the state line.

> **12:29 PM Jun 23rd**
> state number 12 : just made Michigan.

Into the twelfth state on the trip, and the one that looks like the palm of your hand. What's that? You don't know that Michigan vaguely resembles the palm side of your hand? That's ok – neither did I, until I met someone from MI down in Charleston just a week before the trip and have it explained it to me.

If you can find a map of the USA right now ... then do so, and look at it. Michigan is up the top, to the right of the middle. OK now look at the palm of your right hand. See the resemblance! That's right! Me neither ... Oh, *ok* then – it does look like it's vaguely shaped like your hand. Just don't mention the 'UP' – that's the Upper Peninsular part of the state that doesn't fit quite so well into the hand analogy.

Point is – if you ever meet someone and they tell you that they're from Michigan, just say 'Oh really? Whereabouts?' and raise up your right hand palm facing them, and without question they will then poke your hand with their finger whilst naming their town. Look at the indentation now left on the palm of your hand – that's where that town is.

> **12:30 PM Jun 23rd**
> Michigan billboard: 'Beef Jerky Unlimited, Exit 6'

The same name place we are heading for is a suburb of Detroit called Royal Oak, slightly north of the centre of the city. And I think I know Detroit, and its location, and yet what I don't realise is that it's actually so close to the border of Canada – so when signs for Intestate 75 and border control start appearing, I get a little jumpy and make sure that Katie does not get in the wrong lane. We will *not* be going to Canada today!

> **1:15 PM Jun 23rd**
> on I-94 eastbound. Exit signs for Canada! Shall we pop across?

Detroit is of course famous for its car industry ... or rather the lack of one nowadays. I'd like to say it's famous to for being where Eddie Murphy is supposedly from in the 'Beverly Hills Cops' series of movies, but you're gonna argue that that's not really some famous for it to be remembered by, right? Except ... for me it is, because if you're English and you grow up as a kid watching all these American movies, you just dumbly take it all in ... the action ... the shoot-out scenes ... the Eddie Murphy one liners and the terrible the sequel that is BH Cop 3, and you don't really have an idea of where Detroit is, or how far away it is from Beverly Hills in California. Taking the trip, and looking at a map is now putting all these places into, err ... place for me.

And you can't mention Michigan, or Detroit and the now-failing car industry without a nod towards Michael Moore and the documentaries he makes on the plight of the city – in particular his hometown of Flint, just a few miles away that has suffered so badly with its economy since all the car giants pulled out.

> **1:06 PM Jun 23rd**
> we're at 'Oakwood', MI – but that's not our destination...

The SatNav is having trouble homing in on Royal Oak. But I know it exists because I've confirmed it on Google Maps this morning ... on my laptop at the campground Internet connection. So after driving in the 'burbs of Detroit for ten minutes and seemingly getting lost, I get Katie to pull over and I get the laptop and the Internet dongle out, and we try to work out where the hell we are and which way we have to go.

Stopping like this to check where we are makes us aware of our surroundings. When you pull over to the side of the road, you sort of also instinctively look up to take in your surroundings. The area is not good.[10]

> **1:04 PM Jun 23rd**
> Michigan in 1 : Industrious. (because 'shit hole' would be unkind, right?)

> **1:08 PM Jun 23rd**
> ok, that's a little unfair. Michigan as a whole is great. Detroit however seems unsavoury.

But as we start to look more, see more and take in our environment a little more, a creepy feeling starts to come over me ... like when you get chills up your arm that something sinister in a horror movie is about to happen. We both find ourselves hit with a gloomy and depressing feeling. It starts off with small things – like when we pass a gun shop which has bars on windows. Not so unusual right? It would make sense for a gun shop to have that sort of protection. Then we both notice something

---

[10] Weeks later, after the trip was over and I was back in Charleston, I got an angry tweet one day from my friend Grace – who is from the town of Ann Arbour in Michigan. 'You said my home state was a shit hole!'. 'No, I said the part of Detroit that I was in was a shit hole, what's Ann Arbour like?' 'It's lovely!' she said directly. 'Ok, I'll be happy to write up in my book then that Ann Arbour is a lovely town and not at all like the part of Detroit that I was in, okay?'

weird about the gun shop. It's not a gun shop. It's actually a pet store. That's right, our natural instinct that surely only a shop selling weapons would have bars on proves wrong, as it seems like we've entered the most salubrious of neighbourhoods, where everything is tatty, beat up, in need of repair, and the places that are still in use all have scary looking fences up. You know you're in a bad part of town when even the local church has got a sign up about security patrols.

> **1:23 PM Jun 23rd**
> there's a pet store, with BARS on the window, i thought it was a gun store. I wish I was kidding.

It's a hot day too ... I haven't expected it to be this warm so far north up, but as we cruise around getting lost in the ghettos of Detroit we get hotter and hotter and more depressed at the run down state of the place we are in.

> **1:48 PM Jun 23rd**
> it's 90 degrees! What the hell? In Detroit! Having to run A/C for the first time 'coz it's too nasty and hot.

And then the road we're driving along becomes really bumpy and bad. It seems to disintegrate and have pot-holes everywhere. At one point, the road is so wide when it bends that I don't realise because there aren't any markings and I suddenly realise that I am driving on the wrong side of the road. It is like being back at home. I correct myself.

We pull up at some traffic lights. By now, we are starting to get jumpy about the neighbourhood we're in and we want to get away from here, but before we do are accosted by a family of four trying to make a living.

In London, you get people trying to wash your windscreen and ask for money. In Detroit what looks like a complete family – husband, wife and two kids stood forlornly in the middle of the junction trying to sell you a bottle of chilled water for two dollars a time. A cooler lays on the sidewalk by the side of the junction, the dad with his beady eye on it making sure that no one else is going to touch the only thing that will make them money that day. Suddenly I find myself comparing their world to mine. When would they ever get to drive around 48 states of their homeland? Answer ... most likely never.

And it is *depressing*. It really is. And weird. I haven't been expecting it. I know Detroit might be a depressed town, but it is only now driving through it, being sucked into it and seeing it for real that I can start to comprehend it and it is making us feel terrible.

We drive around just getting more disheartened, commenting more and more to each other about the desperate state of the streets and houses that we are in, until eventually we run out of things to say and we're saying nothing to each other really – except just plotting a way south, away and out of Detroit, out of the burbs and out of the grimy run down part of the city.

In the USA
Royal Oak, Michigan
On the Tube map
Royal Oak
(Hammersmith & City and Circle Lines)

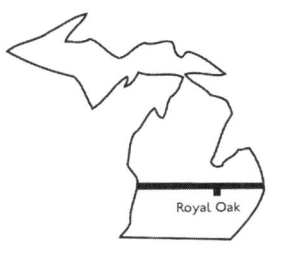

So, an immediate confession to make – we never make it to Royal Oak.

Yes, I'll write that again. We never make it Royal Oak. I skipped one. I know, *really* I know. Just thirteen 'stops' into the trip, and I have already seen enough, and I don't like what I see.

And even now writing this later, it's hard to say why we don't feel inclined to do it. At the time I would say it's because it is a hot horrible day, and the SatNav is having trouble finding it and we don't want to stop to ask for directions. Or because we are in a sketchy part of town, and we feel like Royal Oak would be even sketchier – perhaps even worse than where we are now, and we don't want to visit it at all.

Or is it really because as I sit and type this now, I know it's because somehow it feels wrong to intrude upon a desperate area, where we want to rock up and be all like 'Hey! We're here because of a same-named place in London!', and wanting to find someone to talk to … and that being weird, and that making us feel awkward. And that we shouldn't invade these people's lives and world and we should just let them be.

> **1:55 PM Jun 23rd**
> Detroit: it's a far cry from the rolling green hills of Virginia. It's depressing, lots. Expect a blog post on this.

Except now of course I realise that this is patronising. Of *course* we should have gone and seen it, and written about what it's like, and maybe we'd have met the nicest person on the whole trip, or find that at Royal Oak there would be something amazing to see[11] … so now, right now as I

---

[11] I looked it up later on Google Maps. Royal Oak looks lovely – there is a library, a book shop, a Farmer's Market – and course, there's a railway station - 'Royal Oak' Amtrak which would have been just perfect, and yet I never made it.

sit and type this I just find myself thinking 'I should really go back to Royal Oak one day', and do it justice by visiting it.

Sorry Michigan, I'm genuinely sorry.

We drive on. Getting the hell out of wherever we are, and head back south. Strangely, the temperature starts to drop.

> **3:58 PM Jun 23rd**
> just passed a sign 'prison area: do not pick up hitchhikers'

Heading south on the Interstate we look out for rogue escaped prisoners in need of a lift, Katie – who has been really quiet since the gloom of the morning – suddenly perks up when on the 'next exit' board the name 'Cabela' popped up.

'What's Cabela's?' I ask. 'It's a huuuuge camping store chain!' she says quite excitedly, and we both know – without having to confirm to each other – that we are going to go there –as something, anything to do to try and raise our spirits and have a bit of fun.

> **5:09 PM Jun 23rd**
> at a Cabela's superstore, Dundee MI. Camp equipment mecca

Cabela's are the best camping superstores in the whole of America. Except it's not just camping stuff – it's the complete outdoor experience. Camping, climbing, shooting ... you name it, they've got it covered.

I buy myself a new pen (pocket) knife, as I'd lost my other one a week before the trip. The inside of the store itself is so huge that it warrants a photo. But the good news ... they do have the correct size of gas canister for my stove, and so I snap up several containers of them and Katie has to pull me away before I buy anything else. The general rule of camping stores? They have GADGETS. And where gadgets are involved, you can always follow the mantra 'They sell stuff that you don't really need, but you really really want'.

> **6:50 PM Jun 23rd**
> made KOA Petersburg MI for the night. This part of Michigan is pretty, it's just Detroit that's depressing, sorry but it is.

We make our KOA that I've booked ourselves into online for that night whilst it is still daylight, although far from being a cute little campground with just tents and backpackers, it's more like a children's holiday camp. There are loads of kids running around, and hot dog van, and a 'DRIVE SLOWLY – 10MPH!' sign up, and I duly get shouted at by a member of the campground staff for driving at 12mph. 'Too fast!' he says (how does he know, secret radar gun stashed away in his golf cart?)

Annoyingly, my camp stove won't work – I thought at first it's that the gas canisters has run out, but having bought THREE new ones in the camping store earlier, my logic tells me that they can't all be faulty, and that instead the compact stove that I paid over $100 for just last month has broken after a week. So I end up driving *back* up to the Cabela's camp store, just fifteen minutes and buy a newer – less than half the price – stove, which then works perfectly ... and for the rest of the trip too. Who says buying cheap never works?

> **10:56 PM Jun 23rd**
> cooked dinner on my camp stove. on my NEW camp stove that is, after my original (now old one) broke. aaaargh!

The next morning over breakfast after we've slept on it for the night we discuss the possibility of driving back north to do Royal Oak, but I fear that this will put us behind schedule. So again the conversation turns as to why we've skipped it out, and before I know it, Katie is reaching for my laptop, asking if she can write a post on the Underground : USA blog which I normally do most days, and she writes a guest post. I think we both finally need to get it out of our system, and what she composes sums up both our views perfectly.

> When I learned that my leg of the trip with Geoff included Detroit, first, I figured out why this leg had not been picked up by somebody else already, and second, I knew I would be in for something different. Little did I know how big of a mark Detroit would leave on MY map.
>
> You could smell the desperation in the air even driving in on the Interstate. We were driving along with the beautiful country farm fields in our view then all of sudden BAM. Industry and smog filled the car. The roads became cracked and broken, and looked almost downright unsafe. Trash littered the sides of the highway, and literally within seconds, our moods changed as well.
>
> We pulled off onto a highway, and ended up in ghetto suburban Detroit. I noticed a small boy, not older than 7, selling bottles of water on the side of a very busy intersection. Then, I saw his brothers and sisters, and even Mom and Dad. The businesses all looked like prisons, bars all over the windows and doors. Pet shops, hair salons, even churches were all barred. One school even had a sign begging the public to donate money to keep its doors open. The trash got higher, and more and more children were peddling on the side of the roads. I cannot express just how desperate it was. Not even Geoff could find anything funny

about this place. Detroit looked like a devastated war zone, a wasteland of failed industry and societal regression.

We finally get our bearings and turn onto another Interstate, and within a matter of minutes, it was like a different city. Malls, shops, affluent suburbia America had appeared. While my fears of being mugged and shot dissipated, a very deep anger grew instead. Then I saw several large corporate offices lining the Interstate. They belonged to none other than Ford and the other 'struggling' big car manufacturers. I kid you not, I broke down into tears.

Ironically, I finished Kurt Vonnegut's 'Man Without A Country' this morning, and he gave a very interesting quote: 'What can be said to our young people, now that psychopathic personalities, which is to say persons without consciences, without senses of pity or shame, have taken all the money in the treasuries of our government and corporations, and made it all their own?'

I can say that I have never been more disappointed in my country than I was yesterday. How can people sleep with themselves at night after begging from the private jets for billions of dollars in DC, and then let a poor 7 year old beg for change not even ten minutes away from their cushy corporate offices?! My bleeding heart does not understand how we can be so greedy, then just sit and watch our own fellow citizens fall into such poverty.

Needless to say I was in a bit of a funk for the rest of the day, and once Geoff and I set up camp and started sorting out the day's events, we both asked each other why we hadn't been to Royal Oak – the stop we were meant to go to, nor had we taken any pictures of Detroit. Looking back I wish we had, but at the time, we just couldn't bring ourselves to do so.

So this is the real Underground USA, folks. It's not all sunshine and roses, quirky roadside attractions or charming American towns with idyllic smiling faces. Although those things are much appreciated and equally noted, you have to acknowledge the good with the bad, and the current societal and economic state of the US overall is not a good one, and heaven forbid that what is happening in Detroit spreads elsewhere

~ ~ ~

The next day, we're not in a hurry – we are not going to visit a Tube-named town. Today, I am going to edit some video.

When I'd prepared the schedule/itinerary for the trip I'd been very careful to allow more time for things than I thought was necessary, and – every week or so – add in a whole day of NO travelling to allow me to catch up with things, and more importantly – do some video editing, as I really want to make sure that I kept up with video logging as I went along.

So today is not about really getting anywhere in particular or having to be at a same-named stop, instead ... we can cruise along at a gentle pace. I'd casually looked at Google Maps before we set off that morning, and decided that Columbus in Ohio looks like a big enough city for us to stop in, find a Motel for the night and do a little video editing.

Destination chosen for the day, I turn my attention to eating something.

> **9:13 AM Jun 24th**
> burning scrambled eggs on my stove for breakfast. back to Ohio today

Now I haven't really thought about the effect that my tweets might be having as I send them out – in some bizarre way I think that really the only person who might be interested in where I am and would be 'following' along on a map would be my mum. Little do I know at that point, but my previous tweet about Ohio would generate some very specific interest.

> **11:17 AM Jun 24th**
> on the road this morning : I75 south, goodbye Michigan, hello Ohio again. Heading for Columbus tonight.

With that tweet, I have clearly been specific about where we are now heading, and so as we cruise well within the speed limit that morning, south on I-75, a lovely lady called *Betty* is sending me an email, that I will not get until later.

> **12:58 PM Jun 24th**
> on US-68, OH. 'God it's like road kill central' – Katie. Counted at least 20 squashed things in the last hour.

Before we get to Columbus though, we have to go somewhere that is on the way anyway – to the town of Bellefontaine.

In keeping in line with visiting some of the 'World's largest' attractions that America likes to offer (I plan to do the Ball of Twine later in Idaho), my roadside travelling guide has pointed me in the direction of something that is not the largest – but the opposite – the smallest. Actually, to be perfectly accurate, it's actually the *shortest* of what it is. Welcome to the World's Shortest Street.[12]

---

[12] It can be quite hard to find, so I'll tell you right now exactly where it is. Go to your computer, fire up Google Maps and type in: **N 40° 21.692 W 083° 45.840** and it'll take you straight to it. Unfortunately, at the time of writing this Google Maps hasn't got to it yet on Street view, and there

McKinley Street is named after William McKinley, America's 25th President who held office for just one term between 1897 to 1901. I can't help but think that they missed a trick here, and that they should have named the street after the President who was in power for the *shortest* amount of time – one William Henry Harrison, the 9th president of the USA, who unfortunately popped his clogs after just thirty-two days in office back in 1840, poor guy.

I'm expecting some kind of big banner, or landmark sign saying 'WORLD'S SHORTEST STREET' proclaiming it from a long way off with big flashing lights. But no – instead, in the same font and colour (white on green) as all street signs in the use, we see a small additional sign that simply says 'World's Shortest Street' and there is a defunct electrical store on one side of the road ... and a railway line sort of passing through it on the other.

'You couldn't make it up could, you?' I laugh at Katie. 'Make what up?' 'A railway line, a bloody railway line. Even when I come to a place that is a non-Tube-stop-named place there's still a bloody railway line'.

Bellefontaine is having a dry and hot dusty day, and I look around to see if there is a gas station anywhere nearby to get a drink – there isn't. The street connects two roads together which converge just a little further on anyway, forming a small triangle, and there is a mixture of local residential traffic and a few trucks doing about their business.

We get a couple of strange looks as we proceed to take photos, and I shoot a lot of video too. From the biggest tire to the smallest street, right? I like the road connection seeing as we are on the road ourselves.

And then after pacing the whole thing out (Twenty-three feet, I make it), Katie and I 'race' each other at running it, crouching down in Olympic-Runner style, 'On you marks... get set... go!' – to see who can run it the fastest. I win. In fact, I win all three times that I make us do it just so that I can video it from different angles – ever the pro, me – see?

Unfortunately, it isn't until we get to the motel/hotel room later and I look it up to see exactly where we have been that I discover something a little controversial – that another street, this time in Edinburgh, Scotland is now in the Guinness Book of Records as the world's shortest street being just 6ft, 9inches long. Oh. Dammit. We've gone slightly out of our way to go to ... the world's second shortest street! Ah well.

---

aren't even any photos of it there either. So you'll just have to believe me when I tell you that it's there.

The motel that I refer to by the way is the one that we've checked into about 3pm in the afternoon, and it is not – by hotel standards, the best. The whole hotel itself does not look like it has been purpose built as a hotel ... but I can't tell what it has previously been. Just ... office space, I think. The reception is bare, and grimy, and if anything reminds me of a hospital waiting room with a piece of sliding glass as the reception window. The lighting is dim, and the bored Chinese looking woman who serves us speaks in a low mumble.

Even the local paper – The Columbus Dispatch – is sat in a 'free' rack, except that the sign has been scribbled over and you have to pay the cover price – 75 cents for the paper.

'Oh my God' says Katie surveying the room 'This is the type of room where they're riddled by bugs in the sheets' and pulls a face to suggest that she does not want to sleep here tonight. Well ... for $55, what else do you expect?

> **3:59 PM Jun 24th**
> i know i've gone quiet. i'm in Columbus, OH. editing video ....

What it *does* have though is a desk which I put my computer on and set it up, and whilst Katie naps, I busily get on with editing some video. And whilst that is rendering out, I check my emails as I haven't done it all day, and find the wireless Internet to be working surprisingly well for a cheap hotel room, and I enjoy my online time. During that period, I receive – to my surprise – a lovely and unexpected email from a stranger.

> Hi Geoff!
>
> You said you will be in Columbus tonight and that's where I live. I hope this doesn't sound weird, but I have a poster of the London Underground and was wondering if you'd be willing to sign it if I brought it to you tonight :)
>
> Betty

There is more to the message explaining who she is, how she's been to London a few years ago and loved it – including travelling on the Underground, and I realise now that Betty isn't a complete stranger as she has indeed already left a few comments on my blog in the past few weeks in the run-up to and during the first couple of weeks of my trip ... and here I am, inadvertently stopping in and ending up in her home town for the night! Would I like to meet up with here? Of *course* I would. It's just ... I would have to explain to Katie that I want to meet a 'random' stranger off of the Internet.

'How do you know she's not a weirdo?' 'Because she's not ... I can just ... tell'. 'But how do you KNOW she's not!' 'Because ... we'll I've dealt with random people emailing me before and you can sort of tell' 'Geoff...' 'No, really! She's commented on my blog ... and besides ... she says she's not a weirdo, let's meet her!'

This is mainly how the conversation goes for a few minutes when Katie wakes up from her nap and I present her with the idea of what I want to do. For a moment I wonder if we are heading for a big argument, and I will storm out slamming the door and driving off anyway, but after a few moments of going round in circles Katie realises that I might just be right ... it would be ok ... and that I am going to go and do it anyway, no matter what. Meeting random strangers on a road trip is part of the whole road trip experience.

So I email Betty back ... give her my number and wait ten minutes, she emails *me* back and gives me her number, and arranges to meet us in a local park that night. A what? Yes, that's right ... a local park. You'll find out why if you keep reading on.

> **6:12 PM Jun 24th**
> new video uploaded! And we're off out in a minute to meet a stalker – I mean – fan/follower!

We have to eat first though, so before anything else we find the delightful Adriaticos Pizza place which Katie has found out by Googling around. The Ohio State University is in Columbus, and this pizza joint appears to be a favourite of the students. Works for me.

We get chatting to the two girls working there as servers, and I allay Katie's fears a little more about meeting up with someone out the blue. 'Isn't that what a road trip and journey is part meant to be about anyway ... doing random things like this?' and in the end, she calms right down and sees that it will be fun.

We're paying up for the Pizza when I get a worried phone call from Betty. 'You are coming, yes?' she asks ... 'Only it will be getting dark soon'. And I apologise for not realising that time has slipped away a bit. We dash back to the car, and punch in the address of the park on the SatNav and make our way as fast as we can.

Dark? Yes, because we've chosen to meet them outside. Or rather Betty has told us to meet them outside in a place called Whetstone Park[13]. *Them*? Oh ... yes ... going for safety in numbers herself and just in case *we*

---

[13] Only weeks after did I put 2+2 together and remember that there is a Tube Station on the Northern Line called 'Totteridge & Whetstone'. You really can't make things like this up sometimes, it's just life, and it just happens.

turn out to be a bunch of nutters, Betty has led us to her knitting circle group which is meeting that night ... outside ... in a park.

> **7:56 PM Jun 24th**
> Ohio is nice. Columbus is pretty. Now off to meet Beddy ....

In my head I can't help but be faux-American and soften the T's to D's. Instead of Betty, she is now Beddy. And a song forms in my head ... the only song I know which has 'Betty' in, and thankfully my iPod has, and Ram Jam is soon pumping out and we make our way through central Columbus.

The SatNav unfortunately knows nothing of the roadwork's and diversions that delay us getting there, but we finally pull in and park about 30 metres way from where we can see they are all sitting. We look out of the front windscreen to a park bench partially undercover by a tree, where there is a small group of women sitting round. One of them – obviously Betty – waves at us. And it's at that point that Katie turns to me with a puzzled look on her face, and said 'Geoff... what are they doing? Are they ... *knitting*?' 'Yes' I say drolly. 'Very much so'. 'Welcome to the monthly meeting of the Columbus West Side Knitters!', at which point Katie finally smiles and realises that what we've been invited to is not a bunch of weirdoes at all – but a bunch of genuinely lovely people.

For the next forty-five minutes I 'schmooze' them – This is the exact word that Katie later uses when re-capping the experience. 'It's like you were famous!' she giggles 'And you turned on the charm totally!! You were a famous Geoff!' she repeats, killing herself with laughter.

But all I've just been is reciprocal on the friendliness that they showed us, and that it is easy to show back.

Famous? Well, as far as Betty is concerned I am niche-Internet famous. She's been following along my website and blog for a while now and loved it to bits, but never imagined that she'd ever get to meet me in person on the trip. 'When you went to Greenford, Ohio', she says 'And then carried on up to Detroit, I was real disappointed! I thought that there was no way that you would come back down here ... so when I read on your twitter that you were coming back and staying in Ohio, I got really excited'. The power of twitter.

This evening is already planned and is their regular place to meet. A small group – women, all women – often meet here to knit, talk, oh and eat some delicious foods too! There are boxes of cakes and scones and muffins strewn about, and they sit around and discuss the world and everything that needs to be talked about, oh ... and knit too. One girl – I forget her name – is making ...'Is that a Harry Potter scarf?' I half laugh and exclaim ... it is!

As also promised, she has brought her large poster-sized Tube map with her that she once bought on trip to London, and asks me to sign it. 'There's no stop called Columbus' I muse. 'There should be!', and in the end sign it ... 'Mind The Gap' in a white space part of the map.

We take photos – Katie shoots some video, and is generally amused by all the middle-aged women that are now fussing around me, and until it gets dark we have the loveliest time just hanging out and chatting about nothing and yet everything.

Suddenly – in the middle of it all, I think back to just two days ago. To Detroit, to a part of America full of despair and crime and places that I did not feel comfortable in and wouldn't want to visit again – to here, just a short drive down the Interstate to the next state down, to a world where a group of knitters met up and hang out in a park, eat home baked food and swap stories. And I love it ... and I find myself being able to think that there is nice in the world too, but yet bizarre that the two places can be so close together and yet worlds apart.

> **9:57 PM Jun 24th**
> i confess, I did not expect to encounter knitting at any point on this trip #random

Daylight eventually goes, which is the cue for the knitters start to pack up. We say our goodbyes, but not before Betty has given us some muffins & flapjacks as snacks to see us on our way, and we drive quietly back ... the music on low, through the dark streets of north Columbus lit up by street lights.

'That was nice, that was ... really nice', says Katie.

'I've had worse evenings' I smile back, and consider how someone that has followed my blog from 4,000 miles away eventually gets to meet up with me as I'm passing through her home town. It may be a world apart from Detroit, but it can also be a small world too sometimes.

Day 10 – Thursday 25th June

What we need now, is Liverpool

*'I see the fear, I see the fear in your eyes,
When they keep you afraid you believe all their lies.
In Liverpool, what we need now is love.'*

I think that during the night I dream that I am Tom Baker in the TARDIS. I wear a long scarf as knitted by the all the ladies we'd met the night before. I use my sonic screwdriver lots, and do a lot of running. And then I wake up and realise I haven't set an alarm and it is already quite late.

> **11:03 AM Jun 25th**
> a late start to the day, ouch. Not good. Still in Columbus OH. I have a headache. Need coffee. At least we have food though.

Cheap Days Inn coffee really is just like brown water that you'll be lucky if it has any flavour, so back over at the Gas Station where we've filled up the night before we get a proper caffeine injection and hit the road – it is time to go find same name stop Number 14 – Liverpool, in West Virginia.

> **11:31 AM Jun 25th**
> today's same-name Tube stop : Liverpool, West Virginia. The SatNav is having trouble finding it though ...

> **12:18 PM Jun 25th**
> so we're heading for cooler weather, farewell Ohio, hello West Virginia. We want rain, we're so hot ....

Our day has started so late though, that it's nearly lunchtime by the time we get going, so when Katie spots a Jimmy John's sandwich place for lunch, she more-or-less insists that we stop and we are made a little bit later still, but I have at least been introduced to the world of their delicious gourmet sandwiches, and it's a small chain so it don't feel like I'm giving money to the man for once.

We head south east out of Columbus down US33 and a few miles out from Ohio River – the snaking major tributary that defines the state line between Ohio and West Virginia, we both get the urge to go to the toilet ... handy, because at almost the exact moment that we both proclaim it (what, are our bladders in sync or something?) a rest stop appears ahead.

We pull in and see that it's quite a basic rest stop. Somewhere to park, a place for your dog to run, a water fountain and a block of buildings which look like they must be the toilets. Strangely there is no coke machine – usually a basic function at most other similar rest stops that I am used to down in South Carolina. We lock the car and wander over to the toilet block … and … that's exactly what it is. The closer we get the more shabby we realise it is, and I suddenly have images of a prison movie where the protagonist is sent to solitary for a week for trying to escape … a rusty old corrugated iron building is where he's consigned to.

Well that's what it feels like walking into this now – somewhat dark, dank and dingy rusty old structure desperately trying to pretend it's a toilet.

I can honestly smell it before I see it. I twist and turn into the small entrance corridor, and then in the dim light can see where it is that Ohio State wants me to relieve myself … into a hole in the ground! What the fuck?

This is *not* a toilet … not if you are look up the definition in the Geoff-Dictionary that is, as all there is, is a horrid old metal ring which I guess is pretending to be a seat. Is it? No! I think it's just there as a guide for you to see where the hole in the ground is properly.

Part of me wants to peer into it, the rest of me doesn't, and suddenly my urge to go to the toilet diminishes, and I find myself backing out of the structure.

A waft of – what is that? Oh, that's right! Clean fresh air – hits me as I go back outside, whereupon I realise that Katie must have met a similar fate in the ladies' toilet. And by the look on her face of her standing there, I think it's clear that she has.

For two to three seconds, we just stare at each other, waiting for someone to say it first … but no one does, because in the next moment, I smirk, which makes her giggle, and we both then pissed ourselves – but of the laughing kind.

'It's so *disgusting!*' she squeals. 'It really is quite bad isn't?' I say being more of a man about it. 'And you know what I need to do, don't you?' 'What?' 'Video it!' I reply, still laughing and nip back to the car to get the video camera. By the time I get back Katie is talking to another woman – to whom she is warning of the pit of turdy doom inside the solitary confinement shack.

'Ah, that's ok, I travel down this road a lot and I'm used to it' says the woman, and Katie looks appalled. 'But it's so *gross!*' she again squeals to me, as I hit REC on the video camera, and duck back inside the male compartment.

I have to confess whilst I am in there, the urge to wee does get the better of me and I do end up taking a leak. I'd like to point out that I don't capture the moment of my urination – simply an overview of the squalid facilities instead.

Back outside, Katie offers squirts of hand-sanitiser to the other woman who accepts it, and I happily take up a globule of it too myself to clean up my hands.

'Wow. Thanks Ohio for some basic toileting there' I say out loud to no one. 'I still need to go' replies Katie. 'Can we stop at the next gas station we see?' We can Katie, we can.

> **2:04 PM Jun 25th**
> Ohio in 4 : Your rest stops suck. (And it's all on video!)

The next gas station doesn't come for a while because we end up following the SatNav down some winding country back roads – so windy in fact, that the SatNav has trouble keeping up and/or its data for the road we are on and we end up coming 'off road' as far at the navigational box-of-tricks is concerned.

We stop by some farmland to take some pictures of more abandoned rusty cars that I spot, and as we pull away from that a totally random moment of serendipity[14] occurs on my iPod as the random shuffle plays 'Kingdom of Rust' completely by chance. Images of rusty corrugated toilets structures pop back into my head, and only when it gets sung in the second verse do I realise that it has the word 'Preston' in the lyrics too – 'But Preston is tomorrow, not today' I say happily, pressing down on the accelerator in time to the beat to whizz us perhaps a little dangerously fast around a bend in the winding road.

The music is good, we are making progress and I am happy. And a few more minutes later the country road that we're on shrouded by high-top trees opens up into a clearing, which becomes a triangular intersection of three roads with what looks like a small General Store on the corner, and I realise that we have arrived at Liverpool.

> **2:36 PM Jun 25th**
> Thank you for travelling Geofftech Road trips. You are arriving at your West Virginian stop. Have a nice day.

---

[14] I apologise as it seems like I'm using the work 'Serendipity' too much in this book, so I've just used the Thesaurus feature on my word processor and it's suggested 'Kismet' as an alternative. So I promise you I will use that word next time instead.

In the USA
Liverpool, West Virginia
On the Tube map
Liverpool Street
(Central, Metropolitan and Circle Lines)

What has looked like being a General Store is indeed a shop, and even though they sell no gas they do have a toilet much to Katie's relief.

The shop itself has obviously seen better days and lots of the shelves are sparse and empty with dust collecting in places where no goods have obviously been stocked for a while. I try to catch the eye and smile at woman behind the counter, but she is engrossed in ... playing on her phone? No ... paper, a crossword? Ah! A *Sudoko* puzzle by the looks of it, and I realise that this might be one of those places where yet again I won't get the local conversation I am looking for.

Katie appears back my by side, her bladder now empty. 'Got anything', 'Nope, can't think of anything I want'. 'Twizzlers?', 'They don't have them ...' I say a little sad – 'But ooh! They do have ... !', and for some reason at that moment my eyes focus on a pack of mint flavoured Skittles right by the cash register – so we buy some along with other sweets and drinks and as I am paying to attempt to engage in conversation with the woman serving, but she doesn't go for it. Strange – they surely can't get *that* many people in here judging by the look of the shop can they? But no friendly local stranger banter seems to be forthcoming apart from some standard small talk. Curses. We go back outside.

An old rocking chair that has seen better days, a rusty metal sign to play the lottery, and an old plastic kid's car, the sort that's big enough for a child to sit in are all outside, not *littered* exactly, but all obviously in an unused discarded kind of way. We find a wooden bench and sit on it, and I open up my packet of sweets.

'It's kinda nice, even though it's quiet isn't it?' says Katie. And we look around the triangular junction with grass and wild-flowers growing in the middle, and the STOP sign glistening in the sun, reflecting rays of light off onto the ground, and I get my camera out and snap a couple of arty photos.

3:02 PM Jun 25th
Liverpool, WV : quiet, but cute.

We sit, enjoying the peacefulness and the sunshine for quite a while, during which time only two cars pass through with neither stopping at the store, making me wonder quite how the business survives.

'No checks please' says a sign on the door as I go for one final look around the building, and almost tread on an upturned rusty rake that has been left in the grass round the side of the building. I notice another pile of children's play toys – trucks, cars, and random wheels in a pile, all faded by the weather.

Katie is back in the car looking at a paper map that she's picked up.

'Hey!' she says beckoning as I approach. 'Do you want to drive us to Charleston now?'

SAME NAME TOWNS TALLY

Something there and enjoyable
Plaistow, Gloucester, Kew Gardens, Harrow, South Kensington, Greenford, Liverpool

Something there but not that exciting to be honest
Putney

Nothing there but somehow being in the middle of nowhere made it OK
Epping, Acton

Nothing there, and not that exciting either. Oops.
Warwick, Wapping, Camden

4:45 PM Jun 25th
i'm back in Charleston. That's ... Charleston, West Virginia ... ho ho!

Charleston in South Carolina is my current home in the USA, and on the outskirts of same-named Charleston, West Virginia we stop at proper grocery store, and get some dinner for the evening. We find the local KOA – at a place called Huntingdon, and revel in the fact that we've made good progress and we will actually camp and stay here for two nights – not one – leaving us all day to do Preston tomorrow without being in a hurry. Royal Oak may have momentarily popped into my mind, but with a literal shake of my head I dismiss it, and I fumble for the camping gear in the back of car and help Katie set up the tent for the night.

Day 11 – Friday 26th June

The Kingdom of Rust

'The Road back to Preston was jutted out in the snow,
As I went looking for that stolen heart for you.
My God, it takes an ocean of trust, in the kingdom of rust'

No trains today – instead it's the noise from the kids in the next tent over that initially wakes me up, and when I eventually summon the effort to stick my head out of the tent I find more than just the morning dew, but a light splattering of rain over everything where it has been wet in the middle of the night.

> **7:56 AM Jun 26th**
> Huntingdon, West Virginia: it rained last night and so everything is moist.

I quite like it though, as it feels as if everything has been washed clean – ironic a little, as we've left the plastic plates from our camp-stove cooked dinner out overnight on the bench, and they have indeed been washed a little more.

I get an instant kick out of realising that the benefit of staying somewhere two nights means that we do not have to pack all the shit down, and even leaving some non-valuable stuff under the cover of the tent too, is possible.

Our tube-map stop for the day is Preston in Kentucky and somehow we are up, showered, breakfasted and on the road by 10am according to the clock in the car – the earliest I've been on the road in a while.

It takes us three minutes to drive down the road and cross the state line into Kentucky. It takes what feels like about another three for me to realise that I'm not wearing my watch and have a little panic about where it is, and then remember that I've left it hanging up in the shower block back at the campsite, so we turn around and go back to retrieve it - generally wasting another twenty minutes to the start of our day before we actually properly start out.

A Queen song comes on the radio – excellent! Halfway through a powerful third chorus I yell out to Katie to stop. 'Ooh! Stop!' I shout, noting that the gas station ahead is in fact in the new state of Kentucky that are in, and I'd be able to buy some Ale-81.

Now that's 'Ale-Eight-One', as opposed to 'Ale Eighty One'. And if you really want to go all out phonetically, then really it should be pronounced 'A late one' as you rhyme all the words together.

'What's Ale Eight One?' asks Katie, and a little moment of pride surges up in me that it seems there is a tiny part of American culture that I (the immigrant) knows about that Katie (the local) doesn't. Ha!

Ale 8-1 is a drink I'd found only in Charleston once, mainly because it is predominantly stocked in its home state of Kentucky. It's ginger ale essentially ... but with an additional bite to it, on the bottle it says 'A ginger and citrus blend' and is supposedly better for you than other soda drinks in that it contains less calories.

> **1:22 PM Jun 26th**
> gas station stop, KY: Bought a bottle of Ale81 (go Google it)

Katie takes a swig. She approves. I tweet her opinion.

> **1:23 PM Jun 26th**
> gas stop in KY: Katie , 'man that shit's good!'

But what is really taking me, is the gas station itself. There's a woman inside smoking which I think is illegal.

> **1:24 PM Jun 26th**
> gas stop in KY: The woman in line in front of me to pay was smoking a cigarette. Classy.

> **1:25 PM Jun 26th**
> gas stop, KY: The cashier draaaaawled like, the most ever, and my polite British accent clearly startled her.

Then I realise of course that it's not *just* a gas station. It's a convenience store, a restaurant *and* a gas station all in one – and I guess that it being a combo of these things and not 'just' a gas station makes it OK for someone to smoke on the premises. Weird, maybe the smoking laws are different in Kentucky.

Back in the car, the SatNav says that Preston, KY is just 19 minutes away and I check my watch as we pass the 'Welcome To...' sign that greets us as we hit the outskirts of Preston – and it really is nineteen minutes later, just as it predicted it would be. We swig the rest of our ginger ale during that time, and are now wondering what Preston would have *in store* for us.

We drive past an old dingy building with a US flag hanging from it, spy a wooden white painted church, a few houses, a sign of an upcoming sale of some sort, a field with cows, another old house juxtaposed nicely in the next part down by a much more modern and practically brand new house ... and that's about it. I pull into the side of the road, hmm. I am hoping it would be more than this,

'Shall we turn around, see if we missed anything?' I say to Katie. 'Sure, do it'.

Driving the same road in the way back a bit more slowly this time, we pass the same buildings – but strangely it looks different from this angle. I quite often find that when you walk, run, cycle or drive a route in reverse that you think you know well you often see things that you don't see when you pass through it in the other direction – and so it proves to be with Preston.

I realise that the beat up old building with flags hanging from it is actually a small hive of activity, as I spot three old men sitting on the porch and only now do I see a sign that says 'Blevins Grocery'. Ok! If all Preston has to offer is a grocery store, then that would suffice.

Oh, how little do I know and how wrong I could have been …

In the USA
Preston, Kentucky
On the Tube map
Preston Road
(Metropolitan Line)

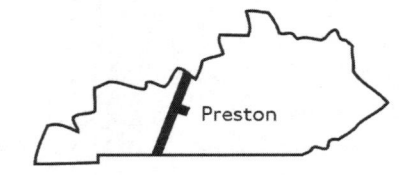

Oh my.

Oh my, oh my.

> **1:45 PM Jun 26th**
> Underground USA has arrived at : Preston, Kentucky. And there is a brilliant old general store here.

I think goose pimples may have actually rippled up my arm when the doorbell 'clanged' as we went inside, and we instantly stepped back in time. Within a second, I know that we have just hit the jackpot and I have found perhaps I think what I have been looking for.

Welcome to Blevins General Store, Preston Kentucky.

Welcome to lost-in-time, perfect small town America.

There is an old man wearing a hat behind the counter of the store – the store which is dimly lit but you can see oozes with character and history and has been here a long time and sells practically every item that a local community can want – and has obviously done so for a very long time.

'Hello', we say. 'Hello' he gives us with a friendly smile straight back. We have just met *Rube*. But wait for it – we've just met Rube *Blevins* – yeah, the original owner of the store which he and his wife Helen have been running now for almost 50 years.

The shelves are stocked with goods, old and new – but so much more besides. For some reason a top shelf in the corner has a line of trophies too – awards, given to the shop? Who knows? But they sell groceries and hardware and stationery. It's like a Sainsbury's with a Robert Dyas and W.H. Smith's all mixed into one ... but in a rustic old country store with an old friendly owner.

I have a flashback to being a child at my grandmother's house (my mum's mum) who has a proper pantry[15] and inside the small dark room where there are food product with names and labels that I feel that I have never seen before and I wonder how long they have been there. This is just like that. There are packets and boxes and tins of goods resting on dark wooden shelves, seemingly out of order but when you inspect them closely you realise that the food stuffs are grouped into similar categories.

Rube suddenly speaks up! Asking us if we are after lunch – and we have to truthfully say 'no' because we've only just eaten at the gas station less than an hour ago. This is a shame because it turns out that the store is also a popular place for a steak sandwich – made from bologna (or ham, if you want the more expensive variants) and they're rather popular in these parts – all washed down with some Ale-8-One of course.

I explain to Rube that there is a 'Preston Road' railway station in London and his eyebrows raise, and I think he is going to ask me questions, but all it does is lead him to tell me a short history of his Preston here in Kentucky where he has been born, raised, worked all his life and 'Not long to go now until I die I expect!', he chuckles.

As he laughs, I can't help but notice on the counter behind him there is a picture of President Clinton. Hang on, is that *here*, has Clinton been here? I am just about to ask when he seems to recall that I've mentioned another Preston.

'This is named after a railroad in London?' chuckles Rube again. 'We used to have trains – two, every day that went west and two that went east. They tore up the old Railroad a few years ago now though. The workers used to come here for their lunch everyday'.

I nod, taking this all in and smiling too as I just look around the store with joy. 'SMOKING ALLOWED!' says another sign right next to cash register – and again, a rustic looking old rack to hold cigarettes with stickers and labels advertising tobacco products which I don't think exist anymore are still on it.

---

[15] America does not use the word 'Larder', they all say 'Pantry'. When things were going to shit in my marriage with my wife, I would often use the British word for something on purpose just to annoy her. I feel like now would be a good time to apologise for this, but I'm not going to.

'Folks don't smoke as much as they used to anymore' says Rube wistfully, 'We don't stock as many brands as we used to'.

This is a present day grocery store, and also now a museum of products from the past. And it's perfect, just *perfect*.

> **1:46 PM Jun 26th**
> it's a perfect 'leave your door unlocked' town, with a rundown general store, guy in a hat has worked there for 40 yrs

We do feel though as if we should be good customers and consume something, so we buy some bottles of Ale-8-1 which are perched up on wooden shelf next to some cans of Pepsi that are *not* tapered at the edges and still have proper old ring pulls! I have not seen a can of drink like this in … Wow, goodness knows how many years.

Rube rings them up – literally – on an old fashioned, non-electronic cash register, that goes *kerching!* And a satisfying *whump!* As the register pops out, he works out our change in his head. Oh my. This is bloody brilliant.

We stay in the store and look round some more, and find some newspaper cuttings stuck up in one corner – with pictures of Rube standing behind the cash register in his hat in the store in which we are now standing. Others it seems have found this pocket of the state that has almost frozen still in time, and there have been plenty of features on the Blevins store over the years.

Did I mention it was perfect? Because it is. Absolutely spot-on, and I want to come shopping in here every day.

But more than anything, the store is still a place for the community to meet, hang out, swap gossip and generally maybe just sit and idle some time away in the world. As we leave with the 'clang' of the bell from the door again, one of the guys say on the bench looks up and nods us a 'farewell' and I notice that that guy next to him is working hard away at a whittling stick.

> **2:01 PM Jun 26th**
> there are four old guys sat on the front porch, one of them was ACTUALLY whittling away at a whittling stick!

'We did it!' I exclaim back in the car to Katie. 'That was amazing' she says and we both sit there for a moment letting it soak in what we have just experienced. For almost a whole minute … silence.

Perfect small town America still exists and is still out there. At my fifteenth attempt of trying out of the 48, I find a place that I love. Except now of course I want there to be more of them.

I get out my paper notebook that I am jotting things down in, and put a huge tick next to 'Preston', with a smiley face. And I look at the categories of the places that I have found so far and realise that it needs a new one – all to itself – which I happily write in.

SAME NAME TOWNS TALLY

Perfect Small Town America
Preston

Something there and enjoyable
Plaistow, Gloucester, Kew Gardens, Harrow, South Kensington, Greenford, Liverpool

Something there but not that exciting to be honest
Putney

Nothing there but somehow being in the middle of nowhere made it OK
Epping, Acton

Nothing there, and not that exciting either. Oops.
Warwick, Wapping, Camden

The next morning it is time to move on again, and after having a slight altercation with Katie which I mentally flag up as our first row (And I then spend the next hour worrying about the fact that I have mentally flagged that up ... because only if you're like a *proper* couple in a relationship does that sort of thing become important, right ... right?) and I'm not sure if it is important or not, dammit.

> **10:16 AM Jun 27th**
> the Journey Continues, today: Heading for Tennessee.

An hour down the road and we stop at a gas station and my trusty UK credit card that I've been using to fill up almost every day fails to make the payment. 'ERROR – PLEASE SEE CASHIER' says the display of the pump non-helpfully, and so I have to use my American one instead. It is about then that I have a thought as to what's happening and decide to call my bank in England.

Of course, beloved cost-cutting outsourcing of the Credit Card Call Centre Company means that you never actually call England anymore. In fact, the funniest thing was once when I called my bank back in the UK, and it was 2pm in the afternoon in America, meaning it was 7pm in England, and the guy that answered the phone said 'Good morning!' To which I replied 'Well it's neither morning in the country I'm calling from or the one I'd hoped to be calling *to*, so where in the world are you?'.[16]

> **11:53 PM Jun 27th**
> am on the phone to Barclaycard explaining that yes, all those gas stops ARE me, and no, my card hasn't been stolen.

What then follows is the most fun day of just driving on the trip. The morning's argument is forgotten and as we drive our way along the road that seemingly straddles the state line borders of both Kentucky and West Virginia; we play music loudly.

> **2:04 PM Jun 27th**
> Katie's MAKING me listen to Bluegrass. Help! 'it's fitting' she says. that's not the verb I'd use.

> **2:06 PM Jun 27th**
> have just passed a town in WV called 'Kermit', brilliant! But can we play the Muppets music? No .... Bluegrass.

> **2:14 PM Jun 27th**
> re-entered Kentucky on way to Tennessee. Is that how you spell Tennessee?

Finally, after over two hours of blue-grass-recourse, it becomes my turn to drive and my insistence that I now choose the music. And of course when I say *I get to choose* something, what I mean is that I get to choose

---

[16] He wouldn't even tell me – really, he wouldn't 'For security reasons', he said.

something that still has to meet with Katie's approval. Remembering the Queen song from yesterday, I put that on.

> **3:51 PM Jun 27th**
> we're on the 'Country music highway', apparently, US23 south. Except we're listening to Queen now. And singing loudly. That'll learn 'em.

We've been steadily climbing up higher and higher and I haven't really noticed until my ears pop to let me know that we must be at altitude. At this point, there is a huge lay-by on the curving road up into the hills, and we stop to take photos just because it's a stunning vista.

> **4:24 PM Jun 27th**
> we must be high (no, not like that), but high up – our ears are popping.

We roll over the border from Virginia into Tennessee much earlier than I've predicted and I feel good … in fact I feel *great*. It has been a bloody fun day of music, singing, driving through scenic winding roads and taking silly video and photos and talking and chatting so much it's just a whole lot of fun. We haven't been tired at any point because we've both been awake and alive and our natural energy pushes us on, and so when we get to Kingsport earlier than I expect I celebrate by splashing out on a hotel again – I shouldn't really have done, but we've made such good progress and Katie points out that we can stay with her sister for the following two nights and save money, and so we do.

> **7:40 PM Jun 27th**
> we're in a motel in Kingsport TN for the night. The business card of the manager here says 'God Bless' on it. If I didn't know I was in the south, I do now

The girl that greets us behind the reception is *very* Southern. Super sweet, super fake-polite, super drawly, super, err... just *Southern*, and when we get to our room for the night and I turn on the TV, the first thing that comes up is the Dukes of Hazzard. Yup, I'm in the South.

Day 13 – Sunday 28th June

Amersham Time

*'Do we need our passports, do we need our sunglasses
do we need any jabs or inoculations, in Amersham,
be sure to set your watches to Amersham time'*

'Hold still'. 'Hold'. There's movement. 'Seriously don't try to move' 'But it's gross' 'I know it's gross, but I've almost got it'. I'm peering in towards Katie's hair very closely, clutching my nail scissors with my right hand, separating the golden curls of her hair with my left, trying to attack, attach to, and remove the little bastard tick that is burrowing its way into her scalp. Gross.

> **8:45 AM Jun 28th**
> just removed a tick from Katie's hair. kinda gross. but good morning, Tennesseeeee

Tennessee would be a much better state name if they spelt it with five E's. They can make it the only state that has a three letter abbreviation code instead of two letters, by making it 'TSE', abbreviating the five E's down to just one. I'm full of good ideas, me. Why doesn't anyone ever listen to them though?

Our destination this morning is the top left corner of the Tube map – Amersham – only obviously we are doing the version 4,000 miles away to the west of the London one.

Like the starting point of Epping, Amersham is not actually in London, so it should really be part of the 'Buckinghamshire Underground'. Except that it's not underground of course, so it should be the 'Buckinghamshire Overground'. Whatever. Amersham is (along with Chesham) are the two stations that you're most likely to start the Tube Challenge at – which is what inspired this road trip in the first place, so there is yet another a moment of kismet[17] for me, feeling like I am visiting the same-named place where a lot of my Tube jaunts have started.

Amersham, in Buckinghamshire is pleasant enough. There are trees and woods, and old people with proper rambler's sticks marching through on summer Sunday afternoons. There's a quaint old tea shop, and more than one antique shop in Old Amersham Village. It definitely doesn't have

---

[17] Told you I'd use that word.

McDonalds or any high street 'brand names'. The Tube may have made it to Amersham, but the rest of London has not.

Amersham, Tennessee? Will it be a quaint old village, or something more akin to trailer park? As it turns out – neither – but somewhere more of in-between. 'Welcome to Amersham Village!' says a friendly wooden sign as we approach what I soon realise is an entrance slip road to a ring road which is what Amersham is – an average housing estate on a road that goes round in a loop.

In the USA
Amersham, Tennessee
On the Tube map
Amersham (Metropolitan Line)

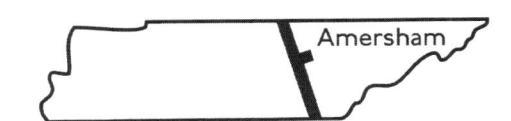

I pull up, wind the windows down, and turn the engine off and we both stare out of our respective windows of the car, looking at ... houses. They aren't run down horrible nasty houses, but they aren't a place where posh rich people live either – it is just an average run-of-the-mill community area, with basketball hoops in the front of people's drives, and large American automatic cars parked in the driveways and on the street.

Oh, and obviously there is train line running right through it – because you've started to realise now that *obviously* there is always going to be a railway line running through it that I have not planned and do not know about, but there it is – fifty yards before the entrance slip road, some 'RAILROAD!' black on yellow warning signs, and tracks that form a level crossing that looks like they have infrequent use – not abandoned, but certainly no regular 07.18 fast Baker Street service on a daily basis.

> **11:57 AM Jun 28th**
> at Amersham, TN. It has a train line!

There is no one about though. I've lost track of what day it is – is it a work day or a weekend? I have to stop and think about it for a moment – oh, it's a Sunday, so is everyone is at church, or still in bed, or perhaps just having a quiet morning? Hmm. We do a slow loop of the circular road, looking closely to see if we make any curtains twitch (not that I can see), snap a photo of the friendly welcome sign, and then realise we are going to get nothing more out of Amersham, and so head towards our next destination instead. I put my iPod on.

> **12:27 PM Jun 28th**
> is it too predictable to play Arrested Developments 'Tennessee' whilst in TN? No, I didn't think so either.

> **12:52 PM Jun 28th**
> if you put the letters of all the states we did yesterday together, it spells the word WVVAKYTN. Today thought it's just NC

We head east – and immediately enter the state of North Carolina and through the Cherokee National Forest, and towards the town of Boone. I must have visibly tensed up because Katie spots it and asks me. 'You okay?' she says looking slightly worried about me. 'Ex-wife territory' I reply perhaps a little too curtly, so immediately repeated myself this time saying it more solemnly. 'Here?' 'Yeah... well... her family really. They have a mountain house and I came up this way a couple of times, and this all looks ... just ... I dunno, a little familiar', and I go very quiet for the next few minutes lost in thoughts of memories past – memories that I am now trying to eradicate, memories that as far as this trip is concerned is part of the reason and the point for doing it. I don't want to be reminded of her or anything of that part of my life – I am having a new exciting time, a brilliant part of my life without her, and here we are driving back through it, but only for a small while.

We push on through and soon get out of vaguely familiar territory, filling up our stomachs at a classic style diner in the town of Wilkesboro certainly helps too, and my mood lightens again as we laugh, joke, and play music far too loud and head east again on Highway 421. After about half an hour the highway turns into an Interstate road, the cars get denser, the roads more polluted, and Greensboro appears on the horizon.

Katie has dozed off whilst I have been driving, but a gentle nudge from me wakes her up and she rises from her slumber to give me directions to guide us to her sister's house where she has arranged for us to stay the night tonight. This feels good – a proper place to stay – saving money in the process – a proper bed, good company and best of all – I am a day ahead of schedule and have lots of great video that I can spend a leisurely day all day tomorrow editing and getting online. I am *really* looking forward to tomorrow.

> **6:36 PM Jun 28th**
> made it to Greensboro, NC for the evening, will spend two nights here, cut video tomorrow.

As I creak open the driver's door on my side of the car in the parking lot outside the row of condos where her sister lives, Katie asks me a question which I didn't know at the time, but would really shape the rest of my whole road trip experience.

'Shall we bring all the stuff in now?' she asks, nodding towards all the expensive video and computer equipment that is in the back of the car. 'Nah', I say nonchalantly, 'I just want to get inside and chill out for a bit, I'll grab it all later before we go to bed', although I do have my phone in my pocket, and my laptop in my bag, I figure it would be OK to leave the rest of the stuff here for a moment and then grab it all later before I go to bed. And with a swing and a *thud!* The car door shuts, I click the remote to lock the car, and we walk over the grass verge to Katie's sister's house with her already standing in the porch waiting to greet us.

I will come back out later to bring the rest of my stuff in, definitely.

Day 14 – Monday 28h June

Robbed

The only reason I know what I am doing is because in the back of my head I have a mantra that says 'You're supposed to be recording all the details of your road trip', and seeing as I have my back-up shaky-cam video camera, and Katie is there to record it for me, that's exactly what I am doing. There is no plan, I don't know what is going to happen next, I aren't out to look sad and pathetic or to beg people for money … I just know I want to get this moment down on video if I can.

Of course, if this had been an expensive over-the-top production I'd have had a dedicated cameraman and crew following me round and they would have captured the actual moment when I first got upset when I discovered the break in. But now it's a few minutes later, and I've had my moment of getting upset and it isn't going to happen again … or at least that's what I think until I get to the end of speaking for a few minutes and talking about what has happened, when at the end of the video, I blub 'It's not fair' and burst into tears. Real tears. Proper 'What the fuck am I going to do now, I can't believe those bastards have broken into the cars and stole all my stuff' kind of tears as I turn into a mess on camera.

To this day … months after that happened as I sit here and type this, I can't actually watch it back, I really can't. I tried to watch it back just now so that I can transcribe the audio here to write into the book, but it's so painful to watch that I have to click pause the moment the awkward part comes on the screen. I don't want to watch it, still. Not even after all this time.

But I speak on video for about a minute. I explain what's happened, Katie records the whole thing the whole time and at the end of it I realise I'm standing without any shoes on in broken shards of glass and it's digging into my feet when I start blubbing and Katie stops filming.

Obviously, if you put all the events into perspective it's easy for someone else to be cynical about it. No one's died, worse things have happened to other people in the world. But yet I don't really like that form of reasoning sometimes, because it's still an event which on a personal level has had a huge effects, and so relatively speaking I know that it is justified in my head to still be angry about it.

Back in the house I upload the video. I write a blog post, and attach the video onto the end.

This was recorded by Katie on my crappy backup second camcorder video camera this morning, and hence the poor quality, apologies. *Note:* There is some strong language.

They took my main kick-arse video editing PC. My Sony HVR-A1U DV video camera. My Nikon D200 stills camera. About $6000 of technology, taken, stolen, gone, kaput. And without it, I don't know if I can carry on.

They also got the SatNav, my iPod *(and with my PC gone, all my music that I've built up over the last five years, and if you know me you'll know how much that hurts)*, and Katie's iPod & work cell phone. Gone gone gone.

I did bring my laptop in, so I've got that, and my cell phone, and my crappy camcorder video camera. Otherwise you wouldn't be reading and seeing this shaky video right now.

Yes I should have brought it all in overnight. I know. Don't tell me that. I know.

The road trip was meant to be the answer to the *'So what now?'* question with regards to my life, and now it's fucked, totally fucked.

I don't think I deserved this. Maybe you think different. Maybe I should just give up and go home. I don't know, I just don't know.

What do I do?

I hit 'Publish' on the blog. It's time stamped at 11.39am. I then send out a tweet that links to the blog post and the video.

> **11:44 AM Jun 29th**
> Please play this. Please, please. And let me know what the fuck I'm supposed to do. http://is.gd/1i9xl

Just after midday, my phone rings. It's from 'Dan Conover', my friend Dan who I have worked with at the local newspaper back in Charleston. Before I'd left on the trip, I'd made a video which I'd published with Dan interviewing me about my trip I am about to go on. Dan is one of life's good guys, a great friend. After today though, I am going to have to think of further accolades for him.

'So you saw the video I guess?' I say answering the phone a little shakily. 'Hey man. We saw it. And we're doing something about it, how are you?' 'Err ... just ... dazed and confused, and wondering what the hell to do next, really' I say. 'Well look. It's gonna be ok. I know that might sound a bit odd, but we've got you covered. You just sit tight there for a bit and stay in touch on your phone ... it's okay for me to give your number out, yes?'

'What do you mean you've got me covered? What's going on?'

'Greensboro is an old stomping ground of mine ... lived there for a few years, I know people and will get people up there on your case. Plus it seems that you made a few friends down here in Charleston and they all want to help you!'. 'Help me? How? They're not just gonna give me six thousand dollars'.

Dan chuckled. A beautiful low southern chuckle that oozed character and wisdom.

'Just hold tight, and wait and see buddy, ok? We're on it', he says.

I don't really know what I am supposed to be holding tight to, or what they are on exactly, but Dan ends the call and Katie looks at me quizzically. 'That was Dan', I say, not sure how to explain what he is doing because I really don't know what he is up to. 'I think he's doing something, but I'm not sure what.'

Over the next hour, I have a tea (because every good Englishman drinks tea in a crisis, and also because they haven't stolen my teabags from the car) and I send off a few emails – including one to my mum telling her that I am OK and she should not get her knickers in a twist or panic about it.

We sweep up the broken glass, we tidy up the back of the car and I confirm that everything that I think is missing is indeed gone. I use my crappy backup video cam to take some more footage, and then sit on the grass outside in the ironically beautiful sunny day that North Carolina is serving up, and get a little more upset.

And then I remember that about an hour ago, I'd posted on my blog and I go back inside to see if anyone has replied yet, or if anyone has emailed.

Now, people talk about jaws-hitting the floor, but in reality they're just 'jaw dropping' moments when they happen. I am standing over my laptop, working out whether to check my email or my blog first, but I can already see that my blog is getting quite a few hits. I look at the comments ... what the ... fuck? It is up to 27 comments already, in less than an hour.

I flicked to the email window. Again – extreme jaw movement happening in the area at the bottom of my face. The emails are – almost literally – flooding in.

'We got you covered' Dan had said.

He'd meant it.

It isn't just Dan. As far as I can tell, another mutual friend of ours – Chrys – has spotted my tweet first and alerted Dan too it. My friend Kathleen has also seen my blog post and immediately sends an email round to people saying that they need to help me and start something up.

And then there is Ken – whom I have most recently worked with in Charleston on a new website and produced video for and *he* is all over it too.

To this day I'm still not quite clear on who actually did what and when. When I later ask Dan about it in person he just smiles sagely and says 'I'm not too sure who did what either buddy, but hey - the important thing is that we did it'.

And this is what they did.

Firstly, they set up a whole new twitter account @helpgeoff to tweet about what is going on. They use a link to and setup a funding page where people can donate me money.

Ken writes a blog piece about it on his news website. He embedded my bad video, and again links to the place where people can donate money.

> Many of you know our quirky British videographer, Geoff Marshall, and many of you know that he's gone on sabbatical to experience the grand 48 states over three months.
>
> Well, bad news: Geoff had $6,000 worth of equipment stolen from his car overnight, which not only sucks but it also threatens an early end to his documentary – Underground USA
>
> Geoff's a good guy and I think this a great project, so I'm hoping that folks can come together to put the show, quite literally, back on the road. I don't think that we can generate $6,000, but if we could get even a fraction of that together I suspect it would be

enough to get him the minimum amount of equipment he needs -- if nothing else the moral boost I'm sure would be substantial.

I've set up this campaign in cooperation with others in the Charleston community that want to see this wrong righted. So, go on and donate below.

For my part, I'll drop $50 now, and $50 for every $1,000 donated by others. I'll also cover all of PayPal's modest fees.

Then, I discovered that Dan and Chrys have also setup a whole new blog called 'HelpGeoff' where again they wrote a little about what has happened and urged people to give a few dollars.

Let's help Geoff get back on the road

For those of you who don't know Geoff Marshall, he's a Londoner who moved to Charleston, SC, in 2006 and recently set out to shoot a documentary film about a 48-state road trip across the U.S. And on the morning of June 29th he awoke in Greensboro, NC, to find that roughly $6,000 of computer, video and photography equipment had been stolen from his car while he slept.

Geoff set out to tell a story about America, and we'd sure hate to see that story end like this.

So here's what's happening: The online community in Charleston, SC, is raising money to help Geoff get back on the road. And bloggers in Greensboro have been checking in to see what they can do to help. Meanwhile, Ken Hawkins, Geoff's former boss at TheDigitel.com, has offered to cover the PayPal fees for anyone who pitches in.

Sure, eventually we'll give Geoff plenty of grief about leaving his gear in the car. But right now, we just want to make sure that this story has a happy ending.

So Ken has instantly given $50 and offered to donate another $50 for every $1000 made in total by others. A friend Paul who I really don't think I know that well has given $200. People that I have never heard of before – like, I really don't know who they are when I see their names come up on the donations list – start to give me money. Five, ten, and twenty dollars.

> **3:46 PM Jun 29th**
> i am overwhelmed with the genuine kindness of many people. thank you. my head is spinning. a cognitive plan of action is forming.

My emails go crazy – actually crazy, as there are too many to read. People comment on the blog, and by the end of the day there are over 100 comments from it, absolutely everyone saying the nicest things and donating money.

Dan gets in touch with the local Mayor of Greensboro, who sends me a nice email. A newspaper reporter comes round and writes up a piece on me, I feature in the paper the next day. It actually gets to the point where it becomes too much to try and keep up with what is going on. Someone emails me to tell me that the hashtag **#helpgeoff** is being used, and at one point during the afternoon it appears in the top 10 of trending hashtags in Charleston. Someone else emails me to say that they have gone into their local grocery store and overhear some people that they don't know talking about me and the stolen stuff. 'Oh do you know Geoff too?' they ask, get chatting, and they all donated. This is *madness*. How the fuck can I be a topic of local conversation and a trending topic?

> **4:54 PM Jun 29th**
> a reporter from the local paper just came by. Will run story tomorrow.

From jaw-dropping I have gone to 'head-spinning' and I actually feel a little dizzy trying to take it all in, so much so it makes me get all emotional and upset again. Even more so when I click onto the 'donate' page and can see that it is already up to $2000. That. Is. Incredible. I don't know what to say, or do now, to anyone.

By the end of the day, just over four thousand dollars has been donated. This boggles my mind. (By the end of the next day it totalled up at just under five thousand, that's an extreme amount of mind boggling).

Ken sends me an initial list of the people that have donated. Some I know, but most names I have no idea who they are – names and eMail addresses that I don't recognise. 'Who are these people that I don't know?' I email to Ken. 'Hey I don't know, I guess they just like you!' he emails back, and I start to well up.

Hidden away in the archives of the shaky-cam video that will never ever see the light of day (and again, I can only watch the first few seconds of it back myself before getting too embarrassed and stopping it), is an additional minutes worth of video that I make Katie shoot of me, sitting at my laptop talking about the people that are donating their dollars. I end up blubbing like a girl for a second time that day.

> **4:55 PM Jun 29th**
> i'm aware of the support round online, not had a chance to take it all in yet though, but i humbly thank you #helpgeoff

At six o'clock, I've had enough. I need a drink, I announce it to everyone – 'I need a drink', and we duly head out to purchase alcohol.

> **6:51 PM Jun 29th**
> i am now going to do the requisite thing in this situation. I have bought Vodka and i am going to get drunk.

Katie drives us all to the local liquor store. I buy vodka. I am going to drink it all I decide. We get back, and I make a start.

> **9:54 PM Jun 29th**
> more humbling. Made the Greensboro local press: http://is.gd/1iBA9 Oh, i am very drunk by the way.

Not too drunk to tweet though, and I also *kind of* remember talking to my friend Andy on the phone back in Charleston and wishing him a happy birthday (it's his birthday and I am missing his birthday party), and that I loved him very very much, and by ten o'clock I send my final twitter of the day.

> **9:58 PM Jun 29th**
> i lve you al; very veru mch. yes. yes i do. mroe vdka please. i thakn you.

That is the actual tweet that I write with my drunken fingers on my phone... I'm not making that up or making it look worse than it is – that's how it came out. And then I must have read it back, because I am aware of how ridiculously drunk that must make me look and hey – my mum's out there following after all – and so I spend the best part of the next ten minutes *carefully* crafting something more respectable.

> **10:11 PM Jun 29th**
> head spinning. too many people to thank. drink more geoff. tomorrow=better & will start again. took me 5 minutes to spellcheck this.

And sometime shortly after that, I shower (because somehow I drunkenly remembered that I haven't washed or cleaned myself all day) and fall into the sort of sleep that a drunk person does ... i.e. a deep and sound one.

~ ~ ~

The first thing that you do when you wake up after the day that your car has been broken into is worry about the fact that the people that did come back for seconds, and so I go outside again and check on the car – and the window is broken.

That's OK though, because it is still just broken from the day before, because by the time we'd got to auto-glass shop they had been closing up for the day and so I've had to postpone it until today instead. Which meant leaving the car out overnight with the window still smashed out.

> **6:24 AM Jun 30th**
> awake. early. cold. *shiver* car still there overnight tho. that's a plus. running on not-a-lot-of-sleep today

Then I crawl back to bed and try to get a couple more hours in before starting the day proper.

The day is a little surreal. Katie has to fly back for an appointment in Charleston that day and she says she feels like she is abandoning me. Her sister still feels bad because the break in has happened whilst we've stayed at her place. And I am being left all alone again to get it fixed and muse over the fact that everything is gone – really gone – and that I've got to make massive contingency plans to get over it.

Greensboro is hot too – up into the nineties and normally that's my rule for running the Air Conditioning in the car. Up until 89F you have to suffer in sweaty silence, but as soon as the in-car-temp gauge registers 90F, then the A/C can come on.

Unfortunately, to maximise the efficiency of the AC ... you have to have all the windows wound up in the car, and the car is kinda missing a window right now.

> **10:33 AM Jun 30th**
> dropped Katie off at PTI airport. Now to find the autoglass place .... without a SatNav to aid me, d'oh...

I remember looking at landmarks along the Interstate to make a note of where to turn off on the way BACK to find myself in Greensboro again.

I stop off at the first gas station that I see, and wait a whole five minutes for a car at a particular pump to finish, because I want to go in that spot, because it is the best spot for me to be able to see the car from inside ... and I want to go inside in a moment to buy a physical paper map of Greensboro that I can navigate for the rest of the day, and I'd have to leave the car effectively 'open' with the non-window as I go inside to buy it.

> **10:52 AM Jun 30th**
> doing some old-school navigating. Stopping at a gas station, buying a map, and asking for directions!

I get lost, but eventually find the glass shop ... to discover that I should have called yesterday and they can't see me until the afternoon.

> **11:23 AM Jun 30th**
> can't get window fixed until 2pm. What to do in Greensboro for 3 hours when i can't leave the car out of sight?

Well, it is time to eat again, obviously. Comfort food.

> **11:27 AM Jun 30th**
> that's right .... You go to a Sonic to cheer yourself up with bad fast food. I'm a Sonic virgin, be easy on me No.4 combo

> **11:28 AM Jun 30th**
> this is fun, they bring the food out to you, cool. I should be videoing this! Oh ...

Sonic's are just another fast-food burger chain (Burger, Drink, Fries, the diet of all obese Americans) but the fun part is that you pull into a parking space which has a console and menu in every space, you speak your order in when they ask, and then ... they bring your order out to you on roller-skates! Stay where you are in your car, have someone bring your food to you, and then be on your way again – genius. I've seen them all over the place in Charleston, seen the commercial on TV and everything, but have never actually been to one before. Now it is time to go to one.

> **11:29 AM Jun 30th**
> she brought the food out on a red plastic tray to hook to my window .... then saw the broken window and said 'oh ...'

The Sonic burger is not bad, but I decide that the vanilla milkshake that I am drinking is *the best* vanilla milkshake that I have ever consumed from any fast food place. So I make a very big mental note there and then to come back to a Sonic again at some point on my travels and have another milkshake at the very least.

As I drink I consult my map, I realise one very annoying side effect from the robbery – I will have to miss another one of my stops.

In the USA
Finchley, Virginia
On the Tube map
Finchley Central
(Northern Line)

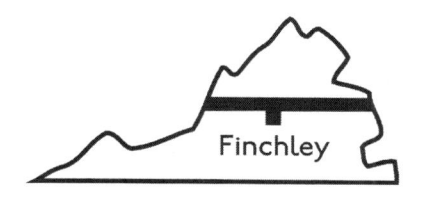

Having all my stuff stolen means that I have already re-ordered (using the money from **#helpgeoff**) some equipment, but I would need time to set that all up and restore everything. I'd planned to be back home in Charleston for the July 4th weekend – a holiday in the USA – just to have a few days off, but now I calculate that if I want to do this properly, I will definitely need time now to setup my computer all over again (that I have yet to buy), get software loaded, configure software and my new camera that I hope to pick up.

In other words, I need time to setup everything from almost scratch again, and I need to go to shops when they're open (and not closed for the public holiday) which is going to eat into my time – meaning that I think I am going to just have to head straight back to Charleston. I don't think I will have time to do Hampstead either.

First Royal Oak, now Finchley and possibly Hampstead too. Fuck.

I'm feeling pissed off about this, I'm slurping up the last bits of the vanilla-ness when my phone rings with a number that I don't recognise. I answer it. 'Heeey!' says a friendly voice – a voice that I do recognise.

It's my old colleague Melissa – whom I have worked with until last year down at the Post & Courier newspaper in Charleston. She is also the girl that had called me up the day that my battery had died a couple of week ago up in Harrow, Pennsylvania. Maybe she only calls when I have car trouble? Either that or she's seen me in the paper.

'Oh Geoff!' she says in beautifully friendly way, 'Are you okay? I saw you in the paper'. 'Why? Are you in Greensboro now?' – and it turns out that she is … well, about an hour away, where she's moved to be with her fiancée and has come into Greensboro that day to sort out stuff for her wedding in a few months' time, and she'd picked up a copy of the local paper and sees me in it!

> **2:14 PM Jun 30th**
> meeting up with my friend Melissa – used to work with her at the P&C! She's in Greensboro too today, small world.

So an hour later when I'm down at the glass shop getting the window repaired, Melissa meets up with me and gives me a big friendly hug which cheers me right up.

She's quite chatty too - to me and to the people in the glass shop, where she proceeds to get me a discount! There is a copy of the paper in the shop and she shows it to the woman behind the counter, and before I know it she's made a deduction, which then prompts me to go and get my t-shirt which I'm getting people to sign, and she signs that too.

> **3:10 PM Jun 30th**
> glass shop just gave me a 10% discount when i showed them my article in the paper!

> **3:11 PM Jun 30th**
> and then i got them to sign my t-shirt, too! "Sorry you were robbed", Heh.

> **5:37 PM Jun 30th**
> window: fixed, caffeine: hit, Raleigh: next destination, navigating using an old-style-map. Remember those? maps: foldy paper things

I drive to Raleigh – stopping at Best Buy on the way to pick up a new SatNav system, and get one that isn't as expensive or as nice as the one I previously owned to come away with on the trip.

But as I open up the packaging – the smell hits me. The smell of a factory fresh product – of consumer goods, on something that I've just spent a couple of hundreds of dollars on – possibly because of the money that people have donated to me, and as that smell hits the senses deep inside my nostrils it triggers a thought that I don't see coming.

My mind is taken back to Detroit just a few days ago. To that family out on the streets selling bottles of water trying to survive. With their children that they may have taken out of school to help them do that. A family who would most likely never in their life be in the privileged position of owning a SatNav for their car – they probably don't even own a car.

And that thought goes further. What does that say about our society that we're all happy to give around $4000 of money to me – someone who you can argue doesn't really need it, but a family struggling to make ends meet in poorest Detroit does.

What if – the day after Detroit – I'd have put a post on my blog saying 'My trip partly revolves around expensive consumer electronic goods I don't really *need* to survive – the basics I really need are food to eat and a shelter above my head. Therefore, can everyone I know please donate money to me, and when I get $4000 I'll drive straight back to that family in Detroit that I saw and just give the money to them – as they obviously need it more than I do.'

If I'd have said that – almost no one would have given money, right? They only donated because they know *me* and they see *me* upset, and they can relate it to it, and they want to do something to help.

How far do you take that thought? To a perfect socialist state? Where no one is allowed any luxuries in the world at all, and we must all as a world continually ensure that everyone is fed, clothed, and educated in a home, and anything beyond that is just a bonus?

And then I appreciate what a privileged position I am in. Yes – I've had my stuff stolen. Yes it is upsetting, but I've recovered quite quickly out of it. And not everyone can recover. Not everyone is in a position where other people will rally round for them. And yet I would say that ALL of the people that donated me money are good people at heart, so why did they give the money to me – someone privileged, instead of someone who really needs it?

My head hurts thinking about it. I want to be with a group of people that I can have this conversation with and talk about it, and work out why it is that the world works this way. I want to justify the fact that people have given me thousands of dollars and that's OK. I really want to get to Charleston for the 4th July weekend where I can have that conversation.

Tonight though I am heading to see *Jamie*. Jamie is the sister of *Natalie* who will be one of my later companions on the trip, and she has kindly offered to put me up for the night. We go for dinner, over which I tell her the story of the robbery, how I want to head straight for Charleston and skip Finchley and Hampstead, at which point Jamie tells me that her boyfriend *Nick* lives near Hampstead, and so one quick call later and she's arranged for me to stay at his tomorrow night, and after that I can head back properly to my American home to recuperate for the weekend.

Day 16 – Wednesday 1st July

Limbo Land

*'When you're at the end of the road,
and you've lost all sense of control
and your thoughts have taken their toll,
when your mind breaks the spirit of your soul'*

The next morning as I sit at Jamie's breakfast table, watching ants crawl across her work surface wondering if I should tell her or not that she has a minor infestation, I pump Green Day out of my tinny laptop speakers.

> **10:19 AM Jul 1st**
> totally loving the new green day, '21 guns'. i'd download it but i don't have iTunes or an iPod anymore (!)

Unsure of what to steal out of Jamie's cupboards to eat, I recall what'd kept me going when up in the north east and look online for the address of a Dunkin' Donuts. There's one nearby, except when I drive down there I find that it has become a Bruggers Bagels instead, but one breakfast muffin and coffee later and I am a happy chappy, back in the kitchen, online, and still getting everything back into perspective. The music is definitely helping.

> **10:43 AM Jul 1st**
> playing '21 Guns' off of YouTube on continuous repeat. because it's one of those days when you need to a hear a song on continuous repeat.

There has been a freaky occurrence when I've popped out to get my morning grub ... I'd parked the car last night much further down the drive at Jamie's house than I'd realised, and there is a moment when my heart skips a bit when I can't immediately see the car in my line of sight when I emerge from the house, and panic that it has been stolen again. It hasn't of course – it's fine – but it does remind me again and reinforce the fact that I am in a heightened state of paranoia about such a thing happening again.

I go online shopping this morning. I spend the money that everyone has amazingly donated and get a new stills camera on order which will be delivered over the weekend when I pass back through Charleston – that is fine, but the video camera is trickier – it will take about a week for it to be delivered because it isn't in stock. In fact, I'm a bit worried that it might not *get* in stock in time at all and then be delivered to me, but I can't worry about that now and place the order anyway. Thinking ahead of where I will be on the trip, I allow a week and get in touch with my friend *Tami* – whom I know I would be seeing in New Orleans and give them her address for everything to be delivered to.

I drink more coffee, play the Green Day song again several more times, and write a blog post to bring things up to date.

> **12:47 PM Jul 1st**
> pun of the day: Thanks to everyone for Raleigh-ing round.http://is.gd/1kmQ9

I leave just after 1pm … far much later than my plan, but I am still catching up on emails (and there are a *lot* of emails) and text messages post-break in, and I'm still processing a lot of it in my head. My next stop tonight has already been planned ahead too – Jamie's boyfriend, down in Wilmington in North Carolina … and the same name stop for the state is the small town of Hampstead, so that's where I head to next.

> **3:49 PM Jul 1st**
> stopped for late lunch, eating. But all i do is look out the window every 30 seconds to check on the car. Sigh.

It's a boring arduous hot drive south down the I-40, and nothing of interest happens. It doesn't help that my mind is in a funk. Really what I want to do is go straight back to Charleston, 'home' for the weekend and recover and recuperate. I want to see Katie and say 'Hi' to some of the people that have given money to **#helpgeoff**. Oh, and I want to go shopping and buy a new computer too! I'm lost in thoughts, many thoughts, and force myself to go on and drive and just continue to recover.

> **5:08 PM Jul 1st**
> I-40 south. Sign on giant billboard: 'Jesus has your number, repent NOW!'

Well how the hell does he know my number? I don't remember calling him. It would be handier if he has the number of the people that stole my stuff. And anyway, why don't I have *his* number? Does he have his caller ID barred or something? So selfish.

> **7:12 PM Jul 1st**
> i'm in Hampstead NC. Another crossroads town with a CVS & Food Lion

In the USA
Hampstead, North Carolina

On the Tube map
Hampstead (Northern Line)

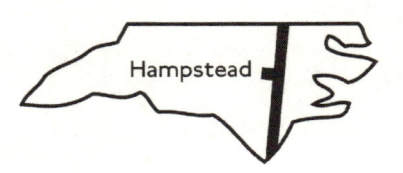

I realise on the drive down towards the coast that day that I do still in fact have my small back-up video camera on me which is able to take some still photos and low quality video. Which is why that evening in Hampstead, you would have found me in the car park of a CVS, balancing the video camera on top of the car and me talking into it.

'This is Hampstead ... it's basically a crossroads with a CVS and a Food Lion at it – like most other towns in America! The sky is pretty though!'

I drive a few blocks up and down and all the usual culprits are there – the McDonald's, the Food Lion, The Lowe's, although I do realise that Hampstead *does not* have a rail road anywhere in town that I can find! That seems like a first (although it isn't), and so I don't add Hampstead to my additional 'Railway Towns' list that I'm making.

For a Seafood Capital of the state (as the 'Welcome To...' sign proclaims), I only see one restaurant that seems to sell seafood, and I would have gone in, except that a nice piece of tuna is the most fish that I handle, and everything else seems a little slimy and disgusting to me, and I'm not tempted at all.

It is an average town. With average looking people going about their business, and knowing that I really just want to get back to Charleston to see friendly faces doesn't want to make me stay here and engage in anyone or anything. I think about the break in again. I then try not to. But it is still dwelling on my mind and is clearly affecting my motivation to do anything.

So on the way back out of town, I do a convoluted about-turn on the highway going out of town just so that I can snap a the 'Welcome to...' sign which I haven't done on the way in, so that I can feel like I've done *something* here, and whilst still in the parking lot use my laptop to confirm via Google that there really isn't anything outstanding about Hampstead worth noting.

I get grumpy again – my stuff has been nicked, I don't have my proper video camera or camera with me, and I am companion-less again. I want to head for Charleston for the weekend, get my shit back, and recuperate.

I head for Wilmington.

> **7:13 PM Jul 1st**
> staying in Wilmington tonight tho which is a much nicer/cuter town on the coast.

Nick greets me into his flat, once I have safely parked the car and I explain that I need to bring *all* my stuff in and not leave it in the car. Two nights at Katie's sister in Greensboro, one night at Jamie's and another now at Nick's and I realise I have actually saved myself quite a lot of money by not camping or staying in a motel anywhere.

> **9:01 PM Jul 1st**
> in Wilmington NC, with my new friend Nick. He's letting me crash on his sofa bad. I have also just fixed his WiFi router!

Nick takes me out that night, and we do what all men should do once in a while: Hang out, drink beer, eat pizza and shoot pool. Obviously back at his that night whilst I update my online presence I play the Green Day track so many times in a row that Nick coyly observes 'So ... you really like that song, huh?' before he lets me crash out on his couch that turns into a bed.

~ ~ ~

The next morning, we exchange farewell pleasantries, Nick heads off to work, and Geoff heads off down the coastline for a drive that I've done a few times before actually – through Myrtle Beach and to my American home of Charleston.

> **11:22 AM Jul 2nd**
> haven't shaved since Sunday & have 4 days of growth on my face. that's about 4 hours for a normal person. now to take a photo of it, oh .... no camera. stolen. oops.

> **2:02 PM Jul 2nd**
> sat in a waffle house in myrtle beach. I am the ONLY customer. That's coz it's 2pm and not 2am – I'm 12 hrs off.

And at just after 5pm, almost three weeks after I have left it, I roll over the huge Cooper River Bridge that is an icon for the town, and head home for the weekend.

I spend four nights back in Charleston – my American home – including the 4th July weekend, and do all the important things that I need to do. I catch up with Katie and we lament again over the finer points of the break in. We put a call in to Greensboro police to chase them up, but they never call back.

I also chase the order for the video camera and have no joy, but *do* go and pick up from the local UPS depot the new stills camera that I've ordered – so I can now take photos again.

I drop into Best Buy and in a hurry I purchase a suitable PC that I can edit video on again. I install all the software on it and make it video-editing ready. I have fun re-installing iTunes too, but then also have a galling ghastly moment when I realise that all the metadata that has gone into my music collection that I have pain stakingly built up over the past few years is not backed up and has been eradicated.

I joke about camping in the back garden of the house, but don't ... I stay in the house as normal. I do make some tea with my camp stove on the counter of the kitchen though just for the hell of it.

I go down to the local Apple store and buy a new iPod – a small mini one though and not a full sized one. I feel like I can't splash out on a full price one. But I've lost all my music though and scraped around in vain looking on discs at home for old backups which I don't really have – so my music on my iPod isn't really there save for a few tracks.

Basically, I spend the time I need recuperating, getting all of my shit together, washing my clothes, tidying up the car some and rationalising the amount of gear I am taking on for another 7 weeks, and pick more pieces of broken window glass out of the car.

On the Sunday night – we all go for beers down our favourite local bar, and that makes me feel a whole lot better.

Dan who has orchestrated the **#helpgeoff** campaign and his wife Janet are there, and they make me feel good about the whole thing. Some people have that knack. There's not many people I have met in this world that I can say what I'm about to say, but Dan is just one of them

The first time we'd met, I knew within about five seconds that we thought alike and we would be friends – that's not to say that we haven't disagreed about stuff over time[18], but he is cool, laid back, creative, always thinking of fun ideas, and it's effortless to be friends with him. Some people I really hate because they make a hard time of you being their friend, and almost make you feel like you're doing something wrong. With Dan, there is none of that. And I love it. And we have a fine evening of drinking, reciting and sharing anecdotes-a-plenty, and by the time Katie

---

[18] So, my favourite kinds of friends are those that you can argue with but still remain friends with. I consider it a 'workout' for the brain. It's marvellous if you have someone that you get along with but occasionally you discuss something where you have different points of view, but still remain friends at the end of it.

delivers me home a little tipsy, I realise I am already starting to get over having all my gear stolen.

And by Monday morning, with all my stuff packed up in the back of the car, I am ready to go again.

Day 21 – Monday 6th July

On the road again

*'On the road again – Like a band of gypsies we go down the highway
We're the best of friends, Insisting that the world keep turning our way'*

Unfortunately, the beers from the night before are taking their toll, and I don't have a particularly early start getting my arse in gear on the Monday morning. It is in fact, the afternoon.

> **12:21 PM Jul 6th**
> on the road again. Isn't that a Willie nelson song? I-26 north/west.
>
> **12:22 PM Jul 6th**
> and it's raining, it was raining last time i left Charleston.

I've sent a few tweets out over the weekend that I've been back, but not loads. Now that I'm back on the road again, I feel the need to update almost every time I take a breath.

> **12:23 PM Jul 6th**
> yes, you can tell i'm back on the road 'cause the tweets are comin' at ya thick and fast!
>
> **12:28 PM Jul 6th**
> and i'm about to pick up my new companion for the week. Cute girl, or ugly boy? Hmmmm.....

I'm sure J.J. won't take offence – or least not much offence – if I say he isn't a cute girl. But I wouldn't go so far as to say that he is an ugly boy either, after all with a haircut and a shower, he scrubs up quite well. I pick him up from Summerville where he lives – a town just outside Charleston, and we head north.

We stop at a gas station first though, which we use because we see that it has a vacuum cleaner that you can use on your car, and there are *still* bits of broken glass down in the deep crevices of the car post-break in that haven't been cleared up.

I also call Barclaycard again who decline my transaction and explain patiently for a second time that I am on a three month road trip across America, and yes I would be getting petrol from different states all over the country for the next few weeks. 'I'll make a note on your account sir', says the friendly voice at the other end.

It feels nice to have a companion again, and J.J. is up for not driving on the Interstate either. 'The smaller the road the better' he suggests in a dry/wry tone that I already know and love, but would get to know even better over the next week with him.

One small flat windy road in particular we find feels *very* off-road, and is covered in almost-dried red mud that kicks up dust behind us as we skid down it, and also sticks to the car. As I look in one of the wing mirrors I can see the whole of the bottom side of one car caked in red mud, and the tyres changing colour to match as more and more of the not-quite-dry dust sticking to the car – it looks kinda cool.

We find an old abandoned 'Gull' gas station, and a multitude of rusty abandoned vehicles and I merrily snap away, like a pig in shit. This is going to go nicely into my 'Abandoned Autos' gallery that I am slowly building online.

On the outskirts of Orangeburg, we see a real gas station – and the cheapest one I've seen so far on the trip, and soon after, we are arriving at out next 'stop' … Woodford.

In the USA
Woodford, South Carolina
On the Tube map
Woodford (Central Line)

Woodford on the Central Line is a cute little station in North East London where you wait for ages for one of three trains per hour to go around the Hainault loop.

Woodford in South Carolina is a large open town with a small population of 200 people, about 80 houses. Oh, and with a train line running through it.

> **2:52 PM Jul 6th**
> underground USA has arrived at … Woodford, SC. The next stop on the route. There is a water melon seller here, and a train line, obviously.

I think Woodford is the first time – and place – that I realise that actually … hang on … a *lot* of the places that I have visited have a train or some sort of train line running through, don't they? But this hasn't been on purpose, I really haven't planned it that way, and yet here they are – train lines popping up in same-name-places as the Tube map.

'There doesn't look like there's much here' says J.J. dryly, as I pull in and apply the brake with a satisfying CLUNK. 'Nope', I reply 'But there appears to be a market stall over there which looks colourful, and I want to go and take a photo of something'.

We wander round what there is of the town for ten minutes, across the tracks, back again, snap a picture of the Woodford Stores which is closed, and come back to what is the only open thing ... the market stall. Actually, predominately they seem to be selling water melons more than anything else, and a small teenage child eyes us suspiciously as we approach.

'OK if I take a photo?' I ask politely, and he looks at me as if I've spoken in a language other than English. 'Photo', I say again trying to be more monosyllabic. 'OK to take, yes?' And this time he gets it, nods and mumbles 'yes', but then seem to get very shy and runs out the back towards a trailer where some more people are.

I take one interesting colourful snap of the water melons and wander back to the car. It is hot. Woodford suddenly seems very dry, and I want to have a drink.

'I need a drink'. 'Me too.' 'Where are we?' and at this point J.J. does something quite defining ... he passes me a map book.

Remember, up until this point I've been using my SatNav system which I thought would see me right – but I'd learned on my second night when I couldn't find the KOA in Putney that that might not be the case, and I thought perhaps I should buy a proper atlas. I haven't done so – but here is J.J. nicely presenting me with one which would prove to be invaluable for the rest of the trip for me to actually have a sense of where I am. 'Thanks J.J.' I say sincerely and graciously. 'You're welcome', he replies.

At this point, I think I'm then aware of someone approaching me to my right. I turn to see a man till a distance off but close enough for me to see that he looks a little angry and is pointing his finger at me and talking quite loudly.

'Was it you taking photos?' 'What for!' 'What are you doing with them?' he says quite nastily at me. I start the engine. 'I think we should go' I say to J.J. and wind up the window and start to drive off before the guy can get any closer. It suddenly doesn't feel like a very friendly place, and I don't want to hang around.

> **3:17 PM Jul 6th**
> water melon seller got all jumpy wanted to know why i was taking photos. Bet they have no business license!
>
> **3:34 PM Jul 6th**
> so J.J.'s description of Woodford: 'typical podunk sc town with American flags on every telephone pole'

SAME NAME TOWNS TALLY

Perfect Small Town America
Preston

Something there and enjoyable
Plaistow, Gloucester, Kew Gardens, Harrow, South Kensington, Greenford, Liverpool

Something there but not that exciting to be honest
Putney, Amersham, Hampstead, Woodford

Nothing there but somehow being in the middle of nowhere made it OK
Epping, Acton

Nothing there, and not that exciting either. Oops.
Warwick, Wapping, Camden

I let J.J. drive – I figure this will be a good time for me to look at the map more closely, tweet some and choose some music on the iPod.

> **3:36 PM Jul 6th**
> feels good to be back on the road, actually. Nice to have the momentum back. I'm excited again

Unfortunately, J.J. has other ideas about the music – and as he politely, firmly and annoyingly absolutely correctly points out – whoever is driving, gets to call what music comes on, and with a little too much glee as far as I can tell, fires up something country-sounding-ish to me. At least I can complain to the online world.

> **3:38 PM Jul 6th**
> J.J. is playing some TERRIBLE music on his iPod! Can i get me a country-music rescue package? Help!

> **3:47 PM Jul 6th**
> just passed sign for place called 'North'. Always wondered where north was on a map? We just found it!

Although I've lived in South Carolina now for over two years, the trouble with the state (and indeed the whole country) is that as previously mentioned... its size. South Carolina itself just seems too big to get a handle on, as I'm comparing it to the wrong size in my head. Back home, if you live in a county you can easily say 'Oh I live in Hertfordshire, or Kent', and have a reasonable feel as to how the rest of the county might shape up. Here I am making the mistake of comparing a state to a county, rather than, err ... a county – and South Carolina is just too big to that. Thus, as we drive through winding back roads slowing making our way west, it feels like a whole other world.

> **3:53 PM Jul 6th**
> south carolina you have not failed me. Abandoned gas stations, rusty farm vehicles and dry dusty dirt roads. Lovin' it

But eventually, we cross into Georgia, hit the outskirts of suburban Atlanta, and get onto the Interstate for the last hour of the drive to tonight's stop.

> **5:05 PM Jul 6th**
> we're 100 miles out of Atlanta. I'm happy to report nothing has been stolen today ... so far.

See? I have a sense of humour.

As does J.J. who –for the whole of the week he is with me – would chat about (especially when *he* is driving) the most diverse of topics and at least one gem per day is too good not to tweet when he comes out with them.

> **5:40 PM Jul 6th**
> quote of the day from J.J. – Hitler had some good ideas, it's just that he was a f'ing nutjob with a load of bad ones too'

> **5:41 PM Jul 6th**
> .... we were discussing which country built motorways/Interstates first. Germany did, Hitler's idea. Just in case you thought we were secret Nazi's or something

At almost exactly six o'clock, we get to Atlanta.

> **6:01 PM Jul 6th**
> welcome to Atlanta, GA. With a giant 60 foot high purple and yellow sign – 'Church of the Now'. Uh hu.

> **6:05 PM Jul 6th**
> Atlanta: 'Birthplace of Chick-fil-a', apparently. Mmmm, chicken.

I fire some text messages ahead to Russell. Who's Russell? Oh, sorry – he's the nice chap that we will be staying with tonight which means I save money by not camping or moteling. Russell is a friend of Mike & Melissa (whom I'd stayed with in Boston), and I had met him a couple of years in a row in Charleston when they held their annual 10km 'Bridge Run' event which he'd attended. And when he'd heard about my trip and asked if I am coming through Atlanta, he immediately suggests that I drop by his and stay the night.

Russell texts me back to tell me that he is going to be working late – which means we have some time to kill. With an extra hour to spare, I crack open the laptop – get online and look us up some nearby Geocaches in a local park and we search for them successfully.

> **7:16 PM Jul 6th**
> left the car unattended for whole 15 minutes & not broken into – progress! [Geocaching in suburban Atlanta.]

Whilst that wastes half an hour, we decide we can spend more time eating. Time to go and hit one of those Redneck Starbucks that J.J. keeps fondly telling me about : Waffle House.

> **7:46 PM Jul 6th**
> at a waffle house. Server has topped up our drinks 4 times now, as we're the only customers and she's nothing else to do

> **7:55 PM Jul 6th**
> sign in toilets: 1. Wet hands 2. Use soap 3. Rub 4. Rinse 5. Dry 6. Breath in/out 7. Tweet this sign, etc...

Our own stomachs successfully filled, it is time to fill up the car with something that it needs too : Engine coolant. On the drive to Atlanta this afternoon, a brand new light on the console that I've never seen before flashes up, and after a moment of panic, J.J. calmly informs me that I just need some coolant which is cheap to buy, and easy to put in. Phew.

Well – it's easy for him to put in so I let him get on with it. In fact, I am so happy that he's covering the broken down car angle that I decide that this will be a moment worthy of getting on video. I haven't really done much videoing with the backup camera since the break-in because the quality is not very good, but having a car maintenance moment somehow prompts me into wanting to put something up online. So as J.J. tops up the car, I crack out my mini video camera.

> **8:16 PM Jul 6th**
> reasons for inviting J.J. #1 : He knows stuff about cars; engine coolant successfully topped up!

At Russell's we pull into the drive, nicely blocking his 2003 Nissan Maxima GLE that is in the drive – I must remember to move my car later I think to myself. More importantly though, is that as this is my first night back on the road away from home with equipment on board again and that means one thing – bringing it all inside Russell's house. Me, he and J.J. therefore troop with a precision of gear and equipment, placing it all down inside his door.

> **8:51 PM Jul 6th**
> made it to place i'm staying for the night. Guess what i'm doing? That's right ... TAKING ALL THE STUFF IN FROM THE CAR

And we settle down with a nice cool beer.

I get Russell to sign my t-shirt – for the state of Georgia. 'You only want me for my bandwidth', he writes with the date, which is partially true, I *do* have a progress map to update after all

> **9:40 PM Jul 6th**
> progress map update for Monday, July 6th. Am in Atlanta, Georgia: http://is.gd/1pnne

And a blog post to write about our day in Woodford, only for me to be halfway through and for J.J. to shout 'Finished!' across the room at me, like a child would when doing a test paper or exam ... and J.J. has beaten me to it on *his* blog of the day's events, dammit.

> **9:56 PM Jul 6th**
> J.J. (my companion this week) has blogged about today already .... beat me to it! http://is.gd/1povj

We chat some more, quite a while actually before it just gets to that point where we are all knackered and we turn in.

'I've got to be up at 05.30 anyway!' says Russell a little too cheerfully. What, do people *like* getting up at that time, or something? 'Yeah, well try not to wake us ...' I say cheerfully back, thinking that I will set my alarm for a much more reasonable 08.30.

'Goodnight then', 'Night!', 'Thanks for letting us stay', 'No worries', 'See you at the bridge run next year then!'. 'Ok!', and we all head to our respective rooms for the night.

~ ~ ~

My mind dreams that night. It dreams of the previous three weeks that I've been on the road leading up until the few days that I'd spent back in Charleston for the July 4th weekend.

It dreams of curling curvy roads though glorious West Virginia, of the little tiny general store in Kentucky, of hours and hours of I-95 Interstate driving on the way *up* to Maine in the first place, and it dreams of a map of the USA and the slow line that I am plotting across it as I travel all over. But mainly I dream of getting my stuff stolen again.

I think I may have dreamed that I received a phone call. A call from the police in Greensboro telling me that they'd made a raid on a house and have recovered a load of stolen good. Can I come to Greensboro the next day and identify what they think is my stolen stuff? It's a nice dream. But can I interrupt my road trip? Can I go back and ruin my schedule just to go back and get my stuff?

Suddenly there is an audio interrupt into my subconscious stream of thoughts – Tap! Tap! Tap! Somebody is tapping on the door of my dream. Tap! Tap! Tap! The taps get a little louder each time. Then they became very loud, and then they turn into a feeling ... of someone tapping my shoulder in real life, and then a voice – J.J's ... that says 'Dude, I need the keys ... to move the car', and somewhere around that point I come out of the dream world, and into the real-world, but still half asleep.

And in the darkness of Russell's guest room, I dangle myself out of the bed, scrabble for my jeans on the floor and fish inside the pockets for the keys to the jeep and hand them to J.J. so that he can move the car where we are blocking Russell in so that he can drive to work. 'Thanks', comes the whispered response. 'Mmmmumm', I mumble back. Flip back over into bed, and squash the pillow on top of my head.

Day 22 – Tuesday 7th July

In the Temple of Love

*'Live in me Jerusalem, Here you live Jerusalem,
Here you breathe Jerusalem, While your temple still survives'*

I flick open the blinds on the windows in Russell's kitchen more than they already are, and it seems as if a second sun in the sky beams in new warm rays of light. J.J. enters.

'Why the hell did you get out of bed to move the car this morning?' is the thing I immediately want to know as I try to work out how to use Russell's coffee maker.

'Dude, I didn't get out of bed this morning to move the car'. 'Yes you did, you tapped on the door to my room this morning to get the keys'. 'Uuuh, no I didn't' replies J.J. in his surely tone and as I think about it ... and think about it some more ... I realise that he is of course right. Russell has been the one – obviously and logically – to come in that morning to grab they keys, but in my dazed and confused state, I thought for some reason it has been J.J.

So Russell has kindly let us stay, drink his beer, use his Internet, and block his car in in the morning probably making him late for work, and you know how we repay him? In the nicest way possible – and I'll tell you because you'll never guess – we knock over his mailbox on the way out.

J.J. has offered to drive first, and after we have loaded the car back up with all the gear, still joking about me getting confused over who has moved the car that morning so that Russell can get out, J.J. gently reverses up Russell's drive, and turns too early to curve onto the street – and there is a small but prominent 'crunch' sound as we back into Russell's mailbox, knocking it over to some weird 45-ish degree angle.

'Oops' says J.J. 'Nooo!' I join in with half seriousness, and half laughing, and jump out to inspect the damage. It's OK. I straighten it up. Try to push it back into the ground harder, and try to justify it in my head by wondering that we probably aren't the first people to have done this. I scan the neighbour's houses around and can't see anyone that has seen us do it, and so we decide there and then not to mention it to Russell, ever. Well, except maybe if he's reading this now – yes, the only reason that he knows about it after all this time is because he's holding a copy of this book in his hands right now. Sorry, mate.

8:14 AM Jul 7th
headin' for Alabama .... But first we've got to go visit a giant wooden chicken

Temple is our 'same name' Tube stop destination for the day ... in fact we are going to hit two in one day, but before that there is a 'big thing' that I want to go and see. I think everyone has heard of the giant ball of twine, or the giant ball of rubber bands ... somewhere in some small crazy midwestern town in American there is a tourist attraction of the 'the largest paintball in the world' where over many many years, someone gets a glob of paint, and paints on it ... and paints some more and now it's just one giant solid ball of paint. However, today ... *we* are looking at a big giant chicken.

I've seen it on the website **roadsideamerica.com** when I'd been doing my research, only to be honest ... now that we are here it isn't *that* impressive. It's more sort of medium sized in my mind rather than enormous, and it is a flat wooden panel in the shape of a chicken. Although there is a mechanism whereby the eye of the chicken does spin around – this makes it marginally more interesting. Oh, and it is part of a KFC restaurant – it isn't just some random chicken on the road side for hell of it, it is very much part of the building and a huge advert for the greasy chicken chain.

The smell of that greasy chicken then suddenly makes me hungry as it occurs to me that I haven't eaten anything for breakfast ... and then almost simultaneously, the overwhelming smell suddenly makes me really *not* want to have any chicken right then. J.J. does get a drink though.

10:21 AM Jul 7th
J.J. is drinking a soda for breakfast, eugh. how can anyone drink a coke at this time of day?

10:28 AM Jul 7th
and we're off again.... to our Georgian Tube-named-place, which is about 45 minutes away

---

In the USA
Temple, Georgia
On the Tube map
Temple (District / Circle Lines)

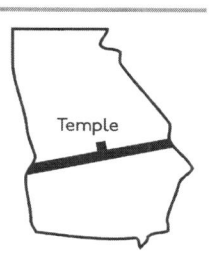

Temple I should tell you is *one of* my favourite Tube stations in London on the Underground because I swear it has a unique smell. Well – that and Great Portland Street – do actually smell similar that if you were to blindfold me before entering one of those two stations I feel fairly confident that I can identify where I am without my vision, just by using my rather large nose.

And while this is a same-name trip it's worth mentioning that 'Temple' is the only station in London that also shares a name with a station on the Paris Metro. There it's named after a demolished Templar fortification that dates back to the 12th Century. I wonder if we would find any templaric remains here in America?

> **11:29 AM Jul 7th**
> and welcome to ... Temple, Georgia. Your next stop. All change please, change to www.templega.us

A few minutes driving into the town and it is obvious that this is not a historic place, but it looks like a lovely cute town all the same, it makes me smile. It definitely has a bit of what Preston in Kentucky has – a bit of cutesy town USA.

We pull up in a car park outside the City Hall, and go for a wander around. There are neatly trimmed bushes, and flower beds that have obviously seen a lot of attention. The Temple Veterans Memorial and ... what is that over there, a Temple? No! It is just a simple church, the Temple Church of Christ but it's close enough for me – Temple's temple, and I *snap* a picture of it as J.J. walks over to investigate.

I leave him to it, and decide to wander off in the other direction and am immediately faced with a rival – a big sign with an arrow pointing me in the direction of the Liberty Christian Church. Ooh, a two Temple town! But then I notice that the sign is attached to a side of row of .... Well, I'd say houses, but they are shops, shop fronts all of which are falling down and looking in bad need of repair, but they have decayed in a nice way and somehow the discoloured bricks from rain water where the guttering is broken, peeling paint in the hot sun and a rusty canopy over what looks like it used to be a café somehow looks nice, rather than ugly.

'TOM UPHOLSTERY' says one of the shops that still seems to be surviving. Run by a nice bloke called Tom, no doubt? That is until I see the 'CUS' part of the sign lying – propped up – on the ground and realise it should read 'Custom Upholstery'. Oh.

'The Church is just a church' says a voice behind me – it is J.J's, looking unmoved about the whole experience, and I'm just about to comment on how he never seems to get worked up by anything when a familiar 'clanging' sound starts up. We look down the street a little more, and only then do I see it for the first time – I'm not sure how I have missed it – the railway line that runs right through the middle of town.

> **11:45 AM Jul 7th**
> and unbelievably ... There's a train line here. Honestly, i don't plan these things.

'Is there a station here?' I ask, but not really asking. J.J. shrugs. 'I don't see it on the map – it does seem to be though that I've got a knack for picking places with railways in, even though that isn't my intention', and J.J. kinda smiles at that.

> **11:46 AM Jul 7th**
> and ... There's a train coming, nice!

Now I am fully expecting to see a couple of huge locomotives pulling a dirty long freight train, so I'm therefore a little surprised when instead around the long bend comes into view a long shiny silver Amtrak train instead – a passenger train for once! But not stopping here, instead making its way west and south all the way to New Orleans – where we will end up in a few more days' time ourselves.

'Fancy catching the train instead?' jokes J.J. and I look around wondering if there used to be a train station here. 'I know where we can find out!'

I'm right. Back down in City Hall the chatty *Irene* is more than happy to tell us about the lovely town she lives in, and even digs out some old newspapers for us, one in particular being a 1983 edition of 'The Temple Enterprise' which is celebrating the town's Centennial – and the picture on the cover of the newspaper ... is a big old steam train. 'The good ol' days' she says, 'Back when the trains used to stop here! Now they just cause a traffic jam for a few minutes at the crossing every time they pass through – ha ha!'

The phone rings and Irene has to answer it, but I stand and read the rest of the front page of the cover of the paper whilst J.J. stands next to me looking a little awkward and a little hot too. It is a warm day, a drink would be in order, I decide.

~ ~ ~

I swig on my tasty bottle of orange vitamin water as we cruise west on the gorgeous hot day with the windows wound down and the wind ripping and rippling its way into the car bringing us a wave of air, and the noise that comes with it all at the same time. The road – the Interstate – curls down into a valley and up into the distance beyond some trees many miles ahead, and it gets me thinking.

I've now lived in the south for three years. It was May 2006 when I had first come to South Carolina, and when May of 2009 passed I noted that I'd been here long enough not to make a fuss about my anniversary of being here, or the time spent. It was different when I'd been here six month, a years, a year and a half, but somewhere just after the year and half marker I realised that I had stopped worrying about how long I'd been here. So if anybody ever asks you 'How long does it take to settle and stop being homesick?' the answer is 'About eighteen months', no kidding.

In all that time though, I'd never really been into the middle states. Oh, I'd been up and down the east coast a lot and been to Boston, New York and Chicago – I'd even done a fly-over and been out to California for a little while, but I'd never really *been* anywhere out in the middle.

So driving from Georgia towards Alabama down the Interstate all of a sudden feels quite interesting and exciting. I've been to Georgia before – the state we are leaving, and although there is nothing *that* spectacular about the stretch of road we are on (in fact, an RV sales lot looms into view not long after crossing the state line), as we drive down the Interstate and I realise where I am, I have a little creeping sense of realisation sweep over me for the first time in three weeks.

Yes – I really am driving round all the states. I really am going to go to countless number of places that I've never been to before, I really am going to see some intriguing sights, meet weird people and have a journey and a story to talk about for the rest of my life, and for the first time on the trip I have a genuine twinge of excitement.

'I've never been to Alabama before' I say to J.J. Wanting to tell him that I'm now excited to be here and explain how it feels like I am now breaking new ground, and how wonderful that is, and that this would be the way into that conversation.

'Yeah, you've not missed much' comes his instant droll response.

> **12:00 PM Jul 7th**
> i don't think J.J. likes Alabama much. But how can he not? It's home to the world's largest chair...

As well as finally feeling like I am starting to get somewhere, and feeling excited, something else rather intriguing happens as we cross the state line and entered the Deep South – we get staked out by a cop.

Now when I say *cop* of course, then you have to realise that there are numerous different types of law enforcement agencies in America – a bit like England has City of London Police *and* the Metropolitan Police and all the county Police and then Community Support Officers and so on.

Well it's a bit like that in the USA but *even more complicated*. So complicated in fact that I'm not even going to dare and try and explain how all the different agencies combine and who's in charge of what – except for the one fact that at regular law enforcement level (i.e. Not the Military) the highest level that you can get and the ones that you want to be wary of – are the State Troopers.

Even J.J. who can be quite nonchalant about such things is wary enough, and so when he says to me in a slightly disconcerting tone 'There's a State Trooper checking us out', I know that he isn't messing.

I perk up in my seat a little, and look in the rear view mirror – yup, the State Trooper car that has been sat on the median (Central Reservation) a moment ago as we crossed the border is now just behind us in the next lane over matching our speed perfectly – what *is* our speed? I check the dashboard – phew, 62mph. He can't pull us for that

'What *is* he doing though?' I ask out loud – I guess towards J.J. 'Running our license plate through his computer, make sure it's not stolen'. 'What, the car? Why would it be stolen?' I reply, vaguely aware out of the corner of my eye that J.J. is fiddling around in his seat and trying to get something ... out of his pocket? But I can't look properly because the trooper is making me nervous and I am looking very carefully at where I am driving, and to make sure I don't go over the speed limit.

'We've got out-of-state plates' explains J.J. 'That's why they do – sit on the Stateline, and any car with out of state plates, especially with two guys in, they check out'. 'Why two guys?' 'Because ... we might be drug dealers?' says J.J. with humour in his voice, but he means it too.

It is about then that the State Trooper then suddenly speeds past us in the outside line, then brakes and turns hard into a reversing area on the median so that he can go back down to his spot where he's been previously- satisfied obviously that we are no threat. The 'Welcome to Alabama' centre looms up on the right, I indicate to come off.

I see J.J. reach down into the pocket of the door and retrieve something. 'Is that knife!?' I exclaim. 'No, it's my Leatherman'[19]. 'We're you hiding it ... why are you hiding it?' 'Well if we *did* get stopped by the cops and they searched us, I just don't want to give them a reason to give us a hard time. And I'd rather they find my Leatherman in the car, rather than on my person'.

---

[19] A Leatherman is a multi-function tool that includes bottle opener, screwdriver, oh ... and a knife blade.

I pull into a space in the car park, switch off the engine and just look at J.J. for a moment, silently, and perhaps a little glumly.

'Welcome to Alabama', is all I can muster.

> **1:19 PM Jul 7th**
> just got totally scoped out by a state trooper (cop). Two men, SC plates, and a full car. We're suspect drug runners!

The nice man behind the counter in the Welcome Center – sorry I mean Centre - who gives us a map of his state makes me feel slightly better, but already Alabama is sinking low to the bottom of my list of 'favourite states' with its over-zealous police force. We both use the loo and then move on quickly, not to a same-name town, but to something a bit silly that I just want to see.

> **1:26 PM Jul 7th**
> we're in Anniston, AL. The world's largest chair is here, it's in the 1982 Guinness book of records.

It's built and owned by a local company – Miller's Office Supply who simply want to call attention to it when they created their business in 1982. So the owner built the world's largest chair in the space next to their building. It's 33 feet tall, with a 15-foot-square seat and Guinness World Records officially recognise the feat as the world's largest chair.

Me... a Tube world record holder, up against another world record. It seems fitting.

We take photos, I pose for a photo, we wander round the chair legs, some people in cars driving past hoot at us, probably because we are ridiculous tourists paying attention to what is just really a very large and silly advert. But I still like it.

> **1:27 PM Jul 7th**
> but enough of .... large .... things today, we have a Tube-named stop to go make, 30 minutes away ...

We drive to the next same-name stop. I decide that it is a bit like being in the English countryside. Slightly hilly winding roads, trees and fields to either side, it is only the driving-on-the-right side, and the fact that there's a yellow line down the middle of the road instead of a white one that gives it away. Well that and J.J. playing some more terrible country music on his iPod that is. I can see I am going to have to have words with him about this before the week is out.

Not-so-long-later, the SatNav guides us in and we turn off the Interstate, and onto the rather brilliantly named 'Kelly Creek Road', and then suddenly – we arrive at Brompton.

In the USA
Brompton, Alabama
On the Tube map
West Brompton
(District Line / Overground)

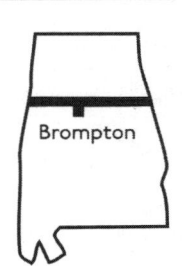

We pull into a dusty lay-by off the side of the road, and look at the triangular junction that is Brompton. It really is just a road junction ... with a Citgo gas station off to one side. The occasional car and truck trundles by.

> **2:37 PM Jul 7th**
> you are now arriving at ... Brompton, Alabama. It's just a big oak tree and one Citgo gas station. Uh huh

'Umm, I think this is it', I say to J.J. a little forlornly looking at his face and getting a look from him that says 'Is this it Geoff? We've come to here to look at ... a Gas station'.

'I know what you're thinking; you're thinking we've come all this way just to look at a Gas Station'.

'I didn't say that',

'No, but you were thinking it.'

A brief silence entertains the inside of the car, two men sitting there looking at a truck pulling out with a loose ladder tied on the back that goes 'clang' as the one of the tyres hit the kerb.

'Maybe there's more to it, maybe the main Brompton town is the other side of the Interstate?' I suggest, knowing that really I am clutching at straws.

I drive back down the road, but all we find is where the railway intersects with the road – yes the railway, again ... I think maybe on the same line that passes further up through Temple, and I can't help but have a small chuckle to myself that another random small town picked purely because shared the name of a Tube stop in London, *does* have a railway running right through it.

At that moment, the lights on the crossing flash, and the bells start to clang – a train is coming! And it jumps me into action to get out my crappy backup video camera, and shoot a few shots of the train coming through. I want to record that Brompton at least has something – trains!

A locomotive pulling a loooong set of trucks starts to pass through and takes a good two to three minutes to pass by. I capture it all on video, flashing lights and clanging bells 'n' everything. Yeah ok, it's just a train but it's something.

After it passes, we go back to the crossroads of Brompton, and unsurprisingly nothing much has really changed since we've been there twenty minutes ago. We make use of the facilities at the Citgo though, and J.J. snaps a picture of the car's license plate that is parked in front of us on the forecourt.

> **3:01 PM Jul 7th**
> just seen a license plate that read '4ST GUMP'. Love it, and yes it was Alabamian.

And I consider the two places we've been to today, including the previous stops, and make a note in my diary again of the same name places so far.

SAME NAME TOWNS TALLY

Perfect Small Town America
Preston

Something there and enjoyable
Plaistow, Gloucester, Kew Gardens, Harrow, South Kensington, Greenford, Liverpool, Temple

Something there but not that exciting to be honest
Putney, Amersham, Hampstead, Woodford, Brompton

Nothing there but somehow being in the middle of nowhere made it OK
Epping, Acton

Nothing there, and not that exciting either. Oops.
Warwick, Wapping, Camden

I do a quick count and realise that Brompton is same-name place number twenty-two. I still am not halfway through the count yet, and what's more I know that on the eastern side they have all been spaced relatively closely. As I head out to into the Wild West, they would become more spaced apart, and I judge that really, I am only about a third of my way through the trip.

We drive south, heading for Florida, and take some more pictures for the gallery of some rusty cars – I get J.J. to film me using the small mini backup camera, but the quality isn't very good and all it does is agitate me that I haven't heard about the delivery of my new camera that I've ordered.

I decide that as much as J.J. is my friend, I don't want to spend the night with him in a tent, so I plump for another cheap crappy motel when we get to Tallahassee in Florida. However, it is the sort of cheap crappy motel that means that the wireless isn't working, and no amount of chatting with the girl at the reception desk seems to be able for it to be fixed at all. At least she signs my t-shirt though, with a welcome 'Welcome to Tallahassee!' scrawls in the Florida part of the map that is printed on my T-Shirt.

It's drizzling slightly as I go back to the room where J.J. geeks out by using my 3G internet dongle and laptop to check his email, and writes his own blog:

> **Day 2: free internet!**
>
> Well, not so much – We're at a Days Inn tonight – in the hopes that the promised free internet would allow a certain amount of updating upon our progress.
>
> Well, you get what you pay for. Namely, nothing. nowt. nada. zip.
>
> Spent a heck of a day on the road today – we hit three state capitals (Atlanta, Montgomery and Tallahassee), and drove through what seemed like the entirety of Alabama.

'Hungry?', I ask 'Maybe', he replies without looking up, and I step back out into the drizzle remembering that when we'd turned in there has been a KFC across the street. The KFC across the street whose lights are now off and looks very much closed. I check the opening times on the side of the door, it has closed at 10pm. I check my watch, it is 10.04pm. Bastards.

So, one filling meal of crackers from the gas station later, and it looks as if we might as well turn in. I nab the laptop back and update my progress map.

> **10:41 PM Jul 7th**
> made it to Tallahassee, FL for the night. Did two 'Tube places' today, and over 600 miles of driving, progress map: http://is.gd/1qCRa

I look up suddenly – disturbed by some grunting noise. On the TV? The water pipes gurgling? Or a car problem outside? No ... it's J.J, who has fallen asleep fully clothed on top of the bed with the lights on, and is now emitting a very annoying snoring sound.

I throw a shoe at him – miss – but hit the side of the bed. 'J.J. – Ssh!' I say, and in his sleepy state he mumbles something incoherent and turns over, half wrapping the sheets around him, making a sub conscious effort to get under the bed clothes properly.

I roll over, do the same, and flick the light switch off.

Day 23 – Wednesday 8th July

Into the Panhandle

'It's had its ups and downs
And turnarounds but we will never regret
The ways we've changed for better for worse.
I am who I am and I'm proud of the progress'

I'm quite proud of myself that I've managed to find a song called 'Lancaster' to match up with today's destination – I am even more thrilled when I find out that it is by a band called 'Texas in July', but ultimately I am disappointed that the Lancaster is in Florida, and not Texas, otherwise it would have just been just ... perfect. But that's ok. You can't win them all.

I put down my iPod which I've picked up when J.J. goes into the shower and survey the motel room for food. There isn't any. Well – there *are* some crumbs of crackers left over from the night before. I hoover them up gleefully off the tips of my moistened fingertips ... ah - a healthy diet – and set about editing a video of yesterday's antics.

> **9:46 AM Jul 8th**
> just cut a new video, a little rough, but totally watchable. FTP'ing it up right now .... will post very shortly

I'm not best happy with the video, as it has all been shot on the back up camera, and the sound quality is mostly poor. But it's all I have, and better than nothing until I get to New Orleans at the weekend and my new video camera will be there then. I drum my fingers on the desk, and watch the progress bar slowly sneak up to the 100% mark as it uploads.

> **10:00 AM Jul 8th**
> video's up. http://is.gd/1r6tH

Video uploaded we check out of the Days Inn, sneaking in some of their complimentary breakfast (read: toasted bagels) as we go. I know we've got time to eat properly later, but I want to get going because I also know that our 'Tube stop' today is seemingly a slightly pointless detour.

When I'd first found a place in Florida, it has been about halfway down the state – and would have taken a lot of extra driving to get to. Then – quite by chance, I'd searched on 'Lancaster' (for Lancaster Gate) and find a place right up the top near Alabama in the panhandle – that's more like it! Not as much driving to get to, but also obviously looks like being a more middle-of-nowhere stop.

Overall, I don't think that Florida is the most exciting state in the USA. I've even heard plenty of Americans describe it as being weird. Tampa bay is particularly weird. And yes – it really is full of old retired folk who go there for the warm weather – *very* warm weather. I'd once been in a gas station in Charleston on a day when it was 32C, overhearing an old lady telling the server that she couldn't wait to get back to Florida as she would prefer it down there as it was 'much warmer'. Yikes.

> **10:36 AM Jul 8th**
> back on the I10 eastbound. 60 miles to our 'Tube' stop.... then we u-turn and drive the same 60 miles back, sigh.

The rain comes out to play with us for a bit as we drive, and then the weather-whistle is blown, and it abruptly stops. And … then very vaguely starts again. And then seems to half go away and just leave a fuggy moist environment in the atmosphere. I battled with the wipers trying to see if there is an ultra-low setting that can cope with the fact that it's somewhere between dry and hardly-spitting-with-rain at all. There isn't. Which means I have to give the wiper blades a manual 'flick' every 45 seconds or so, which really agitates me. Fortunately, a few minutes later, it starts to really chuck it down, and I can switch the wipers to regular automated mode.

> **10:41 AM Jul 8th**
> ah …. Florida rain. Very wet, very excessive. Forgotten how tropical the climate can be.

Just after 11.30, after driving down some tiny dirt roads, but surrounded by a forest of pine trees we come to the Tube stop for Florida. Hello Lancaster.

In the USA
Lancaster, Florida
On the Tube map
Lancaster Gate (Central Line)

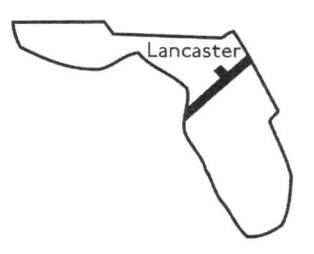

Wow. I've managed to do it again.

I find myself at a crossroads in the middle of nothing. So much so, that I can only let my tweets do the talking.

> **12:08 PM Jul 8th**
> we've just been to Lancaster, Florida. Only tweeting now, because there was no cell reception there.

12:09 PM Jul 8th
we did take lots of photos though. Mainly of ... the car parked at the crossroads.

12:10 PM Jul 8th
to liven things up, we took one of the car at the crossroad with J.J. sticking his head out of the sun-roof. I know, mavericks eh?

12:11 PM Jul 8th
i went for one final walk around Lancaster to make sure I'd not missed anything. It took 30 seconds, tops.

12:12 PM Jul 8th
oh, and only tweeting now because there was no cell reception there.

12:13 PM Jul 8th
there was an advert though for logged pine trees, surrounded by, umm.... lots of pine trees!

Except that as you'll have gathered these are all retrospective tweets as it is so desolate there is no cell-phone reception and we have to wait until we have signal again before I can use my phone.

I make up for the lack of tweeting that morning.

12:15 PM Jul 8th
btw, we're heading west again now on the I-10, target for tonight: Pensacola, FL.

12:16 PM Jul 8th
email urban legend: A woman once called Delta airlines and asks for a flight to 'Pepsi Cola, Florida'. Heh.

Enough tweets now, Geoff. What's that? Oh no, apparently not.

2:02 PM Jul 8th
entering Central Time Zone again. Freaky .... just watched my phone auto-update itself. At exactly 3pm, it became 2pm!

2:28 PM Jul 8th
church sign: 'Jesus is coming soon'. Really? How soon?, i've got to run to the shops in a moment, don't want to miss him

If you haven't worked it out by now, you're starting to get the fact that I'm not really into the whole religion thing, aren't you?

We pick up at Geocache and stop at a Denny's restaurant (because I have never been to one before and J.J. is quite keen on taking me to virgin places) during which I have a surreal conversation with my cousin Phil via Facebook instant messaging back home.

'Where exactly are you now? I've been following your trip!' he asks, 'In a Denny's in Florida' I reply as our server puts down some hush puppies on our table.

Over the course of the next few minutes (and whilst we eat – terrible table manners) I chat to Phil and he says that he wants to come out and visit America himself now at some point very soon. We make a plan for him to come and visit once my trip is done.

SAME NAME TOWNS TALLY

Perfect Small Town America
Preston

Something there and enjoyable
Plaistow, Gloucester, Kew Gardens, Harrow, South Kensington, Greenford, Liverpool, Temple

Something there but not that exciting to be honest
Putney, Amersham, Hampstead, Woodford, Brompton

Nothing there but somehow being in the middle of nowhere made it OK
Epping, Acton, Lancaster

Nothing there, and not that exciting either. Oops.
Warwick, Wapping, Camden

With J.J. doing the driving, we call a halt just outside Pensacola and stop in Milton, FL for the night.

> **6:27 PM Jul 8th**
> made camp for the night, literally. Here: http://is.gd/1rvlp Just about still inside Florida, heading for New Orleans by the weekend.

Dinner comes courtesy of J.J. taking me to a Hooters 'If you've never been you need to go' is his reasoning, during which we make a list of every 'chain' burger joint in America that we can think of.[20]

We don't stay in a KOA that night – but I again I elect not to go down the tent route, and we stay in a campground *Kabin* instead. It's only after my week with J.J. is over do I realise that we don't sleep together in the tent for the entire week that he's with me.

---

[20] Arby's, Blake's Lotaburger, Bojangles, Burger King, Carl's Jr., Checkers, Church's Chicken, Five Guys, Hardee's, In-N-Out Burger, Jack in the Box, KFC, McDonald's, Sonic, Steak 'n Shake, Taco Bell, Wendy's, Whataburger and Wimpy.

Day 24 – Thursday 9th July

From FL to AL, from AL to LA

*'Big wheels keep on turning, Carry me home to see my kin
Singing songs about the Southland, I miss Alabama once again
And I think it's a sin, yes'*

12:18 PM Jul 9th
it's too hot, and it's 'only' 88 degrees. What will i do in Texas when it hits 100?

The next few days are strange ones as we are heading for New Orleans where I plan to hole up for the weekend, hopefully take delivery of my new video camera, and get the proper videos rolling again back online.

We are to meet up with my friend Tami, before J.J. then flies back to Charleston, leaving me alone for a week to drive up north to Chicago by myself.

When I first planned this part, I did have a plan for a friend of mine – Steven – back in the UK to come and join me for this leg of the trip, and he'd agreed – only to disagree quite late on leaving me with no-one to go with on this part of the trip. Which was OK, it had bothered me slightly at first, but now I figured I would be alright about it.

12:20 PM Jul 9th
we're leaving Milton, FL. Heading for Mobile, AL.

1:13 PM Jul 9th
in Mobile, AL. We're gonna check out the USS Alabama, big old warship, #chs : like Yorktown, but older & even bigger

We have fun in Mobile, AL where we go and visit the USS Alabama. Think … HMS Belfast on the River Thames – only bigger, with more guns, and very American. When J.J. agreed to come on this part of the trip, one of the stipulations is that we take a tour of this ship. Tick, done, lots of joy.

On the way out of the parking lot from the Alabama we cruise round looking at car license plates, I'm still missing one from New Hampshire where I've forgotten to take one a few weeks ago when I was up there. So now anytime there is a concentration of cars, I'm on the lookout for one. Cross, can't find one here, less joy.

Heading west, we swap the driving role a few times, and roads too alternating between the Interstate and US Highway 90 that runs alongside it, just to break up the scenery a bit, we whizz straight though Mississippi quickly stopping for a free drink at their state welcome centre.

> **4:09 PM Jul 9th**
> the Mississippi welcome centre gives you a free water/soda/coffee. How nice! Can't imagine that at a place in England

A big card-board cut out of Elvis adorns the entrance to the visitors centre; I query this with J.J. - 'Elvis? In Mississippi? But Elvis is from Tennessee isn't he?' 'He worked and lived in Tennessee' I am wisely told, 'But he was *born* in Mississippi'. Oh. 'Birthplace of Elvis'. Tenuous.

And into Louisiana.

> **6:46 PM Jul 9th**
> made it to NOLA! (that's new Orleans to you)

J.J. teaches me that everyone knows what NOLA means – New Orleans, LA – where LA is the two-letter short state code for Louisiana. Goddit.

> **7:15 PM Jul 9th**
> just met Tami, my police officer friend downtown. She's escorting us to our hotel!

So the weekend is a bit strange, I'll try to summarise it briefly.

Over the weekend, there is a lot to take in. First I need to explain that Tami is a friend whom I had made online a few years previously. She's a Police Officer in New Orleans Police Department but also a huge Anglophile, and when in the wake of the 2005 terrorist attacks on the tube in July of that year, I had arranged a charity mass-participant event for people to do their own tube challenge and visit all the stations in one day.

Tami had booked a ticket and flown out just to take part in that – as that's how much she loves London. Her trip took a dramatic turn though when during her time in England, hurricane Katrina hit her home – and she was stuck in the UK for a few days until she could get a flight back. So – Tami knows I am coming to New Orleans, and we meet up several times over the weekend.

She's even done the nicest thing and pre-arranged for a hotel for me to stay in. It's nice to be in a decent hotel and spread out and relax and put my feet up. There is internet for me to hook my computer up to, although it's not free – in fact, it comes in three tiers of service depending on what speed you want. Have you noticed how the nicer and more expensive hotel you stay in, the less free the Internet becomes? Stay in a cheap $50 a night crappy motel and you'll get free Wi-Fi. Stay in a plush hotel, and it becomes 'Well as you can afford to spend $150 a night here, we've got no qualms charging you an extra $10 a day for the Internet'.

J.J. and I hit the French Quarter on the first night and just take in the atmosphere – and by 'atmosphere' I mean people getting very drunk in public, in one of the few places in America where it's legal to carry alcohol on the street. People are selling beads, wearing beads, and aside from the numerous bars, there are t-shirt selling shops and numerous strip clubs. Although it's only a Thursday night, it feels like the weekend such are the number of drunken masses staggering around.

Home of Mardi Gras, and with a reputation as a party town New Orleans is obviously the place to come to let your hair down. That still doesn't quite prepare me for though what I see as I walk down Bourbon Street (the main 'drag' as it is) when going back to the hotel. Perhaps my tweet would best summarise it.

> **2:20 AM Jul 10th**
> i just saw some dude with his head up a girls skirt, orally pleasuring her in the middle of the street. a crowd gathered to encourage #nola

You might think I'm making this up, or I've seen something that *looks* like this when I see this, but as I'm not prepared to take a photo *(even though others are)*, I make sure that this is what I am observing – and it is. A circle of people have gathered, and at first I think it's a fight, only for me to then see a girl in a white dress, stretching out with one arm to balance herself against a lamp post, and a guy on his knees down on the ground with his head quite clearly up her skirt. And she is making ... *reciprocative* noises. I think she may have had a drink or two.

Bizarrely, one of her friends is also tugging on her other free (non balancing) arm, seemingly oblivious to what is going on down at her waist level, whilst what must have been the guys' mates are being quite blokey by standing round and cheering him on. *Cheering him on*, yes.

I look around, to my sides to look at everyone else looking on. Then I try to focus hard – is this *actually* what I am seeing? Yes. Yes it is, and everyone apparently seems to think this is quite quite normal.

Public cunnilingus ... welcome to NOLA.

~ ~ ~

The next day on Friday, J.J. and I meet up with Tami and the first thing she does is to deliver me a bag of video camera goodies that I have ordered. There is the light, and spare battery and charger and blank tapes ... but – hang on! There is *no* actual video camera. This is not useful! So I go straight online to find that the camera is still flagged as 'Out of Stock' which is why one has not been shipped to me. I ring the store that I ordered from and they say they don't know when they'd get it in stock, but they take my number and tell me that they will call me hopefully later in the week and send it to wherever I am then. I have to accept this and hope that it will work.

The second thing Tami does is to then take us on a tour of New Orleans – around the areas that were flooded when Hurricane Katrina has passed through causing massive devastation back in 2006. Then she takes us to where she works – at the local 911 call centre, but as we drive there she asks me casually to get something out of her glove box for her, and I open it up, to see a rather large handgun inside, a 40mm Glok, just casually sitting there. 'Is it loaded?' I ask tentatively. 'Uh huh', nods Tami. I say no more, and shut up the glove box not daring to touch the gun.

After being shown round the call centre, we stop outside in a nice park and sit on bench and using my not-very-good backup video camera talk to Tami about her time back in 2006, after the hurricane, and how it affected the people and the City, and how long it took to recover. 'Well I was living on a boat for 6 months!' she reveals, something that I had not known, something which many people did whose homes had been completed flooded.

Whilst J.J. held the video camera and gets all this down, I can't help but think that this is one of the best conversations that I've had on the trip, and yet I know really from the background noise of where we are that the crappy video camera won't pick up the audio properly. This annoys me – right up until the point again when I remember that people have died in this city in the hurricane, and thousands more affected who still may not ever recover, and I feel over privileged again and perhaps I shouldn't be making a fuss. My mind struggles again with trying to rationalise this all.

I finish talking to Tami. She has been great to us the whole weekend (the next day she even takes us out for lunch – she pays – with her sister and we have a lovely time), and yet she is someone who I feel should not be messed with. Ignoring the fact that she's a Police Officer, something tells me that I would be unwise to get into her bad books, or do something to upset her! I think that's a characteristic of most people that live in New Orleans actually – they are tough cookies, and is something to be admired.

On the way back to the hotel – there is an odd moment where J.J. opens up to me and tells me that he's been quite affected by what he's seen too, and later he writes about it on his own blog:

New Orleans

I hadn't intended to post any more about the trip until i got home to South Carolina, but today's 'sightseeing' kind of hit me.

> We drove into town yesterday, spending a goodly part of our jaunt on US 90 – picking it up in Biloxi and rolling along to the vicinity of Waveland. It was somewhat disturbing to see all the empty foundations and hollowed shells of buildings – but not like what we saw today.
>
> Today, we stood on the levee bordering the Lower Ninth Ward at the location of one of the major breaches – and, except for scattered new construction, there was nothing in front of us.
>
> Makes one thankful for having a roof overhead, among other things.

~ ~ ~

The next morning on the Saturday, J.J. and I have a bit of a falling out. Not that there is any arguing *per se* but the weather is so damn hot that after ten minutes of walking outside we just both get grumpy and on each other's nerves. We walk around trying to find one of the local classic tram services to ride on, but neither of us has seen the signs saying that it is closed for maintenance, and in the hot heat making us miserable I think we both blame each other for not spotting it sooner. Humph. But it's okay … just. When it comes to J.J. leaving and heading to the airport, there is a rather subdued 'Well, thanks … see you soon' and a limp handshake and he is off, leaving me by myself.

I spend most of that Saturday afternoon inside my hotel room not wanting to outside into the real world. It is nice and air-conditioned, and I have now paid for Internet on my PC, meaning that I can download and watch some British TV on the luxury of my computer, which I do. For several hours.

I also spend the evening editing, and put together a new video for the blog – and lament the fact that I do not have a companion to go with me for next week. Well, except for the fact that … I *have*!

As actually, over the weekend, I've received a surprise message which I hadn't expected and it changes the whole week ahead of my road trip.

Day 27 – Sunday 12th July

The Mother of all Road Trips

*'Road trippin' with my two favourite allies,
Fully loaded we got snacks and supplies
It's time to leave this town, It's time to steal away
Let's go get lost, Anywhere in the U.S.A.'*

9:31 AM Jul 12th
what's this? ooooh look, a new mystery companion has turned up for the next leg : New Orleans up to Chicago .... revealed later!

The elevator door 'bings' and rapidly reveals to me in the parting of the sliding doors the figure of my mum. My *mom* as the Americans would say. My mother! Here – in New Orleans! How did that happen?. My littl' ol mum who has decided that she wants to jump on the crazy-train with her travelling son and be part of the road trip.

When I'd planned the trip six months back and I drew up in my head a list of people that I would like to come with me – I admit that my mum is not one of them. Instead, I'd pencilled in one of my best mates from home to come with me and we swap many excited emails back and forth about the upcoming trip.

The many emails slowed down to a trickle and then stop completely when I start to ask tricky questions such as 'So have you bought your ticket then yet?', and in a slightly awkward phone call about two weeks before I set off, he admitted that he hadn't and that he can't come after all.

This leaves me with a gap in my schedule and the ominous thought of having to drive up the middle of America following the Mississippi river as I go by myself. Not such a big thing really, except that I know the week after I am already going to be by myself – one week is fine, but I'm not sure that I can manage two.

So I've mentioned it on the blog once or twice ... 'Does anyone want to travel with me from New Orleans to Chicago?', but I get no real responses. Right up until I am in the hotel with J.J.

When we'd booked into the Harrah's hotel on the Thursday evening, I know that I am staying for four nights – J.J. two, as he would fly home on Saturday. What I really didn't expect is for my mum to replace him and for her to spend the latter two nights with me and be my companion for the next week – but that's exactly what happens.

My mum has read my blog upon my arrival in New Orleans on the Thursday, where I mention – yet again – that I still have no companion for the next week and am now getting rather desperate. And my mum reads it, reads it again, checks her bank account online to see if she can afford a ticket – and then gets in touch ... *by twitter.*

Not a phone call, not an email, not even an internationally-sent text message, but a direct twitter message from my mum to me.

Now I like to think that my mum is technically savvy – more so than a lot of other friend's mothers I know. People in America always seem impressed when I've been in a bar of an evening and my phone would beep. I'd check my phone. 'It's just my mum sending me a text', I'd say. 'What from England?', 'Yes we have mobile phones there too', I would reply.[21]

But my mum has got twittered up earlier in the year when I had been taking part in a 10km run, and she is trying to follow it from home. 'Send me texts and let me know how you're doing' said one, and I rapidly realised that this would be inefficient.

'Or you can just follow my twitter feed along with everyone else', I sent her a text back, and included the link to my twitter page.

An interesting side effect of this is that my mum (like many) does that thing where she assumes that she has to be signed up to twitter herself in order to be able to read my feed ... but you don't. You can read anybody's twitter page (unless they've protected it), without having to sign up. But sign up she does ... and I think it takes her a little while to get her head around it, but after a few weeks I notice one interesting thing ... that my mum would no longer send me text messages. No – she would just send me twitter direct messages instead ... because it's free!

Why spend 25p/25c on an international text, when you can send a direct message to that person's cell phone via twitter? So that's what we now do – send direct messages to each other. And late on that Thursday evening in New Orleans, my phone beeps, I check it, and there is my mum on twitter to me with a direct message:

Onionwoman
How desperate are you for a travelling buddy? Is this just a request or is it essential? There is a flight on Saturday morning from LHR :)

---

[21] During my time in the USA, some Americans would get my sarcastic sense of humour – some would not. The 'litmus' test that I ended up perfecting would be whenever I was asked 'Where are you from?', and I would say with a straight face 'London, England. It's a small town of about 8 million people that you may have heard of', and if they smiled and or laughed and got it, then I knew that I liked them. Others however would just look at me oddly and not know how to respond to that – I generally found myself unable to get on with those people.

I reply to her, and the next day – Friday – she buys a last minute ticket, and on Saturday morning hops on the plane, getting to New Orleans about midnight on Saturday.

> **9:16 AM Jul 13th**
> alright NOLA you've been fun, but it's time to move on .... back on the road today.

We're up and out at a reasonable time on the Monday morning ... although worryingly now my mum is feeling rather ill and sick. Possibly a combination of jet lag, the exceedingly hot and dry New Orleans weather, or maybe the rich food that she's not used to means that my mum spends most of the day in the passenger seat feeling very poorly.

I load up all the gear into the car (several trips, multiple up and downs in the elevator) and help her into the car, where she starts to snooze, and I drive a mere two hours in a strange silence – no music playing – trying to get accustomed to the fact that my mum is here, to her first, and my twenty-third same named place.

In the USA
Bond, Louisiana
On the Tube map
Bond Street (Central / Jubilee Lines)

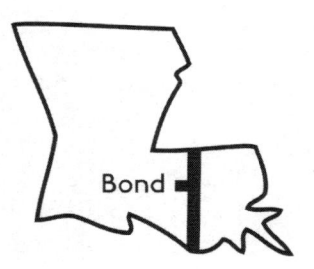

Wow. Remember Florida? With its dirt-track roads that led to a crossroads in the middle of some tall pine trees. Welcome to Bond ... which isn't even that – because it is the junction of just *three* roads – a T Junction in effect where three dirt roads meet in the middle of some trees, and umm ... that's it. No really. Nothing more.

'We're here' I tell my mum, but she's concentrating on putting a cold flannel from the ice-box on her forehead, and trying to feel better rather than be an engaged as to where we are. Not that there is anything to be engaged in.

This is a proper nothing – no road signs, no random mailbox, no advertising hoardings, no rusty cars, no abandoned train lines, a proper nothing nothing nothingy kind of nothing. It's rubbish

All of a sudden I am hit with a wave of grumpiness and I stomp about the sandy dirt roads for a few moment pacing up and down as if something this would miraculously get something interesting to appear up in Bond – but of course it doesn't.

I'm annoyed. Back at the car I get out my notebook and add Bond to the 'absolutely nothing here' list, and I realise that I think it feels like I've just driven my mum to nowhere, with nothing interesting to show how – not a great start for her trip.

But then I look at my mum dozing in the passenger seat of the car, not looking very well, and my grumpy feeling immediately dissipate and I suddenly feel more concerned about her than anything else, and want her to be better.

We head back east, and I remember that there is something on my map that might be fun to go and do and perhaps perk my mum up – the birth place of Britney Spears in Kentwood, Louisiana.

> **3:08 PM Jul 13th**
> i've come out of my way a little bit to go to the Britney Spears museum, in Kentwood LA ... and it's closed ffs.

Museums it seems, are closed on Mondays in America. This would be the first – but not the last time that I would be caught out by this on the trip.

We head off again. My mum is still looking ill, and now I'm starting to worry. Has it really been wise for her to come over here at the last moment? Shouldn't she be taking it easy watching Coronation Street back home and making tea by the gallon? Instead, I've convinced that *yes* it would be a great idea for her to come out and join me on a crazy jaunt for a few thousand miles north across America, and yet now she is suffering for it.

So my mum is sick, and I am annoyed with myself. Bond has been a washout, and the phrase 'What if these places turn out to be nothing towns?' reverberates around my head, the Britney Spears museum that we also made a detour to has been closed ... and all these things are annoying me ... but most of all there is one thing that is *really* fucking me off, and that is my lack of video camera.

> **3:27 PM Jul 13th**
> I-55 north. Long, boring, 5 hour drive ahead. And i am fucked off.

I suddenly feel like I am really stupid. *Really* stupid. I'd got the vibe from the website that the camera was out of stock and might take ages to come, but I've been stupidly kidding myself that a week is plenty of time and that it would be in New Orleans by the time I got there.

> **3:52 PM Jul 13th**
> so i need a HDV camera. I still don't have one. Who wants to loan me one? Deadly serious. #helpgeoff

I don't remember much about the drive north up the I-55, because I am too busy on the phone calling people. As my mum lays half passed out, recuperating in the passenger the seat, I fume like a petulant child, annoyed with myself for not realising that I needed to sort this out sooner, and as I am driving I do the only one thing that I can do to try and sort things out – I call people.

I call anyone that I can find as I scroll through my address book, anyone that I think can help me who might be sitting in front of a computer right now, and able to look up online a retailer in Memphis – where we are headed for – that would sell the video camera that I want. I give all my friends that afternoon the task of going off and Googling round to help me find a shop where I hope I can just cruise into town and go buy a camera.

At a gas station at Grenada, Mississippi, my mum awakes and we use the toilet. I am still on the phone, talking to people trying to locate a shop that would sell me what I need. And by the time we cruise over the state border, although I haven't manage to locate a place that sells it, I feel like I have tried and have made the effort, and I am starting to feel better again.

> **7:49 PM Jul 13th**
> resolute.

The KOA campground we stay in that night is actually in the state of Arkansas, and as we rattle over the cantilevered Frisco Bridge with the sun setting I say 'hello' to my 25th state on the trip.

> **8:24 PM Jul 13th**
> hello Arkansas …. At least i know how to pronounce you properly.

The campground is located right off the Interstate … but I'm not bothered because normally all the tent pitches are towards the back of the camps away from the traffic noise. Unfortunately, no one in West Memphis KOA has received this memo, and they put us within spitting distance of the rumbling traffic – as well as being next to some sort of sewage cesspit a few metres away, which even though it is fenced off you can tell it's attracting lots of bugs flitting round living off the muck and grit that seems to hang in the air.

With the tent up, I make myself and my mum (who has perked up a little, thankfully) some tea, leave her snoozing in the tent and go off to the laundry room on site.

Yet again the laundry is a respite from the heat with its delicious air conditioning, and has a table where I can setup my laptop. Somehow though, the bugs from the inside are being sucked in through the air conditioning and doing their merry dance around the glowing screen of my laptop. Every 30 seconds I swat at thin air trying to get them away from the email inbox which now greets my eyes.

I run through all the emails which all my friends I have called earlier and they wonderfully provide links to shops and retailers in Memphis who sell video cameras. But an hour later of going round them all – and doing some Googling of my own – I have found no one that sells the model I want at the price that I can afford, or they don't have them in stock – and I find my frustration returning once again.

> **10:21 PM Jul 13th**
> most longest, tiring & fruitless fcuking day of the trip so far. There will be better days, surely?

I distract myself from the agonising quest for a video camera, and write a blog post and update my progress map. I swat at more of the little bugs doing their dance around my glowing laptop screen. My mood darkens again.

I can't call anyone now ... I'm an hour behind Charleston now and it's too late. I stare at my screen. I do not have a video camera. My mum is sick. The only consolation is that I know we would be staying here for two nights, so maybe tomorrow would be better and bring more joy.

There are days – quite often actually – where I find in life that you plug away and work hard, and try your best to get somewhere and achieve something, but it just doesn't all seem to come together, and you go to bed feeling like you achieved nothing. Then – after a night's sleep the world *does* seem to be a better place as if magically the curse is lifted whilst you sleep and everything in the morning is better.

So I decide to go to sleep, and hope that this would be one of those nights that turns into a much better day. I crawl over my mum already asleep in the tent, onto my side, curl up in my sleeping bag and send my last tweet of the day.

> **12:53 AM Jul 14th**
> i'm in a bug infested, right-next-to-the-noisy highway KOA Campground in Memphis.

Day 29 – Tuesday 14th July

A little more information and a lot less showmanship

*'The Mississippi delta was shining, Like a national guitar
I am following the river down the highway,
Through the cradle of the civil war, I'm going to Graceland'*

8:43 AM Jul 14th
i've just spent the night sleeping with my mum, and it's not every day you get to say that in your adult life

8:49 AM Jul 14th
memphis #koafail Too near the road, noisy and riddled with bugs. Eugh.

I think I'd gone to sleep last night worrying about bizarre things. Actually I *know* I'd gone to sleep in an outrageously grumpy mood, so I think I subconsciously distracted myself by having odd thought about sharing a tent with my mother – i.e. what if I farted in my sleep? What if I started playing with myself – worse still, what if *she* started doing any of these things?

On a bright and breezy Tuesday morning, I grasp the one massive perk to having my mum on the trip : Tea and laundry. A day of me driving whilst my mum just dozes in the passenger seat plus an early night for her and twelve hours of sleep has appeared to have done her the world of good – it is probably just the jetlag. As soon as she hears me stir and moves and rise to go to the loo, she is up herself … eager to get on, and by the time I come back from the toilet, she has the camp stove on boiling water and is making tea! Fantastic. My day has got off to an excellent start.

As I sup on my tea, and I talk to her about 'Where the hell do I get a video camera from then at short notice?' I realise I am scratching my feet. And my lower legs, hmm… lots of bugs on this site, and now we've been bitten – my mum too, we compare lower legs and can see that they are very much red are starting to come up in bumps, dammit.

9:18 AM Jul 14th
KOA campground info rack has 55 brochures. 23 of them pertain to Elvis. #Memphis

We have a cooked pancake breakfast in the KOA kitchenette, and I leave my mum talking to the lovely chatty girl serving us, I go back to the laundry and set myself up for a couple of more hours. We are planning to go Graceland and see Elvis today, but this morning, I simply HAVE to get a video camera on order that morning, one way or another – hopefully delivered by tomorrow before we set off again.

> **9:32 AM Jul 14th**
> ok, Paul Simon 'Graceland' & Mark Cohen 'Walking in Memphis', any others for my soundtrack today anyone? #Memphis

At one point ... I come close. Close to getting a Sony camera. To the point where it is in my shopping basket of an AV website of somewhere that I can't even remember – I just know that they can have it delivered for me tomorrow. Then I remember that all the accessories I have are for the other type of camera and not compatible with this one, and so I hit 'cancel'.

> **11:37 AM Jul 14th**
> nowhere i've called in Memphis can sell me a pro video camera today. nowhere. I'm almost giving up.

At another moment, I find myself on a shopping website, almost ordering a different camera altogether but one that *do* work the accessories I have – but then find out that they would not deliver to a campground address! Ridiculous.

> **12:02 PM Jul 14th**
> un-fucking-believable. Last measure: I call B&H to order different a video camera (more $$$), but THEY DO NOT SHIP to hotels/etc.... FFS.

> **12:03 PM Jul 14th**
> they don't even ship to FedEx facilities or post offices. must be a residential or business address. incredible.

And then my phone beeps ... with an incoming text message, and I check ... and it isn't strictly a text, but a direct twitter message from my friend Rudi. Rudi who is back in D.C. that I'd stayed with for a night on the way up to the start at Maine, and Rudi who is avidly following my journey as I go.

> **Randomduck**
> @geofftech I've found you the exact video camera model that you need, it's on Amazon at ...

... and there then follows a shortcut link to their site.

My heart *might* have skipped half a beat in that moment. I certainly draw in a sharp breath as my finger hesitantly hovers over the mouse left-click button, knowing that a tiny exertion of force in the index finger of my right hand could lead to a buying page of pleasure. Has Rudi really found me a place that is selling it? Or would it prove to be another dead end?

Click!

'Yeeeesss!' I think is all that I utter from under my breath, and my mum chooses that exact moment to stick her head round the laundry door to see how I am getting on and to wonder if we are leaving to go to Graceland soon.

'I think I've got a video camera!' I say, the syllables doing a little dance and my voice trilling higher as I say it. And I click and I click and I click, and I type my credit card number and I click some more as I do all the necessary steps to order up a replacement camera – the same model as I've had before, that I would know how to use, with all the accessories that I got back in New Orleans ... and at that moment ... I mean *really* at that moment, I want to kiss Rudi – and let me stress here dear reader that he's not even that pretty by boy standards ... and yet I really want to kiss him.

12:20 PM Jul 14th
ok, i *think* i've ordered something. But even tho I chose 'next day delivery' it's telling me estimated delivery is 2-3 days. FFS, again.

'Does this mean we can go and see Elvis now then?' asks my mum politely. Yes mum, yes it very much does indeed.

* * *

Paul Simon plays on my mum's iPod in the car. I've had to download it especially that morning as my iPod is still not full of music since it has all been stolen, so 69p has been spent on purchasing one very specific song to play as we drive to see Elvis. And I start to tweet.

3:05 PM Jul 14th
i'm goin' to Graceland ....

3:37 PM Jul 14th
$10 just to PARK at Graceland! Duh. And an entrance ticket is going to be . . . how much?

3:41 PM Jul 14th
wow. Choose your level of fandom: VIP tour: $69, Platinum tour: $33. Mansion only: $28. I think that's a rip off. #elvis

3:48 PM Jul 14th
additional 'stable' tour (e.g. horses) for $15. Oooh. #Elvis #Graceland #expensive

3:50 PM Jul 14th
silly audio headset guide device has been thrust upon me. With a big orange plastic strap to hang round neck. #graceland

Those five tweets in which you read above there look just like regular-rambling tweets similar to any I've written so far in this book, and at the time are just regular tweets. But what I didn't know at the time (but clearly do now), but the trip to Graceland is the reason that you're reading this sentence right now – or to be more precise, is the reason why you're holding this book in your hand right now, reading about this whole trip.

For some reason – tweet fever takes over as I tour round Graceland – probably initiated by the fact that I can very rapidly see that it is going to be a tourist trap where they try and extract as much money out of you as possible, and thus the tweets come thick and fast as we take our tour.

3:51 PM Jul 14th
and now we're on a bus .... I feel like such a tourist, which ... is because i am, duh. #Graceland

3:53 PM Jul 14th
i refuse to wear the headset and look like a geek. So i'm pressing one side of the headset to my ear instead.

4:07 PM Jul 14th
carpet on the ceiling inside Elvis's house, brilliant! 1970's kitsch all over. #Graceland

4:20 PM Jul 14th
i'm seeing lots of Elvis artefacts, but am not actually learning anything about the man, or his life. #Graceland

4:21 PM Jul 14th
i bet it won't cost me $28 to Google information when i leave and actually read up on a few facts ..

4:46 PM Jul 14th
elvis automobile museum: that's more like it! Much more impressive. #Graceland

5:02 PM Jul 14th
tour over. Geoff has left the building. I'm all shook up, (sorry, couldn't resist) #Graceland

5:10 PM Jul 14th
you don't seem to be able to buy any Elvis records.cd's in the gift shop. Odd. #Graceland

5:12 PM Jul 14th
the all-Elvis Sirius satellite channel actually broadcasts from here! There's a studio .... that's cool. #Graceland

5:25 PM Jul 14th
i've just found the CD's for sale. Reason? There are FOUR separate gift shops here, different stuff in each. #Graceland

6:48 PM Jul 14th
actually, now that i've had time to consult the map, Graceland Exhibits=7. Restaurants=2. Gift shops=14. Gift shops win.

To save you sanity (and keep the word count down) I've actually *deleted* some of the tweets that I wrote that afternoon as we indulge in Elvis – but when I got back to the campsite that evening and I sit down to blog it all, the blog post turns out to be what would be the template for this book.

i.e. I guess most normal writers tend to make notes – and later use these as the structure to write the rest of their book. But by tweeting continually every day what I'm doing – even down to a handy date and time stamp – I've unwittingly been making notes for my entire journey so that I can come back later and read them all and instantly be reminded of what I am doing and be able to write about it.

So I write a blog post that evening – mainly concerning how lame I think Graceland is in that it is just a showcase for Elvis artifacts, and not a museum on any level where you can learn information or read anything in depth. And as I write the blog post, and read it back to edit it, I realise that I can do this for the entire road trip – use the tweets as the bones of the book, and flesh it out with several hundred thousand or so other words, the result of which you're reading now.

~ ~ ~

I put the Sirius Satellite radio on as we pull out of the Elvis parking lot. I wonder if my mum is going to ask me to put the Elvis channel on that we've just seen being broadcast, but instead she wants to know if we can go to the grocery store and buy some supplies, and it reminds me that I want some more camping bits – some tea lights and a box of matches at the very least. And maybe a new gas canister for my stove.

I call up the campground where we're saying and ask them where the camping shop is in Memphis – a city with a population of 600,000, the largest in Tennessee – and have a rather depressing conversation.

'You'll want to go to the Wal-Mart' is the answer that I get back. 'Isn't there an independent camping store anywhere in the city?' I ask, maybe a little desperately. 'We usually just go to the Wal-Mart' is the response that I get back again.

I'm left feeling a little disheartened by this. It's not that I am completely against The Man™ because there are obviously times and places where it is massively convenient, but I don't want to feel like it has actually completely taken over the world ... the world of course being America.

So if you – the reader – have some better knowledge that I do, or of the campground staff, and know of an independent camping shop in Memphis, then please feel free to get in touch and let me know. It would be nice to think that The Man™ has not run the campers out of town, as I may be back in Memphis one day.

The shopping experience itself is a little surreal. I leave my mum in line at the checkout to nip to the loo, and by the time I come back she's telling her complete life story to the stranger behind her – I swear my mum likes talking to people more than I do sometimes.

Within a few seconds me returning my mum announces to the whole line 'Oh here he is, my son', and it seems the whole line is chatting to each other as if my mum has infected them with the chatty bug, until it becomes our turn to be served, and I find myself being overly talkative with the woman on the checkout.

> **7:30 PM Jul 14th**
> am chatting far too much with sales assistant in Wal-Mart, she's gotta be at least 50 and loves my accent. She just said so!

And then something even stranger happens ... I find myself balking at the total amount. We've only bought a few cheap items from the camping section, and yet in the back of my head I've done that thing where you total it up roughly and I figure that it's going to cost no more than fifteen dollars. Instead the total is twenty two dollars, and for some reason that extra amount (About four quid, in my real monetary world) leaves me reeling – silly, but true.

> **7:36 PM Jul 14th**
> oh my God, i've finally gone native. Am in a store complaining about Arkansas's sale tax – 9.25%, higher than SC!

And then I realise why ... I have been caught out *again* by the 'What you see is NOT the price you pay' plot as each state has its own set sales tax, plus and local taxes added onto that, and 9.25% more has been added onto the total. I later find out that Arkansas has one of the highest sales taxes in the lower-48 (Hawaii has the highest of all the States), and then annoyingly ... if we'd gone to the Wal-Mart five miles back down the road in Tennessee, buying exactly the same the goods would have cost us slightly less. And *that* is one of the things that still winds me up about America.

The evening goes past nicely. My mum & I cook a somehow-tasty macaroni cheese meal on the stove, drink tea and play a game of cards under candle light until my mum retires for the day. I make some calls, and slink off again to the air-conditioned launderette to write up my Elvis blog for the day, and lay the foundations for this book.

> **1:02 AM Jul 15th**
> a little less Elvis, and a lot more twittering, my Graceland review: http://is.gd/1zhcO #Elvis #Graceland

Day 30 – Wednesday 15th July

Rewind

*'The place I was born in stays crooked and straight
I see innocent blue eyes, go blind every day.
If you could rewind your time, would you change your life?*

Wednesday morning noisily starts with the gentle overnight rumble of the trucks on Interstate 55, to the morning roar of all the traffic coming to life as the sun rays warm up the day, and my mum asks me if I would a like a cup of tea. It's a formality really, she already knows the answer.

I scratch my morning self away, then scratch myself some more. Then scratch and scratch and *really* scratch at my leg hard – my lower legs down by both the ankles which I notice are red. Are they red because I've just scratched them so hard, or had they been like that already before I started to scratch them? Now I'm not sure, and probably would have thought about it some more at that moment except that my mum then appears at the flap of the tent opening with a tea in a plastic cup in her hand.

Over breakfast pancakes again, my mum does her best to tell her life story (and mine) to the woman serving, but she does actually seem to really appreciate our friendliness, and it ends up with her taking a picture of us 'posing' next to a cardboard cut-out of Elvis that they have in the breakfast room.

My mum carries on snapping pictures, whilst I get online and check the UPS website for the whereabouts of my video camera. It is good news.

> **9:37 AM Jul 15th**
> the sweetest phrase of the day: 'OUT FOR DELIVERY'. Video camera in Memphis on a UPS truck somewhere, standing by ...

Having a day 'off' yesterday and hanging out in Graceland has done me good ... it has been a day of not driving for hours and hours and feels like a nice rest day. Getting a video camera on order and on its way makes me feel even better – it feels as if everything is back on track ... they just need to deliver it! Today is the day when I want to crack on and visit *two* same-name places, but I need the camera before I can go there.

> **10:52 AM Jul 15th**
> time to get moving again. I've got two 'Tube' stops to do today, one new state, and a new video camera to pick up .... hell yeah.

The first 'stop' is actually retracing our steps slightly ... so keen I have been to get to Memphis two days ago where I know that we'll camp up for two nights, that I have driven right past where I want to go next without actually stopping. The town of Oxford is about an hour back south the way we have come, and we can't sit around in the campground anymore waiting for the video camera to turn up ... so we will go and do Oxford, and then come back later that day and pick up the camera. The staff at the KOA are wonderfully helpful and say that they will indeed hold it for me when it arrives ... they even take my number so that they can call me later and let me know when it has turned up.

My mum pops to the loo though just one more time before we leave. So with all the stuff packed up in the car, I pull up outside the campground store and my mum jumps out to use the toilet, engine running – I am all ready to go, except at that moment ...

... out of the corner of my eye, I see the brown vehicular blob gliding into the campground. I realise later of course that I have been sub-consciously checking all morning any movement involving trucks and cars coming into the campground, and now – at 11 wonderful o'clock in the morning, the man-in-brown in his UPS truck is bringing me a gift, like an early Father Christmas.

'You're like Santa Claus to me bringing gifts!' I say smiling at the dude, inwardly congratulating myself smartly for the 'Father' to 'Santa' translation that I've just done, and point my crappy hand camcorder at him that I've grabbed from the back of the car the moment that I see him arriving.

I suspect he thinks that I'm being odd, but the fact that I am grinning like the proverbial Cheshire cat and calling him Santa obviously makes him like me.

My mum appears – she takes over the shooting, and so rather wonderfully I am able to capture on my poorer-camcorder the moment that the nicer quality new replacement video camera turns up. And I *am* like a kid at Christmas, ripping open the box in the reception of the campground with perhaps too much vigour, spilling the polystyrene packaging over the floor such is the hurry I am in.

> **11:34 AM Jul 15th**
> video camera delivered !!!!!

We thank the campground stuff profusely again, I thank the UPS man, and I make my mum drive so that I can open up the video camera properly and get it setup again. Our destination? Oxford Circus...

> **11:42 AM Jul 15th**
> on the road .... Heading back to Mississippi for next Tube stop

---

In the USA
Oxford, Mississippi
On the Tube map
Oxford Circus
(Central, Victoria and Bakerloo Lines)

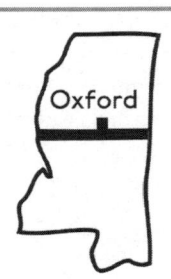

My initial impression is that Oxford, Arkansas will be more comparable to England's famous Oxfordshire and not the bustling London Oxford Circus junction and Tube station, but hey – it's the same name that counts.

> **1:42 PM Jul 15th**
> hurrah! It's a proper quaint little place, with a town square & everything. Result.

> **1:45 PM Jul 15th**
> there's not a chain store in sight, Oxford MS is super independent – love it!

It *is* pretty, and pretty soon too we discover that it is a College (University) Town, the University of Mississippi is based here, and within seconds I see a college girl wearing a 'Ole Miss' T-shirt crossing the street as she walks briskly by.

> **1:50 PM Jul 15th**
> ah – it's a college town, 'ole miss', 'the Harvard of the south' #oxfordms

We soon find ourselves in the central square of town known as 'The Square' which is clearly the hub of the town, with many beautiful buildings dotted around the outside. My mum and I get out and wander round, and whilst I can't find a visitors centre per se, we do seem to end up in City Hall – similar to what I'd been in back in Plaistow in New Hampshire.

I take a handful of free mints that are on offer, and read the many many posters up on the wall advertising just how lovely Oxford is to live in, with its history and list of famous musicians that have come from the town, and all the movies that have been shot here over the years. Only that I'd heard of just one of the musicians, and none of the films listed.

My mum wanders off in search of a toilet, and we agree to meet back in ten minutes. That is enough time for me to do a lap of the square and find 'Square Books' – which itself has a sign in the window advertising the fact that it has recently been voted as 'Best Independent Book Store in the USA', and popping my head in briefly does indeed reveal a wonderful smell of books, and an old beautiful building where every nook, cranny, and alcove has artistically been designed to house thousands of books. It's charming.

> **1:57 PM Jul 15th**
> .... which would explain the numerous book shops. #oxfordms

'This is really nice, isn't it?' says my mum as we meet up a few minutes later back at the car. 'And not a Wal-Mart in sight!' I reply. (There is ... of course, a Wal-Mart a few miles west out of the town, but the small delightful square of downtown Oxford is fantastically cute, and chain-free.)

'I think I'm proper hungry though' I say, the delicious vanilla scoop from 'Fortunes Famous Ice Cream' that I have just picked up is filling a small hole, but is not a proper meal.

> **2:02 PM Jul 15th**
> local newspaper: 'The Daily Mississippian'. Try saying that after a few drinks.

> **2:03 PM Jul 15th**
> remember Marty McFly's home town in 1950's Back To Future? There ... that's Oxford MS for ya, totally unspoilt, brilliant

> **2:09 PM Jul 15th**
> ah .... and there's the British nod, tucked away in the corner of the square – that's right, it's a red phone box.

I get my mum to snap a picture of me outside the phone box, and then to fill our food needs we find an Abners Chicken down the street on the corner. We sit inside and at the next table over to us sits four distinct law enforcement types – what from I can see there is a local cop, a city police officer, the country Sheriff and a State Trooper all in their different identifying uniforms but all with guns in holsters on their belt, and they discuss who is getting promoted in light of the recent news that one of their colleagues is leaving to move out west. My mum and I discuss where our next stop is ... back up in Arkansas.

We do talk to the gas station owner on the way out of town. Mainly because he is clearly not a local as when he speaks to us it's with a Brummie accent. Yes – a Midlander here in the middle of Mississippi, now running a petrol station. I leave my mum talking to him with him telling her how much better life is here than in the UK, whilst *I* go to the toilet for once, and when I come back, I have to nudge my mum out of the door to stop her talking, wary that we have to move on and get to our next Tube stop.

2:35 PM Jul 15th
now departing Oxford. Please mind the doors.

6:02 PM Jul 15th
you are arriving at ... Victoria, Arkansas. Population, 59.

In the USA
Victoria, Arkansas
On the Tube map
Victoria (Victoria / District and Circle Lines)

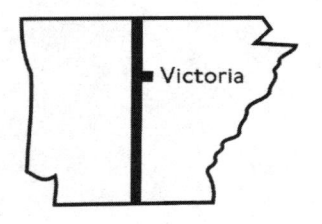

'I already love it, look!' I exclaim to mum as we pull off the road and into ... well, a sort of dusty dirty patch of non-road set back from the road. And in the middle of this all? An old steam train!

> **6:03 PM Jul 15th**
> and i've done it AGAIN. There is a rusty old train line here, with a rusty old steam train, i fookin love it.

Yup – I've done it again. Found a railway – of sorts. There has obviously once been a railway here, but now the only stretch of tracks that are left are those that the train and four wooden carriages that are behind it are standing on.

'A relic from yesterday?' asks my mum. 'Must be!' I say, excitedly snapping a picture of the train. 'If I sit on it, can you take my photo?'

It has a No.73 plate on the front of the boiler, but no name. A 'Railroad Crossing' sign has been preserved as well, Victoria it seems is a farming town. In the distance we can hear the hum of industrial machinery but there is no one about – no one to talk to. However, it isn't the kind of 'nothing here with no one to talk to' place, it is the 'nothing here but it's brilliant because there IS an old steam train!' kind of place.

We wander around for a few moments, and the only other thing of note I can find is the 'Welcome to..' Victoria sign, which also pronounces that the population is that of just 59 people.

> **6:05 PM Jul 15th**
> so it's a farm town, tractors, barns, grain silos .... or is it cotton. Cotton fields in all directions of the horizon.

I can't see any houses though – just large barns, grain mills, and huge warehouse type buildings from within which farm noises are emanating.

Back in the car, I open up my laptop to get online, and Google it. The only other one fact I find new is that it is named after a sister of the town's fonder – one Robert Wilson, a rather big name in these parts it would seem for founding a company of cotton plantations. Ah! Cotton Mills – is what those big silo-looking things are then.

My mum comes up to the car, camera in hand where she's been taken photos too. She snaps a picture of me sitting with my legs dangling out of the car with laptop on my lap.

'The car's a bit dirty' she notes, and I look – and indeed, I don't think I've washed the car since the start of the trip – have I? Err ... yes I have - just the once when passing back through Charleston. But now it is covered by a layer of dust with dried hard mud stuck to it in places.

'I've got an idea!' I say, grinning – recalling something I'd seen just down the road thirty seconds before we pulled up by the train. My mum gets into the car, and I drive back down the road from where we've just come, and slowly approach a damp spot in the road. 'Look!' I say, pointing, and to my right a large field of cotton that is slowly getting watered by an automated watering machine, a large frame spanning the fields, only... every time it gets to this end some of the water sprays out onto the road. We wait two minutes, and I see it coming – so I hop out the car with my small video camera and catch the moment a huge spray of water comes over the car, and then carries it on its way.

My mum winds her window down. 'We got wet!' she says. 'Yup, all we need now is a sponge and we're good to go!'

Victoria. A farming town. With a train. And almost a free car wash.

SAME NAME TOWNS TALLY

Perfect Small Town America
Preston

Something there and enjoyable
Plaistow, Gloucester, Kew Gardens, Harrow, South Kensington, Greenford, Liverpool, Temple, Oxford, Victoria

Something there but not that exciting to be honest
Putney, Amersham, Hampstead, Woodford, Brompton

Nothing there but somehow being in the middle of nowhere made it OK
Epping, Acton, Lancaster

Nothing there and not that exciting either. Oops.
Warwick, Wapping, Camden, Bond

We head back to the Interstate, and head north. We've enjoyed Victoria. I am glad my mum is with me for a good one, and it hasn't been a 'nothing' stop. We are in good moods. I put the radio on, and press a bit harder on the gas pedal.

> **6:45 PM Jul 15th**
> a bug just went SPLAT on the windscreen. It's the Men in Black opening sequence!

> **6:46 PM Jul 15th**
> and i'm making my mum listen to a God radio station, just as we pass an adult store. #nicelyjuxtaposed

Now, did I mention yet how cool my mum is? She's in touch with the twenty first century ... mostly. She gets online, she uses the Internet, she emails, she texts, she tweets[22] ... and best of all, she has not given up on her pop music either.

My mum has the original Beatles albums on vinyl (Ok, even though I've stolen them off of her), but a nice memory as the dark Missouri sky rolls

---

[22] Actually sometimes she calls me, I don't answer so she leaves me a voicemail. She then send me an email telling me the same that she called about, and then sends me a text to tell me that she tried calling me and has now sent me an email. And then she'll tweet me a little later on if I don't reply soon enough asking if she's seen her text message. I'm not making this up, this has actually happened.

in as evening approaches is the playing and singing of the Black Eyes Peas 'Boom Boom Pow!', as we speed up the Interstate.

Hang on … what? Evening? It didn't get dark this early yesterday. We haven't travelled so far have we that we've shifted enough for it to get dark already, surely? And yet it is dark. OK … getting *darker*. And then I realise why as a few spots of rain hit the windscreen … it's not evening drawing in, it's dark clouds drawing in. The weather is changing upon us.

Within a very short space of time the weather deteriorates really quickly, and from it being a pleasant drive, I have a slight pang of concern that it might be wiser to get off the road.

The sky then becomes *really* dark, and the rain is hitting so hard on the windscreen that even the fastest blade setting can't keep up … and I can see my mum starting to look a bit panicky too. It's time to get off. And just as I'm wondering where, I see to the side of the road ahead a very familiar arched glowing 'M', and never have I been more grateful to randomly find a McDonalds.

> **7:26 PM Jul 15th**
> holy shit! THUNDERSTORM! Drove right into it … Black sky, lightning, it's insane. We've pulled off, taking refuge.
>
> **7:27 PM Jul 15th**
> others in McDonald's saying there is a tornado … 15 miles to the south of us
>
> **7:59 PM Jul 15th**
> BOOM BOOM POW! Whoa! … horizontal forked lightning! That i have not seen before. At least the rain is washing the car tho.

We grab a coffee and hot chocolate each, but not food as I am really trying hard to not eat in a McDonald's. Ten minutes later though, and I've succumbed with a Big Mac in my hand – mainly because my mum offers to buy it for me. After half an hour when the worst of the weather has passed, we carry on.

> **8:45 PM Jul 15th**
> I-55 North. Three is a juggernaut completely blown over onto the median, cab crumpled. Fuck, scary. Cops only just arriving.
>
> **9:16 PM Jul 15th**
> made it to motel. safe & dry. we're in Sikeston, Missouri for the night. update map, blog and video comin' up.

It's only another half an hour under normal driving conditions to our next stop for the night, but I take it slowly because – well, everyone is taking it slowly. By the time we check in, and I plug in my laptop to check my email, I have people telling me (who've seen my tweets) the reason for the bad weather.

SEVERE WEATHER STATEMENT (NATIONAL WEATHER SERVICE MEMPHIS TN)

6:26 PM CDT WED JUL 15 2009

A SEVERE THUNDERSTORM WARNING REMAINS IN EFFECT UNTIL 645 PM CDT FOR SOUTHWESTERN LAKE, PEMISCOT AND SOUTHEASTERN DUNKLIN COUNTIES (DUNKLIN MO-PEMISCOT MO-LAKE TN)

NATIONAL WEATHER SERVICE DOPPLER RADAR CONTINUED TO INDICATE A SEVERE THUNDERSTORM PRODUCING NICKEL SIZE HAIL AND DAMAGING WINDS IN EXCESS OF 60 MPH. THIS STORM WAS LOCATED NEAR HAYTI, MOVING EAST AT 20 MPH

PRECAUTIONARY/PREPAREDNESS ACTIONS – IN ADDITION TO LARGE HAIL AND DAMAGING WINDS, CONTINUOUS CLOUD TO GROUND LIGHTNING IS OCCURRING WITH THIS STORM. MOVE INDOORS IMMEDIATELY!

LIGHTNING IS ONE OF NATURES NUMBER ONE KILLERS. REMEMBER; IF YOU CAN HEAR THUNDER – YOU ARE CLOSE ENOUGH TO BE STRUCK BY LIGHTNING.

Wow. Suddenly it feels like maybe we've had a lucky escape from something possibly quite treacherous – or at worst we are some unlikely extras in a real life version of 'Twister' or something, but apart from me being puzzled about how there can be MORE than one 'number one killers', I am mainly just pleased that we are alive really.

Day 30 – Thursday 16th July

Roll with it

'I think I've got a feeling I've lost inside
I think I'm gonna take me away and hide
I'm thinking things that I just can't abide
I know the roads on which your life will drive'

'Yes, all those are my transactions'

'Yes, yes that's right, I'm driving across America all summer using my credit card to fill up with petrol, so there will be more of this'

Pause.

'Ok, great – but this is the third time I'm calling you now because you've declined me and I've had to verify who I am, is there any actual way that it's not going to happen for a fourth time?'

Pause.

'OK, thanks', and I hang up.

There are to be no same-named-towns the following day, so instead en route to our next stop we take in some slightly odd attractions instead. First, we stop at Lamberts Café for a brunch which turns into lunch, and it's a place made famous for the fact that to serve you bread, they throw it at you from across the other side of the restaurant.

> **1:08 PM Jul 16th**
> at Lamberts Cafe, check out www.throwedrolls.com where they serve large portions of outrageously tasty food whilst throwing bread at you, natch.

> **1:14 PM Jul 16th**
> and the main wall is covered in HUNDREDS of license plates, oh look a New Hampshire one! #lamberts

Out of Missouri and into Kentucky via a road that makes me feel like I don't know where I am.

> **5:26 PM Jul 16th**
> eh? I've slipped back into KY. How'd that happen?

Someone, somewhere is making a terrible gag out of the fact that I have just typed 'slipped' and 'KY' in the same sentence. Oh yes that's right ... me.

We stop in Metropolis, Illinois which is not the town that the Superman film is named after specifically, rather though is the town that has taken on the mantle that this *will* now be a town about all things Superman – hard to avoid when you're standing next to a giant model of the man himself.

> **5:53 PM Jul 16th**
> i'm standing next to a giant 20' tall model of Superman. Yes, i'm in Metropolis, IL…

A friendly guy in the gas station earlier has told us that the tiny tip of Illinois that we are in is actually considered part of The South, but hitting the town of Metropolis would put us firmly in the North.

> **8:27 PM Jul 16th**
> is southern Illinois part of really pat of 'The South'? Where does the mason dixie line intercept?

> **9:25 PM Jul 16th**
> my mum's driving, north up I-57. we just went past a GIANT white cross that's almost 200 foot high, no kidding

As my mum drives, I do the coolest thing – book where we are staying tonight on my laptop using my 3G dongle, all in a matter of under a minute – as I find a KOA campground ahead in Terre Haute. I'm not sure how to pronounce Terre Haute, but I like the words and consider it would be a decent place to stay just based on its name.

We rock up, and are given our tent pitch and see that two pitches over is a much larger and much grander big blue tent that looks like it can house a whole family. Instead it contains just two people – what looks like a father and son, and as the father sees me looking over in their direction he smiles and shouts 'Good evening!' to us.

Ten minutes later, and we are tucking into hamburgers courtesy of that gentleman – *Tyler*, and his son, *Daniel* – who are making their way back west across the country to go home. Tyler has been out to New York for a job interview and has flown out – but has managed to take his son with him on the promise of a fun camping road-trip back across the country to California.

As the sun sets, we talk loads – tell them what we are doing, have a beer and really enjoy the moment of having nice company with complete strangers. After a couple of hours, everyone is tired though and it's time to turn in.

We thank Tyler again for the burgers, shout goodnight to his son who is now audibly playing a Star Wars video game from within the confines of their cheaper-than-mine and yet-so-much-bigger tent, and turn in for the night.

It has been a very pleasant evening – and what a lovely man.

~ ~ ~

Oh my god. What a FUCKING annoying man. How can this be?

> **3:15 AM Jul 17th**
> ffs! I have been woken up by the dude snoring in the NEXT TENT OVER to me. *that* is loud

It is – to be honest – my night from hell. I was expecting to have one at some point on the trip, because everyone has 'a longest night' and it turns out that this is to be mine. Firstly, I can't sleep because I am still scratching myself to bits. Both my mum's legs and mine are still red and bumpy from the bites from two days ago, and at one point, I sit up bitching, unfurl my penknife and using the pointy end of the cork-screw attachment, start rampantly scratching my right leg up and down VERY hard. I succeed in momentary relief, followed by streaks of blood where the corkscrew has gouged up chunks of skin out of my leg. But it feels good though – so I do it again, cutting deep down into my leg as I go. That's gonna scar, oops.

Secondly, Tyler snores. Yes – that's right, not my mum, but the nice burger-patty giving man is now snoring so loudly that we can now hear him from over 100 feet away, THAT'S A LONG DISTANCE PEOPLE! But in the dead of night, and the quietness of the Terre Haute campground, it's distinctly audible.

My moving and scratching obviously wakes my mum too. 'You okay?' 'No, you?' 'Your moving about woke me up', 'Sorry about that'. I decide to get out of the tent.

I walk over to campground shower block and have a mild shower. Then I dangle my rashed up legs in the shower stream, hit the tap to COLD and scratch them for ages as the soothing cold water runs over them ... that feels better again. So I dry myself, and not wanting to go back in the tent yet go and sit in the car.

Half an hour later I am undressed again, back in the shower with my flaming red legs with the cooold shower spraying onto them again, scratching like hell, and wondering – now at gone 3am – if I am actually going to get any sleep tonight.

Back at the tent, I can no longer hear Tyler snoring. I pity his son, but the wonder maybe if the kid has smothered him to death with his pillow. Who knows? Exhaustion is now creeping up on me, and I crawl back into the tent, desperately hoping that I will drift off to sleep before my legs flare up again and make me want to have a shower once more. I do, and the next thing I know it's the morning.

~ ~ ~

The next day is a long boring day of driving north. There are no same-name places to visit, and there aren't any attractions to visit either. It is a bit of a nothing day. My mum has somehow slept the night before whereas I haven't meaning that I make her do a chunk of driving again whilst I snooze in the passenger seat.

Snoozing in a car of course is not easy at the best of times. When you're 6' 3" like me it gets really tricky, especially when the seat belt has this nasty habit of cutting into the side of your lip when you head lolls to one side as you drool, and then BAM! My mum's heavy foot presses too hard on the gas pedal of Beverly's delicate Jeep which wakes me up at every intersection that we get to along the way.

The camping misery of the night before makes it an easy choice of what we are going to do tonight; we are going to stay in a hotel, so on the drive up with the Internet-dongle plugged into the laptop again, I book us in at the Days Inn in Lafayette, Indiana.

> **6:49 PM Jul 17th**
> we're in Lafayette IN for the night. i'm going to treat my mum to Crackerbarrel and show her a good time.

I do end up taking my mum to a Cracker Barrel though – a chain of 'Country style, home cooking restaurants' with a tacky gift shop attached to the side which I think my mum will like – she does. What we both like even more though is our server, who is unintentionally amusing.

'What reason did you come to Lafayette for!?'

Our server *Naomi*, is having a rather hard time trying to work out why we are here.

> **8:49 PM Jul 17th**
> our server in Lafayette IN – 'Why are you here? This is my hometown and i hate it'

I'm not making this up ... really this is what she says. With her short brown hair with curly bangs, and deeply rounded mesmerising brown eyes to match, Naomi is lovely and yet every time she speaks she give us yet another damning indictment about her home town and state.

> **9:01 PM Jul 17th**
> server: 'and don't stop in Gary, it's the crime capital of the states!' Me: 'really? I thought that was Detroit?'

It becomes a bit of a game ... every time she comes to serve us she has something bad to say about her hometown. We take our time eating, and as patronage thins out in the restaurant, she spends more and more time chatting to us, and before the evening is out, we know that she has a child, that the father has run off on her, that she lives in a horrible condo that she detests, and generally thinks that the whole of Lafayette is ghastly. So when she gets to asking me what I'm doing driving through her hometown, I try really hard to think of an alternative to 'Having the trip of a lifetime, and seeing more of your country than you'll ever do', because that wouldn't have been the best thing to say, would it? 'Umm, just ... heading for Chicago' is my meek reply. Naomi nods, and goes on to tell us about the drug problem in her hometown.

~ ~ ~

11:51 AM Jul 18th
i'm starting to agree with my server from last night: Lafayette – Could be better. A lot better.

Lafayette doesn't look that great come the morning either – industrious and it's a bit of a grey day to match. No magic Voodoo has taken place overnight, instead Naomi's words of 'Get out of here!' have resonated, and all I want to do this morning is hit the road as quickly as possible, and leave.

12:06 PM Jul 18th
i'm getting the hell out of Indiana ... via a Tube stop though

Actually, I think I'm about to be quite rude here. If you're American and/or especially from Indiana then you're not going to like what I write next, maybe skip this paragraph?

It's not massive spoiler to tell you now that by the end of this book, I make it round all 48 mainland states – I drive through, see, and experience them all – seeing what they have to offer and soaking up the environment around me as I am in them. And I have to say: Indiana is *dull*. Sorry, but it is. It has no National Parks, no great claim to fame, I think the most major 'attraction' or famous thing that you can attribute to it, is the Indy 500 car race in Indianapolis that takes place every year – except what do you do if you don't like speed car racing? Leave the state, I suspect.

Sorry, Indiana. But somewhere has to come last – and I think you're it.

That's not to say that Lafayette is all bad though, because something happens here this morning which I won't forget which really does cheer me up. My mum offers to drive as we set off and I am more than happy to let her do that. 'Can I put my iPod on too?' she asks which is fine by me too, so she does.

It isn't until about the fifth or sixth song in though (all of which I have enjoyed) that I realise that I am enjoying her mix of music. 'This is almost like listening to my iPod!' I joke. 'They're all my songs, how weird is that?' My mum gives me a funny look. 'They *are* all your songs' she says

'Don't you remember?', and suddenly a memory comes flooding back to me, and I *do* remember.

My mum had been out to visit me in Charleston last month – she thought it would be the last time she would see me before I went on my trip, and at that point no way do either of us think that she would come on the trip with me. And when she was with me for the few days visiting, she took advantage of the cheaper US prices and bought herself a new iPod Nano for her to take home to the UK – but before she leaves, I give her a copy of about 2,000 of *my* songs onto it, so that she has something to listen to on the flight home.

When she got home – she plugged it into her own computer, and synced it all up with her music, overwriting my music and she would be all set. Only – well, she'd not done that last bit.

'Hang on, but that was over a month ago! Did you not sync your iPod in all that time?'

'I never got round to it, I've been busy'.

Too. Many. Thoughts. Going through my head right now.

One, I am physically flinching over the fact that my OCD tendencies would never 'go a month' without syncing and setting up a new iPod, that would like, be the *first* thing and top of my to-do list when I'd have walked in the door (even before tea making, perhaps!) Two - actually never mind two - because something else is stirring in my head.

When I'd had my computer and iPod stolen in the break-in I'd lost all my music. ALL my music. It has all gone, several thousand tracks of it, and it was a daunting task thinking about getting all back again. But I don't have to ... because my mum has inadvertently kept a backup for me. YES!

That night I know I would check in at a hotel, I know I will plug my mum's iPod into my computer, and get a lot (not all, but a *lot*) of the tracks back that I have lost, but can now recover again. It is a beautiful moment, and I actually high-five my mum in the car as we drive along.

Lafayette, Indiana – My iPod recovery moment. Well done you.

Kingsbury next.

In the USA
Kingsbury, Indiana
On the Tube map
Kingsbury (Jubilee Line)

'Is that a train line I can see?' says my mum, as my SatNav informs me we are moments from arriving at Kingsbury, Indiana. 'Looks like it!' I say with a smile, and remind myself that I *really* need to make a list of which of the places completely by chance have had railways in them.

I turn off the highway, into the town of Kingsbury, and we find ourselves pulling up by a level crossing at 'Railroad Street', a certain giveaway of train activity. Overgrown bushes and an old building suggests that there might have at one time been a station here, but now it looks like many other railroads in America – it's a freight line only and there is no longer any passenger activity here.

There doesn't seem to be much town-folk activity either as we slowly drive around looking to see if there is a café that we can stop at, but all we find is an old battered sign indicating that a nearby white building is the Post Office (which is closed) a church, and what may have been a hardware store – but again with no human life present.

'So what do you do when there's nothing of interest to take a picture of?' asks my mum, and I think about a good answer, before realise that I don't have a good answer. It's not that there is nothing here, there is *something* here, but it's just rows of houses in just-about-looked-after streets with trees, but there is no hub-bub, no central location of activity going on, and I can see that we are going to struggle to find something else.

In ways, this is worse than when you turn up to a crossroads in the middle of nowhere and there really *is* nothing – here there is something, but … well it isn't anything interesting.

And then I remember what state we are in – Indiana, isn't it? Oh I'm sorry. I'm *genuinely* sorry if you're an Indianan reading this, but I realise that what feels to me like the most boring state on the trip so far has served up a totally bland and not-at-all-interesting town too.

After another lap of the backstreets where we see a man walking his dog in the pleasant afternoon sunshine, we go back to the railroad, to the level crossing and I take a picture of the road sign for 'Railroad' way, before I realise that I haven't even seen a sign saying 'Welcome to Kingsbury!', because ... well there isn't one.

We need to leave you behind Indiana.

We need people.

Activity and a bustling metropolis perhaps? It's time to head to *a much better place*.

> **3:55 PM Jul 18th**
> Chicago skyline on the horizon ... Sweet. I love this city.

We check into a hotel, and I get online and update the blog, along with some photos and everything else Underground : USA related in an online way. And yes – I then leave my mum's iPod copying over songs for an hour whilst she has a nap and I make some tea. Ghostbusters 2 is on the TV – nowhere near as good as the original movie.

I watch the progress bar in Windows copy the names of familiar songs over – flashing in front of my eyes as I get about 2,000 of my tunes back.

> **6:11PM Jul 18th**
> I HAVE THE MAJOROTY OF MY MUSIC BACK! Feels great. #thanksmum

> **7:08 PM Jul 18th**
> all hail the Park & Ride. We're on the train. Coming down the blue line on the L into the city #Chicago

> **8:12 PM Jul 18th**
> And tonight, i'm taking my mum to a Taco Bell for dinner. Yes i am that classy. #roadtripfood

We spend the evening downtown in Chicago, going to an Improv show and ride on the subway – that makes me happy. We eat Taco Bell across the road from the lit up Wrigley Stadium, and then go to an improv show at IO. After, we walk the streets soaking up the atmosphere. Dammit, I like Chicago.

~ ~ ~

On Sunday morning after a short lie in, we sit on the bonnet of the car and record my mum's thoughts of America and her trip this week. Well, what I do is set up the video camera and ask her this question, and I am hoping for an answer with some depth – perhaps her thoughts on the sights she has seen, people we have met or even something pertaining to society or the economy. Instead, her most telling line of the interview is when she says 'I've eaten a lot of bagels for breakfast'.

Thanks mum.

> **3:20 PM Jul 19th**
> Dropping my mum off at O'Hare airport #Chicago

3:28 PM Jul 19th
The drop-off area is called 'kiss & ride' – cute. #Chicago #ohare

3:36 PM Jul 19th
And suddenly, i'm all alone in Chicago

I've been to Chicago just once before in my life – last year, the previous summer I'd come up here on a one-way flight and then did a sixteen hour drive road trip drive back down to Charleston with a girl friend of mine.

I'd gone to improv shows, shopped, soaked up the tourist spots, travelled around on the 'L', and gotten very lucky with the weather the week that I was there – one of the hottest on record for the city it later transpired (as I perspired!).

I don't really remember my mum leaving. I really don't. I'm thinking back trying to remember the layout of the airport, or the way the one-way system worked to drop people off and I don't recall it. I can remember it for all the other people that came with me on the trip – but not for my mum. And I think I know why; it's because I'm not that sad that she is leaving.

I've been in America for the best part of four years now, and I'd only gone home five times in all of that time to make trips back and I have – of course – always gone to see my mum.

She's actually come out *four* times to see me – once for my wedding, once for a trip, once for a surprise visit where I bought her a ticket, and once where she wanted to come and see me before I went on my road trip.

As I'd dropped her off at Charleston airport on a previous occasion I remember that I had got sad. I cried, and then went back to the car and got on with my day. And here's why I'd got upset … because I wasn't sure when I would be seeing her again.

And yet when I dropped her off this time … I was much less sad, I was almost positively jubilant, because here's what the last week has taught me. You never know what's gonna be thrown at you in life next, which is a cliché but in this case oh so true.

I have no idea that my mum – just a month later – would appear in the hotel in New Orleans. When I drive in with J.J. knowing that I was there for a few nights, I have no idea that I would be driving *out* with my mum. And yet here she is – sharing with me a very exciting week of her life. How insanely brilliant is that?

And so sadness … because I think for the first time on trip, something is creeping across me – it may even be giving me some little goose bumps up my arms now as I type this – that it's perfectly OK to head out into the unknown sometimes, as not knowing what's going to happen, but dealing with it when it does can be the best experience ever – sure, bad things will happen, but good things will counter them too.

Life is basically a whole pile of bad things, mixed in with a whole pile of good things, and one would hope that on average, that you have more of the latter and less of the former. And my mum randomly coming out like that has added to my pile of good things. And if that can happen unexpectedly, then what other good things can suddenly come into my life? And that's why I am feeling very much OK about it.

I spend the evening catching up with some old improv friends from Charleston who are now here in the windy city – at Henry's house we drink – they smoke dope, I elect not to – we chat shit into the very small hours, and I eventually give Henry a ride home halfway across town to his abode.

'You can't say you've been to Chicago though until you've survived a winter here though', Henry tells me wisely. But I remember thinking also that there is something ... just *something* about this city that I like, and although I'm not really sure what it is, I tuck the *something* to the back of my head and log it with my brains background processor – I know that the reason why would pop up and present itself to me when it is ready.

> **11:39 PM Jul 19th**
> Well I like Chicago, same thing. I don't know why, but it just feels right. Love this city. #Chicago
>
> **11:40 PM Jul 19th**
> And the L just rumbled overhead on a bridge, all lit up. Pretty sight. #Chicago
>
> **11:41 PM Jul 19th**
> There's just a vibe about this city that i love, seriously. How does it do that?

I drive halfway back across town to the hotel. I zig-zag across its highways and intersections that break up the city at anything-but right angles, as the subway rumbles overhead, I roll down the window, turn down the volume on the radio and take a deep breath and soak up the city.

Now I'm not completely naïve – Chicago has its problems like any other big city, but I think it's fair to say that any urban density of this size is going to have its problems – it's impossible for it to be crime free, but if you just get a vibe about a certain place ... then you should just trust your instincts, and do with it, right? A bit like when you have a crush on someone.

> **12:22 PM Jul 20th**
> you know when you like a girl, because it just feels right ... you sort of can't put your finger on it ...

All I can remember for a while is that when talking about the great cities of America, then people would obviously rave about New York. If that person is slightly more laid back and 'West coast' tendencies then obviously they would rave about San Francisco being the place to be. But why has no one ever told me how great Chicago is before?

New York is fine, sure ... it's a hell of a big city. But on the few times that I'd been there it always seems *too* big and *too* overwhelming. And with Manhattan being laid out on the typical block-by-block system which Americans know and love, it kinda loses some of its edge, some of the charm that London has.

San Francisco is fine, but is so laid back that it feels too messy and unstructured to me.

But here is Chicago, with a population of almost 3 million, 9 million under the metropolitan 'Chicagoland' area *(which stretches into the states of Wisconsin and Indiana – not just Illinois)* and it just feels like the perfect big city size. It has the big sky scrapers of New York – but not too many – if that's what you want, it has the colourful characterful suburbs of San Fran - if that's your thing – it seems that there is a suburb and a district and a little part of that town to cater towards whatever your leaning is in life.

And as I drive down Ogen Avenue and stop at the Circle K for some bad (and by 'bad' I now mean 'good' because I am really starting to like it) gas station coffee, I realise that at some point in my life I would really like to come back and spend more time in Chicago.

Day 35 – Monday 20th July

I'm in a wide open space

*'I'm in a wide open space, I'm standing
I'm all alone and staring into space
It's always quiet thru' my ceiling
The roof comes in and crashes in a daze'*

10:58 AM Jul 20th
I've got a lonely week ahead, but that's ok. Geoff's road trip runs on Dunkin. Good morning Chicago, it's time to leave.

I know chains are bad. I know. I know, I know, I know, don't look at me like that —okay? But there's just something about Dunkin Donuts bacon breakfast bagel that just has everything in it *(you know, like – preservatives and saturated fats)* that just fires me up in the morning, and all fuelled up like the car- I'm ready to hit the road again.

12:29 PM Jul 20th
Leaving Chicago. This makes me sad, heading for my next 'stop' though, which i confess is a bit tenuous

1:30 PM Jul 20th
On I-90 west. They have service stations! Except it's called an 'Oasis', serving both carriageways connected by a bridge

Seriously, that's what it's called. Not a rest stop, not a service station, but an 'Oasis'. I *may* be tempted to play some Oasis right now on my iPod ... instead; images of palm trees and camels by a pool of water in the desert greet me ... in my mind, as I stop completely unnecessarily at the oasis to see what all the fuss is about. Not much, as it turns out – it is just a service station, so one sandwich and use of the facilities later and I am back on the road to same-named-stop number twenty seven.

3:55 PM Jul 20th
I'm in Rockford, Illinois and i'm headed for a museum that's called ...

3:58 PM Jul 20th
... Swiss Cottage. Actually, it's 'Tinker Swiss Cottage', but close enough. Told you it was tenuous.

In the USA
Tinker Swiss Cottage, Illinois
On the Tube map
Swiss Cottage (Jubilee Line)

'Tinker Swiss Cottage – Built 1865-1878. National Register of Historic Places' says the sign that greets me as I pull into the car park. The car park – which I note, seems to be mostly empty. Oh, that's not a good omen, surely it's not closed is it? It can't be! It's on a week day and it's in the afternoon. It *can't* be closed.

> **4:00 PM Jul 20th**
> Dawning Realisation : it's a Monday. it's a Museum. it's closed. Shit.
>
> *diamondgeezer*
> @geofftech 'The Museum is closed on Mondays.' Sound familiar?
>
> **4:04 PM Jul 20th**
> @diamondgeezer You'd think I'd learn after 'Britney Monday' (which is what we're now calling it), wouldn't you?

But as I jump out of the car and walk along the path to the main entrance, I suddenly remember something. Yes – it is a Monday. And in America – museums are closed on Mondays.[23]

So I'm left to wander about the ground and take photos. Yes, I am standing outside and looking up at a large Swiss-style cottage – which (as the Wikipedia entry tells me) 'Is built on a limestone bluff overlooking the Kent Creek'. I squeeze my way through some hedges where no footpath runs and indeed find a nice view overlooking the creek – *snap* – and take a photo.

I walk around the back of the house but can't get close enough to peer in any of the windows, but worry that that would just look a bit suspicious anyway.

I snap another picture of a sign, 'Museum Tours begin at the Visitor Center & Museum Store', but not on this Monday obviously.

---

[23] Actually, I later discovered that it's not just the USA – around the world and especially in Europe too, museums are often closed on a Monday.

Back in the car I fire up the 3G dongle to find that yes – it's open on Tuesdays to Sundays only, and that I am missing out on the history of how Robert Tinker built the impressive house (cottage), and the chance to see how 'The Museum and Gardens preserves, protects and interprets local history, heritage and culture to promote community and economic vitality'. But it really is closed.

What is really bugging me though is how I would classify this on the list of places that I have visited. I *have* been here, but I can't go in. And I can see that it is nice, but I can't experience it first-hand. Hmm. I think I'm going to have to have a 'closed' category on my list of same-name places, which is a bit odd because it makes it sound as if it's a town which is closed, when it isn't.

SAME NAME TOWNS TALLY

Perfect Small Town America
Preston

Something there and enjoyable
Plaistow, Gloucester, Kew Gardens, Harrow, South Kensington, Greenford, Liverpool, Temple, Oxford, Victoria

Something there but not that exciting to be honest
Putney, Amersham, Hampstead, Woodford, Brompton, Kingsbury

Nothing there but somehow being in the middle of nowhere made it OK
Epping, Acton, Lancaster

Nothing there, and not that exciting either. Oops.
Warwick, Wapping, Camden, Bond

Closed
Swiss Cottage

> **5:69 PM Jul 20th**
> What state am I in? You may ask yourself. 'Iowa' would be the answer, more virgin territory for me.

An hour later down the road I cross the state line into Iowa, as I head west along I-88, Western Illinois becomes eastern Iowa, and the sun reminds me by getting low in the sky across the expansive horizon that I am going to need a place to stay tonight – and I don't know where I am going yet.

> **6:00 PM Jul 20th**
> Iowa: it's a big wide open space. #mansun

But I've been all day on the road without a proper Wi-Fi moment, and there are emails to read and update maps for me to plot so I crack open the laptop and use the 3G dongle to locate the nearest chain-coffee-place (you know the one) where I can get some Wi-Fi for free instead and make myself happy.

What actually divides Illinois from Iowa is – yet again – the Mississippi and I appreciate that I have started to lose count the number of times that I have crossed it so far on the trip, and the city of Davenport presents itself to me – the third largest city in the state – with four liquid-crack outlets available to me – all nearby. This makes me happy, you can always judge the true size of a town by the number of Starbucks that are operating in it. Four is a good number.

I park up. I buy coffee. I open my laptop, started to type – but stop when I'm distracted by two girls – one in particular – who are sitting at the table across from me.

> **8:24 PM Jul 20th**
> just seen a girl who had a pierced chest ... BETWEEN her breasts, on the taut part of the cleavage. ouch. why would someone do that? #pain

> **9:21 PM Jul 20th**
> day 35, Progress Map, into Iowa! http://is.gd/1FLhR

I get my progress map done, catch up on all my email, and even read a lovely friendly tweet from the woman who obviously runs the Tinker

Swiss Cottage twitter account, who'd sent me a message saying 'Sorry you missed us! Come back tomorrow when we're open', and I tweet back to explain that I have already moved on.

I look up a place where I figure I can crash for the night – and head for the Iowa-80 truck stop, the largest truck stop in the whole of the America. Big parking lots, showers, places to sleep, food, 24 hour gas and even a dentist apparently.

I pack down my laptop and realise with dismay that I must have kicked the power cord out at some point – I've been running on battery for the last hour and there's almost no charge left – but that's ok, I know where I'm heading tonight and I'm unlikely to want to get online again at any point, as I am completely caught up in the online world.

> **11:58 PM Jul 20th**
> I'm at Iowa-80, the world's largest truck stop. It's lit up like Christmas!

> **12:01 AM Jul 21st**
> On the road paradise: shower, laundry, barber, library, dentist – even a chiropractor! 24 hrs/day! #iowa80

But annoyingly – the car park isn't as friendly as I'd hoped *because* it is all lit up. I'd hoped I might be able to have a shower and then kip down in my car in the corner of a parking lot somewhere, and in the morning, arise and use the facilities again.

So I do the one thing that I've been considering doing in an emergency, and whilst this isn't an emergency … yet, I think I'm going to have to go and do it. I'm going to go and find a Wal-Mart and park up there for the night and sleep in the car.

When I'd sat down and planned out the trip, I did of course do the sensible thing and budget it all out – work out how much of my savings I can spend, how often I should sleep in the tent, and how often I can afford to splash out on a motel. And right now, I am feeling like I've gone over the mark, and it is time to draw the purse strings back in and spend maybe a night or two sleeping *in the car* to save some money. All I have to do is shunt some stuff around, roll out the sleeping bag diagonally and I will fit in … just. All I need is a safe place to park the car and I am sorted. So where can I park in a secure area all night? In a Wal-Mart car park, that's where.

But it's 12.30 at night, it's late and I'm tired – I just want to find somewhere where I feel safe to sleep and soon. So back in the car I fire up the SatNav and type in 'WALMART' to find the nearest one. 'No results found!' comes the annoyingly cheerful response a few seconds later. Really? Nothing nearby at all? And then I remember ... and type in again 'WAL-MART' with a dash in the middle, and sure enough after a few seconds it finds one 19 miles and 31 minutes' drive away. I hit 'Fastest Route' and head off into the darkness of Iowan farming roads.

The fastest route ... really? Really? Because far from being a nice tarmac surface road as I hoped, I suddenly find myself bumping along in the darkness on very rough country farm roads. Going down these sorts of roads in Kansas in the daytime is fun, but suddenly I realise that this is the first time I've been on a rough road surface in the middle of the night, and my brain takes that moment to kick in and start to give me thoughts that I don't want, such as 'What if I get a flat tyre NOW?', 'What if something major in the engine FAILS!', and I am stuck – all alone – at night not knowing where I really am.

Because that's the problem with in-car SatNav systems. They're great at telling you where to go ... really, there are. But it makes you lazy, because you become over reliant on them, and you don't look at a map to know where you are, and you don't learn the route, or sometimes even look at where you're going – you just blindly and dumbly follow what it says and let it take you where it says it's going to take you and that's it.

Which is why when almost half an hour later, the SatNav announces that 'I have reached my destination', there isn't a light or house or anything to be seen along the two-lane road of Highway 61? Thanks, SatNav ... for taking me to the middle of nowhere.

I pull over onto a track which seems to lead up to a farm. I have a way round it ... and pull out my laptop and plug in my mobile Internet dongle. It's at this point that I remember that the laptop isn't fully charged, in fact ... shit! It's down to 12% power and instantly pops up with a message saying that I should save my work and/or plug into a power source soon. Yes, yes, yes! Just as soon as I've got the actual address of the nearest Wal-Mart.

I hop onto Sam's corporate website and click on the 'Store Locator' link. You can only search by ZIP Code[24] ... what? Well I don't know the bloody ZIP code, do I? So open up another webpage, Google the phrase 'What is the ZIP code for Davenport, Iowa' and then go back to the Walmart.com site with the numbers 52806 in my head,

It plots them all up on a little graph, and I see the nearest one to where I am ... stupid SatNav, it's obviously got the wrong address! But I am on the Wal-Mart site with the right address ... soon be sorted. It's at 3003

---

[24] Zone Improvement Program. What the Americans say instead of 'Postcodes'. Someone didn't believe me once when I told them that this is what is stood for, but it really does!

189

North Hwy 61, Muscatine, IA 52761 – and so I manually type that address into the SatNav.

The SatNav thinks about it …for all of, ooh 0.01 of a second before cheerfully announcing 'You have reached your destination'. WHAT THE FUCK!

Special message to Mr. Sam Walton – Please get onto your corporate store address database, and UPDATE THE ADDRESS with what it REALLY is for the Muscatine branch.

About thirty seconds later, and the laptop gives a gentle 'beep', and goes into standby mode, as the battery is now out of power. I sigh, and shut the lid and sling it back into my bag. I get out of the car to check where I am – yup, on a farm track, on the road side of Highway 61 in Iowa, presumably somewhere between Muscatine and Davenport.

The moon is out, the stars look beautiful, and the temperature is a little chilly. A huge semi-truck rumbles past, and the vibrations shake the car quietly, and I have a tiny moment of 'In a strange way, this is kinda fun…', not really knowing where I am, it being past 1am and I'm standing on a muddy farm truck in Iowa. A big wide open space.

Ok, so it isn't as desperate as it sounds. I am slightly worried by the fact that when I get back in the car and make the choice to head west to Muscatine, which I only then realise that the fuel gauge is just above the 'E', oh shit. This I really don't need.

I can't just sit here and do nothing though, so I get back on the road and drive on – nervously looking at the fuel gage and wondering if I'm going to reach a town soon.

I needn't worry, as literally in under ten minutes of driving – seven miles down the road – and (by my working) at 3200 Hwy 61 (and not 3003) the glowing yellow and blue of a 24 hour Wal-Mart SuperCenter looms into sight on my right hand side, and with glee I pull in and use the toilet. I size up the parking lot, spot where other trucks and cars are seemingly doing the same thing, and after humping a lot of my gear & crap from the back seats into the front, I roll out my sleeping bag in the back of the car at a diagonal angle so that I can stretch out properly, and finally bring my day to an end.

~ ~ ~

The rain starts at about 6am, thumping down in hard TAP TAP TAP heavy droplets on the roof of the car. Plugging my iPod in and playing some soothing music makes it bearable for a bit longer, but about 07.30, I relent, and get up. To the toilets again – inside Wal-Mart – where I swear the woman on the cash register gives me a funny look as if to say 'You were here at 2am, weren't you?', but I am at my grumpiest when I am within the first half an hour of waking up, and so like the miserable git I am, I don't even raise the faintest of smiles at her.

Poptarts and Nutrigrain bars are all that Uncle Sam has to offer in the way of breakfast, so I instead headed off in search of fuel – for me and the car – at the first gas station that I can find instead. They have Poptarts, Nutrigrain AND donuts, as well as the obligatory gas station coffee. #win

> **9:04 AM Jul 21st**
> Stopped at a gas station who are having a 'Customer appreciation day' this Fri. That is a bizarre concept to me

I dash with my coffee in my lid-less cup back to the car as it is still raining – getting heavier I think – and take a big welcoming steamy sip as the moistness hit my lips and floods down into my gullet bringing warmth rays of sunshine to an otherwise dreary wet day.

> **11:07 AM Jul 21st**
> Incidentally, the gas station was called 'Kum and Go'. I kid you not. #iowa

I wish I can tell you that Tuesday July 21st is a lovely, dry sunny day where I see lots of Iowa'n delights – but alas, it rains all day. I come off Highway 61, onto the intriguingly named 'X61' road instead – which purports itself in the map book as a 'scenic' route ... but with the constant whine of the windscreen wipers back and forth, and a dull grey Mississippi river to my left being pelted by rain, I don't observe anything scenic, and nothing inspires me to get out and get my camera wet and take any photos of the damp greyness.

> **11:17 AM Jul 21st**
> i'm on Us Hwy 'X61'. I think there's a London bus route with that number

South through Burlington, and I am soon out of Iowa and back into Missouri and the town of Quincy (I later catch myself humming the TV theme tune to Quincy without realising at first that I'm doing it – I love how the brain works like that), and it rains as I follow the river somewhere.

> **2:37 PM Jul 21st**
> back in Missouri. Hwy 61 south. It's STILL raining.

Only because I'm bored with going South so much do I turn to my right and head west a little instead.

Macon looks pretty, and I do stop to take photos – but again, rain drops on your expensive replacement camera don't inspire you to stick around for too long, and having now been on non-Interstate for the whole day, I head south to the I-70 to get some speed on and see how far west I can head and make by the end of the day.

> **12:47 PM Jul 21st**
> ok, it's been raining all day, i could do with the weather letting up a little, please

It's brilliant being British sometimes, we're *really good* at complaining about shitty weather.

I stop in Colombia for an hour to get online – and look up where I need to be next. The town of Red Bridge – a suburb of Kansas City – I can be at tomorrow morning if I make a bit more progress today, so I book myself in at a campground, put my foot down and within two hours make it to Oak Grove to the east of Kansas city. The best bit? On the way there, the weather finally improves.

> **6:15 PM Jul 21st**
> after eight hours, i think it's finally stopped raining

There's actually an urban myth that the weather 'divides' in America at the I70 – a major Interstate that runs from West to East across the country. And that if the weather is shitty to the north of it, then all you've got to do is come down to below it – the south and the weather will improve. On the slight south-side of the I-70, the weather really does improve. Myth? No – hard solid fact as far as I'm concerned.

The campground is nice, and it is also a little surreal. After the rain and miserable weather all day it feels as if it can't possibly be the same day I am in. It's as if I've gone to sleep and woken up on a new day and not remembered it. I can't believe it is also still light … and sunny, as if the day should be over by now, but it isn't – there is still a couple of hours of daylight to go and it is nice and bright. I set up my tent, nod at the guy a couple of pitches over setting up his tent – a biker dude with a big beard, tattoos and bandana – he looks scary, but I end up having the nicest and politest conversation with him that you can imagine possible, and he invites me to stay with him when I'm passing through Texas later on.

> **8:38 PM Jul 21st**
> The guy in the tent pitch next to me is called 'Bubba'. brilliant, i have never actually MET someone called Bubba, until now, tick!

> **10:52 PM Jul 21st**
> Day 36 progress map, on the outskirts of Kansas City, MO for the night: http://is.gd/1GSP0

The evening eventually does draw in though, and I obviously end up heading for the light and power source of the KOA launderette to get some internet time. I do everything online that I need to and have a chance too to make a couple of calls to people as well. Things feel nice. I am relaxed. I drink some tea out on what counts for a porch and listen to the crickets chirping away in the distance bushes.

Two girls – teenagers – walk past me on their way back to their tent. They point at me and snigger, and I realise that they are laughing at the miner-style head lamp that I wear for when putting the tent up in the dark, only I'd put it on an hour ago when it has got dark just to help me walk around the campground, and haven't taken it off since, but I don't mind. I smile.

Today has been a good day and they can laugh at me all they want to. I am in the heart of America on an epic tour – surviving - and they cannot bring me down.

And for some reason I have a feeling brewing deep down inside of me that tomorrow is somehow going to be rather brilliant …

Day 37 – Wednesday 22nd July

The White City

*'Oh sweet city of my dreams, of speed and skill and schemes
Like Atlantis you just disappeared from view
and the hare upon the wire, has been burnt upon your pyre'*

09:51 AM Jul 22nd
the sun is out. the sky is blue. Kansas awaits, but first i've got to nip to the loo ... (and no, it's not raining in my heart).

I can't explain it, but some days you just wake up and have a feeling that everything is going to be brilliant – and this is one of those days. I fetch some water from the tap that I have now located in the daylight that eluded me last night, and boil it up to make some tea whilst I pack down my tent.

I look for Bubba because his bike is still here even though he is all packed up, but he isn't about. The showers at the KOA are probably the cleanest and newest ones that I have seen so far on the whole trip, and so after I scrub myself clean, I wash myself all over again and even my hair too. And shave. *And* deodorise - it is that kind of a day, I feel wonderful.

My tea is downed, but I have nothing to eat – yet I recall a Waffle House right by the exit where I'd exited the night before. It's time to go and eat.

10:24 PM Jul 22nd
i'm in a waffle house, Kansas, and onto my 3rd coffee refill.

Jenny, her sister Janet and their friend Joanne (Yes, the three J's, if only J.J. were here!) are hanging off my every word. Well, in-between serving other customers they are, and they keep coming back to me to refill my coffee cup and ask me questions about England. In return I ask polite questions about one of them who is quite clearly expecting, and tell them how Missouri is turning out to be one of my favourite states of the trip so far.

I sit and talk to them for long enough to get hungry again, and drink too much coffee whilst I also read my book, but two 'Tube stops' need to be done today and so it's time to get going again.

11:10 AM Jul 22nd
Thank you for travelling Underground : USA. this morning, your Missouri stop is . . .

I leave the Waffle House and turn on the car satellite radio. It instantly starts playing one of my favourite songs of all time. Brilliant! I turn out onto the road, sing along, and immediately into a gas station to fill up and note with glee that the price of gas is just $2.24 a gallon. Also brilliant! That's the cheapest Gas I have found on the trip so far.[25]

11:14 AM Jul 22nd
. . . Red Bridge. A suburb of Kansas City, MO. Houses, park, fire station. Pretty.

In the USA
Red Bridge, Missouri
On the Tube map
Redbridge (Central Line)

To be honest, Red Bridge isn't really a town, more of a residential district as I had suspected, but **placenames.com** has told me that it is a place, and a place it is. And to be even more honest, it is really just a suburb of Kansas City. Actually, it is *really* a suburb of South Kansas City.

Still, I find myself on East Red Bridge road, which is mainly a shopping centre at a crossroads with lots of nice suburban streets leading off of it with pleasant houses. There is a Doctor's surgery, an animal clinic, a beauty salon, a pizza place and of course the ubiquitous CVS pharmacy which is just like seeing a Boots in every town centre back home in England.

I park up and wander around the shopping centre for ten minutes, and in a moment in which I shock myself, I'm not even drawn into the Starbucks as I've drunk far too much coffee at breakfast this morning, and I am in danger of coffee starting to seep out of my ears, and so I give it a miss.

I walk around, and there is an electronic store, and an ice-cream parlour, and a phone shop, and you know ... just all the normal average standard stuff which doesn't do much to excite me. There is nothing wrong with it, there is just nothing special about it, and it isn't inspiring me to talk to anyone or *do* anything here. All it is really making me want to do is to leave and go straight onto the next place which for some reason deep down inside of me I feel will be a lot more interesting but I can't say why.

---

[25] And would turn out to be the cheapest I would pay on the whole trip. Hats off to Missouri

I take a final picture of 'Welcome to Red Bridge Shopping Center!' on my way out of the car park, programme my SatNav for White City in Kansas, slam the gear into drive and press down on the gas pedal.

> **1:37 PM Jul 22nd**
> And I'm into Kansas ... Dorothy.

Shortly after getting onto the westbound I-70 there are signs that further down the road there is a turnpike. I have flashbacks to the north east and the whole of New England where you seemingly can't go anywhere without being charged a toll. It's a little bit of a rude interruption to discover that out here in 'rural' Kansas, they also have turnpikes.

Still, at the least the road signs are making me smile.

> **2:04 PM Jul 22nd**
> Kansas roadside sign: 'Beef! It's what's for dinner!'

> **2:05 PM Jul 22nd**
> Kansas in 2 : Cow Farming.

> **5:01 PM Jul 22nd**
> Graffiti on side of barn: 'No God ... no peace. Know God ... know peace'. #Kansas

The sun is out, the tunes are pumping on my iPod and Radio, and I am aware that there is a lot of steering wheel tapping going on.

As I sit and write this now, it's sort of hard now to look back and think about *why* I knew I was going to enjoy this day so much, or how fantastic White City was going to be ... but in my head I somehow knew in advance that this is what was going to happen.

Now I *could* have just headed directly west on the I-70 and turned due south when I get to the nearest turn off for White City, but where's the fun in that? So instead, soon after Topeka I turn off and then programme the SatNav to take the *shortest* route to get there, and definitely *do not* use any major highway or Interstate roads to get there. And boy does it do it!

After about a minute of churning away in which you can almost hear the electronic-elves inside do their merry dance of computation, it picks a route which turns right, then left, then right, then left, then right. You get the idea – yes? And it is then that I realise and remember all at the same time, that I am in the land of square roads.

The simplest way for me to explain this is for you to go to Google Maps *right now* and type in 'White City KS', and go to it. Then, zoom out a little bit … and you'll see this beautiful little network of a road grid where everything is perfectly laid out in a north/south and east/west configuration.

There's also the joke along the lines of 'How do you confuse a farmer from the Mid-West?' 'Just put him in a European city and tell him to head north'. Because the historic cities that grew over time shaped around mountains and rivers that take twists and turns don't run in straight lines for any long distances at all – unlike here where everything is perfectly straight in the four compass points.

I also soon realise that I don't have to follow the SatNav's instructions that closely either. As long as I turn right and travel west a bit, and then turn left and head south for a bit, I will eventually get there, and so I do that … sometimes going just one 'block' sometimes going three or four, before turning and driving through farmland and trees and beautiful green countryside for miles on end.

> **5:19 PM Jul 22nd**
> Kansas: middle of nowhere farmland brilliance. I am LOVING IT! haven't seen another car/person for the past hour

> **5:32 PM Jul 22nd**
> So do I want to go down a road that 'May be unsuitable for large vehicles'. Hell YEAH I do!

I take a photo of this sign – it has bullet holes in it. I stop and listen to the world and the earth turn … all I can hear is the wind and wildlife in the trees. I look across the fields with animals in the distance and a bee buzzes past me. The world at this moment seems impeccable and picture-perfect.

As I approach the outskirts of White City, I keep an eye out for the 'Welcome to…' sign, as I know there is something that I want to do – I want to get a shot of me driving past it in my car, which of course is tricky because there is just the one of me.

This means that when I see the sign, I slow up and stop by it, and set up my video camera on the tripod with the sign in the foreground, and the road in the background. Then, I hop back into the car and drive off leaving the camera in record mode by the roadside whilst I disappear into the distance.

Two other cars do pass – one in each direction – whilst all this is going on, and maybe… maybe they see the video camera and think 'What on earth?', who knows. It isn't stolen, I get my shot, check that it's OK and drive down into the town of White City proper.

In the USA
White City, Kansas
On the Tube map
White City (Central Line)

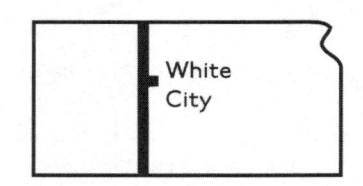

> **6:06 PM Jul 22nd**
> White City, KA : founded in 1871 by English settlers, AND there is a trainline, brilliant!

It takes me all of five seconds to realise that this is it. The feeling that I had when I work up this morning was a premonition coming to fruition – I have hit the jackpot. The goldmine. This is going to be even better than Preston. This is going to be the perfect town.

White City *is* perfect. It has just one main road – MacKenzie Street passing through it, which is cobbled, wide and has a lot of building set back on the sides. From what I can see it has one bar, one small grocery store, one post office, one church – and ah! A liquor store.

To this day I have no idea why I go inside the liquor store first as I'm not in any way after buying an alcoholic drink – I think I just want to go and have a look. Inside I nod a 'Hello!' to the woman behind the counter 'Hello!' she says very friendly back and she instantly knows that I am from out of town by my accent.

'Just passing through?' she asks 'Yup, just gonna get something to eat and drink but liked the look of your store!' I say.

'You'll want the bar down the street then!'' she says, and she comes outside with me to point me in the right direction.

An hour later, and I am having a very enjoyable time in the local bar. It has gone from a table of farmers sitting round a circular table wondering who the hell I am, to two girls – who I later find out are mother and daughter – being the ones to come up and talk to me to find out who I am. When I explain I am from London, and there is a White City there too, it opens the floodgates and soon I have a crowd of people coming up wanting to talk to me.

It is odd though, for about an hour random people keep coming up and talking to me 'Hey Jo! This fella here is from White City in England!' someone would shout when someone new comes into the bar and I'd talk to them for a few minutes and then they would leave me in peace. But after an hour it feels like everyone has had their turn and no one else is going to talk to me. I do get the girl that has first come up to me though to sign my t-shirt.

Back outside in the wide street I go for a wander, just loving how rural and homely it feels – a sense of proper community – and as I do so, stumble back upon the lady from the liquor store. This time she introduces herself to me as *Roxanne* and we sit outside the front of her store on the bench chatting away.

As we do this, a guy that she says 'Hey Brad!' to, wanders up walking his dog and he stops to talk to us and I have an idea.

Being by myself on certain parts of the trip makes it really hard to shoot video with *me* in it, but here is an opportunity where I can do that. I ask Brad if he would mind shooting video, and his eyes light up – 'No problem!' he says, but he ties up his dog first.

And for the next twenty delightful minutes, I sit with Roxanne outside her shop – The Moonlight Liquor store, and talk about life in small-town America.

'It seems like it's a real community here' I half ask and half tell her.

'Oh it is, it sure is' she replies. 'There are about 550 people in the town today – it's got a real colourful history – It's a rural farming community, it's the entrance for the foothills of this state – and it's a rodeo area. There are a lot of horses, cattle drivers and cowboys here!'

'It's been a rearing community from the inception. I bought an old mansion that divided into four houses in the 1930's from Mr. Bingham, who was involved in the railroad when it passed through here. He had one daughter, his wife and daughter died so the so in law divided up the houses and sold them.'

'The trains don't stop though – they mainly carry automobiles and grain. They no longer go coast to coast though; they mainly go between Newton and Kansas City.'

We chatted so pleasantly for such a long time, that I almost forgot the most important thing that I want to ask her.

'What are the best things, and then the worst things about being in a small town like this?'

She doesn't have to think at all, and comes straight out with the answer.

'Well personally for me the best thing is knowing that people can be very comforting to you in rough periods of times in your life, and come to your house to help you. Even on a good day people will just wave 'hello' at each other all the time – that's the best.'

'Along with sitting out in your backyard at night in front of a roaring fire and looking up at the stars – see the sky very clearly. Walking down a country road and knowing you're not going to be accosted. Forgetting to lock your doors and knowing that you're safe as there's very little crime'.

It is sounding more and more appealing.

'But it's not a way of life that I would try to sell to everyone. But when you're at my stage of life, just living close to nature is healthy and comforting', and at this point someone drives down the street, toots their horn and Roxanne looks up mid-sentence and does indeed wave to someone passing by.

'The worst? Is the gossiping. I guess some people's lives are dull and boring that they have to get involved in yours to feel a part of something. But I'm one of the lucky ones, and I don't get involved in that. People come to my store and tell me things, but I don't tell them anything back! Moonlight is a place where everyone comes and are decent human beings'

We chat a little more, and I get it all on video and then hang around to play with the dog and take some more photos. It suddenly goes from me being a new person in town – the focus of attention – to suddenly being a temporary member of the town, and other people having conversations around me, and I suddenly feel accepted. OK with Roxanne – OK with everyone else.

I snap a few more pictures before realise that I should push on. I need to make some mileage tonight to get me in touching distance of where I want to be tomorrow. I say goodbye to Roxanne, to Brad to some of the others that are now hanging around, and with a wave from my wound-down window, depart White City.

> **8:12 PM Jul 22nd**
> I did it. I found it. I found perfect America. That's going to be very hard to beat. #whitecity

So I found it. At my twenty-eighth attempt. Preston – I give you – was good, but it was just one delightful old building amongst an average town, so White City trumps it as the *entire* town is delightful.

To this day when people say 'What was best same named place you found?', then 'White City, Kansas' is the immediate answer without any hesitation. It's time to update my list, and put it at No.1 on my 'same name' list of places.

SAME NAME TOWNS TALLY

Perfect Small Town America
White City, Preston

Something there and enjoyable
Plaistow, Gloucester, Kew Gardens, Harrow, South Kensington, Greenford, Liverpool, Temple, Oxford, Victoria

Something there but not that exciting to be honest
Putney, Amersham, Hampstead, Woodford, Brompton, Kingsbury, Redbridge

Nothing there but somehow being in the middle of nowhere made it OK
Epping, Acton, Lancaster

Nothing there, and not that exciting either. Oops.
Warwick, Wapping, Camden, Bond

Closed
Swiss Cottage

As I head out of the town that I don't want to leave, I check my watch – it's almost 9pm, but I have been deceived as it is still perfectly light in the sky, and I record some shots of me talking into the camera down by where the railroad crosses the main road of the town. I am hoping that a train might come along as I do it, but alas ... no such luck.

I look at the map, and know that I have to head north … but how far I go depends on how tired I am as the evening draws in.

I turn the corner out of White City and immediately am confronted with the lovely sight of some abandoned vehicles, and something that I have been looking for since the start of the trip … an abandoned school bus. Wait for it … *two* abandoned school buses. White City, can you *be* any better to me? No I don't think so either.

I snap with glee the rusty yellow frames of the buses with broken glass and the twisty twines of plants that are slowly crawling up the inside as nature reclaims their structures, and wonder again how long they have been there. I stick my head inside the back and try to imagine the screams of children, lunches in a box on their way to lessons. Now silent, in a field, a cow poking its head over the fence looking solemnly at me.

The road north is US Highway 77, and as I venture on, the SatNav increasing in its latitudinal figures, the sun starts to set. Somewhere between Milford and Riley I stop the car by the side of the road, dazzled by the awesome colour display coming down over the horizon and snap away with my camera. I put it on a slow exposure to capture as much of the dark night colour as possible, and quite by chance get a truck passing through the frame of the shot, its headlights leaving streaks across the digital exposure as the sunset behind it. I am happy. I smile. My day *cannot have been* any better – it feels like the best day of the trip so far, and I push on, encouraged by the beauty of the skies.

Through Randolp and Waterville I drive. I check in with Katie on the phone to let her know that I am doing quite well thank-you-very-much by myself, and that I may just have found the most perfect little same-named-town in the whole of America.

> **11:01 PM Jul 22nd**
> Back in the land of phone reception. White City was /perfect/. I think i may have fallen in love with Kansas a little

I stop at a Casey's gas & store – they're all over the Midwest – for a pack of Oreos and obviously a gas station coffee.

Somewhere beyond Hanover and before Odell I cross the state line in the darkness and say a little sad 'goodbye' to Kansas and 'hello' to Nebraska. The dark road in front of me is lit up by the beams of light. I check the time … just gone 1am in the morning and my plan of hopefully making it to the large city of Lincoln is looking unlikely – I am just getting too tired, and I don't know where I am going to stay.

Beatrice has the answer … a tiny little unassuming town which suddenly appears out of nowhere, and on the outskirts? Another Wal-Mart. It has to be done. It's so late now and I am so tired that it's not going to be hard to fall asleep for another night in the back of the car, so I pull in ... and as I had done two night ago in Iowa, use the toilet of the Sam-Store before I head back out to the car to move stuff from the back seat to the front seat so that I can settle in for the night.

I still feel a bit odd about sleeping in the car in the parking lot of a Wal-Mart. I mean ... is it some way illegal? Or just frowned upon by the Wal-Mart people? Supposing some nosey security guard comes wandering round with a torch at 4am in the morning, and starts looking at all the cars parked making sure that they are OK, and shines it in on me curled up in my sleeping bag?

I can't actually curl up *in* my sleeping bag though, until I've moved all the stuff around to the back seat. Just as I've done two nights ago, I have to go through the chore of transferring all my stuff that is in the back of the car onto the front seats so that I have space to stretch out in the back, and here's where the trouble starts.

I'm just shutting the front driver's door having moved the last of the stuff when I hear two people approach from around the front of the store. I've parked the car down the side of the Wal-Mart – out of the way from where regular shoppers may park, and away from the bright lights ... and into the dimly lit area of the place where the staff obviously park their cars ... and the two members of Wal-Mart staff who are now rapidly approaching.

I just get back inside the back door of the car and quietly shut the door. And here is the weird thing – I am stuck. I can't unfurl my sleeping bag because it would cause noise and movement in the back of the car, it would rock about, and the two people would obviously think 'What's going on in the back of that car over there?' and go and have a look. And so I don't move. I sit perfectly still. They may just be coming out to their car to get something and then be on their way, and then I can make all the noise and motion that I want to settle down. Except ... that's not what happens.

What happens is that they are on a cigarette break. And they've come out to here to lean against it and chat. The car – their car – *that is right next to mine.*

So imagine the ridiculous situation ... I'm sat, hunched up hidden from view behind the darkened windows just a few feet away from two Wal-Mart workers having their cigarette break at 1am in the morning. All I want to do it take my trousers off, unroll my sleeping bag and go to sleep.

Instead for the next fifteen minutes, I have to sit perfectly still and can't help but hear every word of their conversation including the horse race they are going to next week, their colleague James that they don't like working with, and of course ... the bloody weather. And I thought that it's just us British that do that.

At one point, they even comment on the car – my car – next to them, and how the front seat is crammed full of stuff – including the driver's seat where stuff is piled up behind the steering wheel. 'Who's car is that?' says one of them 'And why's all the stuff backed up behind the wheel?', and I'm silently praying that they don't get too inquisitive and peer in through the front window and see me cowering in the back.

It's a bizarre situation, and I of course realise that if I've not moved at the beginning then that might have been better. But having sat here quietly not moving for ten minutes, all I can do is still quietly some more and sweat it out and wait for them to finish.

Eventually – maybe even after they've had two cigarettes, they finish. Stub them out on the ground, and walk back to work. And finally, with pins & needles setting into my legs from the awkward position I've been sitting in cramped in the back of the car, I am able to sort out the rest of my stuff, climb into my sleeping bag, and get as comfortable as I can to settle down for the night.

Day 38 – Thursday 23rd July

Escape

'Couldn't escape if I wanted to, knowing my fate is to be with you,
Finally facing my Waterloo'

Hello, Nebraska. You look beautiful today.

> **9:18 AM Jul 23rd**
> Sitting in a Starbucks in Lincoln, Nebraska. it's a bit chilly this morning. and i was on the road before 7am …

Now I am *very* aware that as you're reading this, you're probably thinking something along the lines of … 'But Geoff … it seems to us that you spend more time visiting Starbucks than you do visiting same-named-places whilst on your trip. Did you?' And you'd have a point … I *do* go to a lot of Starbucks, for one very good reason. Not that I like their coffee (I mean, it's OK to drink), not that it's always fun to have banter with the Baristas … but *because they have free wireless*. Well – they do for me anyway, as I have a Starbucks gold card which gets me two free hours a day – which, if you're on a tech-savvy road trip where using Twitter and Google maps and blogging and uploading video is part of the whole trip, then you need to get online every day – hence, frequent trips to the liquid crack co. of Seattle.[26]

> **9:27 AM Jul 23rd**
> Day 37 Progress Map: http://is.gd/1ITdB Stayed the night in town called Beatrice, Nebraska. Now heading north again

Hence, my Day 37 progress map is posted from the P Street branch of Starbucks in Lincoln, Nebraska where a delightfully charming old man who can't have been a day under 90 years old holds the door open *for me* as I carry my laptop, camera and video camera that I've brought in with me to upload stuff with whilst I have my morning coffee. I didn't know it then … but Nebraska is full of nice old men.

Hang on a sec – I need to recap in case you thought I mis-typed a word back there. 'P Street' I heard you saying back there – 'What is that Geoff – Pavilion Street, Peter Street, Percival Street? You've forgotten to type in the rest of the word beginning with 'P'! … Ah – except that I haven't –

---

[26] I once saw a car bumper sticker back in Charleston that read 'Starbucks – They might as well call it liquid crack'

because all the horizontal streets in Lincoln from bottom to top are labelled by a letter. Yup, from A Street through to U Street (Their local map is even called the 'A to U' and not the 'A to Z') – except that it misses out 'I Street' for some reason, perhaps because it looks too much like the number '1' ? Who knows, but it's not very imaginative on the road naming front, is it?

Lincoln though, is a classic man made grid city system, which are everywhere in Central America. No wonder the poor American tourists get confused when they come to London and get confronted with those tiny twisty turning roads and little streets which are created and evolved over time rather than someone just – BAM! Creating a city in perfect alignment.

> **12:48 PM Jul 23rd**
> Nebraska in three : Horizontal traffic lights

Oh, and if you want to know about the west-to-east count too, well yes… they are all numbered, running from 1st street in the far west of Lincoln all the way through to to 202nd Street, so far east out of Lincoln that it is basically the border road with the first town that you reach – Eagle – when heading out of the city.

Anyway, I digress. We are we? Oh that's right – Starbucks on the corner of P and 12th. I feel like I am in a human game of Battleships.

Not for long though, as I have a same-named town to get to just north of Lincoln.

> **11:03 AM Jul 23rd**
> So tell me tweeters. Where did Napoleon surrender? I bet it wasn't a tiny town in Nebraska … was it?

I zig-zag my way out of town, except … I'm not sure that's the right phrase. A zig-zag line to me, is one that runs at 45 for degrees for a bit, and then at 135 degrees for a bit. It's like lots of 'Z's knocked over on their side as if they'd been in a domino chain and then squashed together.

What *I* am doing is a lot of letter 'L's – err… also knocked on their side by going at 0 degrees, then 90. So I travel due north for a block then due east, then due north. Then head east again … just because I can. I get all the way to U Street and 26th before hitting a proper named road (Vine Street, which instantly makes me think of Monopoly) and then onto Interstate 80, for an hour's drive … for it is time to meet my Waterloo.

Yup … Nebraska's Tube-name-stop is the 450 person populated town of Waterloo. I play Abba on repeated loop about … ooh … six or seven times in a row before even I get bored with the song and tune in to a local radio station instead.

As I pull off the main highway and down into the town I suddenly appreciate how hot it is, and I do that instinctive British thing of winding the window down to get some air in ... but all that actually does is pump some ninety-degree heat into the car. I look up at the temperature gauge to see that it is actually registering 93F[27], and at the *exact* moment it flicks over onto 94[28].

My arrival has just made things a little hotter, it would seem.

In the USA
Waterloo, Nebraska
On the Tube map
Waterloo
(Northern, Bakerloo and Jubilee Lines)

1:06 PM Jul 23rd
More small(ish) town America: Waterloo, Nebraska. It doesn't look as cute as White City, but it's not bad.

1:07 PM Jul 23rd
Oh. And it has a railroad/way. Again – unplanned. Now to sit and wait for a half-mile freight to come rattling through...

I drive up and down all of three of the main roads in the small town – also intersected by three level crossings. The one in the middle which has the local store, bar and eatery called 'The Depot' – decorated with train paraphernalia catches my eye.

But there is no one about ... the streets are strangely empty, and the bar closed and I want to just *meet* someone, find someone local to talk to about the town, so I drive a little further afield, and on the road leading south east out of the town, see some life in the form of a convenience store and some trucks and cars parked up outside – other customers, doing what I am doing – buying drinks on this very hot day.

---

[27] 33 degrees C

[28] 34 degrees C

And that's where I meet *Donald* ... as I come out of the store, I sit on the kerbside of the parking lot and open up my atlas whilst swigging my drink he comes walking slowly out towards his car – wearing a cap, as all good old American men do and nods a 'hello' to me. I smile politely and nod back, knowing that doing this is all I probably need to do to invite him to talk to me. And talk to me he does, and he's *delightful*.

I find myself talking to Donald, a native of Omaha – but who has lived in various towns all over the State. He tells me that he was born in 1927 which I worked out in my head makes him 78 years old – very much retired – and he does that thing where he asks me a question, but before I can really answer it, he is telling me about himself. About his wives – two of them – a glint in his eye when mentioning his first one, and then a true look of sadness when talking about the second. Is he divorced, has she died and he's out lived them? I couldn't ask – he is too sweet to ask, and happy to tell me all sorts of information without me having to prompt him, I don't have to – he just talks anyway which I find most endearing.

'My second wife never liked the trains though ... the worst thing she said was that the coal train used to leave a dirty dust all over the clothes on the washing line!'

'She liked it even less when I then got a job on the trains, as a guard. I never made it as a driver though'.

'Of course, that's not my favourite job' he chuckles. 'When I was a lad, I once worked in an IHOP where my manager was a woman with one leg. Wooden leg she had!' and starts to hobble around even more than as if to demonstrate how one's walking might be affected if you have a wooden leg.

This goes on for several minutes, as I gulp down my drink which by the end isn't chilled at all – it has really warmed up in the middle-of-the-day sun, and by screwing the lid back on and me standing up to chuck the empty bottle into a nearby trashcan, Donald senses that this is his cue to maybe stop talking and bring his one-way conversation to an end.

'So will you send me a postcard then?' he asks, looking at me almost a little sternly as I fumble for my car keys, my indication that it's time for me to go. He wants me to do *what?!* Send him a postcard? I ask him to double-check that that's what he wants.

'At the end of your trip if you make it to California can you send me a postcard?' he asks sweetly. *Of course* I can do that! 'But I'll do one even better' I say with a smile ... 'I don't know when, but at some point I'm sure I'll be back in London, and I'll send you a postcard from there. How about that?' And now it is Donald's turn to really smile, as he gives me his address.

I go for a walk after that and just soak up Waterloo for a little while on the gorgeous day. Smart houses with neatly trimmed hedges and privet fences are in evidence, but so too are the quaint old general store with the bell that go 'Ding!' every time someone walks through it. There is a sleepy dog on someone's porch, a poster on a telegraph poll advertising someone's garage sale next weekend, it is lovely. It is going to have to go into my 'Perfect small town' category.

As always though, time is against me and I become aware that I've only really driven for about an hour today – and I need to go further, much further to make the progress that I want to make. I again head east, going around Omaha on the Interstate system, and then along I-80 towards Des Moines – birthplace of Bill Bryson, a man whose travel writings across America have me in fits of laughter every time I read them – no matter how many times – but I'm not going to be able and pay homage to old Bill[29], because I need to head north as well, which means more 'L' shape manoeuvres across the planes of Iowa.

> **4:31 PM Jul 23rd**
> And ... Back into Iowa. Are you keeping up?

It is like navigating through Lincoln this morning, only instead of going a few hundred yards at a time before turning a block, I'd drive for two or three miles north, before turning right and going two to three miles east.

I also make a quick stop at the Iowa Welcome Centre, which oddly seems to be located about 10 miles *inside* Iowa – where I've been driving for quite a few minutes, instead of having somewhere more obvious – like on the actual state line between Nebraska and Iowa.

> **4:41 PM Jul 23rd**
> am in the Iowa welcome centre: They're having a bread & jam party with oldies sat in a circle playing banjos, guitars & violins

To be honest, I'm still quite not sure to this day what to make of the welcome centre, only that I am confused about being 'Welcomed'. There appears to be a party taking place, and for one moment I honestly feel like I am gate-crashing a wedding, or its reception. Only to realise that there are other people in the place that are ignoring the party in the middle of

---

[29] I've no idea if the USA has a 'Blue Plaque' system similar to what I know and love in London, where the local council mark the birthplace of a well-known person, but if they I would really like to think that there was one on Bryson's house.

the room and looking at the 'Things to do in Iowa' brochures in the racks that are on the outside walls.

> **4:43 PM Jul 23rd**
> oh, and a mouth organ. There's a crazy lookin' woman playing a mouth organ. Welcome to Iowa.

> **5:32 PM Jul 23rd**
> and here ... come ... the ... endless ... cornfields. #northerniowa

I recall again my week long trip to Chicago back in the summer of the previous year, I'd bought a one-way flight up there, because I knew that on the way back I would come back with my friend Eleanor. It's a sixteen hour drive from Chicago all through the night to Charleston, and I'd even made a ten minute video about it. I don't think I actively realised it at the time, but what I was of course doing was having a dry-run of what it would be like to road trip across American and make a mini documentary about it at the same time.

One of the comments I'd made on that video is how I 'Wanted to see the cornfields of Nebraska and Iowa at some point in my life', because although you might think that they're very plain and boring ... because I'd never seen them before, to me that made it exciting to see for the first time.

I turn north and I turn east, then I turn north and then turn east again over the course of a couple of hours, as I slowly cross my way across Iowa, through the farmland and yes ... cornfields.

A few miles out of Carroll, on Highway 30 I stop at a dusty crossroads junction with nothing much going on just so that I can take a photo of dusty crossroads junction with nothing much going on. The wind blows gently across the fields and I just sit quietly for a few moments soaking in the air and the gentle breeze. In the distance, there is a buzzing sound.

> **6:42 PM Jul 23rd**
> I'm watching a crop dusting plane spray the cornfields in Carroll county, northern Iowa. i could be Cary Grant.

> **6:43 PM Jul 23rd**
> If I had an Internet connection right now, I would be adding 'North by Northwest' to my NetFlix queue.

> **6:47 PM Jul 23rd**
> Whoever said cornfields were boring? It's beautiful out here.

I only really have one issue with Iowa ... and that is its smell. For all the open spaces, and big skies, and endless cornfields on the horizon that is has to offer, what you really notice with all the farmland and cows around too, is that whilst *looking* beautiful, it does not *smell* that great. Time for another tweet, surely.

> **7:02 PM Jul 23rd**
> However, I've just realised Iowa smells of cow shit. Sorry, but it does

---

In the USA
Latimer, Iowa
On the Tube map
Latimer Road
(Circle / Hammersmith & City Lines)

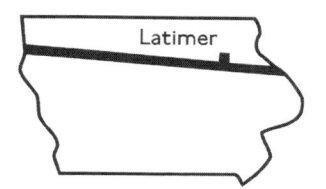

> **10:19 PM Jul 23rd**
> Just got to Latimer, Iowa. It's late, it's dark, and everything is closed. Hmm, i might have to come back tomorrow, Grr

I stop at a Mexican restaurant for dinner, and for the first time on the trip feel self-conscious for some reason about eating by myself. It feels a little as if other diners are looking at me, wondering 'Why is by himself?' On all the other tables there are couples and families and on one, four burly farmer type guys one complete with denim dungarees and hats, and me ...? I sit there all alone, eating my refried beans and look at my road atlas for my next stop.

That next stop is Latimer, a small town right at the top of Iowa, and just off east to the I-35, the main Interstate running north/south through the state. And as I finish up and pay my bill, I suddenly realise that even though I've done a lot of driving today, I am probably going to get there when it is dark, and part of me wonders whether that is right and really if I should visit it during the daytime.

It is indeed dark another couple of hours driving later when I come off the Interstate down a small road and to a crossroads where I know I've hit the right place, due a large sign lit up that reads 'LATIMER – A PROGRESSIVE COMMUNITY'.

A little Googling finds me that the town's official website goes further on this, proclaiming Latimer to be Iowa's 'Northern Star', and that in Latimer…

"Life moves at a less stressful pace, where people know their neighbours and where many visitors decide to call this progressive community home.

We offer a clean, quiet and secure lifestyle with access to big city amenities just a short road trip away. Our prime location offers endless opportunities for both business and family and people will visit for a day and decide to stay for a lifetime."

As I park up the in the quiet, dark main street of the town, I look for signs of people that have just come visiting for a day, but then have ended up staying an entire lifetime. Nope, can't see any, it all seems quiet. *Too* quiet. Hang on! Maybe this is some freaky town a bit like in that Ewan McGregor movie 'Big Fish' where everything is just so perfect that you don't want to leave!

So I find myself wanting to find some imperfection – something that I don't like about this place – otherwise I may just be drawn into it, and be stuck here forever!

I look at the 'Latimer Café' that I am standing across the street from – actually, that looks quite cute. I quite like the little short street lamps that light up the main street too – it seems quite out of character for America *not* to have something large and dominating all over the place. There is a community centre, and post office, an Amoco gas station, all looking small and with character – but it is also very much nearly 11pm at night, and so the whole town really is quiet and closed up.

Back in my car I consult the map, and look to see whether I can stay somewhere here the night, come back in the morning and still have time to get to my next destination. And sadly – I realise that I can't as I have a date to get to Minnesota in couple of days' time to pick up Natalie for when she joins the trip.

Saddened that I haven't got to talk to anyone, or really seen any signs of life I drive back down to the Interstate, and just before I get there I see a Shell gas station that is all lit up and still open – my tank is half full/empty but I decide to pull in anyway to see what's happening.

Scott is what is happening. As he cooks me up a fresh corndog for me to munch on, he turns out to be quite a chatty and friendly cashier – although I think he is just bored because there is no one else here – and he tells me that he's moved to Latimer to be with his girlfriend whom he'd met at college, and she'd returned here after she'd graduated, but they are 'Looking to move away again soon'.

Really, Scott ... really? Or have you'd been sucked into Latimer's progressive community, and you are now in fact going to stay for a lifetime?

SAME NAME TOWNS TALLY

Perfect Small Town America
Preston, White City, Waterloo

Something there and enjoyable
Plaistow, Gloucester, Kew Gardens, Harrow, South Kensington, Greenford, Liverpool, Temple, Oxford, Victoria

Something there but not that exciting to be honest
Putney, Amersham, Hampstead, Woodford, Brompton, Kingsbury, Redbridge, Latimer

Nothing there but somehow being in the middle of nowhere made it OK
Epping, Acton, Lancaster

Nothing there, and not that exciting either. Oops.
Warwick, Wapping, Camden, Bond

Closed
Swiss Cottage

An hour more of driving north, up the I-35 and I cross the Stateline from Iowa into Minnesota. I head for the KOA campground that I know is there in Albert Lea, pay my 'after hours' dollars in the drop-box, find my spot next to a giant caravan on wheels, pitch my tent using the headlights of the car, and flop into my sleeping bag.

Day 39 – Friday 24th July

Spam, spam, spam ...

'Lovely Spam, Wonderful Spam'

When I'd got to the campsite late last night, I couldn't really see much due to the darkness, so there's always that strange moment of looking at it in the morning daylight and taking in your new surroundings, and realising it is nothing like you'd imagined.

Next to me is a large Winnebago that looks like an organised family on the road – they have washing hanging out on lines, shoes lined up outside and an inflatable dinghy (Where have they been using that? The campground swimming-pool?) All lined up neatly outside. Me? I have my towel awkwardly slung over the crack-in-the-window open on the car back window. Hmm, time to shower and get my online fix.

I perch awkwardly in the laundry, and use a shelf meant for storing phonebooks to put my laptop on, and type away.

> **10:00 AM Jul 24th**
> good morning. Had a late one last night, Day 37 progress map is now up online though, I'm just inside Minnesota.

> **10:01 AM Jul 24th**
> today's mission: Head east along the I-90 and into the 32nd state of my trip : Wisconsin.

Today's same name placed in Wisconsin is – I know – going to be a small drag, because I can tell from the map that it is going to be a two hour drive to a middle-of-nowhere place, and then two hours back again to get back where I already am now.

However, I've only been on the I-90 heading east literally a couple of minutes when I approach the town of Austin, and I see a biiiig sign at the side of the road.

> **11:02 AM Jul 24th**
> just seen sign for 'Spam Museum' www.mmmmuseum.com, seriously!

> **11:03 AM Jul 24th**
> and it's not a Monday so it'll be open!

Now I always thought that I am the type of person who would not be drawn in on a whim by large road side signs, but suddenly seeing the sign, and remembering that I am by myself and need something to do to cheer myself up and bit and keep me entertained I realise: I am going to have to go to the SPAM museum.

> **11:45 AM Jul 24th**
> i don't really have time to visit, but sometimes you just have to do these things #spammuseum

And suddenly, just like being back in Graceland and Elvis, I enter into tourist-that-tweets mode, and find myself giving a running commentary on all-things-SPAM.

> **11:50 AM Jul 24th**
> i just has my photo taken next to 'spammy'. I am not kidding. #spammuseum

> **11:52 AM Jul 24th**
> they have a Monty Python exhibit! Alltogether now . . . #spammuseum

> **11:54 AM Jul 24th**
> i'm listening to a re-working of REM's 'stand', substituted 'stand' with 'spam'. Again, not kidding. #spammuseum

> **12:04 PM Jul 24th**
> different flavours of Spam: Garlic, Bacon, Cheese, Turkey, Classic, Lite & Low Sodium. I had nooo idea. #spammuseum

I am suddenly aware that this might be spamming people with all my tweets.

Geddit? 'Spamming'. I'm *hilarious* sometimes. No, really.

> **12:08 PM Jul 24th**
> spam Museum : modern, bright, fun, informative, interactive. Everything Graceland isn't. Spam 1, Elvis 0. #spammuseum

> **12:18 PM Jul 24th**
> choice of t-shirt in gift shop: 'i think therefore, i Spam', or 'Got Spam?' #spammuseum

> **12:25 PM Jul 24th**
> there's a guy walking round offering chunks of cheese flavoured Spam on pretzel sticks. I'm on my 4th one! #mmmuseum

> **12:28 PM Jul 24th**
> annnnd, i'm done. That was (dare i say it) Spamtastic! #spammuseum #mmmuseum

I'm sure you may be wondering how exciting a Spam museum can really be – and you're right, if you're reading this it probably isn't. But it is a well laid out, functional, informative (into the world of Spam production and distribution) museum, that tells me everything about Spam that I never knew I needed to know – but most of all I keep thinking 'This is a lot better than Graceland' in terms of a visitor attraction.

Mind you, everything that I learn about SPAM I promptly forgot after I leave – because let's face it; it's really just something that you might want to eat, and that's the most important thing to most people.

12:36 PM Jul 24th
back on the road : 90 east. Wisconsin awaits.

I cross the Mississippi River *yet again* into Wisconsin, and check in really quickly – dumping my stuff at a Days Inn in the town of La Crosse. Then hit the road again almost immediately.

Heading south-east down US Highway 61 (or is it 14? It is labelled both – something that I never get my head around in America is how the same road can be labelled with two different numbers), it is less than two hours down the road to Green Park ... farm.

In the USA
Green Park Farm, Wisconsin
On the Tube map
Green Park
(Piccadilly, Jubilee and Victoria Lines)

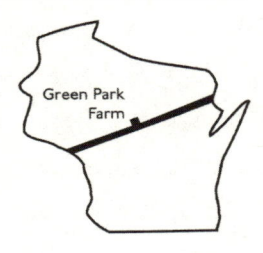

Yes, Green Park isn't a town or a place, **everyplace.com** actually describes it as a 'locale' but it appears that there is also a farm here, which works for me – and as I turn off the highway and onto a minor dirt road I can see the farm building ahead.

So; this looks like it is very much going to be a 'nothing' place, but this time I have a plan, and knowing that it is going to be a 'nothing' sort of place, I'd worked this one out in advance – very simply, I am going to go for a walk.

It occurs to me that I haven't really done this in any of the previous 'nothing' places, I've just rocked up to a middle-of-nowhere crossroads, lamented about the fact that there is a big pile of nothing, and then slightly dejected got back in the car and driven off. This time – there is to be no driving off in the car, there would instead be walking.

I pull up by the even smaller and even dirtier dirt road and get out, and close and lock the car. This is why I have dumped all the stuff out earlier at the hotel – I know I am going to leaving the car for a while.

And walk is what I do, for the next hour and half, and it is *splendid*.

I've been so cooped in the car for so many miles, I think I've forgotten what it is like to walk anywhere for a distance. I end up walking down the road, down a path, across a bridge over a stream, past a field of cows than barely pay me any attention, up and around a huge silo of some description, past some rusty old farm machinery dumped in the corner of the field, and I feel *fabulous*.

I even leave my phone back in the car (hidden, out of sight, just in case) so I can't be disturbed, I adjust to the smell of bovine (of course), I have a good vascular work out air-in-lungs, striding steps, collecting my thoughts, enjoy the green fields, bushes, plants trees and scenery, and it is *delightful*.

At some point, I think my legs muscles may have made a formative line of conversation with my brain. 'Hey! What's with all this walking all of a sudden? We've just been used to pressing a gas and brake pedal for a few weeks now'. 'Ssh', my brain replies, 'It's called exercise, and it's good for you, keep going'. And it is *invigorating*.

I don't talk to anyone, I only see a couple of others cars that have past me, but by the time I get back to the car and the Green Park Farm again, I feel like I've made the most of coming here – more than I have with a couple of other places. And this is a good thing, a very good thing.

Green Park Farm – gets a tick.

> **5:54 PM Jul 24th**
> Green Park Farm : a good place to walk

The rain comes down on the drive back to La Crosse. I buy a Subway sandwich and snap a Wisconsin license plate, and return to the hotel. I go back out again to get some toothpaste that I'd forgotten to buy in the shop, and do the typical thing where I can *see* the Walgreens from my hotel, but I can't walk there – I have to take a convoluted route that takes over five minutes to drive to get there, and back again. And as I park up, the rain really comes down, with a little lightning and thunder too, and I make use of the hotel's heated pool. I feel *very* relaxed now.

> **9:10 PM Jul 24th**
> episode Number 13 is up! (i.e. another Video!). Welcome to White City. http://is.gd/1L8dB

Back in my room, I edit up some video quite quickly, and so relaxed am I feeling, that strangely for the first time in many weeks I head for bed before 11pm.

~ ~ ~

I sleep well that night – a deep night's sleep that I think has been brought on by the walk, but one that my body needs anyway to get some rest that it craves from all the travelling.

I take a slow and easy drive on the non-Interstate road all the way northwest towards Minneapolis, and for the first time on my trip, do something a little unheard of – I get my caffeine and Internet fix at a branch of Caribou Coffee. It's the second largest chain of coffee shops after the mighty S. B. X. but for some reason is only the first time – not just on the trip – but in my life and time in America that I go and get one.

> **5:56 PM Jul 25th**
> it's been a slow day, I admit. Progress for day 40 though: http://is.gd/1MJEV

I don't have to pick up Natalie – my next companion until tomorrow, so that night I stay with my friend Rainy-Dae (yes, that's her real name) – although when I say 'friend' it should be worth pointing out that I've never met her before in my life, she is in fact a reader and commenter on my blog – and has only found my blog a few months ago.

We've chatted over email, and she'd suggested that when I get up her way I could stay at hers for the night, which is lovely of her so I gladly take her up on the offer.

When I get there, we have dinner and conversation and then I find out that she's done a beautiful thing for me – she and her work colleagues have made me a *gift box* of things to help me along my way on my road trip. A CD with some songs on it, a 'Subway' gift card loaded with dollars so that I can by a sandwich at some point, and Minnesotan farming 'Cow' that is a key-ring, but has a button on it so that it makes a 'Moooo!' sound every time you press it. So I press it, a lot.

> **9:57 PM Jul 25th**
> tomorrow companion #4 flies in, and from there on i've got someone with me for almost every day until the end ...

Day 41 – Sunday 26th July

In time

'Reaching for the top and you've been on my mind
they steady trying to stop my shine
but it's always been yours it's never been mine
You always come thru just in the nick of time'

In the USA
Elm Park, Minnesota
On the Tube map
Elm Park (District Line)

Oh.

It's going to be like that again is it?

I get back into my car, plug in my 3G dongle into my laptop and type in the coordinates that I'd programmed in to check that Google Maps really does confirm this as being Elm Park.

I'd driven out up to north of Minneapolis this morning, and as the roads got smaller and the traffic less dense, I somehow knew what I am going to get when I arrive at Elm Park – another crossroads. Another nothing. Another place with trees and fields on all four corners, but ... no, really. Nothing else.

You can only find so many ways of describing that you have arrived at a crossroads in the middle of nowhere – but I have, and there is nothing interesting about it at all.

> **10:51 PM Jul 26th**
> Elm Park : It's a big fat nothing.

It doesn't even have fantastic large pine trees like Lancaster did, or a railway track like Acton. It is just ... the crossing of two country roads that lay perfectly as west/east and north/south to each other.

I try to do a Green Park and explore by walking, but in each direction the road just leads to woods and trees on either side, with no distinguishable features anywhere. I walk in each of the four directions for five minutes and back and find nothing. Upon returning back for the fourth time I put the road atlas on the bonnet of the car, and I hear the sound of another engine – another car passing through – at speed – and I don't think the driver even gives me a second glace.

Sigh.

SAME NAME TOWNS TALLY

Perfect Small Town America
Preston, White City, Waterloo

Something there and enjoyable
Plaistow, Gloucester, Kew Gardens, Harrow, South Kensington, Greenford, Liverpool, Temple, Oxford, Victoria

Something there but not that exciting to be honest
Putney, Amersham, Hampstead, Woodford, Brompton, Kingsbury, Redbridge, Latimer

Nothing there but somehow being in the middle of nowhere made it OK
Epping, Acton, Lancaster, Green Park Farm

Nothing there, and not that exciting either. Oops.
Warwick, Wapping, Camden, Bond, Elm Park

Closed
Swiss Cottage

I feel like I need to find another good one soon – Green Park has really been a nothing, but I've made something out of it. But since the high point of White City, and Waterloo in its wake, nothing else has really hit the spot, and I am increasingly in need of a fix of superb little same name town. Which means I need to drive on, and go and pick up Natalie from the airport.

> **3:54 PM Jul 26th**
> off to the airport (MSP). I have a new travelling companion to pick up …

A boring drive back south again to go down to the airport, and I flick through my phone to check my texts to confirm her flight and arrival time. We've actually spoken yesterday to confirm that she is still coming, and whilst on the phone she goes into a mini rant about a whole bunch of things that she wants to tell me about when she sees me.

> **5:49 PM Jul 26th**
> at Minneapolis airport. I have a new companion on board. I feel like The Doctor more than ever.

Within two minutes of getting in the car, Nat proclaims 'Oh my God', and launches into a minor diatribe about a whole bunch of things that she's obviously been saving up to tell me. I'm starting to feel like it is all going to be about her for a bit now, and not about the trip. We head for the grocery store.

> **6:33 PM Jul 26th**
> companion #4 has food requirements, so we're shopping in Whole Foods. This could be the healthiest week of eating for me

It's worth mentioning by the way that Natalie has a wheat allergy. And is lactose intolerant. Definitely can't do any bread or dairy, or basically any 'fun' foods that I may have been gorging myself on since … er … well since I had money to spend as a teenager on fun foods. Which is why at six o'clock in the evening we find ourselves shopping in the Bloomington branch of Whole Foods – a rather good chain of shops across America that sell what I would call 'health food shit'. Lots of overpriced organic stuff and absolutely no fun-foods whatsoever. I do pick myself up some soap-free shower gel though, so it's not a completely wasted trip – oh and Nat stocks up on food for a week, and packs out my cooler full of weird products that I have simply never seen before in my life.

And we head west to South Dakota along Highway 212, until around eight o'clock in the evening, Nat finally says something that I've been waiting for her to say all day, in fact … if my own Geo-sense is working out right, she's timed it rather well.

'So, with this Tube thing then ... what's that all about? Where have we got to go to?'

Now I'd explained the whole concept of the trip to her when I'd invited her to come on it, and again just before I left. Never mind, I explain it to her again.

'So you've got to go places that have the same names as stations in London?'

'Yes'

'So where's the next one?'

'Well as it happens, your timing couldn't be more perfect, we're in one now'.

In the USA
Kingsbury County, South Dakota
On the Tube map
Kingsbury (Jubilee Line)

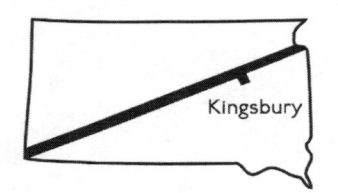

I have to confess though that the place we are in now in South Dakota is a bit of a cheat – on two counts. Firstly, when I'd researched the names of places all those months ago, I really couldn't find a town in the state that had the same name as a place on the Tube back in London, I really couldn't. It seemed that *no* town or city in the whole of South Dakota matched back with anything in London, but I'd got round it, by finding the name of a *county* that does – welcome to Kingsbury County.

The other second glitch is of course that I've already visited a Kingsbury – the town back in Illinois, but you can forgive me for that, right? After all I never said that the 48 places are going to be unique, I just said that they are going to have the same name as a *place* on the Tube map.

So I explain this all to Nat, and that rather fortuitously, we are in Kingsbury County in South Dakota *right now*.

'So ... we're in one right now?' she asks quizzically.

'Yes'

'This is it? This is Kingsbury' she says waving her hand to a dusty road with crop fields on either side.

'Yes'

'So exactly where are we stopping then?' Ah – good question.

The answer lies in the huge collection of photos that I took whilst on the trip. For shortly after I confirm that we are in Kingsbury County right now, something stirs in Nat where I think she feels that she needs to record where we are, so she grabs my camera and starts taking photos. Then she winds down the window of her passenger side, leans out and takes even more photos.

Now I took over 3,000 photos on the trip, and yet it's fair to say that the best photo of the whole trip – wasn't actually taken by me, it was taken at this exact moment driving down the dusty road through Kingsbury county. Nat reverses her shot looking back down the car and the road and *snap!* Takes an awesome picture of the car kicking up dust as we go.

But I still feel like we need to go *somewhere* and do *something* whilst we are here – and across the field to out left, I can see the answer. Two giant wind-turbines which we're going to go and take pictures of.

Now we've seen quite a few of them at a distance driving around already, but suddenly these became a focal point and something for us to 'see and do' whilst in Kingsbury. We turn off the main dusty road, and slowly trundle down a narrow dusty road instead, getting closer to the white fibre glass windmills sticking out of the ground slowly spinning around.

And it's only when we get up close to them do we realise just how big these things are – normally you see them in the distance on the horizon, but we get up right next to them – close enough to find there isn't a fence around them protecting them so we can touch the base of them with our hands, take cool silhouetted photos using the setting sun of ourselves against them, and look up high into the sky ... towering above us by at least 50 metres, maybe more – their three giant blades slowly 'whooshing' round in the breeze.

'How the hell do they construct these things?' asks Nat. 'No idea' I say craning my neck looking up wondering at the moment if a bolt would become rusty and one of the propellers would come down towards me and spike me to death. But then I see the 'bolts' of the things holding the base in place, and they are a foot long, and three inches thick. This thing isn't going anywhere.

I breathe in the fresh evening's summer air – and can't smell the burning of coal or the deposits of a nuclear power station anywhere nearby. This is Kingsbury County, South Dakota – doing its bit to make the planet a little bit greener.

We get back in the car, I start the engine, and I can't help but wonder if the exhaust has just spat out a little bit of oil onto the ground.

Down the road, we fill up with gas once more again and I love how it's still light in the sky, and the setting sun is plastering rays of warmth that bounce across the sky and glints off the car bonnet, to the point where I'm almost compelled to put my sunglasses on.

It's such a weird thing to like so much, but I realise I do have a thing about gas stations – they're important because they mark the refuelling stops for my journey, and as I am going to one almost every day they are markers that progress is being made. But they've also become important to me on a personal level - I love the smell of coffee that emanates from all of them, mixed in with the smell of gasoline – and right now, the sun has obviously been out all day shining brightly heating up the tarmac on the forecourt too and it is warm to touch, and I can *feel* the heat coming up from the ground.

Concrete, caffeine and combustion engine fuel. It's a strange combination, I admit, but it really does it for me.

I think about this as we drive for half an hour more, until the sun finally *does* set, and we turn a corner in the road to see the glow of yellow that is the KOA sign, leading us to salvation for the night, as we pitch up for the night in the tent at Sioux Falls.

> **11:41 PM Jul 26th**
> made it to Sioux Falls, SD for the night. Tomorrow: unto the Badlands and the wilds of north America...

Day 42 – Monday 27th July

Gambler

'I'm a gambler, and I will take you by surprise
Gambler, I'll aim this straight between your eyes
Gambler, yeah I know all the words to say
'Cause I'm a gambler, I only play the game my way, yeah'

The day starts in quite a positive fashion.

> **10:11 AM Jul 27th**
> plotting the day ahead. Flitting between SD and NE. and heading for a town with population of one ... yes, ONE!

I get motivated by strange little things. Visiting a place, town, well ... not even a village really where there is a population of just *one* person, gets me very excited. Nat however has further thoughts about the whole affair.

'Why does this whole state smell or urine?' she says, winding up her window on the driver's side. I instinctively pick up my phone and type without even thinking about it.

> **10:51 AM Jul 27th**
> Nat: 'why does this whole state smell or urine?' #southdakota

I put back down my phone, still on auto-tweet mode concentrating more on the driving. And I would like to point out dear reader, that I – Geoff – do not say this, nor do I really think it. I'm happy to confirm on record that the whole of Iowa smells of farming, cows, and cow shit, but the whole of South Dakota as urine? Come on, that's not fair, is it? I wind down the electric window on *my* side and inhale deeply through my large pointy nose.

Oh.

Where's my phone again?

> **10:52 AM Jul 27th**
> to be fair, it smells of pigs and cows too, but she's got a point.

Smells aside I'm enjoying South Dakota very much, with its big open spaces. Even bigger and open-er than Iowa I figure. There is just one thing that concerns me though – that there really is so little to around here that all there is to is gamble away what little amount of money you do make?

> **1:17 PM Jul 27th**
> A gas station name to rival 'Kum & Go', i'm at a 'Pump 'n' Stuff', brilliant. #southdakota

There has probably been a few before it, but I think I first notice it when we pull into a gas station in Yankton, SD – just before crossing the bridge over the river that will take us back down into Nebraska. It's called a 'Pump 'n' Stuff' which I find such an amusing yet buoyant name that I spend several more minutes than is probably really necessary taking a photo of the sign – and trying to be all artistic too by lying on the ground taking it so as to get the sun in just the right place that I want it. I go inside when done, where Nat has disappeared a few moments ago to have a wee, only there is no toilet … just a load of fruit machines.

> **1:21 PM Jul 27th**
> There is a mini casino, INSIDE the gas station! WTF?

I don't know *why* I find it so odd to see – well, maybe because probably because it *is* so odd to see, to the point where I turn round and speak to the cashier serving to check that there appears to be a legal place to gamble inside the gas station.

'So do all gas stations in South Dakota have slot machines?' I ask, smiling hoping to have a jovial conversation with the cashier about it. Unfortunately they either miss my smile, or don't care, and I end up having a very serious conversation for a couple of moments about the fact that – yes – a lot of gas stations do have one armed bandits, and that's very normal in these parts, thank you very much.

When I think about it, it just completes the picture really. Back in Kentucky last month I'd found that gas station which was a gas station, grocery store, café and obviously a general focal point of the community – so is this place, it's just that they are tagging on fruit machines into the mix as well. And the more I think about it, the more it makes sense, so you know – when in Rome, be Roman.

> **1:28 PM Jul 27th**
> So i gamble $1 on an electronic poker game … And win $6! Sweet. Time to leave whilst in credit…

The rest of the day is fairly straight forward. We head south on Highway 81 over the Missouri River – well, it isn't *that* straight forward in that the SatNav system tries to take us over Meridian Highway Bridge, to which we abruptly find a 'Road Closed' sign and discover that this rusty old relic built in 1924 is now for cyclists and pedestrians only. A shame as it is a 'two deck' bridge with two levels – where the northbound traffic drives *on top* of the southbound – and we don't get to enjoy that. Instead, we head a few blocks west to the shiny and less-than-a-year old Discovery Bridge which has replaced its predecessor 84 years to the day later. Traffic flows on both sides here in a regular fashion – nowhere near as much fun as a two level bridge.

That takes us into Nebraska where we continue to wend south and west and south and south and west some more before picking up Highway 12 – a near deserted Highway 12 – and head for our next same-name place.

But we make sure that we stop at Minowi en route – famous for having an official population of just ... one person, even though the sign saying 'Welcome' on the outskirts says 'two'.

The last remaining resident, a lovely lady by the name of *Elsie Tanner* – her husband passed away a while ago, and no one has done an update to the sign to reflect the correct population number.

> **3:45 PM Jul 27th**
> first cell signal in over two hours! There is life here Jim, but not as we know it. #Nebraska

> **3:46 PM Jul 27th**
> just went to tiny town of Monowi, Nebraska. Population of 1, her name is Elsie. She made us grilled cheese sandwiches. #Nebraska

At some point on the drive west and slightly north which takes us back into South Dakota we gain an hour on ourselves when we go into Mountain Time. I'm not really paying attention because I've kind of given up on looking at my phone (which also serves as my main clock) a few hours ago, when I realise that we are clearly going to be in a part of the country for a few hours that has no mobile phone coverage.[30] Maybe a bar of signal pops up here or there as we drive through small towns, but I don't really notice.

And I'm glad that I give up my techno-vice for a while because it means that I am then just able to consume the view that Nebraska and South Dakota serves me up.

Somewhere west on Highway 18 it comes to the point that I think is suitable that I've been looking for a while and pull the car over to the edge of the road. Taking my camera, I am able to literally lie down in the middle of the road and take a wide-angled shot, very low down of the road sprawling out into the distance and into the vanishing point. There are no cars in front or behind of me as far as the eye can see. Gentle

---

[30] So, having driven across the whole of America, I can recommend which phone company has the better mobile/cell coverage – Verizon does. Often when I'd have no signal on my AT&T phone, Natalie (or others) would have coverage on the Verizon network. Sorry, AT&T but that's the truth.

winds blow across the plain splashing fresh air onto my face into my nose and down into my lungs. We are out in the country land where you rarely pass anyone else, and we are able to feel disconnected and away from the world, and it is *magnificent*. I soak it up. Nat grins at me as she too enjoys being as far away from anyone else as possible, and we both breathe the fresh clean air. Everything is peaceful. I feel like a bit of an old hippy with all my worries dissipating. Something inside of me wishes that I could live out here every day. I wonder how far it is to the nearest Starbucks though.

We stop briefly for drinks, snacks and another gas top-up in White River which appears to be an Indian influenced town. We drive on, heading for the KOA campground as near to the Badlands as we can get for the end of the day.

We turn up a narrow farm road, as I want to shoot some video of us kicking up dust in the middle of some dusty farm roads. Again, we have this complete and utter sense of freedom with no one else around. The winds whips up making me instinctively cover the microphone on the video camera to try and protect what Nat is saying. We carry on a few blocks more, and across in the distance to our left ... is that ... a mini-tornado? More likely what the locals would call a dirt devil. We see what looks like an inverted triangle of dust moving its way across the field in the distance, only for the weather to then change, less blustery and almost as quickly as we've seen the cone of dust appear it disappears.

'Woah! Mind OUT!' screams Nat, as I'm not really looking where I'm driving as I've been looking at the dust the wind is kicking up, meaning that the baby deer than has suddenly ran out into the road in front of us I haven't really seen and I almost hit it. It isn't to be though as it's running incredibly fast, and carries on straight into the crop fields to our left. 'He's in a hurry!' I observe.

Two minutes later when we get to the intersection and turn left we see what must be the same baby deer, now slightly up the hill off to our right, still running away from us full pelt up into the distance, heading for ... who knows where? Somewhere urgent, with energy, with the string winds of South Dakota blowing in its wake. I wind down the window and stick my head out, the wind roars against my head and I scream 'Woooooah!' for no other reason except that I can.

We are out in the wilds of America, and I am fucking loving it.

A few miles south of the town of Interior, SD on Highway 44 and we reach our destination for the day. I have this strange sense when we find it because I really feel like I've lost track of where we are exactly – the loss of mobile phone signal has made me feel out of touch. I'm not really sure where we are on the map, and the instructions in the KOA guide as to where the campground is are a bit vague, and so when we literally stumble upon it along the side of the road I am a bit surprised to see it.

We pull in, pay for a hook up for the night and set up camp. Dinner on the camp stove that night comes out of a tin. Their Internet doesn't really work so I am unable to get online and blog or post any photos which makes me slightly grumpy. There is however for the first time since early that morning a mobile phone signal, and so I put my washing on in the launderette, and as I motion my head in circles watching it spin, I make some phone calls and check in with the world that way.

> **10:33 PM Jul 27th**
> UndUSA is alive! All day, we've had NO CELL SIGNAL. Now at KOA Campground in Badlands, SD and there is a VERY flaky wireless signal

> **10:36 PM Jul 27th**
> ps. Now in Mountain time. Note to UK peeps: that's 7 hours behind. CHS peeps, 2 hours behind. Goodnight!

~ ~ ~

I wake in the morning to find Natalie missing from the tent, and my camera gone too. Clearly someone has snuck in in the middle of the night and ran off with her, and stolen my camera. Well either that or she's just got up early to take some photos. Fortunately, it turns out to be the latter as I find her about 100 yards away over the edge of campsite, through the bushes and onto a sandy plain which slopes down onto a river. The just-risen sun is low in the sky, and the warm rays of light are bouncing off the slight ripples in the water as bugs skim their way across. We dip our toes in, and just breathe in the air, and revel in the surroundings. It. Is. Lovely. But we have to move on.

The lack of cell coverage means that I can send no emails or do any texting or tweeting all morning. And after about an hour of checking and re-checking my phone every two minutes, I concede and just decide to just enjoy the trip, rather than attempt to log it all the time and we head for The Badlands National Park.

To tell you exactly what a 'badland' is in the National Park, is kind of tricky and it would be much easier if you were to be able to see a picture of one. Unfortunately, you have elected to buy the non-photo version of this book, which means you'll just have to reply upon my terrible description instead.

The dry rocky mini-mountainous terrain flanks us on either side of Highway 240 which snakes its way through the volcanic-looking rock.

The majority of the landscape is sandy red in colour, and if you're sitting anywhere near a computer right now or smartphone, then go search on the word 'scoria' too for more detail that you can shake a stick at.

Nat gets her National Park logbook stamped with the 'Badlands' logo, and then I get her to operate the video camera whilst I interview a Park Ranger, whose hat I really want.

We shoot some more stuff on video in the Badlands – generic shots of us passing through as well as a whole bunch of photos. I don't think a rugged rocky landscape has ever been more scenic to me before, it is impressive.

As we get back into the car after shooting the final piece of video, Nat asks me quite a pertinent question. 'Ummm, Geoff ... where's the tarp?' with a quizzical look on her face, and I immediately look on top of the car where it should be. Every morning when we pack the tent down I fold up the tarpaulin and stuff it under the roof-rack bars on top of the car. I never tie it down though because it is always folded enough times for it to be thick enough to be jammed under without it needing to be tied. And there it stays all day flapping in the breeze as I drive along, drying out nicely ready for its next use at the campground that night. Except now it isn't there, even though I distinctly remember putting it there this morning. This means that at some point between leaving the campground and driving to the Badlands this morning, it has been blown away and is now littering the beautiful South Dakotan landscape somewhere. Shit.

'Shit'. I say summing up the situation succinctly with that one word. 'We can't use the tent without one – we'll have to go buy another', thinking that the last one I'd bought from a Lowe's DIY store in New York on my way up to Maine. No branches of Lowe's out in the Badlands, so we're going to have to find a camping store instead.

> **3:19 PM Jul 28th**
> trying to find a Lowe's or camping shop in Rapid City now tho, because we 'lost' the tent tarpaulin.

As Nat drives, I look at the map – the proper paper map – not an online Google thing, and for the first time in a while marvel at where I am, where I've been, and where we are going to that day – and still what lies ahead and what is to come.

I start to feel good. I start to feel really happy. I start to like South Dakota because it makes me feel this way, and so naturally I have to share.

> **3:21 PM Jul 28th**
> South Dakota in 3: Pretty fucking cool. #southdakota

We get briefly snarled up in a traffic jam in Rapid City as we stop at a gas station to get some ice, and the SatNav gets confused about if we should go left or right off of the forecourt. For a moment, I panic that we won't make it to Mount Rushmore that day in time, but it is only a brief jam, and we sail on out of civilisation, along a quiet highway road again and into the Black Hill National Forest. An hour's worth of driving and we get to the town of Keystone – full of tacky looking souvenir shops and overpriced restaurants. I think of the Keystone Cops – I'm sure everyone does, as we sail on through.

> **5:56 PM Jul 28th**
> so Mount Rushmore is 2 miles out of the town of 'Keystone' – a tacky tourist trap mecca if ever i saw one. #mntrushmore

We go round a bend in a road, and another, and another, and go on a bit more and make another bend, and I start to wonder if we've missed it when I see the sign to turn in. Unfortunately (well I think so anyway), as you make the turn to take you in up the windy road you can glimpse the monument of the faces carved in way up on high.

> **5:58 PM Jul 28th**
> why hello, Mssrs Washington, Jefferson, Roosevelt and Lincoln …

> **5:59 PM Jul 28th**
> and yes, you do get to see it from the road before you get, unavoidable but disappointing i guess. #mntrushmore

> **6:03 PM Jul 28th**
> it's 'free' to get in. You have to pay for a $10 parking ticket valid for your car for a year. #mntrushmore

> **6:12 PM Jul 28th**
> ok, it's a National Park (Black Hills) so it's well run. Good layout & information. Hundreds of people tho. #mntrushmore

Mount Rushmore is of course one of those things that you have to take photos of – and if you're me documenting it all on a road trip, then you have to video it as well. I take a lot of shots from different angles, get Natalie to record me … before remembering what I'd done at the Badlands that morning – interviewed one of the National Park Rangers, and that's how I ended up talking to *Jeanette*.

'So what's the question you get asked most then?' I say struggling to come up with an idea of an interesting question. So I figure that my best way of starting would be by *not* asking the question she gets asked the most.

'It's actually probably people wanting to know where the bathrooms are!' she says chuckling, and I grin joining in the moment that it is nothing at all to do with Rushmore itself. There is a brief pause, where we all look at each other and smile and I am aware of the *whirr* of the tape heads on video camera to my right where Nat has been shooting the whole thing all this time, until my temptation just gets the better of me and I have to say it.

'So, can you tell me where the toilets are then please?'

Nat's phone buzzes in her pocket at that moment and she answers it, and I realise that I really do want to go to the toilet – perfect, as I already know where they are!

> **6:46 PM Jul 28th**
> note to self: when sitting down on the toilet, unplug & remove radio mic from pocket first, avoids testicle entanglement

I recall all the times in the past when I've been videoing people and they'd leave the radio mic switched on whilst I'd waited for them outside, and I can hear them peeing in my earpiece. If you *ever* have a radio mic attached to yourself for something you are recording, please make sure you always turn it off, or just take it off completely when going to the toilet, thanks.

> **6:41 PM Jul 28th**
> Natalie is on the phone to her mum: 'yes, it's g-e-o-f-f-t-e-c-h dot c-o dot u-k. Yes that's Geoff with a G'. Funny.

Post-toilet-trip and back outside, Nat – still on her phone - gives me the 'smile, nod and raised eyebrow' look, and I just grin back. I turn and soak in the view of the four presidents again, and generally revel in all the people milling about on this pleasant summers evening.

> **6:42 PM Jul 28th**
> A bird soaring high above just landed on Jefferson's forehead. #mntrushmore

By the time we have to leave, I don't really want to. I keep thinking 'this is nice, I like being a tourist, I am amongst other tourists and we all have a happy-on-holiday-feel amongst us'. There are families with kids, old people cheerily having their photos taken. Rushmore is nice, just ... really really nice, and I think for the first time on the trip I realise that at some point I am going to stop doing things like this – visiting places – and I will have to go back to the real world of work and taxes and relationships and responsibilities. I'm not sure I want that.

We drive back out through Keystone – still looking tacky – on the way to the KOA that I've booked us into to camp that night which turns out to be one of the oddest KOA's I would stay in on the trip – it's more like a Holiday Camp than a campground. A huge plot of land with numerous facilities, and reception that is more akin to a proper hotel – I later confirm in the guidebook that we have stumbled across the second largest, and most commercial of all the KOA campsites. I don't like it. It's too much, too commercial, and overbearing.

I end the evening sitting in the bar yes – *bar* – i.e. a pub that is on site, having a local beer and using the limited bandwidth connection which hundreds of people are all trying to use at the same time thus making my progress slow, as I upload and share my latest bunch of photos.

> **11::57 AM Jul 28th**
> drinking Fat Tire beer, in a BAR at a Koa campground, mount rushmore. yes they have a BAR at a campground! That's a first.

> **12:32 AM Jul 29th**
> blogpost on Minowi, Nebraska now written up. Town of population with just ONE! And we met her: http://is.gd/1S6IB

Walking back to the camp spot I realise how tired I am again – I know, I know. I also recognise that I am being grumpy again – I know, I know. I fathom in my head that a typical day would start with me feeling refreshed and energised, and then we'd visit somewhere cool, but by the end of the day there will have been a lot of driving and we've not eaten properly and I will just be feeling tired and grumpy again. It is a proper day of highs and lows – every day.

But I am also starting to realise that I am two thirds of the way through the trip, and so therefore at some point, it is all going to come to an end. And I don't like that. For all the highs and lows, I really don't want it to end.

Outside the tent, I can hear it start to rain.

~ ~ ~

There is a distinctly damp feel to the morning when daylight comes around, and I am awake before my alarm goes off, which is never a good sign. I check my phone to see what time it is and to tweet-grumble about being awake so early when I realise that I will be unable to do so.

Sometime during the night the rain has crept inside the tent due to the slope that we are sleeping on, and water has got inside and made my phone wet, so that it is displaying the message 'INSERT SIM CARD' even though it is already inserted. Shit. I take the phone apart, wipe it down with a tea-towel and place it on a clean piece of kitchen roll in an attempt to let it dry.

I go and sit in the car and start the engine and put the heater on. About a minute later when it is still cold I recall a conversation I had with Beverly before I set out back in Charleston 'Everything works in the car ... except for the heater'. Oh.

I find a discarded Oreo that has fallen out of the packet and onto the floor but I don't care and eat it anyway. Nat joins me and informs me that it's 7am, and that she's cold too. So we sit, inside the car, with the engine running being a bit miserable. On the plus side though, my phone comes back to life.

> **7:07 AM Jul 29th**
> it. is. cold! First time that I'm wearing a sweater on the trip. #southdakota

We start to banter to cheer ourselves up. I decide to shoot some video, and realise that I want a picture of us taking some video, except the lens on my camera is so big and heavy that it keeps falling over whenever I try and point it back at us positioned on the dashboard in self-timer mode. Eventually, I find another Oreo cookie on the floor of the car to use a lens rest, and I am able to take a photo. The mood lightens as we enter 'multimedia mode', and half an hour later, the sun makes a half-hearted attempt to break through the clouds. It warms up slightly, so we eat some bad campground food, and pack up and hit the road.

At Hill City, we fill up with petrol. As I make a note of the coordinates of exactly where we are[31], I realise for the first time that the 'West' coordinates on the SatNav are now a-hundred-and-something, which I don't think I've ever really registered before.

> **1:16 PM Jul 29th**
> i'm at N43 56.031 W103 34.546 – the furthest west i've ever been!

The damp gloomy Wednesday morning that we had woken up to continues, and carries on so that it becomes a damp and gloomy Wednesday afternoon. A hot breakfast and hot coffee still doesn't quite seem to warm me up – I have to get used it and realise that we've come quite a far way north now, and the 100 degrees temperatures of the south are a long way behind.

What's weird is that it kind of reminds me of being at home in England ... where you expect this sort of weather, so you don't mind. But having been used to a lot of warm sweltering weather for the past few weeks, I feel slightly indignant about it.

> **2:37 PM Jul 29th**
> Deadwood, SD. It's just 48F !

We head up north on US Highway 85, through windy roads and through the cute towns of Deadwood and Spearfish. Deadwood in particular is

---

[31] Every time we stopped at a Gas Station on the trip, I made a note of the SatNav coordinates of where we were. Sometimes it's important to have a list of everywhere in life that you fill up with petrol, trust me on this.

nothing like its name and is a grand tiny town full of independent shops, artistic brick buildings and a chilled hippy but cool attitude that really would have warranted a stop. But like I say it's also raining and a bit dank and cold, so whilst I lazily study the map and worry about gas for the rest of the day Nat drives, and also lazily snaps shots from the driver's window. A car toots its horn at her when she stops at a junction and leans out the window to take a photo, not realising that the car is behind us, waiting to turn.

> **3:02 PM Jul 29th**
> in Spearfish, SD. Heading slowly north to ND, for our northernmost 'same name' stop. It's gonna be a looong day.

As we approach Spearfish we both lament the fact that Deadwood would have been a cool place to stop, so we should probably stop in Spearfish instead … which turns out to be 'OK', but just not as nice as Deadwood overall we feel. We luck out though and find probably the cutest café in town, and over some excellent coffee we geek out on their free Wi-Fi and before I know it over a whole hour has gone, I don't feel the time slipping by, and I realise that we need to push on.

I drive, and we get more gas at a faux-rock'n'roll museum-slash-gift shop that has an Elvis section and a Route 66 section. But this isn't Tennessee, or anywhere along the Mother road – it feels odd seeing this stuff out here in South Dakota, and it fails to lift the damp spirits. We head out through Belle Force and I look at the map and realise that north on this road, there is … well … nothing and we should probably fill up at every opportunity – just in case.

> **4:17 PM Jul 29th**
> and we're now in 'when we see a gas station – fill up', mode. Whether we need to or not

We try to find the Geographic Center of the U.S. – On the road atlas that I am now looking at it appears as a little red square blob on the side of the road with a label, so I figure that in real life there may be a sign, or a visitor's spot or something to park where there might be a huge stone saying 'Center of the USA here!', but there is nothing … the long, lonely US Highway 85, a road full of a lot of nothing.

And we keep going, and strangely as we do, even though the day is wearing on and we are heading north, the day eventually seems to get slightly brighter and warmer and our moods finally lift.

'I think I need a photo of me on one of these hay bales' observes Nat. And there are a lot of them to choose from. Apart from the tiny town of Buffalo and Ludlow (and to call them 'Tiny Town' is too big of a description for them, they just look like farmhouses and, err... that's it ...) the road is strewn on the side with hay bales. And so seconds after she says it, I am pulling off to the side of the road, getting my camera out to snap a photo.

'Do you want me to drive for a bit?' asks Nat, as I load the camera back into the car. I do. But this makes me stop and look round and take in our surroundings.

'Look!' I say.

'At what? There's nothing'.

'Exactly!'

At which point I start to shoot video – and it's one of my favourite pieces of the whole trip, me standing in the middle of a long and empty road looking in both directions down the empty US Highway 85.

'In that direction ... North Dakota, we're in South Dakota right now ... Someone tweeted me this morning telling me that this road was just miles and miles of nothing ... they weren't kidding'

It invigorates me. I feel refreshed, keen, agile, alert, aware and in awe of the nothingness of my surroundings.

Nat does drive, and we press on ... thirty miles down the road getting to the North Dakota state line, and there is even a little pull-in for cars, where obviously everyone parks up so that they can take a picture of the 'Welcome to North Dakota sign'. 'Legendary' it says, and I count 37 bullet holes in it too.

Fifty metres back down on the other side of the road going the other way ... the 'Welcome to South Dakota' sign. Really? So the bit in-between the two signs is just – no man's land?

I think back about that spot and it makes me excited. How on earth can anyone get so excited about *nothing?* Dunno, but it exhilarates me. The slow wind whipping up the plains, across the fields allowing me to feel comfortably snug and warm when I get back into the car a few seconds later, and slam the door shut. It just feels ... *great* to be here, out in middle of nowhere where we've only passed two cars in the last hour of driving. And just typing this paragraph in has made me go look it up on Google Street View and have a yearning to go back there again.

Once again, I am loving being in the middle of nowhere. It's time to tell the world.

> **8:00 PM Jul 29th**
> in Bowman, North Dakota. Crossed state line about 20 miles back. MIDDLE OF NOWHERE stuff, awesome. #northdakota

Not knowing when we are going to next see a gas station, we fill up with petrol.

> **8:02 PM Jul 29th**
> heading east a bit, then north lots more, looking for 'The Enchanted Highway'

A same-named destination is our ultimate stop for the night, but en route we make our way along to the town of Regent, to find the Enchanted Highway – a collection of the world's largest scrap metal sculptures constructed at intervals along a 32 mile stretch of road.

A local artist has conceived the project, started to build it in 1989 and maintains it to this day. At 'Pheasants on the Prairie' we're standing next to three giant sizes pheasants, towering above us all twisted into shape out of coloured metal, and it is fun and impressive. But as we take photos we realise that the light is fading, and so we jump back in the car to get going. Except that as I start the engine there's a 'Ding!' of a pitch that I've never heard before, and I notice that the yellow 'Check Engine' light has come on. Really? What! Oh not now. Please not now. Ok, I will get that looked at the next time I get a chance too, promise.

We get onto the Interstate … west on I-94 and have one of those infuriating and yet glorious moments all at the same time because we have to decide where to stop to eat. It's glorious because you have a complete moment of utter freedom – being able to choose where to stop and go, and infuriating because your stomach is grumbling at you and wishing you'd stop being so whimsically free and easy and can you just get some protein and carbohydrates down into it for it to process as fast as possible-thanks-very-much.

Our target for the night – actually our target for the last couple of days – is Watford City – still a good 100 miles drive away. I consult the map. There are four towns off of the Interstate – Gladstone, Dickinson, South Heart and Bellfield.

Nat is driving. I'm navigating. 'Where are we going then?' she asks. 'I'm hungry'.

'I think we should try Dickinson', I say without looking up from the map 'It's in the largest boldest font out of all four'. 'Uh huh' she nods back with her approval, and yet within 90 seconds we're whizzing past Gladstone looking down onto the cute little lit up town with all its businesses and no doubt lot of happy content people eating yummy food in independently owned diners and we look at each other and think out loud as to if we've made the right choice.

'We're good, it'll be good, I know it's gonna be good', I say confidently, hoping that Natalie doesn't detect that I'm just saying that.

'You don't know, you're just saying that' she laughs back, and it's only a few miles down the road we're get to see who's right.

'Dickinson looks like a two gas station town to me.'

'Two is that all? I think it's gonna be more like five or six'

'Well', I say peering at the map some more, 'It IS in bold type, but it's in sentence case, not lower case so it's probably not going to be as many as that.'[32]

Dickinson looms – lit up in the fading light – from the side of the Interstate in all its regular strip mall glory, but you can tell from the lights behind it that there is more to it than that. Natalie snaps a photo of the 'Welcome to ...' sign 'I have a friend called Dickinson – I have to send him that photo', and with our stomachs now very much leading the way, head into the proper part of the town.

I laugh when I see the sign for 'Historical District' mainly because I always laugh when I see America pointing it out that it has a 'historical' part. To them, that means 100 years at most. I know men who would be prepared to keep underwear for that amount of time. Dear USA: You can't call anything 'historical' until it starts to become at least 500 years old. Thanks, the UK.

'The Dakota Diner, Dickinson' appears on our right a few moments into town after the 'historical' sign.

'It's a Diner!' I yell, 'It's in Dickinson!' comes back Natalie, 'And it's in Dakota!' I add ... and we roll into the parking lot to find ... that ... shit – although the lights inside we can see are on, we can also see that it is closed, the chief giveaway being the 'Sorry we're closed' sign now up at the entrance.

We can also see inside though that there are a group of people gathered round – the staff? – looking like they're having some sort of meeting. I check my watch, it's ten past eight. Oh no, is this going to be one of those places where if you don't eat dinner between 6 and 8pm in the evening then you're forced to go hungry?

'Dammit!' I say, and immediately inadvertently start a game that I know I am going to lose.

'Dead Diner' more like, comes back Natalie. 'Dinner's off', I add.

'Dude ... Don't Do that'

---

[32] One day, when I am in charge of all the maps in the whole of the world, it shall be perfectly clear from the case and the boldness of the type of a place name on a map, exactly just how big it is.

'Deliberate?'

'Definitely'

'Drat'

There's a pause of about twenty seconds. You can hear our brains ticking over.

'Difficult to start every sentence with a 'D' isn't it?'

'Decidedly so'

'Didn't mean to start doing this'

'Did'

'Distinctly, I did not …'

There's silence. As we look at each other trying to think or more words that begin with 'D', but before either of us a can – a Mexican restaurant appears ahead, and we both instinctively know that we're going to go there for food.

Post dinner, we try and find a hotel to stay in for the night – I'd rather go to Watford City in the morning when it's daylight, and places will be open and there will be people about, but we try *every* motel and hotel in Dickinson, and they are all full. In the end we get desperate and find a place on the other side of Watford, and make a booking online. It looks like we're going to Watford tonight then. It's a bit of a drive away – two hours exactly it turns out.

1:32 AM Jul 30th
and welcome to … Watford City, North Dakota

In the USA
Watford City, North Dakota
On the Tube map
Watford (Metropolitan Line)

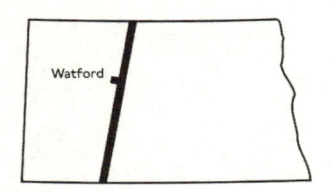

We make it to Watford in the early hours of Thursday morning. This *is* ridiculous. We've come a long way to go out of our way just to go to a town called Watford City, just because there is a place in London called Watford.

And it's dark. And everything is closed.

'Welcome to Watford City' says a large wooden sign as we arrive at the town, I pull in and jump down to take a photo.

'Watford City is the 1999 North Dakota CITY of the YEAR' it proclaims. Plus a whole load of others signs including one intriguing one saying 'Ancient Free and Accepted – Masons'. Uh huh, is this a large Masonic town then?

> **1:36 AM Jul 30th**
> Watford City was voted North Dakota's city of the year in 1999, woot

With everything closed, it seems the only sensible thing to do is to drive through the neatly-lit 'high street' and see what we are missing out on, 'Do it best – Badlands Hardware' catches my eye, we've left the Badlands National Park back in South Dakota, haven't we? That is *miles* away – why the reference to the Badlands here, I wonder?

We stop at a crossroads and I get out. Nat looks like she'd rather be asleep and generally doesn't seem to be getting in on the spirit of the fact that it is called Watford.

> **1:39 AM Jul 30th**
> we've arrived at 00.30 but it's well lit up, semi cute. The Kum & Go 24hr gas station is open still

'Nat?' I ask making a face that says 'Come out and join me in the streets of wonderful Watford!', but she isn't having it. Maybe she needs to have visited Watford Underground station in London like I have many times to be able to appreciate this on the same level that I am. Yes. Yes that's probably what it is. And is probably why she just gives me a grumpy stare back.

> **1:37 AM Jul 30th**
> Nat just gave me a look that said 'so we turn up to a dark empty town in the middle of the night, takes photos and leave?'

We pull back in by the 'Welcome to Watford City' sign. I position the car so that the headlights light up the sign. I insist that Nat takes a photo of me standing in front of the sign.

> **1:42 AM Jul 30th**
> and. Erm ... Yup, that's pretty much it. 300 miles excursion and $45 in gas to visit a town with the same name. At night.

> **1:46 AM Jul 30th**
> so i think that'll do for the day. Tomorrow: Montana

I want to back come in the morning – when it is bright and daylight and shops and businesses will be open. I spot a diner across the street that looks *brilliant* and suddenly realise that if Nat isn't with me, I'd be all for pulling over into a side street and kipping down in the car for the night and exploring Watford by myself in the morning. As it is, we have reservations for a motel that is still yet a little drive away, and Nat now looks like she is going to kill me if she doesn't get some proper rest soon.

I get out my logbook, and add Watford to the bottom of the list.

SAME NAME TOWNS TALLY

Perfect Small Town America
Preston, White City, Waterloo

Something there and enjoyable
Plaistow, Gloucester, Kew Gardens, Harrow, South Kensington, Greenford, Liverpool, Temple, Oxford, Victoria, Kingsbury County

Something there but not that exciting to be honest
Putney, Amersham, Hampstead, Woodford, Brompton, Kingsbury, Redbridge, Latimer

Nothing there but somehow being in the middle of nowhere made it OK
Epping, Acton, Lancaster, Green Park Farm

Nothing there, and not that exciting either. Oops.
Warwick, Wapping, Camden, Bond, Elm Park

Closed
Swiss Cottage, Watford

We do another thirty miles of driving that night to get to our motel in Williston. To be honest, it's amazing that we get there in one piece because it's so late, and we are so tired that I can't even remember who drove. I'm sure not a lot was said. Anything could have happened in that twenty minute journey and I don't think either of us would have clearly remembered it. It was that kind of journey where we just wanted it to be over.

The hotel is 'functional' – and I'm not going to say anything more than that. All I know is that at two-thirty in the morning, the last thing you really want to be doing is lugging in equipment from the car, but that's exactly what we have to do. The one slightly comical moment may have been where Nat takes the fly screen off of the window to our room, and I just pass my PC and video equipment in through the window from the car park outside into the room because it's quicker than walking down the corridor back and forth several times to bring all the stuff in from the car.

~ ~ ~

In the morning, I spread out a large foldable paper map of the USA over my bed – the bed which I'd slept *on* but not *in* the night before. Nat is in shower, and I'm taking this moment to consider the next stop, and I feel concerned.

I'm worried that since Nat has been on the trip, I'd kind of strayed off focus a bit. The trip is about visiting all 48 states, and hitting up one same-named-town or place in each of them. Also, on the side it's the time out and time of my life to give me thinking space about what I want to do next in my life, stay in America or go back to England. And then – along the way – I am allowing myself to visit some of the major National Parks, attractions and scenic places that America has to offer, because I'd be a fool to pass right by these places, and not visit them whilst I have the chance. I know I'd like to come back again to these parts, but realistically I don't know if I ever will in my life or not, so I've got to take that opportunity now.

I already feel like I have rushed through Latimer the other night, Kingsbury County had been a bit of a cheat with Nat what with it just being a county and not a town. It felt at Watford as if my standards are slipping, and with Nat on board and me not really being sure that she's 'got it', I can feel the standard slipping even more.

To add to that, the next couple of days do not help either as there are no same-places to hit just yet, just driving and driving to fantastic, scenic, places – but none of them Underground themed.

I want to be able to write and tell you about more same-named towns and places that are very interesting that we discover, but I can't do that, because what we do is become tourists for the next couple of days.

We have breakfast in a kitschy café down the road, where I eat kielbasa for the first time in my life. We stop at a gas station that also sells shotgun ammunition as casually as selling gum by the cash register. We stay the night in a simple but-nothing-interesting KOA at Miles City. The next day our morning starts at a hippy-shop that is also a café where the lovely *Linda* serving us is happy to sign my t-shirt. 'What shall I write?' she asks with a pleasant smile?

'How about … Montana – it's full of casinos!' I cheekily suggest.

'Oh, but it's SO much more than casinos!!' she retorts is a nice but at the same time serious way, and before I know it, that's the exact phrase that she's written on my t-shirt, and to this day it remains my favourite out of all the people that signed it.

We drive up the Beartooth pass – a scenic road that is only open during summer months, but all it is doing is making me feel more like a tourist, and going off track as to my real journey intent. I should probably check my 'same name' list actually, just to make sure that I am still on course with that, but my notebook is currently buried under all my video equipment on the back seat – I make a mental note to check when we next stop.

> **4:39 PM Jul 31st**
> we're about to go drive 'The Beartooth pass', into Yellowstone. 'The most scenic drive in all America'. cool.

The pass takes us into Yellowstone Park, where we don't stop and stay, but again it isn't the real purpose of my trip.

> **3:37 PM Jul 31st**
> made it to Billings, Montana. As Montana goes, this is a huge city. #billlings

> **3:39 PM Jul 31st**
> there's a casino on every block. Is that all Montanans do – gamble?

> **4:04 PM Jul 31st**
> i've just counted 17 Casinos driving through Billings, MT. I wish i was kidding, but no. #gamblinganonymous

We stay the weekend at a campground in Livingstone, during which Nat and I have a 'day off' and she takes the car and explores Yellowstone by herself – I would go with her the next day.

I sleep, swim in the pool, edit some more video and have a lovely conversation with *Brenda* the woman running the campground shop with whom I'd had a brief conversation with the day before when buying some stuff, so today when she recognises me again she's even more chatty.

She ends up asking me what the purpose of my roadtrip is, and I go into extensive detail about tube stations and the 'same name' part for a good minute, and then tag onto the end the bit about me being recently divorced. Brenda instantly smiles.

'Sounds to me honey like you're just doing it to get over your marriage' she says with a brilliant smile. 'Which I think is what you need to do – you're doing the right thing you know, just follow your bliss!'

I'd never heard that expression before now (I think it's an American thing) before and to be honest it sounds a bit cheesy – it did then and it still does now, but the underlying meaning of it really resonated to me for some reason.

'You don't think I'm doing this to explore the fascinating country that is America then?' I say with a smile.

'Oh sure you are honey, but you're also doing it to get some perspective on your life and figure out what to do next, am I right?'

Wow. Yes! You are *exactly* right. My face must have said this, because I don't actually say anything for a few seconds as I wonder instead how she has figured all this out.

'I thought as much!'

We chat some more – actually, the conversation for five minutes in the KOA Kampground store may just have been my favourite thing of the whole weekend – even beating Yellowstone itself. Sometimes, it's the little moments that count.

'Take care honey!' she says, as I leave the shop with the door clanging behind me.

On the downside, by the end of the weekend, I have also mistakenly eaten some McDonald's breakfast, shouted at the Wi-Fi in the campground for not working, had yet another small argument with Nat, and burn a hole in the bottom of my stove pan by heating it too hard for too long.

I'm fully aware that we've been on the road for four days and not hit a same-named town for a while, so tomorrow, I am going to drag us right back on track.

Day 49 – Monday 3rd August

Popular

*'You were the popular one, the popular chick
It is what it is, now I'm popular-ish
Standing on the field with your pretty pompom
Now you're working at the movie selling popular corn'*

Over some dreadfully made camp ground coffee I look at the roadmap of where we have to go today, and inwardly chuckle to myself at what it is we have to do. Essentially it is just a 400 mile detour ... 200 miles there, to drive to a tiny same-named town, that I just *know* in all likelihood is going to be a completely nothing crossroads in the middle of nowhere – and then 200 miles back again from practically the same direction where we have come from, just so that I can say I have been there. I am happy with that. Nat maybe less so.

I close down Google Maps on my laptop and fire up the Underground : USA Facebook group instead and spend the next few minutes busily uploading some of the stunning pictures of Yellowstone that I now have on my camera.

> **8:43 AM Aug 3rd**
> added up whole bunch of stunning photos of Yellowstone Park to Und USA facebook group & blog

Nat comes out to cook some non-fat, non-protein, non-white, no-taste, might-as-well-be-eating-thin-air breakfast, only to rapidly discover that the little bit of gas for the stove that we have left, gets used up in just trying to light the stove, and so now we have no gas. Oops. That sets the agenda for the morning then,

> **9:23 AM Aug 3rd**
> in search of gas. Isopropane, that is.

A quick check with the campground staff confirms what we have suspected, that being that Bozeman a few miles down the road and en route to our next stop would be a sizeable enough town to have a proper camping store in, so – going via a quick Geocache on the way – we are Bozeman bound.

> **12:58 PM Aug 3rd**
> Bozeman, MT. Seen three beggars within 2 minutes of being in the town.

12:59 PM Aug 3rd
one beggars sign says **Green Only**.So you'll turn down $10 of quarters in change then will ya buddy?

There is a strange mountainous hippy feel to the town, and I can honestly say that for a non-metropolis's style of town/city, there's an unnerving amount of beggars on the street, asking for change. Despite this, it somehow manages to retain its cutesy charm – and ability to have good shops too, and we stumble across a camping store without even really trying to find it and nip inside.

2:12 PM Aug 3rd
In the 'Northern Lights' camping store. They sell bear-repellent spray, debating stocking up.

2:57 PM Aug 3rd
Is it just Montana that has little coffee 'huts' ? Keep seeing them everywhere here.

3:03 PM Aug 3rd
We're finally heading for our Idaho same named stop on the Tube map, except it is actually a DLR station

---

In the USA
Poplar, Idaho
On the Tube map
Poplar (DLR)

7:42 PM Aug 3rd
i'm in Poplar, Idaho. Yes i know that's a DLR stop, sssh. Oh, and there's nothing here.

With Poplar I am determined to get the purpose of the trip back on track. Since Natalie has been with me, it does feel as if I've not done justice to the places that I've been to, and maybe perhaps overall all the 'not much going here' crossroads that I have been to, I wonder if I can have made more of it. I decide I am going to make more of this one.

'I'm going to make more of this one!' I say to Natalie with a little steel in my voice as I notice the SatNav says that we are now exactly an hour away. 'How's that then?' she rightly asks. 'I'm going to video it, even if there's nothing to video. I want to have a video of how sometimes we end up in nothing places'. 'OK' she says – surprising me, as I thought she might have more to say about it, but she doesn't.

Poplar is – as I suspected it would be – a crossroads with not a lot going on. It isn't strictly 'middle of nowhere' nothing going on. But I make a fuss about taking some photos and shooting some video. I give Nat the camera, and get her to shoot me 'pulling up' and then opening the door of the car – the first thing I see though is a dog further up the road.

'There's a dog running up the road behind you, look!' and as Nat spins to capture him digitally he stares back for a moment before scampering off. I continue to talk to the video camera.

'As we arrived a moment ago viewers, Nat just turned to me and said … *Is this it?* Which I think describes perfectly the sheer and utter silliness of this quest… quest?! Ha! My SatNav says we're at Poplar though, and yes … this crossroad is it'

'So typically what I do now is take a photo of something interesting, although I think it's going to be hard to find something interesting. But at least I can say I've been here, yes?'

I wander off to take photos, and Nat even shoots video of me taking photos, and in the twenty minutes that we are there doing it, the only thing of interest that happens is that the dog reappears and walks towards us a little more, this time close enough for us to see that it is actually limping as it walks. It stares at us from 100 yards away, and then turns and limps back down the road and through a hedge.

Poplar. It sounds a bit like 'Popular' or perhaps 'Population' right? Of which it is, and there is neither at this one.

We press on to where we are staying that night, another KOA.

> **8:03 PM Aug 3rd**
> just passed 'Stinker Stores', it's a skunk-themed gas station, apparently.

> **8:07 PM Aug 3rd**
> Idaho in 3 : potatoes, farms, dusty.

I leave Nat online using laptop at the campground and head back into main downtown Pocatello. I buy some toothpaste. I eat a Jack-in-the-Box cheeseburger.

I come back. Sit in a lonely launderette playing Just Jack and get online myself and Facebook stalk some people.

> **10:21 PM Aug 3rd**
> made it to Pocatello, ID for the night, we drove 200 miles south to get here today. Tomorrow: turn around and go 200 miles north. #crazy

It isn't a bad day ... and I'm not in a bad mood ... but I also am not in the greatest of moods either. It is just one of those days where I recognise that really we've driven 200 miles just to see ... nothing ... and I start to wonder, is that a bit stupid after all? Is it stupid having companions with me that don't really care about that side of the trip and just want to see some of America?

I think about the prospect of doing it at my complete leisure ... taking more of my time and not worrying about where I have to be by or when, but just ... having the luxury of moving along when I want to, or not when I don't want. Maybe next time. Hang on - *Next time?* I inwardly exclaim to myself.

> **1:47 AM Aug 4th**
> completely loving the new Just Jack 'The day I die', just ... lovely. #justjack

What time is it? *Shit!* How long have I been sitting here in the launderette online? Too long apparently, and I head for the tent thinking about the prospect of coming back in five years' time and visiting some of the areas that I know I won't be hitting this time around. *Next time*, indeed. Heh.

~ ~ ~

The next day is practically the reverse of what we have done to come down this way in the first place, and instead of driving 200 miles south, we just fill up with gas and drive 200 miles north instead. There will be no same-name stops to do today, so when the opportunity presents itself to do something rather fun, we can't turn it down.

> **11:13 AM Aug 4th**
> have just seen a sign for a potato museum, and it's not a Monday. You know what this means, don't you folks?

> **11:47 AM Aug 4th**
> although I suspect a running commentary on a potato museum may not be as compelling as Graceland?

Yeah yeah. We park up. We pay the entrance fee, and we take the tour. Twitter overload!

> **21:20 PM Aug 4th**
> did-u-know? The botanical name for a potatoes plant structure is a 'Tuber'. And i'm visiting Tube stops!

> **1:22 PM Aug 4th**
> the world's largest potato chip (crisp) is here. it's 25 inches across, and gone stale – was made in 1991. #potatomuseum

> **1:33 PM Aug 4th**
> did-u-know? The average American eats 142 lbs of potatoes every year. #potatomuseum
>
> **1:35 PM Aug 4th**
> 'spud' comes from the Society for Prevention of Unwholesome Diets, as potatoes were first thought to be bad for you

This is the tweet that causes the most replies to be fired back at me. 'Oh no it isn't!' is the general consensus from people on why potatoes are called spuds. A quick Google search later reveals this to be true, and in fact a 'spud' is the nickname for a sharp narrow spade-like tool that was once used to dig up large rooted plants – including potatoes.

Which makes me wonder, if the potato museum has made *that* fact up – what else is a lie? What if the average American doesn't eat 142 lbs of potatoes every year? This has me worried, I can tell you.

> **1:37 PM Aug 4th**
> McDonalds get on average 36 french fries from 1 potato. You're finding this fascinating, aren't you? #potatomuseum
>
> **1:39 PM Aug 4th**
> Gift shop selling Mr. Potato-head novelty items, naturally. #potatomuseum
>
> **1:44 PM Aug 4th**
> And i'm all potato'd out. See ya later, tater. Time to hit the road again.

We get back on the highway, we do more driving, and we head north. Towards a campground where I know we can hold up for a few days. Both Nat and I need another day off from each other – and it is timed nicely. Tomorrow I have a Tube stop which I can do all by myself, and I also have a date with a Canadian friend of mine, as we are so far north up the top of the USA now, we're getting close to being in another country.

We arrive at the Deer Lodge KOA campground whilst it is still light and we book a Kabin for two nights so we can have time and space to ourselves. Thankfully there is a working Wi-Fi signal but only if you sit out on the porch of the cabin – which is fine because it means I can have the pleasant experience of watching the sun slowly set as I go about the very important task which I've been meaning to do for the past couple of weeks, but not been able to find a moment to do – until now.

I fire up my 'music' folder on my laptop, and start playing songs ... there is no way that I have got everything organised back onto my iPod yet, and so I've been collecting songs along the way and storing them and just playing them off of my laptop.

There are three songs that defined my road trip around the USA, and even though I'm playing them in random order this night, they rotate around in the order that I will chronologically remember them.

Lady GaGa's 'Paparazzi' plays first – which was the first two to three weeks – right up until the point that I'd had all my stuff stolen. I would play the Sirius satellite radio and listen to BBC Radio One from back home, and it was in strong rotation on their playlist. I even remember the moment driving through Delaware sipping on a Dunkin' Donuts coffee thinking 'What *is* this?' and glad that the radio comes with a text service which tells me exactly who it is and what it was. And I love this song.

The day after I get back on the road after I'd had all my stuff stolen, I realise that they haven't stolen the radio! The aerial is complicatedly entangled in the rest of the car and the thieves have obviously thought it too much bother to untangle it, and the hard metal aerial wire doesn't pull apart easily either – you'd need to use wire cutters. So it has been left. As I drive out towards Burlington on the I-40 to the nearby Best Buy to get a new SatNav so that I know where I am, Green Day's '21 Guns' comes on the radio. I've been hearing it a couple of times before I think, but this is the first time that it really resonates and I turn up the Hi-Fi in the car – loud, and blast out as I whizz down the highway. By the next day at Jamie's I must have played it twenty times solidly in row as it fits my mood perfectly.

But none of this can match the obsessive song that I played a few weeks later. I still can't remember where I am when I first hear it, but the first time I do, I know it makes me feel happy *and* sad both at the same time – which is surely a strange reaction for a song to have.

I'd play it a little during my week on my own, but it isn't until the week that Nat comes with me that I start to really get into it.

> **10:54 PM Aug 4th**
> i'm (finally) sending out 'thank you' emails. to everyone that gave money to #helpgeoff

And that's what I do. For two solid hours mainly listening to the same three songs on repeat, I sit and type out individual (no cut and paste!) thank-you-emails to everyone that has given money, I play Just Jack's 'The Day I Died'. I play it once, I play it five times, then ten, I easily play it more than twenty times in a row, I play it to death as I type out all the emails.

'Geoff!' comes the feminine scratchy tone from inside the cabin. 'Can you either turn it down or *please* play something else!'

Oops, sorry Nat. I turn the volume down on my laptop so that I can only just hear it.

I sit and I type and I type and I type that night. I send individual emails to everyone that has given money to the **#helpgeoff** campaign and got me back on the road again. And I really do type them all individually. No copy & paste ... I wanted everyone to get a personal thank you, and as I write, Just Jack is there.

Sometime past 1am, with Nat already asleep and in the dark, I finish and audibly let out a sigh, and feel good that it's finally done – it has been stressing me out for a few days that I haven't done it sooner – but I haven't really had the chance.

I check my email one more time before going to bed – and what? Ah, bugger. An unhappy email from Katie asking why she's not heard from me today. I haven't deliberately not called her, it's just how the day has turned out. I email her back – a carefully crafted email that takes half an hour to write, and at stupid-o-clock again, I eventually shutdown and head inside the cabin, with 'The Day I Died' humming inside my head without me even having to try.

Day 51 – Wednesday 6th August

Epiphany

*'And there's something about this city today,
like all the colours conspire to overwhelm the grey,
and this close to the fire I can feel no cold,
with a rainbow halo, around my soul'.*

I'd always planned to have a day off on this Wednesday, and as plans go it's fortuitously timed because I need a day off to go and do my own thing. Firstly, it is clear now that for all the fun most of the time, I am also driving Nat mad, just as much as she is driving me mad too. I think we are just both suffering from being sat in the same small confines of a car for too long, and we've exhausted all jokes and are just a little bit sick of each other.

Secondly, I need some time out for myself because I can feel I am getting to a point where I am near to figuring out what I want to do, and if I am any closer to knowing if I know I am going to go home or not.

I re-read Katie's email from last night as well. I'd said goodbye to who-is-now-my-girlfriend in Charleston a few weeks back and driven off and she has to cope with the fact that we aren't going to see each other for another two months, and that I am having an amazing adventure and the time of my life without her.

So there's been a few bad emails and texts in the past few days, just because the distance is making it hard – and I want to have some time out, some space to myself, especially when I get an annoying email from Katie all because I haven't sent her a text message or called on one day – the truth being that on that day we've mostly been driving through areas which just *doesn't have* phone coverage … and yet it fucks me off, so when I get up this morning I already know what I am going to do.

I send a twitter update from my laptop, turn my phone completely OFF and then go out for the day – by myself.

> **12:23 PM Aug 5th**
> having a 'day off' today. Going to meet a Canadian friend of mine in Great Falls. Phone going off now.

It's a complicated story about how I know Scott, and when I say 'know' I've only ever met him once in my entire life, when we'd sat in a Starbucks in central London meeting for the first time, and yet chatting like old friends who'd know each other forever.

When I knew I would be up near the Canadian border at the beginning of August, I'd emailed him my schedule in advance, and we'd decided that we'd meet in Great Falls … about a 3 hours' drive for me … and about a 5 hour drive for him! The location? Starbucks, of course.

In the USA
Hackney, Montana
On the Tube map
Hackney Central (Overground)

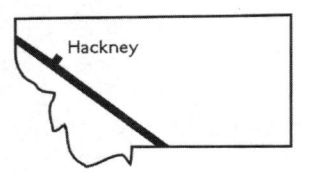

But I do take in a same-named stop on the way. Ten minutes off of the I-15 and up the I-90 instead is the town of Hackney. And by 'town of Hackney', what I mean is 'dusty road of Fairmont'.

I have the good sense to check on **placenames.com** and Google Maps this morning before I leave to see exactly what I am getting myself into, and the website quite clearly states that Hackney is a 'populated place'.

But at the precise Longitude and Latitudal coordinates that it has given me, I am looking at a track up a valley that gets narrower as it goes along. Mountains lie ahead. A river and a line of telegraph poles are down (quite a way down, I am about 5,000 feet up!) to my right. I have passed one farmhouse on the way up here. There looks like there may be another one up ahead.

But most of all, when I had come off the Interstate the road sign has said 'Fairmont', I'd driven down a Fairmont Road, seen a sign for Fairmont RV park which is right next to Fairmont Hotel & Springs resort. As far at the world is concerned, I am in Fairmont and not Hackney.

Bizarrely, I do have a 3G signal on my phone – I think because I am still quite close to the Interstate, so just to double check, I fire up my laptop – get online and check the coordinates for Hackney, and yes – I am in the right place. Only there doesn't seem to be any real 'place'.

Even all the other 'nothing' stops I have been too – in a flash I recall Epping and Lancaster and Bond and Elm Park, there have been a distinct crossing of roads – a junction of some description, but here it is a rough road – one that I wouldn't like to attempt to drive along in the winter – with no discernible Hackney features at all.

I turn the car around. It's OK – I will just chalk it up as another 'nothing' place. I try to console myself and remind myself that some places are always going to be like this and that it's OK – and I am off to see Scott today anyway, so that will make it a good day.

I drive slowly back down the rough track to the main road, and as I do I look out again at the valley that is now deep down to my left, and as I do I see something that makes me double-take, and then smile, and then grin, and then REALLY grin so widely that eventually it vocalises itself in the form of happy laughter – for there is a train down below.

SAME NAME TOWNS TALLY

Perfect Small Town America
Preston, White City, Waterloo

Something there and enjoyable
Plaistow, Gloucester, Kew Gardens, Harrow, South Kensington, Greenford, Liverpool, Temple, Oxford, Victoria, Kingsbury County

Something there but not that exciting to be honest
Putney, Amersham, Hampstead, Woodford, Brompton, Kingsbury, Redbridge, Latimer

Nothing there but somehow being in the middle of nowhere made it OK
Epping, Acton, Lancaster, Green Park Farm, Hackney

> *Nothing there, and not that exciting either. Oops.*
> Warwick, Wapping, Camden, Bond, Elm Park, Poplar
>
> *Closed*
> Swiss Cottage, Watford

I stop the car and jump out and with my zoom lens on my camera look deep down below to see a typically long freight train with ... well, *a lot* of wagons behind it being pulled along, and I laugh once more. I have to laugh. I realise then I would have to count up how many – all by chance let me stress again – that have had railways passing through them. That has never been the plan; it has just worked out that way. I know that at the end I would total up just how many of the places do have railways. I watch the train pass through, and I am left looking at the stunning view of an empty valley with trees and rough land stretching in all directions – mountains too. I breathe in deep, clean fresh mountain air into my lungs and slowly exhale it. I am feeling very relaxed right now, a calmness inside ... it's as if ... I don't know *something* deep inside is coming together – but what? I just know that for some reason this is a moment that is building to something else.

Whatever, I mustn't keep Scott waiting. I press on.

I arrive bang on time, and know that he's already here when I spy the only Canadian plate in the parking lot – 'Alberta, Wild Rose Country' it says as its slogan. He sees me from the window, and comes out and greets me with a big hug. That is nice! And hang on – what's this? He's wearing a T-Shirt with the London Underground roundel on, that's excellent!

Over a coffee we sit and talk. Just sit, and talk. And talk and talk ... and talk, and it is exactly what I need. Sure, there is talk of the road trip, but we also discuss other travel, places, music, news, gossip, technology.

It is lovely. We chat and he gives me some Canadian candy and even some Canadian coins as he knows I've been collecting the American Quarters and he feels like I should have more and more 'strange money' to add to my collection. After a couple of hours though, our time is up, as I have a three hour drive back – but worse for him as he has a five hour drive! I realised that Scott will be doing ten hours of driving today just to come and see me, which is extremely nice of him.

He is sad to see me go, and I'm sad too. The time out talking to him myself is having the effect I thought it might have. Scott is not part of the trip, he's an excellent diversion and we've actually actively talked very little about the trip – instead the brain has been doing what it is really good at doing without you being aware of – processing things in the background, in your sub-conscious, so that there is then a moment when you realise something or come to a decision, and you think that you've only just thought of it then, but actually your brain has come up with it an hour ago. I think it have been first stirred by that *something* at Hackney earlier today, but now I am more aware than ever that my brain has been processing something on the side.

I drive not-too-fast actually back along the I-15 heading south, because it is by no means a fast Interstate. The Flint Creek range on one side, the Boulder Range on the other, the road goes up, and down, and round bends and more bends, snaking its way through glorious mountain scenery, which helps me unwind even more, and I have my iPod on playing a random selection of liked songs of mine.

It starts to rain … the sort of annoying pace of drizzle that isn't enough to have your wipers on the slow speed, but enough that means you have to manually wipe it yourself once every few seconds, but yet I'm loving it. I feel like I have time and space and thoughts and the whole world to myself, and at that moment – on iPod shuffle, not planned – the Just Jack 'Day I Died' tune comes on, and I sing along. I sing louder, and smile as I sing, realising for the first time that I have inadvertently learned the words without even trying because I've listened to it so much over the last few days by playing it to death, as it plays and I sing I am smiling and realise I feel extremely exhilarated.

A lay-by appears ahead on a bend in the road. A lay-by that is there because it offers a view down into the valley below, so I pull over and breath in the delicious damp mountain air and survey the rocky scenery that disappears beyond the crash barriers that separate the road from the valley down into the depths below – it is stunning. And I take photos, the headlights of the car light up the gloom of the mountain drizzle which somehow totally inspires me rather than drags me down, and I smile and yet at the same time a small tear forms in my eye, the emotion of the past … wow … how many days has it been now? I've lost count, whatever – finally, it's all catching up with me.

After a few minutes, the rain gets a little heavier, so I get back in the car but don't go anywhere, so I just sit – and I hit 'back' on the iPod to play the Just Jack song again, and in a pure moment of – yes – *serendipity* again that is impossible to emulate because sometimes in life they just occur like that to make you feel like nothing else on earth, through my window to the left, a rainbow appears in the sky, through the drizzle and between the two mountains, and I *snap* a photo with my camera – capturing the shadowy silhouette of the car at the same time, and I sing, I sing along to every word of the song, especially the 'Rainbow Halo' part – as I look at a real life rainbow, and at that point – at that *exact* point, I know exactly where I am and what it is that I want to do now, and so for the first time today I turn my phone back on and tweet my one and only thought to the world.

7:40 PM Aug 5th
epiphany

It is time to go home.

Katie's email has got me thinking all day in the back of my head about my future with her – but my future with my whole life, her – and everyone else back in Charleston right now that has become my American home, but really on the whole trip I have been subconsciously thinking about where my real home is, and right now I realise that I've worked it all out in my head, and know that the only place that I want to be now is *proper* home.

It is time, I'm done now. I've had my fun, and now I know I have to get back to real life, in London, England. That's where I need to be.

I just have to finish off the rest of the road trip first.

Day 53 – Friday 7th August

Hello Seattle

*'Hello Seattle, I am the crescent moon
Shining down on your face
I will disguise myself as a sleeping pill
And descend inside of you'*

I'm going to sum up one whole day in a single sentence:

On Thursday, we drive west along US Highway 12 – through the stunning Clearwater National Forest, and then we stay the night in a B&B that is built in the shape of a large wooden dog.

~ ~ ~

> **8:53 AM Aug 7th**
> I just spent the night in a giant wooden Beagle. woof!.

I have to get Natalie to Seattle by the end of the week, which is an easy two days driving with no same-name places to stop along the way, just a giant dog. Yes – a giant wooden dog which we sleep in.

When I'd originally planned the schedule for the trip at the beginning of the year, I'd emailed ahead to the Dog Park Barn Inn (a B&B built of wood in the shape of a Beagle, and large enough to have a room inside to sleep in) asking about their available dates, knowing really that I wanted to stay there the night of the 5th of August. And yet annoyingly back in February when I'd booked it, the 5th was just one of two days in August that they are already booked for! So I'd have to book the 6th instead, knowing that what this meant in reality is that that would be a day of long boring driving the day after so that we can get to Seattle by the end of it which is where Nat would then fly back from.

I get up early – about 5.30am to be precise at sunrise, and I spend a few minutes outside with the video camera getting some shots of the Beagle that I can intersperse with the interview stuff from yesterday which I've shot. Only it's raining lightly, so all the cars driving past at that early time in the morning see the ridiculous sight of a man carrying a video camera on a tripod in one hand, and an umbrella in the other shielding the equipment from the precipitation as I get some shots of a large wooden dog. One of the drivers toots his horn and waves at me; I just about manage to smile back.

Back on the road, an Exxon gas station stop leads to a near awkward-moment with Nat as to her dislike of Exxon for environmental reasons, but as there is no other gas station around, and I promise to her not to mention that I've been at an Exxon in the car with her. I may have had my fingers crossed as I make this promise.

> **10:13 AM Aug 7th**
> ooh! We just crossed the state line into Washington. The weather is terrible, bad visibility...

> **11.03 AM Aug 7th**
> emergency bladder stop at McDonalds, Pullman. Natalie will pee in the car otherwise. It is still raining miserably

We pull out of Pullman. Or rather, we pull out of the parking lot of the mall in Pullman, Washington – the 39th state on my trip, and as we do so the yellow 'check engine' light in the car comes on again. Shit.

> **11:13 AM Aug 7th**
> and the yellow 'check engine' light just came on, ah shiiiit ...

The light had come on a few days ago when we'd been driving up the enchanted highway, and like all sensible cross-country road trippers I'd ignored it and hoped that it would magically go away and get better by itself. One night in Watford and the morning after and the light *had* gone off again, and I'd forgotten all about it, right until now this rainy miserable morning, when it comes on again and both Nat and I concede that as we have a little time (and all day) to get to Seattle, we should probably get it looked at.

> **11.21 AM Aug 7th**
> garage No.1 : $68 just to put the scope on for a check engine light? Noooo f'ing way!

We stop at the first garage we see just up the road, which is more like a car-rental place which seems to do auto-repairs on the side. The efficient but not-so-friendly person behind the counter informs us that we will have to wait two hours and pay a not-entirely-small amount of dollars just to get some guy to plug a scope into the car to get the engine codes inspected. We decline.

Half a mile up the road, we spy a NAPA (National Automotive Parts Association) garage which although equally chainy and corporate just looks more like a proper friendly garage in where some guy in greasy overalls called 'Joe' clutching a spanner will come out asking how he can help you.

My vision isn't far off ... the mechanics name is actually *Karl* and he isn't clutching a spanner but he *does* have partially-stained overalls on! We also pull an amazing sneaky trick. Nat elects to pull the cute female card, so whilst I sit outside in the passenger seat of the car, she goes inside making Karl assume that she is a single female in distress. By the time he realises that he's been fooled and sees me sitting in the passenger seat it is too late, as he already has his scope in hand and has offered to have a look for free.

> **12:22 PM Aug 7th**
> the car is ok! It's a minor oxygen/fuel adjustment. Got Karl the nice man to fix AND sign my t-shirt!

> **12:24 AM Aug 7th**
> and we're BAAAACK on the road. Pit Stop! Seattle here we come ...

The weather finally lifts and the sun comes out, I stop to take photos of a rusty truck in a field to add to my 'abandoned' collection of vehicles galleries. We stop in the town of Othello just as we cross into Washington State and eat at a Mexican restaurant (one of six in the town that we count), only realising halfway through that there are bullet holes in the glass of the window by which we are sat – a drive by shooting from a rival restaurant?

> **2:13 PM Aug 7th**
> i'm watching a cop in Othello, WA check out the bullet holes in the Mexican restaurant i've just eaten in

We carry on with our long and relatively dull long driving day. We go west along Highway 26, and eventually and inevitably connect up with the Interstate and keep on the I-90 towards the town of StarSoft. Or MicroBux. Take your pick.

> **8:49 AM Aug 7th**
> hello, Seattle! Can i get me a SBX?

We time it perfectly to hit the snarled up traffic of the evening rush hour, but we eventually sneak into downtown, and some ridiculously expensive parking later, I head off to get some online time[33], and leave Nat to wander round the famous Pike's Place market.

I've been in Seattle before last year and done the market area, so don't have the urge to do it again. I do of course though have the urge to check my email and update my progress map.

> **8:03 AM Aug 7th**
> farewell companion no.4, just dropped Natalie off at Seattle airport ...

---

[33] In one of the 424 Starbucks in the Seattle area. Yes, you read that right – as of August 2007 there were over 400 outlets of the coffee giant in the Seattle area. That's a lot of caffeine.

Dropping Nat off is painless enough, and I think – think – that we are just about OK. I'm sure there is plenty left there to dissect and talk about later when I see her when I get back, but all that can wait. I need to get through the next couple of weeks, get to the end of the trip, get back to US home, and make plans to head back to my UK home.

That night I score a free night's sleep on the couch of my friend Chris. Well – I say 'friend' but actually I've never met Chris before in my life.

Instead I know Chris through his website **septicscompanion.com** which I discovered shortly after moving to America. Chris himself is from the UK (Scotland), and has setup an amusing website as a guide to helping Brits now living stateside. He'd ended up producing a book which actually explains British slang to Americans.

Chris works for Microsoft, lives in Seattle and is married – and one of the first things that his wife does is to give me a look as if to say 'So you're the strange man that my husband has been talking to off of the Internet and has invited you here to stay for the night'. Whereas *I* am thinking that Chris is the strange man that I have only met via the Internet, and I am taking a bit of a gamble crashing in his house for the night. Don't worry, we soon bond – we go out for beers.

> **10:34 PM Aug 9th**
> out in Capitol Hill, Seattle with @pugwonk and friends who i have never met before in my life!

We talk all things English-to-American, I discover that there is a pecking-order at Microsoft and that the 'Search' team are at the bottom of the ladder and get looked down upon by everyone else. And on the walk back to his home gone 1am, we try to help a strange lady start her car, only for me to snap the key in the ignition and make the situation even worse for her – I'm nice like that.

> **02:21 AM Aug 8th**
> i am giving a ride to a complete stranger called Kim whose car key i just broke. Life is very … random, sometimes.

Chris gives me a copy of his book (I now have two, I'd already bought one online previously) signs it for me, and I promise to take a picture of me holding it at London Bridge when I get there in a few days' time … a British thing in the middle of America, it seems appropriate.

Day 54 – Friday Saturday 8th August

Friends will be friends

*'It's red letter day,
the postman delivers a letter from your lover'*

When I wake up on Chris's couch in the morning, I have a moment of panic where I wonder where I am before I remember, yawn, scratch myself all over, and wander through into the kitchen still wearing just a t-shirt and my underpants in search of a kettle – as I suspect that being Scottish he might be clued up in the tea department.

The window in the kitchen overlooks where I've parked the car out the back, and I glanced down in a 'check that it's ok' kind of way, and – FUCK! NO!! I've been broken into *AGAIN!*

I can see the passenger door open, swinging half open in the breeze where obviously someone hasn't shut it properly. I run for Chris's front door, leaving *that* ajar, so it doesn't close behind me, and not caring that I am still wearing just underwear, run round the side I can feel myself welling up again where I think I am about to burst into tears.

Down the side, round the back to the car, and … Oh! Oh hang on. I think I know what I've done here. Oh for fucks sake. I am an idiot. I really am.

I tweet sixty seconds later back in the kitchen where the kettle is now starting to get to the boil.

> **08:31 PM Aug 8th**
> honestly, I am an idiot sometimes. Thought the car had been broken into again – it hadn't, I'd LEFT THE DOOR OPEN all night!

What a fucking idiot I can be sometimes. CHECK THE CAR IS LOCKED GEOFF in future – every time, every night! For goodness sake, I'd brought all the stuff in anyway, but for some reason left the passenger door ajar. Nothing smashed, nothing stolen and nothing broken … except maybe my intelligence.

Chris appears which is my awkward cue to put on some trousers, and we chat and talk and have our photos taken sat on the steps of his house. It's a lovely summer's morning, and I want to stay longer and just hang out, but I have to drive on.

I have a couple of same-named stops to do today though before I pick up my penultimate companion later on, and they are going to be easy ones. I head south from Seattle and only take about an hour down a very boring Interstate to get to Olympia.

12:31 PM Aug 8th
the Geofftech-mobile is now arriving at ... Olympia, Washington

---

In the USA
Olympia, Washington
On the Tube map
Kensington Olympia (District Line)

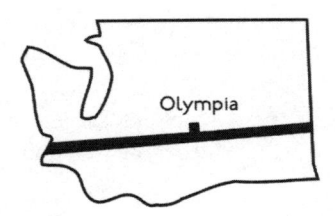

Olympia in Washington turns out to be just lovely, thanks. OK it isn't a quaint 'cutesy' one-horse kind of town, as the population is far too big for that. But even though it is big, it feels like it has character, people nod and give me smiles and say 'hello' to me – a complete stranger as I walk around the main town square. There is a waterfront, a farmer's market is on, and I am very happy and content as I walk around for an hour and soak it all in.

I stumble across the 'Old Towne Bicycle Shoppe', and for one moment considered hiring a bike that they're offering to do and cycling around for a bit more to explore the city. Then I check my watch and realise that I have to drive down to Kenton today *and* then get to Portland to pick up Alice and I don't have the time.

'Can I help you sir?' says a friendly voice behind me, and I gather what must have the proprietor of the bike shop has come outside for a cigarette and she's seen me loitering and wonders if she can help.

'Not unless you can alter time, and give me a bonus few hours to look around your lovely town!' is what I say ... only, inside my head, to myself. And to her I just mutter an awkward 'Uuh, hello, oh ... I'm okay thanks!' as if she'd caught me doing something bad outside her shop.

I pop into the 'Spar' Café for a drink. I find a classic art-deco styled cinema with a ticket seller booth in the middle – and the entrance/exit doors on either side – something you never see in the UK, and then with time against me – reluctantly – I head back to the car.

12:59 PM Aug 9th
Olympia: Big town, but with character. Waterfront, farmers market etc... I'm impressed.

I head on further south down the I-5, where I hit my second stop for that day – the town of Kenton.

In the USA
Kenton, Oregon
On the Tube map
Kenton
(Bakerloo Line / Overground)

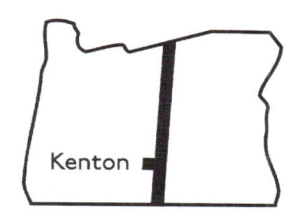

Or at least I'd assumed it's a town – there it is, a network of roads bold as anything on Google maps with the word 'Kenton' quite clearly labelled – it doesn't look as if it is in the middle of nowhere either, which is good. I realise quite quickly though as I come of the I-5 and over a bridge to take me over a river that really I am in the boundaries of Portland already, so most likely it's just going to be a cute suburb of Portland by the waterfront, right?

Err, no. What actually happens is that the SatNav directs me to turn right, over a railroad crossing of some rusty rails that looks like they haven't been used in a while, and into what clearly looks like an industrial estate.

I don't know if America uses the term 'industrial estate' like we do, but that's exactly what I have appeared to have found – a small network of three roads where the predominate thing I can see are trucks and trailers.

'Welcome to Blue Line transport' says an old battered sign as I drive around, looking at men loading up trucks, and lots of industrial looking machinery, dumpsters, and other rusting metal objects lying by the side of the road.

The river does play a part though – but again through industry and business, as I find a Wildlife hunting shop, Newmans Fish and Happy Crabs Seafoods – but again, these aren't jolly shops down a bustling high street, they're all industrial business with no shop fronts, doing their business en masse, plain and simple. And with a lot of trucks loading.

> **1:12 PM Aug 9th**
> i'm in the tiny suburb of Kenton. And by 'suburb', I mean 'a truck haulage company parking lot'

I jump out to snap some pictures, but just as I am steadying my camera a guy in a truck approaches the junction and leans out of his window.

'Can I help you sir?' he says politely but firmly. 'Yes' I say, 'Is this Kenton?'. There is a moment – almost non-detectable – then he replies 'Yes is it sir', and somehow happy that I am looking for Kenton and nothing else, pulls away and leaves me to it ... He slows 100 yards down next to a truck, gets out and starts to unload the boxes that are on the back of his truck.

Later that night at the campground to satisfy my curiosity that I haven't missed anything I get online and zoom into where I've been and check ... yes ... Google Maps confirms that this is Kenton. An industrial park with trailers, lorries and rusty looking equipment, that gives a run-down feeling to the place.

So not *that* much of a difference from Kenton in London then.

Out of Kenton, and it is companion time, but before I do I need to talk about friends first

There's a great statistic that gets banded around a lot that I learned during my time in the USA, and that's that Americans supposedly have less 'close' friends than people in Europe.

By 'close' what they mean is not just a mate, but a *real* proper buddy – the sort of person that will help you move house without you having to ask, who will let you turn up on their doorstep and feed you for dinner without thinking about it, the mate that doesn't mind what time of the day or night that you call them. Proper. Close. Friends.

Out of all the friends that I'd picked on my road trip it transpired that this was going to be my most troublesome week of the trip in terms of companionship. This may sound rude to write, but this story is a true account of what happened, so if I'm telling you like it is, then I'm going to tell you that my week with Alice was not one that I'll remember as being my best companion to go with.

I'd been a friend with Alice a lot of the previous year, and at the beginning of the year she was still enough my friend for me to ask her to come along with me. Alice has never been on an aeroplane before in her life, and certainly hasn't visited any of the states that I am offering her to come with me through, so perhaps in a small way it felt like I was doing her the pretentious favour of her letting her see some of her own country, and that makes me great for doing so with her – terrible of me, I know, right? I acknowledge this and don't deny it.

'Just enough my friend' though, I say – because somewhere between the beginning of the year when I asked her, and June ... when the trip actually started, our friendship became strained and deteriorated. I can't pin it on one particular thing, it's just that over time some friendships develop, and evolve, and then sometimes wither and die – and this was one that was in the process of dying.

When a friendship dies, then ... you let it go and you move on and do other things with other friends and I find to be ok – I know some people don't, but I am comfortable with that. The only problem is I can't do this here, because she has tickets booked to come and meet me at a certain date and time. If it hadn't been for that, I think I would have almost certainly done this stretch alone.

It also hasn't helped either when suddenly a couple of weeks before the trip we'd met up to discuss plans in detail, and she sprung upon me the fact that she is a very nervous passenger and insists on doing all the driving. Not such a bad thing you might think? Well no, because whilst it's nice to take a break from driving, it's also nice to take a break from taking a break, and on the week itself it annoys me greatly that I don't actually get to do any of the driving.

So it is with a huge amount of trepidation that I pick Alice up, welcome her to Underground : USA, and my odd week with her starts.

> **3:52 PM Aug 8th**
> just got to Portland, about to pick up companion number five.

I collect Alice outside her hotel in Portland. 'Hey!' she greets me with. 'Welcome to Underground : USA' I come back with and already I worry that I say that with a slightly forced smile, and as she gets in she proceeds to tell me about an erotic sex-show convention that has been taking place the day before in the hotel where she is staying at.

I'm trying to soak in a little of Portland though as we drive though – if I'd of not walked around a truck stop for an hour earlier then maybe I would have had the time to take in Portland. People from all over the USA tell me that it is a nice, clean, efficient and lovely city to live and work in – and it does look like it from the brief amount that I see.

The tram-like rapid transit system that I watch darting about the place looks wonderfully out of character for an American city of this size, and I am sad that I don't get to explore it more. One day, I would like to go back to Portland and see it properly.

> **4:27 PM Aug 8th**
> just realised I'm in Portland, Oregon having also been to Portland, Maine – east to west, coast to coast!

We head out south east of the city on the highway – not the Interstate – and the conversation already seems a bit strained. With Alice at the wheel

I consult the map and work out where we can get to before nightfall, and start looking for a campground.

We have to stop and pull in to get some gas though, and I am immediately confused again when a friendly guy appears out of nowhere and – pump in hand – asks us what grade we want. 87? Ah ... welcome to the state of Oregon – which along with New Jersey of course – they have to by law dispense the petrol for you.

> **5:06 PM Aug 8th**
> we're in deep Oregon. Where they fill up gas for you, doh!

I get chatting to the attendant – a nice guy called *Mark* who tells me that his job is just a fill-in to pay for his hobby in life – snowboarding. The nearby Mt. Hood is a real Mecca for the boarders, and mostly people come here just for the winter season to participate. Mark however, loves it so much that he got a 'boring job' (his words) here, just so that he can be near to all of the action. We chat some more for a few minutes, my English accent eventually provoking him to ask if I'm staying in town or just passing through, when another car pulls into the gas station and he runs off to serve them instead.

It's at this point that I notice another parked car a few feet away at another pump with no driver in it, and it has Washington State license plates on it. I realise that I don't have a picture of a Washington plate, so I lean into the car and grab my camera so that I can take its photo.

No sooner have I digitally recorded into the cameras memory bank of 1's and 0's do I hear an angry shout come from a way behind me. It seems that some bearded looking young dude who has been using the toilet is the driver of the car and is objecting to me taking a photo.

'What the hell you doin' man?' he snarls at me angrily, and I start to stammer off a reply about collecting all license plates, and trying to take a picture of them all when suddenly I interrupt myself. In a moment I realise that there are some people that are just better left off remaining in their own ignorant world, and letting them believe what they want to believe and it's not worth my time and energy trying to explain otherwise.

But I'll explain here, because I want to put my logic down. The driver is unhappy with me taking a picture of his license plate. His publicly viewable license plate that he drives around with on his car all the time, that he leaves on his car when it's parked in public places that everyone and anyone can see ... and make a note of ... or take a photo of ... and ... what? What does he think I am going to do with that piece of information? It's not his social security number, it's not his date of birth, and it's not his mother's maiden name. It's a six digit number which – by law – he's required to display for everyone to see.

Maybe he doesn't like me crouching down so close to his car (I don't touch his car in the process) to do it. Maybe he thinks I am tampering with his car. But I know that when I start to explain that it is just a photo, he is still angry. Maybe some people are just always angry, or like to behave that way. Or maybe it's just the paranoid fucked up world that we live in.

Britain has been described in recent times as a 'Nanny State' where you are told what to do, and how to do it, and a certain way to behave. My mum often used to tell me that I am better off out of the UK and in the USA because I don't have to contend with that. Well I *do* have to contend with it ... but just in a different way. Is this what it is like now? Is this all post-911 and the fear of everyone in this world where anti-terrorism procedure is now as common as washing your hair?

Above all of this, the friendly gas-pump attendant has been watching the whole time, and the angry driver seems to be a friend of his, and Mark shoots me an apologetic look that his friend is being perhaps a bit of an idiot. It's OK Mark, the world needs idiots too to make it go round, as well as the non-ones. It's like positive and negative neutrons in an atom, it's deliberate and it's mean to be that way. Sometimes thought I do worry that there are more idiots than non-idiots in the world.

I drive off ... *sorry* ... I mean – Alice drives us off along Highway 26 where about an hour later we stop to take some stunning sunset photos on Highway 26, as the sun sets across the devastating landscape. We stop again later at a Safeway's grocery store in the town of Madras to get something to eat for that night (no, it isn't a microwavable curry). We stay in a super-friendly KOA in Redmond that night where there staff working there are ... well, super friendly – and it feels like this is a good place to be for a day or two – except we are only staying a day.

~ ~ ~

The next day is a Saturday, and we spend it just driving. With Alice behind the wheel, I take photos when I can – of the scenery, of number plates. We fill up with gas again, we stop and buy and eat some bad roadside food. I lighten the mood for a while by getting out the video camera and shooting some 'road trip' style footage – of the roads, the mountains, other trucks and cars passing us by and the day eventually feels OK.

We just have to make good enough progress today so that we can get to Nevada tomorrow for our same-named-Tube stop.

Day 56 – Sunday 10th August

Jackpot

*'There's a first time for everything and we have come to that time
From this moment on we will now take people to the top of the world
When they discovered us they hit the jackpot'*

Actually, the next week isn't the most memorable on the trip overall to be honest, save for one beautiful moment and a couple of other minor ones. The next morning – a Sunday, I'd forgotten it is a Sunday – is an ideal time to do some laundry and I crack open my laptop to blog the latest whilst I'm waiting for my pants[34] to dry.

I'm happily minding my own business, drawing in the latest update on Google Maps when a woman who appears to be in her fifties approaches me.

'You haven't seen a copy of The Yellow Pages in here, have you?' she asks, a little direct. I look around – the laundry room is also doubling as a tourist-leaflet handing out point, and has a local map on the wall and does seem to be the sort of place that might have a phone book & Yellow Pages too, but I can't see one.

'I have not' I say, 'But if you want me to look something up for you on my computer, I can if you like', and the woman suddenly realises that I do indeed have the entire power of the Internet at my fingertips.

It transpires she's looking for a church … like I say, it's a Sunday – and she is looking for her particular denomination as the two nearby aren't of her particular brand.

We spend the next five minutes with some difficulty actually Googling around – the town we are in and nearby towns too trying to find a church that is suitable for her, and in the end we do – or at least I think we do. She seems happy enough anyway. Happy enough for her to decide that she should try and enrol me.

'Are you not going to Church yourself this morning?' she asks without a hint of any emotion on her face. I stall for an answer, thinking about how

---

[34] By pants I mean 'trousers' in this case. As I found myself slipping over to the America lexicon during my time there, and hangover of the whole experience is that I use both American words and English words, sometimes mixed into the same sentence, and I can't settle or decide on which I should be using. Sorry about this, just .. bear with me.

to handle this one. Quick Geoff, say something, or she'll ask if you don't believe in God.

Too late.

'Do you not believe in God?' the emotionless face slightly shifting towards one of worry that my soul is going to slither into hell to simmer and burn.

QUICK GEOFF, think of something to say to appease her! Oh, I know.

'Actually my mum did bring me up a Christian' I reply which I do consider to be a brilliantly deflective answer. It doesn't actually *say* 'Yes, I am a practicing Christian person right now, thanks', which would be a lie, but does pertain to having a religious upbringing, which I feel like might deflect any more unwarranted questions from this woman.

And it almost works – *almost*, as she smiles and turns to leave – but then stops and turns back and briefly does something which still annoys me to this day. She comes in close to me – invading my personal body space – rests her hand on my shoulder and says in a hushed tone only a couple of levels above whispering 'It's ok … Jesus has a plan for you', and turns and starts to walk away before I'd even manage to start to think of an answer.

Oh, you can fuck off. What? You think that's rude? No I mean it, she can fuck off.

Why is it ok for her to judge me and force her views onto me, but I bet it wouldn't be ok and she would be really unhappy if I'd of done the same to *her*. 'Don't worry!' I would say resting my hand on her shoulder 'There is no Jesus, and I live in hope that one day you might realise this'.

I try to get Alice on my side in this one – I should have known better.

'But you judge people all the time!' she retorts. 'You're the biggest judger I know!'

Fuck. She might be right. Yeah I judge … but not on religion which is one of those things that you shouldn't judge people on. I look back at Alice, is she … smirking at me? Fuck again. Actually no, she is judging me by calling me a judger. I'm confused now – when does having a strong opinion about something cross the line and become judgmental? How are you supposed to have a healthy debate with someone with different opinions from you and not be accused of judging them? No idea. Or I have no idea about to convey this all with Alice anyway, and she looks at me with a grumpy expression on her face.

And that – unfortunately – sets the tone for the rest of the day, in fact except for a few fun moments (which I will describe, coming up) the tone for the entire week. It feels like me & Alice have officially fallen out, and yet here we are trapped together in a car, in a tent, on a journey for a week – and there doesn't really seem to be much that either of us can do about it.

We have to press on though, and fortunately – it turns out that we do not have such a bad day. We are heading for the next 'Tube' stop on the trip, and to do that we travel south and drop down into northern Nevada.

If I'd have been blindfolded and whisked away in the middle of the night and taken to this part of America and told to guess where I am, it would have been immediately obvious when we hit the first town that we come to in Nevada, as it is called 'Jackpot'.

Established soon after 1954 – which – oddly enough is at exactly the same time that Idaho (the state that we've just left) made all forms of gambling illegal, this small town of-not-quite-2,000 people still thrives today purely due to the abundance of casinos for which it attracts its fair share of Idahoan's to come and play.

Nevada – as I would discover later in Las Vegas – really does put gambling up there as one of its main attractions. I later heard people say 'Well what else have they got? Fuck all! It's nothing but desert! So unless we legalise hookers and gambling, no one is going to come here!', so legalise those two things is what they did, and people came.

For the next sixty miles and hour that we drive after entering Nevada we do indeed see fuck all apart from a dusty desert landscape. A long undulating road which sometimes curves, and sometimes passes through a tiny farming community which no doubt has a one-armed-bandit hidden away inside somewhere, as the Nevada desert spreads out all around us in all directions. I half doze and occasionally check the map thinking about how we are going to find Holborn – the same name stop that in Nevada that we are heading to that day, and we stop at the town of Wells to fill up and for me to look at the proper map.

> **2:56 PM Aug 10th**
> i'm in Wells, Nevada. A town that exists purely because of the Interstate. even then you can tell its seen better days.

Wells itself is not that much more to write home about. Before the Interstate had been built here back in the 1960's I suspect it has been just another one of those tiny little farming towns that you'd pass through, except now a four lane highway passes right through instead bringing with it truckers from all over the county, and where there are truckers – there are trucks stops and gas stations with its coffee and corndogs.

We fill up with gas – a small amount of 4 gallons – we don't really need to because we've filled up this morning in Idaho, but suddenly the phrase

'Running out of gas in the middle of the desert' doesn't seem that appealing to me, so I am taking the chance to top up wherever I can.

I mentioned earlier that I am 'checking the map' to wonder about how to get to Holborn, and you're probably thinking 'Well why don't you use your SatNav Geoff' – and here is the thing. The SatNav *does* know of the town Holborn, because it's on the searchable list of towns in Nevada, but every time I select it, the little box of microchips goes into a techno-spasm, and after more seconds than it should be taking it keeps coming back with the phrase 'No navigable route found!'. Shit. We are going to have to do this one manually.

> **2:57 PM Aug 10th**
> have come in search of a Central-line same named town that my SatNav cannot navigate a route to ... interesting ...

And this is why gas stations are also good ... because in this technology tweeted-up twenty first century of gadgets, they stock something which I am about to fall back upon ... paper maps.

I drink my coffee, eat my corndog, and then head for the back of the truck stop store where there is a whole shelf-load of paper maps adorning it. Now I know from checking Google maps late last night that there *is* a small road that leads out to Holborn, but for some reason my SatNav isn't aware of it. So we have to find it manually.

I find it on page 16 of the state map of Nevada, and make a note of the turning off of the I-80 that we have to take heading east. I step back outside and head towards the car.

'Got it?' asks Alice, 'Got it!', I reply 'We want to look for ...' and then realise that I can't remember at all the name of the town or the turn that it is that we would be looking for, so I go back inside the shop weaving my way through the slot machines for another look at the map. I'm not sure why I am feeling so cheap that I don't just actually *buy* it. I guess I am just that stupid sometimes.

> **3:16 PM Aug 10th**
> and i thought Montana was bad for casinos. naturally it's got nothing on Nevada. Slot machines, like ... everywhere

When I come back out (and with the town of 'Moor' now written on my hand so that I won't forget it), I walk back to the car again only to notice that the car next to us has a license plate I haven't seen before. A Nevadan one? No, a Hawaiian one!

'Are you guys from Hawaii?' I ask the gentle elderly-looking couple inside. They aren't – they are from California, and this is a rental car that they have been given. They too have been wondering why a car rental place in CA would give out a car with Hawaiian plates, and I also aren't the first person to ask them if they are from Hawaii. They're OK with me taking a picture of the license plate though – even if it isn't one of the 48 I'm trying to collect, there is no way that I can't a picture of it. Hmm … maybe I can get an Alaskan one too whilst on my travels?[35]

> 3:15 PM Aug 10th
> i just got a picture of a Hawaii license plate! In Nevada, of all places!

This actually gets me into a mini-spate of running around the rest of the cars in the truck stop parking lot (where, presumably – everyone has parked up to go to the casino inside) still in search of the elusive New Hampshire plate which I still haven't found, and get a funny look from a rather broad looking Texan dude. I know he is Texan from the fact that his license plate says 'Texas' which is about the moment that he spots me and gives me a look. So we get the hell out of there and head for Holborn.

Holborn in central London is a busy place. It's a major crossroads in a very busy part of town, and is actually the Tube station that taught me that lesson that every novice Tube-traveller in London learns early on – that the stations in the centre of the city are much closer together than the ones on the outskirts. When I was young and didn't know London very well I once got on a bus when going for a job interview at the BBC, and paying by cash told the bus driver for a 'Single to Holborn, please!' and he laughed, smiled and then nodded whilst saying 'Holborn? You're already here!' and his nod leads me to 100 metres down the road on the other side where I can now see Holborn Tube station as I'd walked up the road far enough to walk between two Tube stations. Although London *is* a big place, I think at the time I thought it was much bigger than it really is, especially in the central area where it can be quite quick to walk between two stations – something that I still do to this day, if my journey only requires going one stop, I don't take the Tube – I walk it.

Holborn in Nevada I suspect is going to be a deserted place. And *literally* deserted too in that … as we go down a dusty road that I hope leads towards it, I realise that we are driving into the desert.

There are no buses, no Tube trains, and generally just *no* people whatsoever on the sandy road that led out to Holborn, Nevada – or at

---

[35] I never saw an Alaska plate on the whole of my trip … but there may be one in Charleston. About a week after getting back, Beverly informs me that she saw one whilst driving to work one morning. At the time of writing I still haven't seen one (Well apart from all the ones that I saw when on a trip to Alaska last year that I failed to take a photo of)

least what we hope is heading out to Holborn, Nevada because apart from one little tiny sign about six or seven miles back we haven't seen much else.

We miss the turning for 'Moor' at mile 360 on the Interstate (don't ask how), and instead come out at mile marker 365, and turn around and head back again. It is at that point that I first realise how truly remote it is going to be when the exit sign at 365 doesn't actually *say* it is for anywhere, except for the fact that it is exit number 365. At least back at exit 360 there'd been a big sign for 'Moor' telling us we are going the right way.

Immediately off of the Interstate there is a locally made sign – built from wood – telling us that Moor is 0.5 of a mile to the left, and Holborn is 7 miles to the right, trouble is, we've been driving for over 10 minutes now down a winding, sometimes, bumpy and definitely desert sandy road which sometimes makes the wheels skid on the car despite it being in low gear, and I realise that I haven't been looking at the mileage on the car at the sign to know when seven miles have passed.

'Do you think we should have turned back there after all?' suggests Alice – remarking on the turning with no sign that has been on our left a few minutes back. 'I dunno' I reply, and think. 'Let's see what we can see over this next ridge', I suggest helpfully, as a crest is looming up in front of us on the road and maybe when we get there we can see something. And we can! It is ... another ridge! Followed by another, at which point I concede that if we can't see anything after *that* one then we'll stop and have a rethink.

The third ridge leads to something slightly promising – an open gate with a sign next to it, suggesting that we are about to drive onto private farmland, but that it is OK for us to be there, as long as we don't tamper with anything. Like what ... the desert scrubs bushes? There isn't anything about *to* mess with!

And then ... round the bend after that ... we finally get somewhere – to a junction, with a wooden stake in the ground, and a board nailed to it, that says 'West Holborn'.

What! *West* Holborn.

Have we gone too far?

We get out of the car and look around ... yup, desert scrub land in all directions, and this wooden sign pointing to West Holborn that I get Alice to take a picture of me standing in front of anyway. Post picture, I scan the vista again.

'You know what?' as I spin a full 360 degrees checking out the horizon on all angles. 'I think there's someone else coming'. I can see in the distance – coming down the road that we have just come, another vehicle, kicking up the sand from the desert road. This seems to prompt Alice to get back into the car.

'Why are you getting in the car?' I ask Alice. 'Just in case' she says, and turns the key and starts the engine 'Just in case of what?' I say, maybe somewhat naively. Are we really about to chased off the desert farmland by some redneck farmer with a shotgun? Images of *VIZ* magazines 'Farmer Palmer' with his catchphrase 'Get ooorf my land' come to mind, and suddenly I get slightly worried, and shift my weight slightly towards the car ready to move completely in that direction if the need arises.

The dust in the distance gets nearer, and nearer ... as a truck pulling a trailer appears, and then disappears and appears and disappears again as it bobs up and down on road with dips in it that we've just come along, until it comes up one of the ridges again ... and then before we know it, is approaching slowly right towards us.

Hang on. They're not stopping! The guy driving nods a 'hello' at me, but carries on driving slowly past. Aren't they going to berate us for being on their land or similar? Apparently not. So I raise my hand, and say 'Hey!' with an urgency that causes the guys to look back and they slow and then stop. They stop, and the driver gets out to talk to me – and get this, he's wearing chaps! Like a proper cowboy!

> **3:57 PM Aug 10th**
> just met a desert cowboy. For reals. He was wearing chaps and everything!

'Is this Holborn or West Holborn?' I ask, and the expression on his face changes as he realises that I'm clearly not a local, and his crinkly sun-drenched face turns into a smile, and he points off to a side 'road' and says 'The Holborn Railroad is down there', and motions.

The what now? Hang on. No ... really? Not again. Did he just say 'Railroad'.

Oh yes. Yes he very much did. I've managed to do it again.

In the USA
Holborn, Nevada
On the Tube map
Holborn (Central and Piccadilly Lines)

Oh my. Holborn is *fantastic*. Truly.

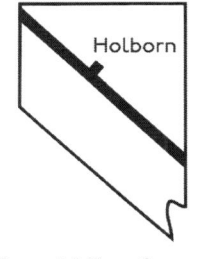

Holborn requires video to demonstrate just how out in the middle-of-nowhere it is. So for the next half an hour or so I shoot video and take photos – including pictures of an excellent rusty abandoned car we find just off of the track. There is a container of some sort in the sidings of the railroad, and I realise too that there are two tracks here – strange, because normally they only have one, and here is a train line in a remote are with double tracks, hmm. I can't figure out why.

We get back inside the car, and for a brief moment wonder whether we can keep going straight on the road we are on as it appears to loop back and head in the direction that we want to go anyway, but all too soon the 'road' as it is turns into rocks and disintegrates into the desert, so we reverse up and head instead back along the way we have just come. Alice is driving, and I wind the window down to take some photos of the landscape. And as I do, an audible instance happens.

'Did you hear that?' I say, 'Hear what?' 'A horn. A train horn – I think a train is coming!'

We've only been thirty seconds back down the dusty road, but I make Alice stop and turn around and drive right back to where we have been. If a train *is* coming through Holborn, then I want a photo of it!

We see it coming round the bend in the distance – slowly – a huge double-length locomotive, yellow in colour with 'Union Pacific 5660' painted in red on the side, and a giant Stars & Stripes too. It spews hot diesel fumes and has a 'chug chug chug chug chug!' noise, like only a train engine can, and for the first and only time on the trip I feel like a bit of a train spotter really getting off on raw motive power.

It's also at this point that my intelligence suddenly kicks in and I realise why there's two tracks here. This is a single line normally, all the way along but it is pulling into the second track, because I bet it's going to let another train pass in the opposing direction.

~~~

'We're actually letting a train that's going faster than us behind, overtake'.

These words are spoken by *Rick*, one of the two drivers of the train. It's a little surreal – the train has pulled into the passing track, past us 'clanging' its bell as it sees us (And probably wonders what the hell we are doing here), and we actually have to drive a little way more down the road to go to where the engine of the train has stopped. I snap a photo, and this prompts one of the drivers to jump down from the cab and introduce himself to us ... hello Rick.

We chat for a good ten minutes during which time he 'Okays' it for us to get onto the tracks and take a photo of the loco close up. I ask where he is from 'Salt Lake' is his succinct two word reply, and they are a slow coal train, and is stopping to give priority to a steel carrying train behind it that is able to go faster. So coal is heavier than steel then, huh?

Most of all though, is that I ask all the questions – but at no point does he ask me or us, what we are doing here at this remote point in the desert, taking photos of trains. Does he think we are a guy & girl train spotter duo that has come to a remote desert location to write down numbers of locomotives?

> **5:07 PM Aug 10th**
> in Holborn! The Nevada one ... Middle of nowhere railway siding. A train stopped and the driver got out and talked to us

I like Holborn. I like it a lot. I like that it is in the middle of nowhere, that we have to look it up on a paper map to get here, that we have a moment of 'Uh huh ... are we in the right place?' that there is a rusty car here, and a train line! And then to top it all over a train runs through where the driver gets out and talks to you. Outstanding.

Out of all the things I do with Alice this week in our week of not-really-getting-on very well, this is easily the highlight. For just a few hours this day and as we then drive east towards Salt Lake City, I feel like I am really enjoying myself again.

SAME NAME TOWNS TALLY

Perfect Small Town America
Preston, White City, Waterloo

Something there and enjoyable
Plaistow, Gloucester, Kew Gardens, Harrow, South Kensington, Greenford, Liverpool, Temple, Oxford, Victoria, Kingsbury County, Olympia

Something there but not that exciting to be honest
Putney, Amersham, Hampstead, Woodford, Brompton, Kingsbury, Redbridge, Latimer

Nothing there but somehow being in the middle of nowhere made it OK
Epping, Acton, Lancaster, Green Park Farm, Hackney, Holborn

Nothing there, and not that exciting either. Oops.
Warwick, Wapping, Camden, Bond, Elm Park, Poplar, Kenton

Closed
Swiss Cottage, Watford

We drive east through the flat, flat white plains of the Salt Lake towards SLC itself, and end up in an AT&T store where I get myself a new phone to replace my broken one – and I finally became an iPhone convert.

> **7:21 PM Aug 10th**
> approaching SLC. Just seen first Mormon (church of LDS) billboard...

The first thing that catches my attention in Salt Lake City is a 'British Store' which has the Union Jack painted all over the front of the shop. I send a badly-written text message to my friend Rudi – in D.C. to let him know where I am as he's from Salt Lake. And he messages me back telling me that – yes! Of course he knows where that store is and he knows exactly where I am. I tweet the same.

> **7:41 PM Aug 10th**
> wecone to Slt Lake Citu, Geoff. 1st thing i see?/? The 'Union Jack' brtsh store! :-)

Now that reason why that tweet (and my text message to Rudi) is so badly written is because my phone is playing up. My nice trusty imported-from-Europe Nokia phone with flip & fold out keyboard is starting to break down as some of the buttons are now starting not to work. Maybe dust or grit has got into the keyboard – all I know is that when I press a few of the keys they sometimes work, but also sometimes don't - or produce a different characters altogether. So hence, new phone.

Post phone-buying, I meet up with Alice in a coffee shop[36] where we she has been waiting for me and we proceed to have a disagreement about something. Then we go for a wander around the main Mormon temple, during which I have another disagreement with her.

> **9:22 PM Aug 10th**
> i'm checking out the LDS temple Say what you like about the Mormons the buildings are impressive

'Is there anything I can help you with?' asks a nice gentleman as I take a picture of the imposing Temple which is reflecting in a small lake, but instead of engaging in conversation I back away as I can see from his name badge that he is with the church, and I fear that he will either try and enrol me, or I will say something derogatory.

The sun starts to set and we realise that we need to push on to get to our campground for the night. We stop at a gas station for bad food, the roads get dark, I play with my iPhone and the conversation drops to a minimum..

We head for the top right hand corner of the state – to the town of Vernal where I've booked us into a KOA to stay in a cabin for two days –

---

[36] I don't need to tell you which one, do I? If I do, then you haven't been paying attention or reading this book properly.

I want to rest up and edit some video. Alice announces that she's going to go on a tour of 'Dinosaur Park' – a local attraction.

Me? I have a date with my arch rivals.

In the USA
Arsenal, Utah
On the Tube map
Arsenal (Piccadilly Line)

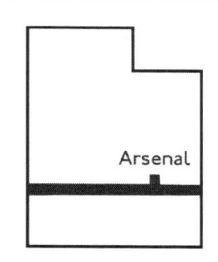

Arsenal

'So I'm confused, is your football team called Arsenal, or the Lehi Strikers?'

'Well ... officially we're registered at the Lehi Strikers, but everyone knows us as the Utah Arsenal', replies *Gary*, head coach of the ladies soccer team – the Lehi Strikers, based in Lehi, Utah.

'Although it's not just girls anymore – I know that in England football as you call is a male sport, and that people think that in the USA it's predominately a female sport, but we're literally getting more and more boys signing up all the time'

'We play at various soccer pitches all around Lehi, at the High School, down at North Lake, Snow Springs field too, which is a real nice field'.

'Our blog is called The Cannon too – we took that from the Arsenal logo, right? The Cannon? In the badge, seemed too good not to use that too!'

'Have you ever been to the real Arsenal then? In London?'

'Ah man, no .. no but I would *love* to. You been there?'.

'Only the old stadium, not the new one .. they opened a new one up a couple of years ago, and I've been here all that time, not been back to see a game there yet'

'Are you an Arsenal fan then?'

'Err, no! Far from it ... I'm a Tottenham Hotspur far – and Arsenal are our closest rivals!'

'Oh you're a Spurs boy! I knew there was something odd about ya!', he laughs.

> 'Bit of old fashioned football rivalry, yup!'. Gary laughs, and I nod.

That's definitely how the conversation went, right?

Yes. Yes it was.

Definitely.

Back at the campground, I edit my latest video.

> **4:40 PM Aug 11th**
> video number 16 is up! http://is.gd/2cpxT

Alice comes back in the early evening just after I've posted the video up, and we almost immediately realise that we both need to eat, so we head out to a local bar and make small talk over some delightful food.

The local beer is good too, and I discover that some Utahans (is that a word?) do have a sense of humour after all when it comes to their faith.

> **8:14 PM Aug 11th**
> in a bar in Vernal, UT. Just ordered a pint of 'polygamy porter'

The conversation is awkward though but I make an effort, and at one point we even agree on a couple of conversational points too, but silence ultimately reigns as we drive back to the campground, stopping for milk along the way at a gas station.

~ ~ ~

In the morning, we stop at the same gas station again to fill up with petrol and look at the map to decide which way south we should take. Going via the town of 'Dinosaur' seems very much the way to go.

> **12:37 PM Aug 12th**
> approaching the town of 'Dinosaur' Colorado.

> **12:39 PM Aug 12th**
> they have 'Brontosaurus Blvd' and 'Stegosoarus Hwy', I kid you not.

We take a scenic detour along Douglas Pass Road, Highway 139 which will take us across the Bookcliff Mountain range, to a height of 8,200 feet. We stop at the obvious pull-in at the top where there is a raised barrier across the road and snap the vista.

> **1:30 PM Aug 12th**
> US139 South. 73 miles of nothing except beautiful Colorado mountains...

We keep heading south and then west a bit back on the Interstate, shooting quickly past towns with fantastic little names – Mack, Cisco,

Sego, Thompson and Crescent Junction. The latter there really is just that – a 'town' that is just a turning to take you onto US-191 and towards Moab and the Arches National Park.

I check the time on my watch. I don't really want to stay in Moab tonight as I want to push on and wonder if we can go the Arches Park, and 'pop in' and do it in a hour and then be on our way again. If I'd have known in advance the beauty I am about to see (a landscape of contrasting colours, landforms and sandstone natural stone arches, fins and giant balanced red rocks) I would have known that this is impossible, and I chuckle to myself now when I think about it.

And talking of chuckling to myself, it's cruel to admit but I really am laughing a lot to myself at the thing that happened next – we get pulled over by a cop.

> **4:11 PM Aug 12th**
> pulled over by a cop! Alice is driving, not me! Oooops …

I haven't even noticed him as I've been busy with my head buried in the guidebook reading about Moab and the local Arches National Park, so the first I know about it is when Alice says 'Uh oh, I'm getting pulled over' and I look up and concur that in the rear view mirror are the flashing lights of a police car.

'Is it a trooper? A State Trooper?' I ask tentatively. She nods. I think 'Oh Shit'. I'm not a fan of State Troopers.

But then to be totally honest, a really small teeny part of me wants Alice to get a ticket. Mean? Yes, and that's why I am laughing at her about it, but there's a reason why.

About a month ago before the trip, a bunch of us has been out in a social gathering one day in Charleston, and Alice had (in my opinion) laid in to me for no good reason at all. 'Oh you're always speeding' she'd said in an accusatory tone. 'You're so going to get a ticket on your way round at some point', and in effect scolded me out for something that I hadn't done yet. And yet … here we are, a few weeks later, and Miss Fussy 'I have to drive all week long' Pants, is the one who's got a ticket for speeding, and not me.

Well except, it isn't actually a ticket.

> **4:13 PM Aug 12th**
> Utah Highway Patrol Section 13 have issued us with …

> **4:14 PM Aug 12th**
> … a warning! 80mph in a 65. Alice is the most relieved person on the planet…

I should like to point that I do good though. I *really* do. The whole conversation from a few weeks back where she's laid into me is going through my head, and I could have quite easily brought it up. Alice knows that I could quite easily bring it up. She must have known at that point that I am thinking about mentioning it, but instead … no … a few seconds silence, and then I say something not at all derogatory towards the situation, and instead try to sound as helpful and as supportive as I can.

I do sent a secret tweet out without her knowing though.

> **4:24 PM Aug 12th**
> Alice's arguing – 'hey it's not a ticket it's a citation' yeah whatever :-)

We go the Arches National Park though and spend a few hours there, and I get one of the Rangers to sign my t-shirt and even draw a sketch of the classic 'Arch' (As appears on all of Utah's license plates) before staying at a KOA campground that night which is medium-to-large sized and a little too corporate for my liking. A bandwidth-restricted wireless connection doesn't let me get much online work done. I go for a wander around the campground and find a soda dispensing machine that isn't chilled but I am so thirsty that a warm soda drink suddenly becomes appealing to me.

There is still not much conversation between Alice and me. How many days left together do we have now? Not many. I plug in my iPod, set it on a low volume on my 'sleep' playlist, and do just that.

~ ~ ~

> **11:19 AM Aug 13th**
> can someone email me 'is this the way to Amarillo', please? I'll need it by the weekend when I get there …

> **11:20 AM Aug 13th**
> in the meantime Utah Saints (I'm in Utah) are in order this morning …

We don't get an early start come the morning, and even then we don't get very far either because just down the road we find the cute Bedrock Store – a general store which has a solitary gas pump outside which has seen much better days, but that's what makes it so fantastic – an independent rustic looking place with a sleeping dog on the porch that flips open one eye to check you out as you go inside to pay, it's lovely.

We chat to the owner from whom I ended up buying a CD of her songs that she's played guitar on, sung and recorded. I get a t-shirt too 'Bedrock Store' that I still wear to this day, and people ask me if it's got anything to do with the Flintstone. It hasn't.

> **6:04 PM Aug 13th**
> ok, so Colorado = mountains. I get it.

> **7:11 PM Aug 13th**
> am 11,300 feet high at Monarch pass in the Rocky Mountains, CO.

At Canon City, I can't help but just think of one word: Gloomy. When I see it, it does not look like a fun place and as we drive slowly through, I initially can't figure out why. Then I do - I see a prison, followed by another, and another. What? A quick search on my new iPhone about the place tells me the facts I need to know.

> **8:40 PM Aug 13th**
> in Canon City, CO. highest concentration of prisons in one place. Guards on the gun towers you can see from the highway!
>
> **8:41 PM Aug 13th**
> mind you, the local Super 8 motel looks like a prison too.

We don't stop, instead we drive slowly through looking at the gloom and right out the other side – and thankfully we don't need to use the toilet either. From Canon City, we head due north and our destination for the night is the KOA campground at the cheerfully named Cripple Creek. We'd stay the night there, and the morning it's only a short drive to the next stop – Monument – that I have to go and do.

The SatNav is predicting that we'll be there in 52 minutes. But a couple of minutes further along the road out of town – a strange thing happens – the time I notice on the SatNav has gone UP to over two hours to get there. What?

The road itself then starts to deteriorate ... it becomes more rugged, more rocky, but we push on because the SatNav *is* showing a route through, and if we turn back now, well then we're wasting time going all the way back down and around through Canon City, to ... well ... who knows where – another campground somewhere perhaps?

The road starts to incline, and then cuts into some mountains. I notice that even Alice is looking cautious. The road narrows, widens, then narrows again and I wonder what we'll do if we meet a car coming in the other direction.[37]

Eventually the road twists and turns and gets so narrow that Alice slows right down. There is a steep mountain wall on one side of the road, and a sheer drop on the other.

'I don't like this, I say. 'Me neither' she replies, and we decide that it would be pertinent to turn around. Alice backs up, but we can't reverse forever, so it gets to the point where we have to turn the car around

---

[37] Later, I realised that we would never meet a car coming in the other direction – no one would ever be stupid enough as us to drive down this road.

properly. The road slightly widens at one point so we decide to do a three-point turn ... except that it is more like a nine-point turn, and I get out of the car to help direct – and I realise that I have Alice's life in my hands. If I fail to shout 'stop!' as she reverses back, she will simply back over the edge of the road, down the mountain and ... *woah!* Horrible thought Geoff – stoppit.

With the car turned around, I programme the SatNav to not take us another way, and use much more major roads instead.[38]

> **9:31 PM Aug 13th**
> we just reversed up and turned around, found ourselves on a narrow windy road hugging the side of mountain with a sheer drop on my side

An hour later and we check in at a different campground. I sit in the fluorescent stripped lit launderette on the KOA site and click through my emails and then update the blog, and the Facebook page – check my twitter too, and look up some photos ... but somehow ... it isn't fun anymore. My enjoyment has of the trip has been sapped out of me today.

I remember being back in the launderette at the KOA with my mum stressing out over having to buy a video camera, and even that somehow felt more 'fun' than this. Not getting on with Alice is tiresome; it feels like a chore now driving around going and getting to places.

Right now it is not how I imagined it, and I close my laptop lid down with a small bang and I sigh ... and exhale out a long breath. My eyes randomly focus on the first thing they see ... happy faces, happy smiling faces. The smiling faces of a fake family set-up shot on the glossy brochure in a rack full of brochures advertising nearby things to do in Pueblo. And I would get to do none of them, I would go off to some nothing town called Monument, and then I would have another tiresome day of not driving again.

> **11:58 PM Aug 13th**
> Underground : USA reality – a cold, dark, damp campsite with 'food' heated up from a can. how much longer is this going on for ... ?

I wander back to the tent. There is a depressing amount of other people about – i.e. none. And in the slight drizzle of rain, I heat up a tin of crap spaghetti which partially fills the empty hole in my stomach. I make a half-arsed effort to clear down the plates, leaving the rest of it in the rain to be cleansed by nature, and crawl into the tent over Alice.

---

[38] As I sit and write this book, I've just looked up the road on Google Maps, and discovered that it's called 'Phantom Canyon Road' – an ominous name! Try it for yourself if you like, search on 'Phantom Canyon Road, CO' and you'll discover something disturbing as I just did – that the Google Street View only goes so far down the road, and the stops. Clearly because the person driving the Google vehicle thought 'Bugger this!' as we did, and dared to go no further.

I plug in my faithful iPod to listen to a podcast – normally really good at sending me to sleep but for half an hour, all I can do is lie awake and feel grumpy again. Actually I'm feeling grumpy about the fact that I'm feeling grumpy. This is the journey and adventure of a lifetime, isn't it? And yet here I am not feeling great about it.

I am looking forward to Texas, to Paul turning up, to going along Route 66, the last few Tube stops and hitting the west coast, to stop and then home. Home, home. *Proper* home.

I start to think about London again. England is calling, and my days on the road are getting close to running out.

Day 60 – Thursday 14th August

Monumental

*'Nobody knows the troubles I've seen,
In a van, on a soapbox for the world to see.
Miles away, and I wish this didn't mean so much to me
To be a Monument for the rest of them'*

A night's sleep – any sort of sleep is usually helpful in making things a bit better, and whilst I'm not entirely cheerful come the morning, the fog that had clouded my mind late last night has lifted a fair bit and I'm in in a reasonably cheerful mood.

I poke my head out of the tent … it isn't raining, but it still feels damp. I leave Alice snoozing in the tent and head off to camp store to get some food for breakfast, but not before I've quickly gone online of course.

> **9:54 AM Aug 14th**
> since I got my iPhone, i've signed up to Google's Latitude. so you can see exactly where i am on the road!

Since getting the iPhone a few days ago in Salt Lake City, I know that there is an application called 'Latitude' that you can get whereby the SatNav coordinates are sent to a central server, and people subscribing to your feed can see on a Google Map where you are. It is something that as soon as I have it wish I'd had from the start as people can literally follow me round and see where I am … a real-time progress map! I am excited. So excited in fact, that I go and buy some bacon for breakfast.

> **10:40 AM Aug 14th**
> is cooking up bacon on his camp stove for breakfast http://twitpic.com/duqzl

The smell of bacon appears to not to raise Alice from her slumber, so I update my Latitude position again – the 200 yards between the campground store and where the tent is actually pitched could be vital.

> **10:43 AM Aug 14th**
> i have seven followers on iGoogle's latitude already! How nice! Not that i've actually gone anywhere today, but i'm about to …

Alice does eventually arise – with all the bacon gone, and she shoots me a look that says 'Thanks for the breakfast… not', oops. So we pack up and head out with the weather now being somewhat drizzly and up the I-25 to our Colorado stop.

1:09 PM Aug 14th
Geofftech Tube Tours now heading for his next same named stop, you are now arriving in Colorado at ....

In the USA
Monument, Colorado
On the Tube map
Monument
(District and Circle Lines)

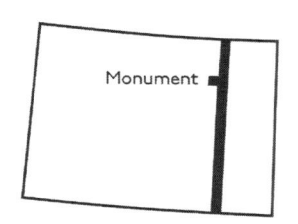

1:26 PM Aug 14th
Monument: Rainy

First things first – we get a picture of me by the 'Monument' sign which actually reads 'Historic Monument' and it seems to have part of an old wall embedded into the side of it. Real or fake, I wonder? (Fake it later transpires thanks to a Google Search).

It almost goes without saying that I've managed to pick a town with a railway connection – the Rio Grand Railroad had come through here in 1872, and the town was built specifically as a stop along the line, and was originally called 'Henry's Station', named after prominent settler Henry Limbach. It changed its name though due to the nearby Monument Creek and Monument Valley. And probably because Henry was a bit embarrassed that they'd named it after him.

We stand around looking trying to make more of Monument than we can ... but we can't. It is a row of shops with not many people shopping in them. Either the rain is not encouraging people to come out, or it's literally dampening their moods.

I smile and say a cheery 'Good morning!' at a gentleman getting out of his car heading for one of the shops, but instead of returning the greeting he looks at me as if he is trying to figure out if he knows me or not, and when he realises that he doesn't, decides that he isn't going to talk to me – all without breaking his stride, which leaves me feeling a little miffed.

We look around at the shops nearby, in particular 'The Love Shop' stands out to me. What? A sex shop in seemingly conservative historic Monument? Ah no, turns out it's named so merely because it's the place 'Where you love to shop' for home decorations, and unique gifts including Vera Bradley and Pandora. And yes, I cut & pasted that last line

289

from their website, because no —we don't go in. It looks too twee and touristy for my liking.

> **1:14 PM Aug 14th**
> Monument: Trying to be cute and hippy?

We do scoop up a drink in the pleasant Coffee Cup Café though, and look at its notice board which really is just a huge advert for 'Art Hop' – a festival that would be celebrating the arts in Historic Downtown Monument, on every third Thursday from 'May thru September'. I check the date – it is a Thursday! Hang on, no it isn't. It is Friday. But the Thursday of next week I'm sure there would be a whole lot of celebrating between 5 and 8pm just like the sign says there will be.

Alice isn't saying much, and to be honest I'm not exactly being loquacious myself to her. The rain is still drizzling down but for some reason I feel inspired to take a picture of a child's toy wet and downtrodden squashed on the pavement. It looks far from being twee and perfect and colourful like the Love Shop is selling. It is real and gritty and also a little bit sad that a child has lost its toy.

'There's not much going on' I say, finally breaking the silence with Alice. 'Nope', she says simply. Which makes it easy for me to add it to my category list later, but not until we've been to the next stop.

In my head, I think of New Mexico. Not that I've never been to New Mexico in my life before, but the images that it conjures up is one of dryness. One of desert, one of sand, one of hot-sandy-deserts, and dryness.

> **1:32 PM Aug 14th**
> alrighty Colorado, your mountains are very pretty but it's all over between us. I have a literal hot date with Texas instead.

Don't panic reader – I've not made a mistake by writing 'New Mexico' one moment and then 'Texas' the next. Yes, we are actually heading for Texas today – that would be the state that we would be in by the end of the day, but to get there – we would have to head through New Mexico, hence my hot sandy dreams.

And I'm not wrong. We get onto the Interstate and head south, and quite rapidly it is weird to see the climate changing in such a short space of time. Colorado is mountainous and a little damp with the drizzle, but it almost feels as if someone flicks a switch as we curve around a bend in the road and enter new New Mexico, and suddenly it feels hot, dry, and desserty and the landscape turns from a Colorado green into a New Mexican yellow.[39]

> **3:12 PM Aug 14th**
> hello New Mexico! state no. 44/48. Their littering fine is only $300, Colorado's was $1000, so if you're going to chuck trash out of your car windows, you know which state to do it in.

We stop for petrol in the town of Raton, just into New Mexico which has one of those terrible Subway's tagged onto the side. Normally I like a Subway sandwich, but somehow when they're part of a gas station they never quite feel like they taste the same.

I have one small moment of excitement – a car pulls up outside with a license plate that I have never seen before – what state is that? I dash outside with my camera to note that the car is from Mexico, and the plate is from Chihuahua. I'm not sure if I should snap a photo or not ... would this mean that I would start on a collection of one day somehow trying to take a photo of all Mexican plates too? I don't like to think about it for too long, but snap a picture anyway, and we get on our way and just after five o'clock cross the state line into Texas.

> **5:13 PM Aug 14th**
> 'drive safe and friendly the Texas way', another state virginity broken. now – what IS the way to Amarillo?

Amarillo is indeed our destination for the evening, and Paul by now has sent me a text message telling me what hotel he is in. We would be there at eight o'clock I reckon; just as soon we've gone and done our same-name town for this state. From the east end of London and the whole regeneration for the London Olympics games of part of a city, to a crossing of two roads in the middle of the panhandle of Texas. Hello Stratford.

---

[39] I picked those colours in my head at my overriding impression of what 'colours' those states might be. It was only later when I thought about that I realised the license plate for Colorado and is white and GREEN, and license plate for New Mexico is red and YELLOW. There's something in that, surely?

In the USA
Stratford, Texas
On the Tube map
Stratford
(Central and Jubilee Lines)

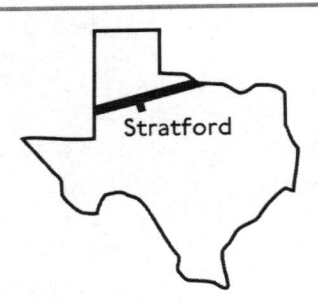

It really is a crossroads – albeit quite a major one. There are *two* gas stations here – one each on opposing corners, and a lot of traffic – a lot of trucks in fact driving about, and a lot of greasy looking truck drivers with scary tattoos eating hot dogs that have been rolling over all day in keep-warm-racks whilst gulping down some of that infamous gas station coffee.

> **7:19 PM Aug 14th**
> Stratford, Texas. It's one giant truck stop with a lot of, well ... Trucks!

Alice takes a photo of me standing under the 'Welcome to Stratford!' sign, which also proclaims to be the Pheasant Capital of the USA. I look around – I can't see any pheasants. What we do see though are some bloody huge great grain silos on one side of the road and to the side of that an abandoned building, an old rusty gas station and my particular penchant – some rusty vehicles.

I don't want to say that Stratford has seen better days because that would give the impression that it is a small dying town – and far from it, because it seems very busy and bustling right now, but clearly it is only surviving because it's an intersection of two busy roads and good spot for the truckers to rest up.

> **7:41 PM Aug 14th**
> a lot of abandoned rustiness here , and a crossroads with two gas stations and populated by trucks.

I snap a few more photos and look around trying to see if there is a local business other than the gas stations where there might be someone to talk to, or something to do, but there doesn't really seem to be anyone, just the gas stations. Alice sits in the car looking bored, and so after a few more photos, I get the inclination that we should move on.

SAME NAME TOWNS TALLY

Perfect Small Town America
Preston, White City, Waterloo

Something there and enjoyable
Plaistow, Gloucester, Kew Gardens, Harrow, South Kensington, Greenford, Liverpool, , Temple, Oxford, Victoria, Kingsbury County, Olympia, Stratford

Something there but not that exciting to be honest
Putney, Amersham, Hampstead, Woodford, Brompton, Kingsbury, Redbridge, Latimer, Arsenal, Monument

Nothing there but somehow being in the middle of nowhere made it OK
Epping, Acton, Lancaster, Green Park Farm, Hackney, Holborn

Nothing there, and not that exciting either. Oops.
Warwick, Wapping, Camden, Bond, Elm Park, Poplar, Kenton

Closed
Swiss Cottage, Watford

7:46 PM Aug 14th
and in the distance ... Dark clouds, and, err is that a tornado???

On the map the drive down US-287 is a small white road less than an inch long, but I know that it is probably going to take about an hour and I've told Paul that we are going be there at eight ... so we are already going to be late. The dark clouds in the distance that we spot start to draw in, and a few spots of rain commence falling upon the windscreen in a rhythmic pattern.

The rain drops get faster ... and faster ... too fast for me to tap my fingers in time to on the dashboard, and then it starts to rain, and rain, and then rain *hard* to the point where Alice maybe sounds a little panicky about how hard as the wipers on top speed are only just keeping up.

A truck roars past us on the outside lane, splashing up a deluge of water against the side of the car and the screen and it's almost as if this prompts the rain to come down even harder. And I am starting to panic because the visibility is getting bad.

'Shall we pull off?' I suggest tentatively to Alice, and for the first time in my whole week with her on the trip she gives me a look that says 'Yes! Please! And for once I actually agree with you!' and as a side turning appears up ahead we pull off the road, onto the side and join a couple of other cars that have also had the same idea.

> **8:02 PM Aug 14th**
> goodness. It's raining VERY heavily! We've pulled off and are sitting waiting for the storm to pass.

Ten minutes later and the rain stops almost as quickly as it has started. Ok – subsides a lot to regular levels and it's almost a case of 'What storm?' and we feel a little embarrassed perhaps to have stopped and not ploughed on through it. Hard storms comes, and just as quickly – they go. I guess that's the way it works here, don't mess with Texas.[40]

> **8:07 PM Aug 14th**
> US Hwy 287 southbound. Is this the way to Amarillo? Yes it is! And it's still a little rainy too.

Forty five minutes more of driving down Highway 287 gets us into Amarillo, the SatNav gallantly directing the way in the tricky multi-lane junctions of complicated downtown junctions. Paul sends me a text again

---

[40] The phrase 'Don't Mess With Texas' comes from a state-wide advertising campaign with the intention of reducing littering Texan roads – the slogan was prominently shown on road signs on major highways and in the media as adverts. Beyond its immediate role in reducing litter, the slogan became a Texas cultural phenomenon and the slogan has been popularly appropriated by Texans as 'An identity statement – a declaration of Texas swagger' and I have to say I quite like that. I find myself feeling the same way about how we in England and the UK think of ourselves as better than the rest of Europe because we are an Island, haven't accepted the Euro and like to do things our own way. Texas is a bit the same – it sees itself as being 'Just Texas' and different to the rest of America, and again I quite like that. I rarely met a Texan that I disliked. It's up there at the top of one of favourite States in the USA. A little bit of a confident swagger is OK in my book.

asking how far away we are, so I call ahead to the hotel and speak to him and get his room number, and tell him we'll be there 'soon', honest.

> **8:51 PM Aug 14th**
> companion update: Alice flies out tomorrow, my friend Paul from England flew in today, and we're just about to go meet him.

I have mixed feelings. On one hand, the harsh truth is that I am glad Alice is flying out tomorrow. My week with her has not been the best of the road trip in terms of companionship, and I am already starting to wonder in my head when I get back to Charleston and indeed in the future just how friendly I will be with her – or in fact, if I will stay in touch with her at all.

Paul is a different proposition altogether. I've known him for four years, but bizarrely have only ever met him about 3 or 4 times in the whole of that time. Paul is a fellow London Underground Tube traveller – he had once attempted the record, and our paths had crossed and we'd become friends in the rather small cliquey world of Tube-challenging, that had later been more solidly bonded by a love of dark humour, sarcasm, and an interest in all things obscure and out of the ordinary.

'So how well do you know Paul then?' asks Alice as the SatNav beeps its 'You have reached your destination' at the Quality Inn hotel where Paul has his room.

'Well' I explain thoughtfully 'I think I've spoken to him more on the phone and on email than in person ... but he's a really nice bloke!'

Paul *is* a really nice bloke, backed up by the fact that within about 30 seconds of him greeting us in his cheap-but-functional hotel room, he poses the one worded question of 'Brew?', to which there is only one answer – 'Yes!' and I think by Alice's puzzled expression it takes her a moment to realise that he is proposing to make tea. Ah ... tea! It's like having my mum back on the trip all over again, except that Paul has longer hair.

As we drink tea made in a coffee machine out of flimsy plastic hotel cups, we shoot some video footage, decide that we are all going to crash in Paul's room that night to save money, and then head off for the one destination in Amarillo that we've all heard about and all want to go to ... The Big Texan Steakhouse.

> **9:37 PM Aug 14th**
> we're headed to the Big Texan steak House. If you can eat a 72oz steak (+sides) in under an hour, then It's free!

With the three of us, suddenly the gloom that has enveloped myself and Alice seems to lift a little, and for the first time all week, I have a nice evening. We eat, talk, and we are even there to witness someone clear his plate and get their whole meal for free – something that doesn't happen too often.

I'm having less luck eating all my food though and as I give up and fail to complete the whole of my plate a rather disappointing third of the way through – I look at my plate of food that is left. I am full, and yet – I've been served dinners in restaurants in England where the amount of food served to start with is only slightly less than the amount that remains on my plate now. My mind starts to wonder off into a world of starving children and just how gluttonous we can be as a society.

> **10:12 PM Aug 14th**
> they've got fried rattlesnake on the menu, comes with a warning! #bigtexan

We find out from talking to our server, that actually how it works is that you do actually pay for the whole meal up front to begin with, and then they simply refund you if you manage to do it.

'That's only the second one I've ever seen' she says laughing, 'And I've been here for five months now'. So it seems that we have good timing to see it happen. They only get about ten people *a year* that manage to do it.

Back at the hotel, more tea is made. I update my progress map for the day, and Paul and Alice sit and chat and flick through the local cable TV channels.

> **1:22 AM Aug 15th**
> at a Quality Inn, Amarillo. They have 'BETV' on the TV here ... Black Entertainment Television.

We also find a Spanish-dubbed version of the Dukes of Hazzard film. When you see Boss Hawg on TV badly lip-synced into Spanish, you know it's time to turn in for the night.

Day 61 – Friday 15th August

It's OK. It's Alright.

'It's OK, It's alright, baby's staying one more night
And just you, and I, maybe we can make it right
If you're sure that the answer is no, I'll take you where you want to go'

'Don't fuck me around you bitch! Get your fucking arse out of bed NOW! And come and help me with this'

'I've had enough of your fucking shit, you bitch fuck you!'

Now – OK, I need to point out that I'm lying in bed slowly waking up all hearing this, and not pressing myself up against the wall using a glass to amplify the sound, but I'm pretty sure that that's what I hear.

> **8:25 AM Aug 15th**
> my morning alarm call: The couple in the next room (thin walls) shouting the F-word at each other, how pleasant.

'Good fucking morning' I say to Paul with a smile as he emerges from the bathroom. 'Fuck you, bitch' he smiles back without missing a beat. Oh, I've missed this! Out of the corner of my eye I can see Alice pulling a quizzical face. I turn and look and translate it properly as a 'I really don't understand English humour' look. This makes me smile inside probably more than it should.

> **9:41 AM Aug 15th**
> taking @paulfraserwebb for breakfast in an IHOP. It's all new to him, he's in for a fun two weeks!

Again – with Paul on board things instantly seem more jovial, and after a filling breakfast we have time to go do one fun thing before Alice has to be on her plane home – so we drive out a little way west to Cadillac Ranch. This is an 'artists' installation, where someone has taken ten Cadillac cars, and inserted them into the ground – bonnet first, and left the rest of the car poking out at an angle. People are then invited to bring paints and colour and anything else they want to do to decorate them, and then you pose by them and have your picture taken.

> **10:55 AM Aug 15th**
> at Cadillac ranch. Ten old cars upturned and buried in the ground. #onlyintexas

Dropping Alice off at the airport is weird. I know she is glad to be going back, I am glad she is going back, she knows I am glad, and I know that she knows. Yeah, it's that awkward. 'See you in Charleston' I just about manage, and then ... she is off with her bag and goes. And I get back into the car with Paul and he just turns to me and says 'So what was that all about then?'

I tell him about my awkward week as we drive to Broom in Texas to see a really large cross.

> **1:19 PM Aug 15th**
> at the world's largest cross in Broom, TX. #onlyintexas

I tell him about my awkward week as we walk around and admire the massive 200 foot tall structure, and I realise it's the counterpart of the one that I have seen just off of the highway with my mum a few weeks earlier back in Idaho.

I tell Paul the rest of the story of my awkward week as we then hit the Interstate and I put my foot down to make some miles and head towards today's same-name town, which is to our east in Oklahoma.

> **5:42 PM Aug 15th**
> you are now arriving at... Warren, OK

In the USA
Warren, Oklahoma
On the Tube map
Warren Street
(Victoria and Northern Lines)

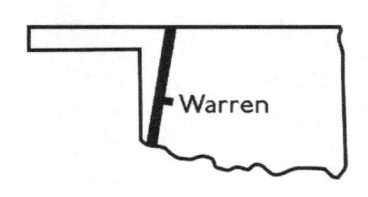

Warren, OK. It looks like a nice tiny town, but it also looks as if everything is closed even though we've come on a Saturday afternoon. Shouldn't there be a mall with teenage kids hanging out somewhere?

Uh, no. *Everything* appears to be shut. There is a white wooden slatted framed building which is just beautiful which is the town's General Store and Post Office. Across the road from that there's a school with a rusty iron gate which swings in the gentle breeze. Some grain mills just down the road are set back by a farm, and an artic lorry parked up at the side with the Stars & Stripes painted onto its radiator grill at the front. Paul takes a picture of me standing in front of the truck.

> **5:43 PM Aug 15th**
> Warren, OK : Two churches and a closed general store

Everything is quiet, everything seems still and if we didn't know better it is almost as if we are on a movie set, left at the end of the day once all the shooting is over and they are waiting for the props people to come in and clear up the set.

'So what do you do when there's nothing going on?' asks Paul wisely. 'Just ... walk around, have a look and take some photos usually', I tell him.

We wander around, we don't bump into anyone, we don't talk to anyone! But we don't need to – because we like it as it is. We take our photos on the rickety bench outside the general store, and then head back for Amarillo again. I even let Paul drive.

6:52 PM Aug 15th
Geoff: 'you're on the wrong side of the road!'. Paul: 'ah c'mon it had to happen eventually'

We swing by the town of Mangum on the way back, where we discover a lovely old ice-cream parlour shop that has been closed for years, but has re-opened *today* and three enthusiastic teenage girls run round serving us, two the daughters of the proprietors, one their friend. I toy with the idea of telling them that back home there is a name of an ice-cream called Magnum, which is a bit like the name of their town 'Mangum', but strangely for me I elect not to.

Instead, they tell us that a lot of businesses in the town have closed down, but they are going to make a go of it and try again. We suck hard on our delicious vanilla malts, and wish them well.

We swing by a movie location too – where Tom Hanks acts out his 'Where Now?' at the end of Castaway – an excellent movie, where he's at a crossroads in the middle of Northern Texas delivering a package to someone. Thanks to the power of the Internet and a website that tells you where movie locations are shot[41], we find the exact same crossroads, and act out a silly scene on video where I pretend to be Tom Hanks. Geoff – trying to figure out what he should do with the rest of his life in the same spot that Tom Hanks character stood and does the same – good times.

---

[41] At **waymarking.com** – the Castaway page is *waymarking.com/waymarks/WMER0_At_the_Crossroads_Cast_Away*

[42] Surely someone must have made the gag by now that IHOP is just a version of a Hop, but made by Apple. No? I'll get my coat ...

We head back to Amarillo with just one last thought in mind: some food. Over the past few days I've introduced Paul to Wal-Mart, Waffle House and IHOP[42] but before we leave Texas there is one place I need to introduce him to : Hooters.

Our server *Tiffany* is a pleasure to chat to and I get her to sign my shirt – 'Don't mess with Texas!' she writes, complete with a lone star just below it, followed by 'Hooters, Amarillo'. And yeah ... she 'dots' the double-O on 'Hooters', and even draws the double 'L's' in Amarillo in the shape of two cowboy boots. Love it.

We're almost alone in the place which is really quiet, in fact – the only other person in the area that we're sitting in – is a guy a few tables over who is sat all by himself. It's quiet enough for us to hear him engage in slightly awkward conversation with our server, and just before we leave it becomes slightly uncomfortable when he asks her for a hug as he's 'feeling lonely'. Wow, that just got embarrassing, so as we leave we both make eye contact with Tiffany to say 'Everything OK?' and she looks back at us and gives us a thumbs up out of sight of the lonely guy and nods an 'I'm alright' back at us.

> **11:24 PM Aug 16th**
> Back in Amarillo for the night, tomorrow : We have plans to motor west

The time is coming for us to get our kicks.

Day 62 – Saturday 16th August

The King of Route 66

'The dream helps you forget, you ain't never danced a step
You were never fleet of foot, hippy.
All the pathos you can keep for the children in the street
For the vision I have had is sweeping.'

It's mildly disappointing the next morning not be woken up by a torrent of swearwords and abuse emanating through the thin walls of the room over, but hey - you can't be spoiled like that every day.

Any number of cover versions of 'Route 66' are an obvious song choice for today's driving, and during that nice moment in bed in the morning when you're awake but you know you don't have to get up just yet and I lay there all comfortable. I flick through the six versions that I have on my iPod – all good, but in the end another song wins out and comes to mind, but annoyingly I don't have it!

> **8:52 AM Aug 16th**
> ok, can someone now send me an MP3 of Prefab Sprout 'The King of Rock & Roll' ? 'coz i'm heading for Albuquerque today …

My first ever memory of Route 66 that I have is back in my teenage years when I remember a picture of Robbie Coltrane (who I loved at the time from being in 'Cracker') sitting on the hood of a Cadillac, promoting his TV documentary from one end of Route 66 to another. It seems that TV producers every five years-or-so say 'I know, let's send someone famous across Route 66 in America and make a programme about it!'[43] as there have been several since, will no doubt be several more in the future – and he we are about to have our own miniature Route 66 adventure.

> **3:25 PM Aug 16th**
> at Adrian, TX. Midway point of Route 66. We've come OFF the Interstate and are trying to drive as much as the old road as possible

> **6:24 PM Aug 16th**
> Santa Rosa, NM. I hadn't bought any souvenirs on this trip do far, but now I'm going crazy on anything Route 66 emblazoned, help!

---

[43] You think I'm joking, but I'm not – During the same time it took me to write this book, a TV producer somewhere said 'I know let's send Billy Connolly off down Route 66!', and they did – making a four part TV documentary about his trip from Chicago to LA. In another few years' time, it'll happen again – trust me.

At Santa Rosa we stop at a local attraction – the blue moon pool. It's actually an old quarry which is now being used as a big swimming pool. As we leave, Paul elects to drive, and ten seconds in he pulls sharply up the street looking for the turn to take us back to the highway. At that moment (and I see him a split second before Paul does, and somehow in that split second know what is about to happen) I see the cop in a police car whose lights instantly flash to pull us over.

'Cop'. I say dryly. 'What?' 'Too late, he's got us', I say with a resigned voice.

> **6:56 PM Aug 16th**
> We got pulled by a cop again … and Paul was driving! Not me!

See now I think it's unfair because Paul is used to driving at a 30mph limit, he isn't driving recklessly, just a little too fast for an over zealous cop who is obviously bored on a Sunday afternoon and likes to give out tickets. Mind you, I think we're going to have some fun with Paul's driving license here.

> **7:03 PM Aug 16th**
> 38mph in a 25, duh. The New Mexico cop looked confused by his UK license.

> **7:05 PM Aug 16th**
> Ok, so if Paul doesn't pay his $80 fine, how are they going to track him down in England?

We have a good look at the ticket that he's issued. First thing to note – he's made a note of Paul's birthday wrong. He was born on the 12th October, but the cop has written it in in US date style meaning that he's put his birth date down as the 10th December instead – with thirty days to respond.[44]

We make Las Vegas – the one in New Mexico, not *the* Las Vegas (that one's in Nevada) whilst it is still light, book ourselves into the KOA and setup camp for the night.

> **9:24 PM Aug 16th**
> Made it to campground in Las Vegas, New Mexico. Not the Nevada/gambling one, there is more than one LV!

---

[44] By the time Paul got home, they *had* sent him a reminder about where to send the money and he did think about contesting it because of the incorrect birth date. But Paul considered that he did break the law – albeit unintentionally – and so he got a cheque raised in US dollars and posted it to them. He couldn't pay online … thank goodness they don't insist that you pay in person. A few days later he got a court summons in the mail – the delay in posting the cheque took him past deadline – Again I'd like to know what they would have done if he'd failed to pay it. Paul put the summons on the fire, and heated his house with it for a few seconds.

~ ~ ~

In the morning, it's only a short drive to our stop for the day.

> **12:03 PM Aug 17th**
> New day. New tube stop. Number 46 will be hit today, the end is in sight ....

In the USA
Angel Fire, New Mexico
On the Tube map
Angel (Northern)

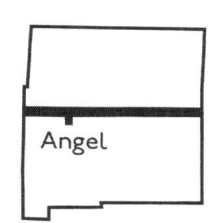

Angel Fire (yes, for 'Angel' on the Northern Line) is a picturesque New Mexican location. We can see a ski-lift up on side of a nearby mountain, a large car park, a bank, a tourist information centre – and of course the obligatory coffee shop.

> **2:14 PM Aug 17th**
> you have arrived at: Angel Fire, New Mexico! It's a skiing tourist town

Several minutes of chatting to the two girls in the café and they tell us everything that we need to know about the town.

'It's a ski-resort!' *Rebecca* tells us, who serves us our drinks. 'They all go up the Wheeler' – by which she is referring to Wheeler Peak, the highest mountain in the whole of the state. High enough for the skiers and snowboarders to enjoy it all year round, not just in the winter.

> **3:09 PM Aug 17th**
> Paul says it reminds him of Coniston, the lakes back in England. Only warmer, drier, and with less cars!

Back outside the café, we head for the visitors centre but before we get there in the field next to us we see a little creature poke its head out of a hole in the ground near us and realise it's a little prairie dog surveying the surroundings.

Then we look and realise that there are *loads* of them all around us ... but the moment we get too close to them (about ten metres away) they would bolt back down into the warren of tunnels beneath the ground we are walking on, and appear up behind us by quite a few metres away.

'They're so cute!' I say to Paul.

'They're burrowing right under our building!' says *Janette* in the visitors centre whom we talk to next (whilst taking a tour of a local artists drawings of the town) who goes on to inform us that as cute as they may be they have to get the exterminators in twice a year to stop them encroaching on the area where the café and other buildings are, as a year back, the toilet block sunk a couple of feet into the ground due to excessive burrowing.

> **3:42 PM Aug 17th**
> we've decided that 'Angel Fire' would be a really good name for a stripper

A pleasant town, in the sun. With mischievous Prairie Dogs. And an ideal place for mountainous activities.

And that's Angel Fire.

We leave town, and push on. Paul consults the map whilst I drive – where else can we go today with the rest of our time? 'How about Santa Fe?' suggests Paul because it looks like a reasonably sized town on the map. 'Let's do it', and hit my foot on the gas and back onto the tarmac road.

> **4:18 PM Aug 17th**
> it's all gone a bit Christmas around here … Santas everywhere. #newmexico

> **6:31 PM Aug 17th**
> is in Santa Fe, NM. it's very … mexican!

Santa Fe is just … *lovely*. Or at least the pictures of the town that hang on the wall in the interior of the Starbucks that I am now sitting in shows me that it looks lovely. I've given Paul my camera, a carte blanch to go and snap photos as he wants, and I iPhone-mapped my way to the nearest Starbux to get my online fix and do some work.

> **7:32 PM Aug 17th**
> there are a lot of hippies here. old crusty blokes with ponytails and loooong grey beards. dusty red brick buildings, ooodles of character.

I may just have been the most clean-cut guy in the whole of the coffee shop though – as I look around me people either have tattoos, braided hair, big beards, musical instruments or sketching something arty on a pad. I feel positively futuristic with my laptop, tap-tapping away, until I finally spot a guy over in the corner with an iPhone, and I give him a nod – and he just looks at me like I'm an old hippie mad guy with a beard.

> **7:35 PM Aug 17th**
> suddenly wishing I was a pot-smoker so that I'd fit in more here.

Two tables down, another guy with a beard who is wearing a crocodile skin hat gently strums a guitar. I assume that he is an official hired performer, until he stops and jots some notes on his pad, and I gather that no ... he is just some local dude that is sitting here spending his time composing a song. I like it.

7:37 PM Aug 17th
i take that back (don't do drugs kids), I really wish I could play the guitar though instead.

Paul comes back ... he's only been gone thirty minutes, but the need for a drink has got to him too, and he joins me at my tiny table. 'Coffee?' he proposes to me, and he gives me his now-signature nod and Churchill dog 'Oh yes', upon which we wander up to the counter.

'It's my birthday tomorrow' I say with a grin on my face to the delightful *Nikki* that is serving us. 'Oh is it?' she says with a genuine smile 'Well Happy Birthday'.

Except of course, this is my passage to a free drink. As I remember that when you sign up for a Starbucks Gold Card (Which I have, back in Charleston many months ago, Cost: $25, and you get ten percent off all purchases, and free Wi-Fi which has been essential on this trip), I remember that it also says that you would get a free drink on your birthday

'How does that work then?' I ask 'Claiming your free drink?'. 'Well they send you a card in the mail about a week before your birthday' she explains.

'Ah!' I say, realising that this probably isn't going to work, 'It's just that I haven't been home in over a month, and home is in fact 3,000 miles away in Charleston, and I can show you my driver's license to prove that tomorrow *is* my birthday ... so ... any chance that I can have a free drink?'

She takes this all in, looks at me quizzically, processing now what she realises is a British accent in the middle of New Mexico, and just simply asks ... 'Why haven't you been home in over a month?'.

Brilliant! Allow me to explain ...

All the Baristas turn out to be exceedingly chatty, and Paul and I step aside every time a new customer comes up to the counter and then step right back in again to carry on the conversation, as I explain the road trip, and what we are doing and where are going and before we know it we are having a conversation about travelling in the USA, world travel, and her own plans next summer to travel to Europe.

I get my free coffee – she even gives me a voucher to have *another* one at some point, because ... well just because I think she just likes us. Which suits my Starbucks obsession just fine thank you. 'That'll feed my

Starbucks Obsession just fine thank you!' I say, only to be immediately outdone.

'You think YOU'RE obsessed by Starbucks' offers up one of her colleagues at the pump making an espresso, 'Show him your tattoo, Nikki!' – and no sooner has this been said, is she rolling up her trouser leg, and placing her foot on the counter (no doubt breaking many cleanliness rules in the workplace in the process) and showing me a tattooed number than she's got on the side of her leg just above her ankle.

'Err… it's a tattoo – I can see that, but what of?' 'My Starbucks staff number!' she replies, and shows us her employee card which sure enough has the number that matches the one that is embossed for life in ink on her leg. 'I like working here so much, I thought I've have the number forever'.

Unable to compete with this level of obsession, we finish our drinks and duck back outside into the pleasant afternoon Santé Fe sunshine. Only at this point does Paul perk up with something that I wish he'd of mentioned sooner.

'Oh there's something you need to see!' he says, 'Follow me!' and strides ahead marching quite purposely on. I'm wondering if he's found some cool monument, or an interesting Geocache, or perhaps even a parked car with the elusive New Hampshire license plate – but it's something even better – a London Underground roundel!

'Underground Gallery' it says, in the proper shape, size and red and blue colours – hanging off of the building above head height is indeed the roundel, the sign for a shop – well, it's not a shop – but is indeed a gallery, that's called the 'Underground Gallery' and clearly they've been to London at some point and have decided to nick the roundel as their sign.

We peer in the window as it appears to be closed, but can't really see anything – so Paul snaps a picture of me standing beneath the roundel, grinning away like an idiot. It's fun.

Day 64 – Monday 18th August

Forever Young

'Can you imagine when this race is won, Turn our golden faces into the sun Praising our leaders we're getting in tune, The music's played by the madman. So many adventures couldn't happen today, so many songs we forgot to play So many dreams are swingin' out of the blue, we let 'em come true'

Somewhere in the middle of the night:

> **2:04 AM Aug 18th**
> ah shit, I've just turned 37. #oldparanoia

Sometime in the morning:

> **9:41 AM Aug 18th**
> there is no milk. happy-morning black tea-birthday to me, d'oh!

I get online before Paul is up, and discover that the KOA shop has no fresh milk in, so black tea it is going to be. 'Mornin'' says Paul in his gruff Lancastrian tone, 'Mornin'' I grump back, and look at him waiting for the greeting. There is a slight pause as he plays with me, 'And Happy Birthday' he says smiling. I smile back … 'I almost forgot it was' I say lying really because what I really mean is that it feels very un-birthdayish being at a campground in the middle of New Mexico, with no cards or presents to open.[45]

There is only one thing on the agenda this morning, and that is for me to go and break my virginity – my Arizona virginity that is, as it would officially be the last 'new' state for me that I would visit on the trip, and the place to do it at … is at Four Corners.

> **7:09 PM Aug 18th**
> i am just about to be in four states at the same time … Yup am at Four Corners! Arizona/Utah/Colorado/New Mexico meet!

Four Corners is a tourist spot right on the place where the four states come together, and there is a concrete '+' marker in the ground where you place both legs and both arms in all the four different states at once and have your photo taken.

---

[45] Reader – that is correct, Paul failed to even buy me a tacky souvenir in the KOA gift shop as a birthday present!

> **7:11 PM Aug 18th**
> it was $3 to get in, and there are lots of tacky tourist shops here. It's windy, too

> **7:13 PM Aug 18th**
> and! As i've been to California before when I go tread in Arizona, I'll officially have been to all the states except Hawaii!

There's actually quite a big line to have our photo taken, and we have to queue up three times to get it done. Once for me to have my photo taken, once for Paul, and then I went back again so that Paul can shoot some video of me entering Arizona officially for the first time.

> **7:39 PM Aug 18th**
> so have now been to Arizona and done the whole lower-48. Still got two 'same name' places to go to though

We haven't really planned where we're staying tonight, but we realise that we're not that far from the border or Colorado again as we've come so far north to get to the four corners. The small town of Cortez looks welcoming in the south-west corner of the state.

> **9:47 PM Aug 18th**
> back up to Colorado for one day, following? Heh. In Cortez for the night, head SW tomorrow ... towards the Grand Canyon!

Having been in New Mexico for most of the day and the previous day, I've really got myself a taste from some Mexican food for dinner – it's one of the things that I've got to like whilst living on this side of the pond is a burrito, and I *really* want one all of a sudden for my birthday.

But it isn't to be. Instead we end up in a mildly disappointing pizza-bar-pub having some slow service and an 'okayish' meal. That's the trouble with excellent service in America, the very few times that you *don't* get it, you seem to take more offence that usual – unlike in England where you just kinda expect it all the time.

> **11:27 PM Aug 18th**
> ah ... Small town America where the restaurants close at 9pm. No Mexican birthday meal for me #Cortez

We get back, light the camp fire – not because we need to but just because we can. Have some tea, and turn in for yet another day.

Actually, for me it's another year – and here's a most incredibly selfish thought. I am (and I am, really) having the time of my life on this trip, but I realise that then on my birthday I don't receive a single birthday present or card, nadda, nought, nothin'. I know the world is full of greed and selfishness, but when you've experienced thirty-six other years of your life when you've at least had *something* on your birthday morning, it's very weird to all of a sudden one year get nothing. I'm looking forward to *not* spending my thirty-eighth birthday in a place where no one can get gifts and cards to me. Happy Birthday to me.

~ ~ ~

On my Birthday+1, we are back on the road, and I am all over the twitter for the day.

> **10:33 AM Aug 19th**
> back on the Route 66 trail today. Grand Canyon tomorrow. tonight i will video edit then and update the blog!
>
> **11:09 PM Aug 19th**
> taken Paul for a Denny's breakfast. 'Did you know in England, English muffins are just called 'muffins' ? – that's confused our server
>
> **1:45 PM Aug 19th**
> Monument Valley on Utah/Arizona border, magnificent scenery. It's impossible to take a bad photo.
>
> **3:06 PM Aug 19th**
> remember the opening sequence to Knight Rider? A black Trans-Am driving through scorching hot desert roads? Well that's us, only in a maroon coloured Jeep Cherokee. Paul is doing his best KITT impressions too, which helps.
>
> **5:21 PM Aug 19th**
> considering staying in a wigwam for the night. (At the WigWam motel, Holbrook AZ). #route66
>
> **6:03 PM Aug 19th**
> and don't forget Winona ... and we haven't! Sucking up '66 heritage attractions and luvin it.10
>
> **10:20 PM Aug 19th**
> Arizona in two: dry. dusty.

~ ~ ~

> **09:22 AM Aug 20th**
> Williams, AZ. Unbelievably cute town where every other shop has a link to Route 66
>
> **09:23 AM Aug 20th**
> and the speed limit is 15mph! I saw the cop car just in time and slowed down ...

A day of being tourists along Route 66 yesterday has brought us to arguable the *most* touristy thing that we can do on the trip ... The Grand Canyon.

In a Williams's café where we wolf down a stuff-us-full breakfast down our necks to last as long as possible, I check the map to see the road to take us to the canyon. In the midst of which I have a terribly embarrassing and humbling moment whilst being served, where the server asks if we are done with our plates and I say 'Not quite, I'm still going' at which point she precedes to clear our plates away anyway. 'Bloody hell, is she stupid or deaf or something?' I say quietly to Paul as she walks away, and it's at that point he replies 'Err, well yes – I think she is' and points for me to look, and only then do I see the hearing aids she is wearing behind both ears. Oh. Genuine 'Oh' and a humbling feeling there, Geoff. We should probably just go to the canyon now.

We toy with the idea of getting a train to it – as there is a tourist train that you can take from Williams – and this is a Tube train related trip after all, but there is only one service a day there and back – a tourist line special – and there is no way that we have managed to get up early enough to catch it, so we drive.

14:34 AM Aug 20th
hi ho, hi ho, it's off to the Grand Canyon we go …

15:36 PM Aug 20th
$25 to get in! Cheaper if I get a pass that'll also get me into Death Valley next week.

15:51 PM Aug 20th
well … I'm looking at a big bloody hole in the ground. You know, like … a mile deep. Wow. #grandcanyon

16:10 PM Aug 20th
it's not TOO commercial which is nice. Mind you, all I'm doing at the moment is driving round the parking lot looking for a New Hampshire plate.

16:15 PM Aug 20th
book in gift shop: 'OVER THE EDGE! The Deaths Of Grand Canyon'. Nice. #grandcanyon

17:04 PM Aug 20th
sat on the edge of the canyon. Slight breeze, peaceful, beautiful. #grandcanyon

17:09 PM Aug 20th
so I'm sat on the south rim, just … looking. Because you can look at it for a long time and never get bored. #grandcanyon

~ ~ ~

The next morning, I have a very direct feeling hit me. For the first time, as I look at the map and can see California getting closer, I realise that this is all coming to an end. I trace my finger from Maine up in the top right corner and loosely take the path that I have travelled all summer round the whole of America, and there is about an inch left to my west to take us to the final state, and the final destination.

'You alright?' asks Paul. I look up from the map. I realise that I have been sat staring at the map out of focus not saying anything for probably quite a while – lost in thought, places, smells, sounds and everything that I've consumed so far. And that it is all coming to an end this week.

'I'm good' I say exhaling air. 'I'm just ...' 'Tired?' 'Ha. Yes, but not of trip. Well I am. But I'm not, not really. I don't want it to end. But I'll sort of be glad when it's over. But also…'

'Also …?'

I paused. Thinking carefully about what I want to say. But I know what I want to say, so hit the internal switch inside of me which will just output the monologue that has been building up inside of me for a while.

'Also, I think I want to do this every summer for the rest of my life, and explore forever having an overall wonderful time, because it's amazing and why would I ever want to do anything else except to travel, explore, meet new people and see new things. And yet, that's obviously just not possible in a realistic world, is it? Because that takes time and money and both of those are finite resources, and yet more people should be able to get to do this and not be ground down their entire lives in in grimy job that that probably don't like, and I realise that I am a fortunate lucky bastard for being able to have the trip of a lifetime.'

I take a breath.

And Paul just does that thing that he is ever so good at doing, and all I want him to do in reply to that question – he just gives me a sage smile, and nods his head in agreement.

> **11:13 AM Aug 21st**
> we're leaving Williams AZ, heading west ... back on Route 66 heading for penultimate Tube stop. #route66

> **12:30 AM Aug 21st**
> just seen first sign to LA – 478 miles. Wow. The end is getting closer…

> **3:26 PM Aug 21st**
> hello Mojave desert ... and it's 100F out there, ouch!

With Oatman and the Wild West behind us we cross the state line from Nevada into California. I remember that someone has told me that California has patrols at all the borders to check for incoming goods into the state, and am expecting some kind of check-point, but there is nothing ... I don't even see the 'Welcome to California' sign, but it must have been there somewhere.

> **8:31 PM Aug 21st**
> i'm in my 48th state for the trip, hello California. Needles, to be precise and good God it's hot! 105F at 8pm at night ...

We arrive in Needles, just as the sun is setting and we are getting hungry ... but for the first time on the trip, I haven't called ahead or booked online at the campground – my confidence is rising in just knowing that would can pull it and get a pitch for our tent even after office hours and just drop some money in the honesty box for a late reservation.

The first thing we notice though as we're setting up our tent is just how empty the rest of the campground is. In one whole section of the campground where we are, there are no others tents and just one small sized R.V. Needles it seems, is not a very busy place.

The second thing we notice is the wind. It is windy. And warm. But it is going to get windier and warmer. First we need to eat though, and as it's late and we are getting lazy, I introduce Paul to the wonders of Taco Bell – yet again parking the car at a spot in the lot where I can keep an eye on it from the window seat inside.

Our stomachs filled with poor Mexican fast food, we head back to the campground and I sit outside in an area reserved for grilling and barbeques, where some white plastic furniture is strewn about, so I up right the chairs and sit up at one of the tables with my laptop. Paul joins me, reading his book. It takes about thirty seconds to discover why the chair has been on its side when a huge gust of wind blows in to knock the chair back over onto its side again.

To escape the wind, I retire to the laundry, and finally get my Route 66 gallery online.

> **11:12 PM Aug 21st**
> day 66! Shedload of cool photos added to the group: http://is.gd/2sWuZ

Only then do I realise that we've had a Route 66 fest on day 66 of the trip! I do love coincidental moments like that that you could never plan, they just... happen that way.

Paul goes to bed ... not just because I'm ignoring him, but because he's worrying that the tent might blow away and his weight will obviously keep it in place. Later, he tells me that once he was inside the tent he was worried that it was going to get zapped by lightning. I join him once I've finished buggering about online.

> **11:45 PM Aug 21st**
> seriously California, 11.45 at night at 102 degrees F? Are you trying to make me naked in a tent with my mate to be cool enough to sleep?

Fifteen minutes later, and I'm starting to realise that sleep is going to be tricky.

Paul is mostly naked ... I can see the moles on his back that I never knew he had. I don't really want to get *that* naked though, I just really want to go to sleep. Badly.

And after two hours of sketchy drifting-in-and-out not very good sleep, I give up, get up and realise that the dryness of the desert heat has made me thirsty and I need a drink. Out of the tent I wander back over to the launderette area where I've been sitting earlier, but realise that the other side of a hedge there is a cut through by the swimming pool that is a quicker way to go. As I turn down the path to go by the pool though, I hear noises – human noises of giggling and splashing around, and some sixth sense tells me stop ... as it sounds a bit ... salacious!

I realise I have stopped walking instinctively which is odd, so I start to walk slowly again and at the end of the hedge of the pool I peer around the corner to see two people – a woman and a man in the pool, and ... oh ... yeah. Oh I see what they're doing now. Memories of New Orleans come flooding back, and so as is the thing to do on this trip, I once again get my phone out of my pocket as I can really only tweet about it.

> **2:39 AM Aug 22nd**
> KOA Needles, CA. Went to get drink from vending machine and there's a couple sat by the pool and she's giving him a blowjob ... #onlyatkoa

I walk back the other way round, get a cold orange drink out of the vending machine and chug it down almost in one go. Thirst quenched, but still awake. I look over at Paul, asleep – bastard. How *is* he managing that? And decide instead that sleeping in the car might be worth a try.

> **5:44 AM Aug 22nd**
> this heat is crazy. It's so windy too. 3.45am and I'm thus wide awake.

So my last night of camping shall be remembered for sitting in the car awkwardly, with wind, heat, and a couple in swimming pool not far away from me having a much better time of it.

I am *really* very much ready for the trip to be at an end now.

Day 68 – Friday 22nd August

Falling Down

'Summer sun that blows my mind
Is falling down on all that I've ever known
Time to kiss the world goodbye
Falling down on all that I've ever known'

'So ... I don't know why the banks don't just GIVE US more money'

'What?'

'Well you know how our tax dollars are meant to be bailing out the banks with 500 million dollars or something, well why not just print 500 *new* million dollars and hand it out for that to be used instead?'

What the .. ? Honestly, I've only popped in to pay the cashier for the petrol that I've just bought (because my Barclaycard has just been declined for a fourth time and I really can't be bothered to have the same repeated conversation with them again this morning) and the guy behind the counter who has a name badge that I can see says *'Phillip'*[46] decides that as he serves me is going to tell me how to solve the world's financial crisis.

'They wouldn't even have to print the money ... it's all electronic nowadays anyway, right?'

I nod.

'Money now only really exists in statements and in computers, so just tell the system that it's there ... and it's there. Problem solved and won't cost us any tax dollars at all! We'll only be spending money that didn't exist before. BOOM!'

He animates the 'BOOM' with waving his arms wide in the air, and it makes me sway back a little away from him. I indulge him though – but just a little, enough to keep him happy, but don't stay so long that he tells me anymore. Has a gas station cashier in Arizona just solved the world's financial problems?

'You alright?' asks Paul, noting that I've been a while.

'Yes, just solving the world's money problems' I come back with sharply.

Paul nods. 'Where are we going today then?'

---

[46] It was a 'Phillips 66' gas station too. Honestly, we're on Route 66 with a guy called 'Phillip' serving us – that's just brilliant.

I know he knows where we're going – he's just asking to make me say it. I give him a little smile.

'London Bridge', as the smile becomes broader and I grin as I remember what the trip is all about – and I feel like it is going to be a good one. It is.

In the USA
London Bridge, Arizona

On the Tube map
London Bridge
(Northern and Jubilee Lines)

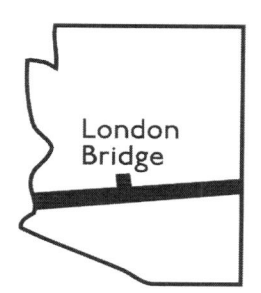

London Bridge, Arizona is the relocated bridge from the 1830's that formerly spanned the Thames until it was dismantled 1967. It's something of an urban legend in popular culture that the Americans thought that they were getting London's more recognisable Tower Bridge when they bought it and brought it over, only to get London Bridge instead. But it is just that – an urban myth.

> **1:46 PM Aug 22nd**
> am at Lake Havasu, AZ ... arriving at my next stop ...

> **2:05 PM Aug 22nd**
> and welcome to London Bridge, Arizona style. My 47th stop on the trip.

> **2:06 PM Aug 22nd**
> and, some might say fittingly, it is pouring down with rain. So much so I've had to get my umbrella out for the first time.

So one of the first things I do is to get Paul to snap a photo of me, in front of London Bridge with my umbrella up. It's odd knowing that just a few miles down the road which we are about to visit, the dry sandy desert awaits us, and yet right now it really does feel like we are back in London.

There are some silver coloured plinths dotted around, with dragons on top with a St. George's flag wrapped around it with 'City of London' embossed on the side. 'The London Arms Pub & Playhouse' is doing its best to cash in on any Shakespeare lovers whilst turning the corner leads us to a fountain – a bit of a mini-Trafalgar Square with lions, and ... of course, a red phone box over in the corner.

2:08 PM Aug 22nd
lots of faux-Brit shops everywhere. And a big union jack, and – of course – a red phone box. #londonbridge

2:12 PM Aug 22nd
Paul: 'but where's the authentic smell of urine that you normally get on British bridges?'. He's got a point.

We decide that the thing to at London Bridge is of course to go for a walk across the bridge. We find the convoluted route for pedestrians which involves two minutes of walking back on ourselves, and then see the big sign better placed for drivers. 'WORLD FAMOUS LONDON BRIDGE' it says, against the backdrop of a Union Jack. 'Surely the one in London is more World Famous?' I ask rhetorically to Paul.

Trudging across, the rain picks up. I would say that the wind blows in off of the Colorado River because if this is really London and it's raining, the wind would be blowing too – but instead, there is just a damp warm drizzle (I am wearing my shorts, it isn't cold) and by the time we get to the other side, the Island Mall Grill looks tempting for a late breakfast.

We have as close to an English fry-up as we can manage, the obligatory hash browns are something you'd never get at home, 'Oh for a slice of fried bread' laments Paul, and of course there is no proper tea, or baked beans, or HP sauce. Come to think of it, it isn't that close to full English, but hey – we tried.

We stay in the grill about an hour after a second lot of coffee including talking to our server who tells us that they have never been to London, doesn't really care *that* much about London – or London Bridge – and they are just working here because 'A job is a job, I don't care what town it's based in'.

Once we've dried out we decide that we should go and get wet again by walking back across the bridge. This time we pay a lot more attention to the stonework of the bridge, and we wonder if they really have moved it here stone-by-stone, or if they've just broken it up into large chunks and done it that way.

Back in faux-London I note that the red phone box doesn't even have a US phone in it. But there are yellow lines painted along the kerbside, which I think is a nice touch.

I am surprised more places aren't open – it is a Saturday after all but it feels like a Sunday. I nab a Geocache that is of course called 'London Bridge', and take a few funky photos of the mini-London. I also get Paul to take a picture of me holding up Chris's "Septic's Companion" book, and post it to the Facebook page for his book – a little bit of promotion for him I hope.

'How does it rate?' asks Paul 'For the list, that is'. 'Ah! The list!' I say, grabbing my notebook out of my pocket. 'I think I'll put it in … '

SAME NAME TOWNS TALLY

Perfect Small Town America
Preston, White City, Waterloo

Something there and enjoyable
Plaistow, Gloucester, Kew Gardens, Harrow, South Kensington, Greenford, Liverpool, Temple, Oxford, Victoria, Kingsbury County, Olympia, Stratford, Angel, London Bridge

Something there but not that exciting to be honest
Putney, Amersham, Hampstead, Woodford, Brompton, , Kingsbury, Redbridge, Latimer, Arsenal, Monument

Nothing there but somehow being in the middle of nowhere made it OK
Epping, Acton, Lancaster, Green Park Farm, Hackney, Holborn

Nothing there, and not that exciting either. Oops.
Warwick, Wapping, Camden, Bond, Elm Park, Poplar, Kenton

Closed
Swiss Cottage, Watford, Warren

317

> **5:26 PM Aug 22nd**
> so ... to Las Vegas, via the Mojave Desert to check out a non-existent phone booth ...

We have to go through the desert on the way to Vegas. Not because it's the most direct route, but because I want to go and see if we can find the legendary Mojave Desert phone booth that has a website dedicated to it. I don't think I need to tell you anymore other than this – there is (or rather, there *was*) a phone booth in the middle of the Mojave Desert, to which random people used to call, people made pilgrimages too, and in its honour – someone made a website about it. And then someone also went and made a movie about it – yes, a phone box. Trust me – I can't do it justice here. Just go and Google the phrase 'Mojave Desert Phone Booth' the next time you're online, and all will be revealed.

> **7:58 PM Aug 22nd**
> wow. We have just survived the rigours of the Mojave desert. Talk about nervous focused energy when we realised we were low on gas

> **7:59 PM Aug 22nd**
> then ... we find a gas station where regular is $3.99 ... ! HOW expensive!?

> **8:29 PM Aug 22nd**
> just crossed back from CA into NV and it's all gone a bit ... gambly! HUGE outlet store on Nevada Stateline with massive hotels and casinos

> **8:31 PM Aug 22nd**
> Geoff: 'what kind of hell is this?' Paul: 'I think it's going to be lot worse in Vegas...'

He's right. It's a *lot* worse.

~ ~ ~

I just want to leave.

I just want to be in any other town right in the whole of America, but not here.

Not Vegas. Not the lights, not the people, not the mess, not the noise ... not the sheer bloody awfulness of the whole place.

It is safe to say that I am not enjoying Vegas.

You know, what I should do is spend a fair few pages writing up my reflective thoughts on the whole of Las Vegas. I should give it a fair crack, I should explain what I liked (very little), and what I hated (almost all of it), but in the same way that I just can't wait to leave the town ... I just really want to rush through this and write-up very quickly about my time there and move on from this part of the book as soon as possible. But – sigh – that wouldn't be fair and it wouldn't make much sense, so I have to tell you a little about it at the least.

I should tell you that Paul and I stay here for three nights in a hotel, a deal which he negotiates and pays for (thanks, Paul) and he gets us a good deal – initially we don't know why.

We soon find out. Vegas is not as booming as it once was. Sure there are lots of people here with noise and money and casinos and outrageously over-charged snacks and drinks and bars at every turn, but compared to how well it used to do, it's currently going through a hard time.

I catch up with an old friend of mine – Rich, who I had worked with in Charleston. He's seen my trip online and when he realises I am coming through Vegas – where he now lives and works, he sends me a message and we all meet up and go out for the evening. As we drive around in Rich's car, he explains that Vegas is going through a tough time.

'Right now it's got the highest rate of foreclosure of any major metropolitan area. The unemployment rate has recently gone up from 4% to 12% – in just three years. And hotels have slashed their room rates to get occupancy rates back up to 90% from a low of 70%'

He takes us on a tour around town and shows us buildings – half complete buildings – which are new hotels, constructions that you can see have come to a halt half way through because there is either no money to finish them, or the company building it realises that Vegas is now not attracting as many guests as it used to.

'The high end restaurants of the MGM have got rid of their $400 bottles of wine and replaced them with $100 ones. The whole of Las Vegas' boulevards are littered by underfunded, unsold and unfinished hotels, casinos and condos.'

And I hate it. By American standards, the main thing I hate is how compressed and compact it all feels. Too many people, bright lights and businesses squeezed into one place. I am used to America being spread out and open, but here everything feels squashed in.

Over the course of the three days that I endure in Vegas, I become aware of an odd thing ... I don't take any pictures. The whole trip, I have done nothing but take countless photos, but here in Vegas it strips me of any creativity, as if it's been sucked from my soul, going with it the urge to take a picture. It is as if I don't want to remember being here. Ever.

As we drive around, I see an advert on the back of a bus. In England, you might see a Direct Line or Churchill car insurance ad. In Vegas? 'Shoot a Machine Gun for 15 minutes for $100!' I start to despair.

Rich continues to tell us how squatting is popular now. In what counts as the 'suburbs', low cheap rent housing have been built, where people live who mainly work in the casinos. But when they lost their jobs, people had nowhere else to go, so some of the suburbs have transformed into near-slums, with people moving from house-to-abandoned-house, squatting and making a living where they can.

'The armpit of America' I remember someone back in Charleston had described it to me – and I am starting to see why. Vegas has no charm, no character that has built up over time, it is enforced and false.

Rich leaves us with one more crazy fact before calling it a night. 'There are schools here which teach kids overnight. There are people that work as croupiers in the casinos that only ever work night shifts. So they drop their kids off at school at 10pm, and collect them again at 6am and go home to sleep'. This … is *insane*. How on earth is that a proper way to bring up a child?

It doesn't then help that for the first time on the trip, Paul then really annoys me. After Rich drops us off, I am all for walking back to the hotel and going to sleep. But Paul is all up for having a drink, having another drink, and getting into the false 'party' spirit of this dreadful place. I am not.

After being dragged around for half an hour, I deliberately lose him in a crowd – feigning to be on the phone so as to be distracted, and then just make my way back. Past the hotels, with fake Paris and fake Venice. Past the hordes of people on the street thrusting cards into your hand trying to sell you a prostitute for the night.

A low-loading truck drives slowly past me to my right, with a picture of a group of women with large fake breasts on the side with a slogan that says 'Need someone tonight?' and a phone number below. Prostitution may technically be illegal here, but it doesn't stop them advertising it.

I don't think I need to tell you again how much I am hating Vegas.

~ ~ ~

It's around this time that the Ernest Hemingway quote from *A Moveable Feast* comes to mind. It's right there at the beginning of the book – you probably glanced at it and or skipped over it but it's there for a reason, and that reason is now. It's been over twenty years since I read it at school, but the quote this morning when I wake up is somehow resonating in my head:

'Never to go on trips with anyone you do not love.'

I'd had my first proper argument with Katie on the trip, then J.J. and I had fallen out in the hot New Orleans sunshine. Nat and I had definitely annoyed each other during our time together, and then of course the week with Alice had been totally awkward - and now here I am again now being pissed off with Paul. Either it's *my entire* fault, and I am terrible to travel with – or as Ernest says, you just have to *really* love those that you are with.

Fuck. Is it my entire fault? Am I awful to travel with? Do I not listen to other people or ask about what they want … even though, it's my trip and thus I am setting the agenda as to where we're going, there has to be some give and take. Or should my companions let me dictate our movements?

I want to go back – to speak to Alice and Natalie, and just say 'Look I realise that we're not getting on right now, let's talk about it and sort it out!', but I can't because they aren't here. Paul is here though, and so I'm not going to let this happen again. This is one I can sort out now.

So I have a 'clear the air' conversation with Paul as soon as I can that morning, and we both seem much more cheerful. Paul wants to party in Vegas – I don't, and so instead we compromise and go and visit the Hoover Dam instead.

It's massively impressive – a huge concrete arch spanning between the edges of the Black Canyon of the Colorado River, and it's right on the border between California and Arizona. Controversially named after President Herbert Hoover, men died building it. It's a huge tourist attraction with hundreds of thousands of people coming to see it every year.

We take the tour, take photos in awe of the massive structure, and walk around in the mixture of Californian and Arizonan sun, and yet my overwhelming memory of it will be that it has the most overpriced café that I have ever seen in America for a tourist attraction. No I do not buy a 'Hoover Burger' for eight dollars, instead we stop at an In 'n' Out Burger on the way back to Vegas, and get one that I suspect tastes much better, and with a much better value for money price at just five bucks too.

> **5:35 PM Aug 24th**
> finally! About to do a In 'n' Out burger – the finest in the world I am informed

~ ~ ~

The next day, I want to escape Vegas again and so this time Paul and I settle on visiting the town of 'Rachel' – still in Nevada but about an hour's drive away, which is the 'home town' of all things alien.

> **2:42 PM Aug 25th**
> it's time to escape Vegas again. This time to Rachel, NV. The UFO Highway by Area 51 …

Actually, that's me just abbreviating is there for the tweet, as Nevada State Route 375 actually has a sign up pronouncing it as 'The Extra-terrestrial

Highway' complete with an image of a B2 Stealth Bomber. The 100 mile road passes right by the US Nellis Air Force Base, home to 'Area 51' the top secret base, and an area where many people have recorded the sightings of UFO's in the area. The small town of Rachel nearby therefore caters for UFO seekers with an alien-themed business.

'Welcome to Rachel' says the sign. 'Population : Humans 98, Aliens ?'. We head for the bar, shop and motel – called 'The Little Al-e-inn'.

> **5:36 PM Aug 25th**
> i'm in the 'Little Al e inn' in Rachel, Nevada. Earthlings also welcome, says the sign. #area51
>
> **5:47 PM Aug 25th**
> the 'A le inn' is selling 'Crop circles volume 6 – the most compelling evidence yet!' So what was in the first five then? #area51
>
> **5:48 PM Aug 25th**
> and suddenly ... BOOM! An air force plane flies past jolting us in its sonic wake, cool. #area51
>
> **5:50 PM Aug 25th**
> and now Paul's wandered off and I can't find him. Maybe been abducted for anal probing by aliens? He'd probably enjoy it. #area51

We spend an hour in the café-cum-gift shop in Rachel, during which we get some food and try to engage in conversation with the guy serving us but it feels like he doesn't want to talk to us.

Over in the corner, there is an old strange looking man who sits at a computer, who occasionally shouts 'I've got another one!' to himself, as no one pays him any attention.

'What's he got another one of?' I asked the behind the counter who had served us. He looks back at me angrily as if it's outrageous that I have asked and snaps back 'You'll have to ask him, won't you!' and turns and walks away.

It then feels as if we are eyed up suspiciously by the guys and another chap that works there for the rest of our time there browsing in the shop. 'Perhaps they think we're a gay couple' whispers Paul to me, as they simply don't seem very friendly or chatty at all.[47]

We drive down a real off-road dusty track, to the edge of the Air Force base itself, to a barrier by a military building with a large sign saying 'No Photographs in this Area!' A CCTV camera is pointing in our direction, and we look across the barren landscape wondering if there really are

---

[47] Which is a shame, because their website clearly says *'We love to meet new people and make new life friends as we have done over the many years. We hope you are to be one of those new visitors and friends in the very near future.'*

aliens buried deep down in secret building below the surface. I think I may have caught myself whistling the opening notes of 'The X-Files' at this point. And then we head back to Vegas.

Just two more days left – one more night. And then it will all be at an end.

Day 72 – Tuesday 26th August

Leaving Las Vegas

*'Used to be I could drive up to Barstow for the night,
Find some crossroad trucker to demonstrate his might
But these days it seems, Nowhere is far enough away
So I'm leaving Las Vegas today'*

With a belly full of IHOP breakfast carbohydrates jiggling around in our digestive system, I let Paul drive and as we head west as I continually check myself for signs that I am getting happier, the further away from Vegas that we go. It isn't really happening, but eventually a wry smile forces its way onto my face when the Eagles come onto the radio … again.

> **1:23 PM Aug 26th**
> leaving Vegas, heading for hotel in California … 'Hotel California' comes on the radio. #perfectserendipitousmomentthatputmeinagreatmood

We are also en route to go and visit something that is definitely piquing my interest … but not in that sort of way. I want to go and check out a legal brothel.

Nevada may be the state for all kinds of pleasure, but the legal brothels are only legal in eight of the sixteen counties in the state. Las Vegas itself is located in Clark County, where it isn't legalised – but if you Google around or look in nightclubs then there are plenty of helpful leaflets telling you to drive west for an hour to Nye County, in particular the town of Pahrump, where all your needs are adequately serviced.

Out of force of habit from looking up ahead almost all towns that I've been to on the trip, I flip through the KOA brochure that shows you where in the states the campgrounds are, and what facilities are there, and note with interest that the KOA in Pahrump *doesn't* allow tents – mainly it seems to only to accept RV's with hook-ups. Only I originally read this though as 'RV with Hookers', like you do.

An hour and a half of hot driving later, and the dusty desert road transforms into some kind of town.

> **3:13 PM Aug 26th**
> welcome to Pahrump, Nevada. Featuring …

> **3:14 PM Aug 26th**
> a visitor's centre JUST for adult services. They tell you about the places to go in town.

I recall tourist information centres back home in Britain – a white 'i' (for information) on a blue circle background. I imagined in my head that that could be changed here to a white erect penis on a dark pink circle. I really should control myself sometimes I also figure.

> **3:15 PM Aug 26th**
> there's also adverts for a brothel museum & brothel art museum. I'm not sure what the difference is.

> **3:17 PM Aug 26th**
> the local radio stations (KNYE) tag-line is 'things that go pah-rump in the night!'

> **3:19 PM Aug 26th**
> surely the local radio station should be KY-EZ. Just sayin'.

The two main brothels in town – the two that are best known are The Chicken Ranch and Sheri's Ranch both located south out of town ... on a dusty road on the outskirts of town.

I wonder if locals get a giggle of watching anyone make the turn to come down here. Has someone set up some digital scanning device to snap license plates which they then post on the Internet to shame anyone that goes here? The mind boggles.

It is only later when I actually look where it is on Google Maps and note that you drive south down a dusty road, to a point where the dusty road comes to an end ... but Google maps says that it doesn't come to and, and that the road carries on south through the desert, and eventually across the border and into California – and then you realise that a lot of their custom probably comes up this dusty road from the south, and not through the main town of Pahrump at all.

> **3:18 PM Aug 26th**
> and we're now outside the infamous Chicken Ranch. Note: no actual chickens were used in the making of this brothel.

So we're looking at the Chicken Ranch. And I want to be able to tell you that it is an amazing building decorated it such a way so at to tempt you in, but really it's just a non-descript building set back from the road, with a parking lot out front and a big sign outside. And it's quiet – dead quiet, and there's nothing going on. I count the cars parked out front – there are six vehicles here. Presumably there is parking for the 'staff' around the back. Does that mean that there are six people in their having sex right now?

'Are you tempted then?' asks Paul wryly and I raise my Nikon camera and *snap* a picture of the sign outside.

I look at him sagely, and nod. And then burst out laughing at my crap attempt to imitate him, and then say ... 'Yes! I'm *very* tempted to get the geocache that is on the other side of street over there – just behind that tree I suspect!' and we trot over to find and log it. But we encounter no prostitutes.

> **3:38 PM Aug 26th**
> and we're off. No we did not go in! But we did do the geocache across the street.

The route west from here to Californian coast means that we pretty much have to go through Death Valley National Park anyway, so on our way through we stop at the visitors centre for a nose around, and note that it feels dry, bright and hot. We stop to get drinks at a ridiculously high priced gas station further down the road, and again I note that it is dry, bright, and hot. And then we head out further west – oddly not taking that many photos – as I mentally note just how dry, bright and hot it is. But mainly, we press on because it's clear now that we're in an 'It's very near the end, and so we must press on', mood, and so we do.

We come out of Death Valley being buzzed by two F-15 jets on military manoeuvres and head for the sizable town of Ridgecrest that we figure will provide food and lodging for the night.

It's a non-momentous occasion to be honest. No 'I'm almost there' tingles of excitement, no 'Looking back at what I've done and how far I've come' moments of reflection, no getting raucously drunk in bar.

No. The last night of the road trip consisted of this : Driving up and down the main drag of the rather disappointing town of Ridgecrest (CVS, Food Lion, that sort of thing) looking for somewhere decent to eat.

> **9:35 PM Aug 26th**
> well, I'm in the nothing town of Ridgecrest, CA for the night. Last night on the road before the final destination tomorrow

After twenty minutes of driving up and down the main drag and trying a few side roads too, we concede that locally owned nice-style restaurants don't exist in this town, and so we end up going to a Perfect Pizza in the nearby strip mall – the only thing that is lit up and seems to be open late on in the evening.

Paul & I sit in the mostly empty parking lot outside the pizza place and munch away. We don't say a lot. We don't have to say a lot. I am tired. Paul knows I am tired. We both know it would all 'end' tomorrow, and whist I am going to be sad to some extent that it is all over. It is also definitely time for the trip to reach its conclusion.

Day 73 – Wednesday 27th August

To the end

'Well you and I, collapsed in love
And it looks like, we might have made it.
Yes it looks like we've made it to the end'

10:36 AM Aug 27th
good morning day 73. It's the start of the end. can i relax now please?

In the morning I feel the need to vent just how tired I am of the whole affair and Paul shoots a load of video of me angrily loading the car by myself (for effect) and generally moaning. That's right, *moaning* – that I've had this marvellous opportunity to drive across the entire country and here I am moaning my mouth off. I know.

'I'm fed up and tired. I haven't washed clothes as often as I should, I've eaten badly, and I'm fed up with lugging the equipment in and out of the car every night'.

I lug the equipment back into the car, and we set off. Down some non-descript highway, stopping at yet another gas station and buying ice-creams to help cool us down on the hot dry Californian summer day, getting onto the congested Interstate of the outer suburbs of L.A.

5:14 PM Aug 27th
ok. So this is it. Were on I-5 heading south, and 30 miles from the final stop

'Feeling anything?' asks Paul, that sage tone in his voice once again.

'Nope', I reply popping the last bit of ice cream into my mouth, failing to stop a bit of it dripping and suddenly ending up steering with my knee as I use both hands to avert an ice-cream disaster.

5:28 PM Aug 27th
am 15 miles out, on a five lane freeway – still feeling nothing'

In the USA
Hyde Park, California
On the Tube map
Hyde Park Corner (Piccadilly Line)

We are definitely in what you would call 'urban' Los Angeles. Actually, it isn't as sketchy as I thought it might be, but it certainly *does* feel sketchy. This morning my mum – still faithfully tracking my progress right to the end – has Googled 'Hyde Park CA' for me, and sent me a link to a local news report from Hyde Park that is all about local crime and drug-fuelled gang wars. 'Be careful!' she writes. 'It's ok! I have Paul with me!' I banter back.

We drive slowly down a road, past a motor repair shop with piles of tyres stacked outside and a large gang of people who just seem to be hanging out there staring at us. Two guys deep in conversation complete with animated hand waving actions also stop momentarily to look up from their conversation to check us out. A main road, a crossroads, down another side road with businesses – some open, some failing, and the smell of industry in the air. A posh suburban district with families with 2.4 children and 'soccer moms' this is not.

Eventually, we see a 'Hyde Park' sign. A sign that says 'Hyde Park Boulevard', as that's all Hyde Park really is – a long road that turns into a Boulevard. I glance at the SatNav, and chuckle when I see a few blocks further down still there is a level crossing with a train track going through. Thanks UndUSA – even on the very last day on the very last stop of the trip, I have inadvertently managed to choose a place with an actual railway running through it.

The next block down gets slightly less sketchy than the previous ones and I see a gap at the side of the road and pull in. I leave the engine running, and get out my phone to tweet something and update my position.

Paul has the video camera running all the time to capture to my reaction, and my reaction is to …take another photo of another 'Hyde Park' sign, and turn to him and say 'Shall we go then?'

We laugh. And then sit in silence again for a few seconds as we both know that on this hot sticky day in the neighbourhood we are in we don't want to get out and explore. More so, because I feel that leaving the car with all the equipment in the back might not be a good idea.

So we sit, chat, watch the world go by, and somewhere in the back of my head, I reflect on the previous places.

> **6:17 PM Aug 27th**
> and I'm at ... Hyde Park, Los Angeles. Sketchyness factor = quite high.

Still no emotional reaction from me though.

> **6:18 PM Aug 27th**
> so ... I guess I'm done. Like that's it.

I can't help but think that somehow the last stop on the trip deserves a better ending, or a bigger send off, or someone should have been there holding a sign or certificate saying '48 Tube map named places ... complete!' But no, it's just me and Paul, sitting in a car that we don't want to get out of on a hot day – and still no big reaction from me.

Instead, we drive to my friend Tatiana's about twenty minutes away, where the neighbourhood is distinctly lovely – with large houses, within which she and her family live in one of them.

The final bit of video of the trip comes with me giving Tatiana an awkward 'Hello!' hug, which for me is quite a big moment – I don't think she realises for me how huge this is because it signals the end of the last three months, and she seems a bit startled at how big of a hug I go in for.

She puts us up in her guest house – a separate building that I think in England they would call a 'granny flat', right? And that night I sleep in a proper bed – ones that are in a hotel don't count as they've not got a homely feel about them – so this, a proper nice bed with a snug duvet which means that when I put my head on the pillow at 10pm, I am out like a light, and sleep solidly for twelve hours – my body and mind knowing that it doesn't have to get up and drive anywhere the next day.

In the morning, I get up and visit the local Starbucks to go online – because that is one road trip habit that is going to be hard to break – and when I return to the house at lunchtime, I am tired again, and find myself having a short nap that turns into another sleep – this time for four hours.

That evening before dinner, I open a whole bunch of post/mail that people have sent ahead to Tatiana's address for me. Birthday presents and cards, from people who had known where my final stopping place is going to be. We have a lovely dinner, I have a birthday drink, and sit on a swing chair in the garden, swim in the pool and for the first time in weeks feel *properly* relaxed. Everyone talks, and mainly I am able to chat about the highs and lows and places and people from the last three months.

And more importantly I am able to think about and consider properly the answer I am going to give to the obvious question which people will now naturally ask me.

~ ~ ~

I stay at Tatiana's for a couple of days – Paul too before he then flies off home. I go online a lot, I blog a final post online, and more importantly of all – I review my list of the 48 'same name' places that I have been to.

I go through my list – to tick off the 48, to sort them again, to list them – or perhaps draw an Underground-style map, but this time with America as the backdrop, and the 48 places marked on them.

As I draw up that list though – I go old school with a piece of paper and pen, sketching a map out of the USA, drawing a line where I've been and plotting the places where I've been, a sudden strange feeling comes over me that brings a few goose bumps to my arms.

I've missed one.

What? No, I haven't, have I? Well, I know that I haven't been to Royal Oak in Michigan because of how depressing Detroit had been, and I haven't been to Finchley in Virginia as that was right after the break-in when everything was a mess, but ... as I count again ... even with those two. *Shit! No!!* It comes out as 47 and not 48!

I look at my map of the USA. And trace the line that I've just drawn with my right forefinger, and pretty soon find a glaring error.

Wyoming! The state of Wyoming and the town of Beckton. *Beckton, Wyoming!* (Yes, Beckton is a stop on the DLR it's on the Tube map, so it counts).

And I stare hard at my map, and harder at my original list of places, and I feel the goose bumps on my arm get hit with a second wave and intensify slightly.

Why the fuck haven't I visited Beckton? I think back ... I *look* back at my notes and my blog and pretty soon realise. That was the week that Nat had been with me, and I'd lost focus a bit – Nat had not seemed that interested in going to any of the same name places, and there had basically been a day where she was so excited about going to Yellowstone, and we were driving up the Bear Tooth pass towards it, that somehow I had totally forgotten. I got caught up in too, and just for the sake of keeping the peace had subconsciously decided not to mention it, and we'd just headed for the National Park instead. *Fuck!*

I sit there, quietly for a moment. Knowing that really I've only done 45 out of the 48 that I'd set out to do. And I draw up my final list.

SAME NAME TOWNS TALLY

Perfect Small Town America
White City, Preston, Waterloo

Something there and enjoyable
Plaistow, Gloucester, Kew Gardens, Harrow, South Kensington, Greenford, Liverpool, Temple, Oxford, Victoria, Angel, London Bridge, Kingsbury County

Something there but not that exciting to be honest

Putney, Amersham, Hampstead, Woodford, Brompton, Lancaster, Kingsbury, Olympia, Stratford, Monument, Warren, Redbridge, Latimer, Hyde Park

Nothing there but somehow being in the middle of nowhere made it OK
Epping, Acton, Poplar, Holborn, Green Park Farm, Hackney

Nothing there, and not that exciting either. Oops.
Warwick, Wapping, Camden, Bond, Kenton, Arsenal, Elm Park

Closed
Swiss Cottage, Watford

Missed
Royal Oak, Finchley, Beckton

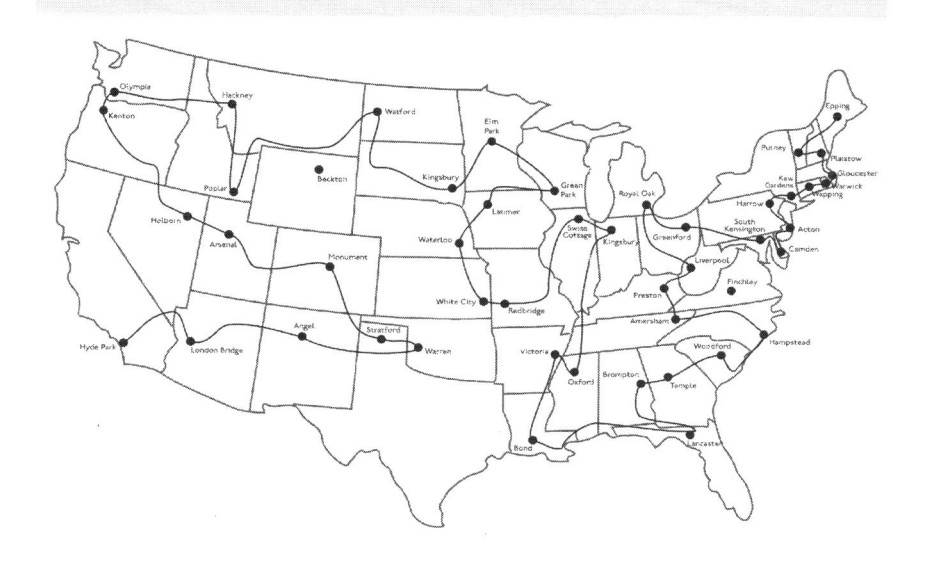

331

The question that people obviously ask me post trip is, 'So what was the best place you went to then of the places with the same name?', and after answering that same question to several people, it became obvious that there are particular places that keep coming up in my answers.

The Blevins General Store in *Preston, Kentucky* had been the first proper 'Oh Wow' moment on the trip, the feeling that I might just be seeing some special small places that are only known to the locals, and perhaps is off the beaten path.

Holborn, Nevada was definitely off of the beaten path – it's in the middle of the desert, and the fact that I randomly turn up there as there is a train passing through made it even better. I am acutely aware that I may have over-used the phrase 'Middle of Nowhere' in this book, but there were lots of those kinds of moments. But Holborn had to be that ultimate nowhere moment though, that beats all the others.

And then there's *White City, Kansas*. Which was just perfect. For the classic 'small-town' community feeling that it gave you, it was the most lovely place that I found on my trip, and part of me would really like to go back there one day. Actually – I would say that about Preston and Nevada too, and that would be the thing that seals it – there were plenty of places that I went to that I was happy just going to once, but like a film that you watch more than once, or a song that you play on repeat (and I know a thing or two about that), here were some places that I wanted to go back and visit again.

I probably never will though, because life is too short, plane tickets are too expensive and America is just too darned big. And that was my ultimate conclusion.

A week after returning back 'home' to Charleston, I sit on the porch of Dan's house, just like I had done before I went on the trip and made a video of me talking about summing up what I had learned. 'You have no idea how big your country is until you get out there and try to conquer it', and he just nodded and smiled in complete agreement.

'If you had to choose *one* place though', Dan asks me 'To live in, where would that be?'

Well that's easy … almost. It would be the in the middle of America. Or in the West. Or in the mountains. Hang on – that's three answers already, bugger. Ok, look *not* on either the west or east coast in one of the major cities. A lot of people think of America as either New York or L.A. and forget about the huge expanse of land that is in-between and the brilliant world of small-town America that is out there amongst the stunning scenery. It's the best, it's real America with real people, and I love it.

Dan is still looking at me – Oh, I'd better reply. I decide to cheat and give him an amalgamation of an answer.

'Well, I love Chicago as a city as it's the right size, but it's in the wrong place climate wise. So what I propose is that we take Chicago and move it down to the four corners of Utah, Arizona, Nevada and New Mexico – that way, I can have my favourite city, but also be near the mountains for when I want fresh air, the desert for when I want a whole of dry nothing and New Mexico for its pretty landscape. Do you think we could make that happen? Move the whole of Chicago out to the west?'

'Sure, I'll get to work on that' he nods instantly, before then pausing, smiling and giving a much better answer. 'Just hold tight, and wait and see buddy, ok? We're on it', he says smiling.

It takes me a second to get the reference, and then I laugh out loud.

I may have left America now, but I know how to appreciate it on a level more than I used to. More than most people do – a land of Hollywood movies, gun violence, or a place where 'No one has passports' – they don't *need* passports, natives could spend a lifetime travelling their own land and still not got to grips with it. I am lucky enough to have sampled a tiny bit of each state of it though, to have a better appreciation – not complete, but more than most.

It's an awkward conversation that I still have even to this day – whenever I meet an American now I ask where they are from and if I haven't been to their exact town, there's a 98% chance that I've been to their home state, so obviously I tell them this. Then they ask why, and when I reveal that I've been to 49 out of the 50 states in the USA they give me a look that says 'Wow, I've not done that nor probably ever will', and I feel a bit embarrassed.

In other words – I know I've seen more of America than most Americans ever will in their lifetime.

I also appreciate what a massive task that it was that I undertook, and how a lot of the time it comes across that I was grumpy, whereas actually it was a mixed bag – everyday.

There would be highs, followed by lows – as driving for long periods of time isn't that exciting when you know you've got to make progress as time is against you, but overall I know that all the good bits outweighed the moments that weren't so good.

It also makes you exceedingly tired being on the road all the time, away from decent home comforts and your own bed. Staying in a tent and sleeping bag is a fun novelty that wears off after the first few nights, and becomes wearisome. Couple this with the ridiculous task I'd set myself of documenting it all *continually* through twitter, my blog, photos and videos – and that's a huge effort and task to undertake – bigger than I thought it was going to be, of course.

So apologies if I come across as a grumpy bugger. I'm really not. I just set myself stupidly high goals and expend a lot of energy and effort trying to achieve them which takes it out of you.

So there. That's it. That's all 48 done. Tick.

I mark them all out on a paper map I've drawn of the USA and on it put blobs with their names written against them. Then I get different colour pens and start drawing lines between them, imagining I am designing a subway system across the whole of America, and I'm now making up the map for their nationwide subway system.

I do a rough draft, and then decide I need to do a better version so I get out my laptop and design it properly – an original map of the USA with my 48 places on them (plus a few other major towns, just for reference), and like it so much that I borrow Tatiana's printer to print myself out a hard copy.

I sit, outside on the wooden bench in the garden with a tea, looking quite proudly of my 'Tube map' of America, and knew that quite soon, I would be back in England and able to ride my real love – the London Underground, in person.

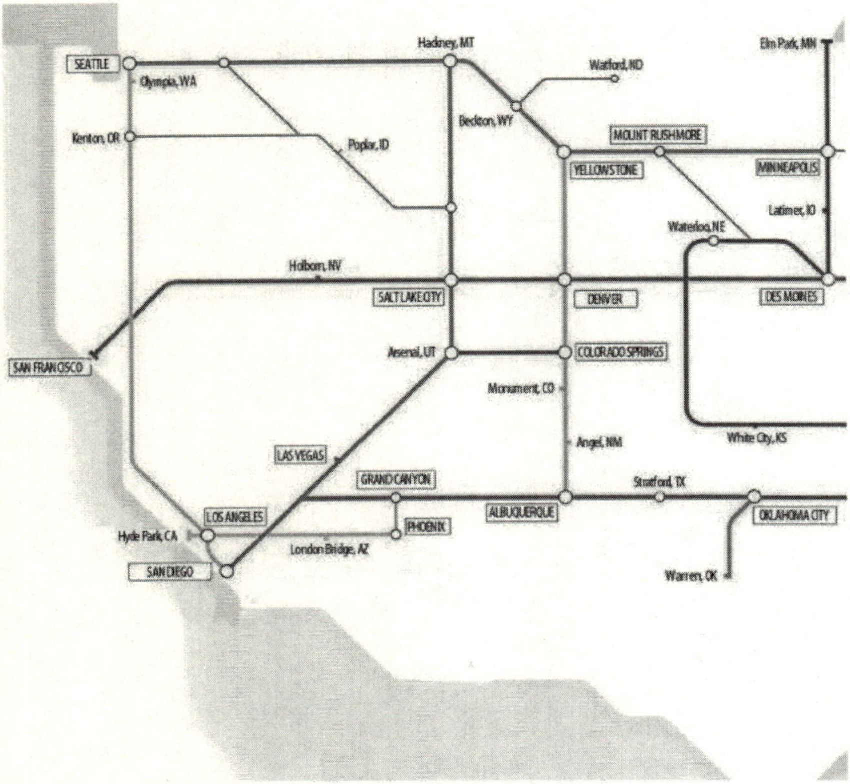
Hackney, MT
Elm Park, MN
SEATTLE
Olympia, WA
Watford, ND
Beckton, WY
Kenton, OR
Poplar, ID
MOUNT RUSHMORE
YELLOWSTONE
MINNEAPOLIS
Latimer, IO
Waterloo, NE
Holborn, NV
SALT LAKE CITY
DENVER
DES MOINES
Arsenal, UT
COLORADO SPRINGS
SAN FRANCISCO
Monument, CO
White City, KS
Angel, NM
LAS VEGAS
GRAND CANYON
Stratford, TX
ALBUQUERQUE
OKLAHOMA CITY
LOS ANGELES
PHOENIX
Hyde Park, CA
London Bridge, AZ
SAN DIEGO
Warren, OK

○ Green Park, WI

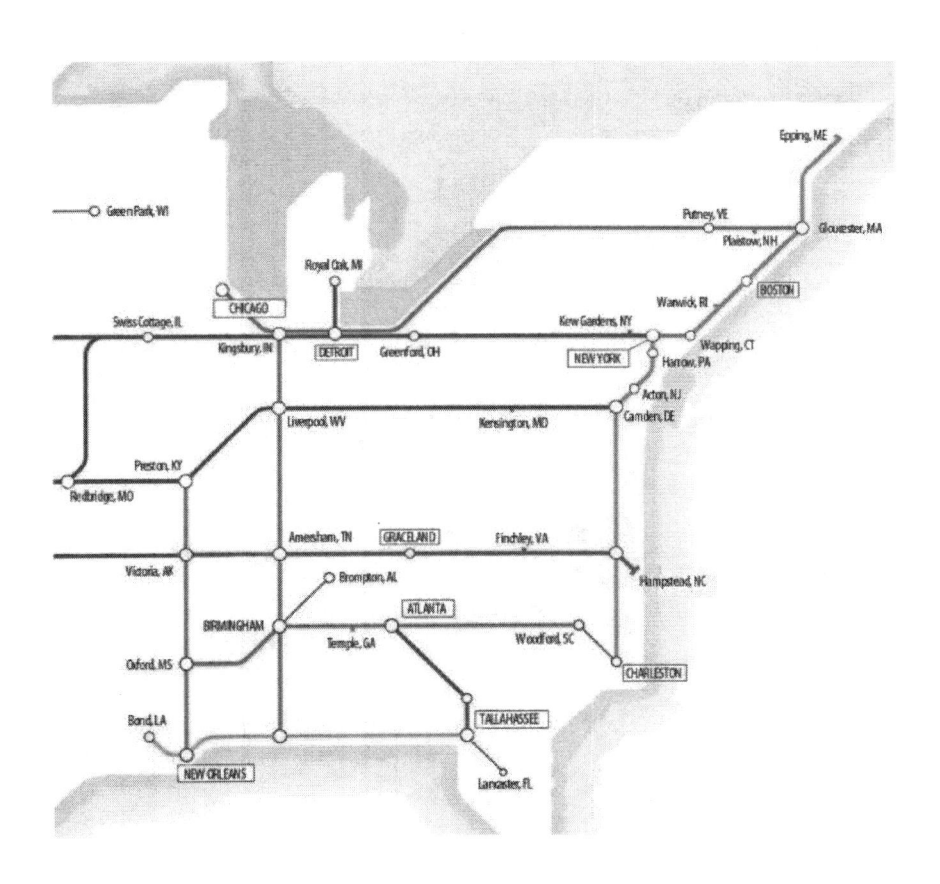

Epping, ME
Putney, VE
Plaistow, NH
Gloucester, MA
Royal Oak, MI
Warwick, RI
BOSTON
Swiss Cottage, IL
CHICAGO
Kew Gardens, NY
Wapping, CT
Kingsbury, IN
DETROIT
Greenford, OH
NEW YORK
Harrow, PA
Acton, NJ
Liverpool, WV
Kensington, MD
Camden, DE
Preston, KY
Redbridge, MO
Amersham, TN
GRACELAND
Finchley, VA
Victoria, AK
Hampstead, NC
Brompton, AL
ATLANTA
BIRMINGHAM
Woodford, SC
Oxford, MS
Temple, GA
CHARLESTON
TALLAHASSEE
Bond, LA
NEW ORLEANS
Lancaster, FL

337

Things that happened post road-trip

- The trip back from the west coast of California back to Charleston was a weeks' worth of driving in itself, and wasn't without a few stories to tell. So I've written a bonus chapter based on what happened on the journey back. You can download it to read at **www.geofftech.co.uk/undusa/**

- Tami (the Police Officer in New Orleans) made a list of 50 places names in England that share a name with a town in America and is planning a trip around the UK, most likely to tie in with the next Royal Wedding.

- My cousin Phil calls me up again and does indeed make a trip out to see me – inspired by my journey, and he got see some of America for himself. Although we did just spend just one afternoon in Charleston driving round trying to find a car with a 'New Hampshire' plate – and we eventually found one! Tick ... all license plates spotted.

- I'm still waiting for the Greensboro police to return my calls to let me know if they ever found any of my stuff. Three calls & voicemails left with them ... and I've heard nothing back.

- I realise that out of all the classic-tourist spots around the USA that I did visit, I never stopped at the world's largest ball of twine.

- A combination of too much diner food, and probably endlessly vast amounts of milky Starbucks lattes eventually took its toll. A pain in my gut which I thought was everything from cancer to ... well, cancer turned out to be Irritable Bowel Syndrome. Most likely, said my doctor – brought on by too much coffee drinking. I have now stopped drinking coffee in Starbucks. Howard Shultz has removed me from his Christmas Card list.

- Shortly after coming home to England, I hire a car for a day and took a trip from Guildford to Portsmouth. It was a surprise and shock to the system when I drove it in just under 45 minutes. The concept of driving somewhere and not spending at least 4 hours doing it *(As had become the norm on a daily basis on the trip)* was a weird one to me. England suddenly did feel really small.

- A whole year later, I put on a pair of white socks - socks that I must have worn on this trip - as summer had come around again. I immediately feel something sharp on my toes and look inside them to find ... shards of glass that had come from the broken window of Beverly's car. I thought I'd cleared them all up, but no – and so here was yet another reminder still of the car being broken into.

- For Christmas the year after, Jono & Katie invite me over again on Boxing Day to just hang out with them again. 'It'll be just like last year', wrote Jono in an instant message to me. 'Yes, only this time let's not find names of Tube Stations in America', I write back.

- Having been to the state of Alaska on a separate trip, I've now got the idea to go and visit Hawaii for my 50th birthday. Literally fly and land on the day that I turn fifty, so that I can then say I went to fiftieth state on my own fiftieth.

- **The Big One!** Three years after coming home myself and my friends *(Chris, Richard, Anthony, Matt, Kate, Kirk and Vicki)* made several attempts to get round the London Underground in the fastest time possible again. After 15 attempts over three years, we finally did it.

On the 16th August 2013, we set a new World Record Time of **16 hours, 20 minutes and 27 seconds** for visiting all 270 London Underground Stations in the fastest time possible.

The certificate hangs on my kitchen wall next to the previous one – a double world record holder.

Statistics

Obviously, the OCD[48] person in me kept an accurate log of statistics as I travelled round, meaning I can present some of them here.

The trip

I spent **73** days travelling – ten and a half weeks from the **16th June** to the **27th August 2009**.

On the road

I filled up with gas **63** times, and my starting mileage was **156,856**. The final mileage was **175,619** giving me a total miles driven of **18,763** which averages at **257** miles per day.

I bought **984.843** gallons of fuel, spending **$2606.26** in the process, with an average Miles per Gallon of **19.61**.

The most expensive place I filled up at was for **$3.99** when coming out of the Mojave Desert. The cheapest was for **$2.24** in Kansas, Missouri the day I visited White City.

I calculated that **62mph** is the most efficient speed in terms of distance versus fuel used.

Overnight

35 of the 73 night those nights I camped *(47%)*, **22** nights were in hotels/motels *(31%)*, **15** stayed at a friend's *(21%)*, and **2** were in the back of car *(1%)*.

I spent **$1100** to stay at campsites, and **$873** staying in hotels. There were a few nights in hotels where the companions paid, the rest were free when staying at people's places.

Same Name with Trains

I did a count in the end, and out of the 48 places, and actually only 14 of them had either a current or old railway line running through it – it felt like more.

My Weight

I weighed 78Kg when I set out, but 83Kg ten weeks later when I got back. On-the-road fast food and no exercise for ten weeks will do that to you.

---

[48] Talking of the OCD thing, it's entirely unnecessary to have this final footnote here by the way, but in doing so I am bringing the total number of footnotes in this book to 48, and I just couldn't resist. I'm sure you understand, yes?

Acknowledgments

Secretly, I always thought that the 'thank you' sections that you got at the end of books were made up, or at the very least bordering on sanctimonious trite.

Did the author *really* have or need the involvement of all those people? I would often wonder to myself?

And then I went through the laborious chore of writing 130,000 words myself, and found out just how arduous a process it was, and discovered that – yes – not only did I need to thank a whole bunch of people that helped me along with the trip itself, but people whose support and encouragement made it possible for it to appear in words as well. Never again will I be so cynical – well, not about 'thank you' pages in books, anyway.

So for coming with me on the trip, for letting me stay with or meet up with you, for providing me with food and gifts, for sending me supportive tweets, for bothering to comment on the Facebook photos, for shooting video for me, for giving me music when I lost all of mine, and for making sure that I wrote the book when I got back, I can't not mention the following people.

Scott Blair, Tami Brissett, Eric Barfield, Betty Blankenship, Pad Connolly, Dan Conover, Pat Durkin, Janet Edens, Steven Francis, Paul 'Churchill' Fraser-Webb. Michael & Melissa Fussell, Melissa Haneline, Ken Hawkins, Jon Hind, Tatiana James, Courtney Kozar, Katie Kozar, Caitlin Lee, Brindolyn McClair, Beverly Morgan, Tina Onions, James Quinton, Chris Rae, James Reaves, Rudi Riet, Henry Riggs, Chrys Rynearson, Russell Shulin, Julian Smith, Philip Smith, Jonathon Stout and Rainy Dae Taylor. Oh and Alice, Natalie and her sister.

And – obviously – to everyone that gave money to **#helpgeoff**

Garion Allen, Jon Allen, Michael Atkinson, John Attebury, Joseph Benton, James Bentall, Steve Berry, Amy Berryhill, David Birch, Cameron Blazer, Donna Bowen, Gretchen Bowles, Helen Brew, Karen Briggs, Dave Brooks, Amy Carter, Amanda Click, Leanne Coleman, Dan Conover, Mark Cooper, Emily Cooper, David Dabney, Stephen Danford, Mary Dalrymple, Patrick Deaton, Leslie Decker, Brian Duncan, Patricia Evans, Faith Ezekiel, Kathryn Fenner, David Gill, Ashleigh Graf, Jason Groce, Leslie Halpern, Vera Hannaford, James Heyward, Doug Hofer, Samantha Hoppes, Katherine Herring, Stuart Hill, Paul Houweling, Martin Howard, Sheryl Hutcherson, Helen Kent, Ronald Krauskopf, David Ladner, Margaret Laverty, Kate Larter, Caitlin Lee, Cara Levy,

Megan Lovett, James McNeil, David Mandel, Amy Nardi Matthes, Carla Marks, Kwadwo Mensah, Mary Morelli, James Moffitt, Sara Miller, Eugene Mah, Miles Mendoza, Liz Michaelis, Gerard Mills, Jessica Mickey, Chris Moore, Kelly Moore, Andrew Murphy, Victoria New, Joseph Neinstadt, Kirk Northrop, Janet Nye, Jonathan Onions, Rachel Parker, Gus Paul, Alan Perks, Kelley Perkins, Erin Perkins, Joan Perry, Kristen Phillips, Emma Le Poidevin, Clare Prochazka, Helen Quigley, Ryan Radford, Scott Rhodes, Angela Rogers, Rudolf Riet, Chris Rynearson, Joel Schooling, Lisa Shimko, Robin Shuler, Seth Siegler, Anthony Smith, Jared Smith, Philip Smith, Rick Smith, Heather Solos, Louise Strasenburgh, Jonathon Stout, Anna Stone, Jeffrey Sykes, Mark Szlachetka, Jeff Thigpen, Amanda Thomas, Jamie Thomas, Anthony Tugwell, Paul Van Slett, David Webber, Catriona West, Lynn Welsby, Allan Williams, Håkan Wolgé, Richard Womersley and Andrew Wong.

To this day, I still don't know who some of those people are!

Special thanks must also go to Michael Furlinger and The Terrace theatre in Charleston, SC for making the largest contribution of all.

And finally *extra special thanks* must go to Simon (You know who you are), and of course to Vicki, without whom there would have never have been a book at all.